Melanie Klein
Today

VOLUME 2

The New Library of Psychoanalysis is published in association with the Institute of Psycho-Analysis. The New Library has been launched to facilitate a greater and more widespread appreciation of what psycho-analysis is really about and to provide a forum for increasing mutual understanding between psychoanalysts and those working in other disciplines such as history, linguistics, literature, medicine, philosophy, psychology, and the social sciences. It is planned to publish a limited number of books each year in an accessible form and to select those contributions which deepen and develop psychoanalytic thinking and technique, contribute to psychoanalysis from outside, or contribute to other disciplines from a psychoanalytical perspective.

The Institute, together with the British Psycho-Analytical Society, runs a low-fee psychoanalytic clinic, organizes lectures and scientific events concerned with psychoanalysis, publishes the *International Journal of Psycho-Analysis* and the *International Review of Psycho-Analysis*, and runs the only training course in the UK in psychoanalysis leading to membership of the International Psychoanalytical Association — the body which preserves internationally agreed standards of training, of professional entry, and of professional ethics and practice for psychoanalysis as initiated and developed by Sigmund Freud. Distinguished members of the Institute have included Wilfred Bion, Anna Freud, Ernest Jones, Melanie Klein, John Rickman, and Donald Winnicott.

The series is under the general editorship of David Tuckett; Eglé Laufer and Ronald Britton are associate editors.

NEW LIBRARY OF PSYCHOANALYSIS
8
General editor: David Tuckett

Melanie Klein Today

DEVELOPMENTS IN THEORY AND PRACTICE

VOLUME 2: MAINLY PRACTICE

edited by

ELIZABETH BOTT SPILLIUS

LONDON AND NEW YORK

First published 1988
by Routledge
11 New Fetter Lane, London EC4P 4EE
29 West 35th Street, New York, NY 10001

Reprinted 1990, 1992 and 1994

© 1988 General introduction and introductions to parts Elizabeth Bott Spillius
individual articles the authors or their estates

Typeset by Mayhew Typesetting
Printed and bound in Great Britain by Mackays of Chatham PLC, Kent

A Tavistock/Routledge publication

British Library Cataloguing in Publication Data
A catalogue record for this book is available from the British Library

Library of Congress Cataloging in Publication Data
A catalog record for this book is available from the Library of Congress

ISBN 0-415-00681-3 (v. 1)
ISBN 0-415-00682-1 (pbk.:v. 1)
ISBN 0-415-01044-6 (v. 2)
ISBN 0-415-01045-4 (pbk.:v. 2)

Contents

Acknowledgements

I wish here to thank the Melanie Klein Trust whose financial help made possible the preparation of this book, and to thank many generous colleagues for their help, most particularly Miss Betty Joseph, Dr Hanna Segal, Mrs Edna O'Shaughnessy, and Dr Ronald Britton who have given much helpful advice and criticism. I also wish to thank Riccardo Steiner who has been especially helpful in giving me the benefit of his encyclopaedic knowledge of psychoanalytic and related literature, particularly in the field of the use of Kleinian ideas by people in other areas of work.

The editor and publisher would like to thank the following for their kind permission to reproduce copyright material: the *International Journal of Psycho-Analysis* and the *International Review of Psycho-Analysis*, Dr Donald Meltzer, Miss B. Joseph, and individual authors for papers published in these journals (Part One: 2, 3, 5, 6; Part Two: 1, 3; Part Three: 2, 5; Part Four: 1, 2); the *Journal of Child Psychotherapy*, Dr Donald Meltzer, and Mrs E. O'Shaughnessy for papers published therein (Part Three: 1, 3); Mrs Francesca Bion (Part One: 1), Jason Aronson and Miss Betty Joseph (Part One: 4); Ballière Tindall & Cassell and Elizabeth Bott Spillius (Part Four: 3), Mrs Ruth Riesenberg Malcolm (Part Two: 2), Mrs E. O'Shaughnessy (Part Three: 4), and Mrs Isabel Menzies Lyth (Part Four: 4).

General Introduction

ELIZABETH BOTT SPILLIUS

In the General Introduction at the beginning of the first volume of *Melanie Klein Today* I gave a brief description of several main themes of theory and practice in Melanie Klein's work and described how her theoretical innovations developed out of her attempts to conceptualize the newly discovered clinical facts that her work with children revealed. In the 1940s, 50s, and 60s the focus of research shifted to the study of psychotic and borderline patients, and this work again uncovered new clinical facts and led to new conceptualizations; it is these ideas that have formed the major themes of Volume 1. These areas of conceptualization have continued, but have in recent years been joined by a further theme, that of technique, which forms a major part of the present volume.

Interest in technique has now become a central focus in Kleinian work. New ideas about it have developed from increasingly close scrutiny of the therapeutic process. There has been much work by individual analysts and discussion among colleagues involving detailed examination of transference and counter-transference and their interrelation, monitoring of patients' responses to interpretations, and comparison of experiences in learning which sorts of interpretation make emotional contact with the patient and which do not.

Bion is the pathfinder in this work, closely followed by Joseph and others. In particular, Bion's use and development of Klein's concept of projective identification started a new approach which even now his colleagues are still absorbing and developing. The products of this development are described in the first section, 'Developments in technique'.

This book also presents examples of detailed clinical work with adults

1

and with children. These papers illustrate the issues of technique discussed in the first section and give further exemplification of the theoretical ideas described in the first volume. In addition they allow the reader to see the variety of individual differences that exists within the broad framework of Kleinian theory and practice.

The papers on clinical work with adult patients indicate a basic continuity of approach since the early 1950s but also show the effect of Bion's work especially in an increasing emphasis on projective identification and the interplay of transference and counter-transference.

Child analysis is no longer the main research area in Kleinian analysis, but the clinical papers on children reprinted here show both continuity with Klein's work and influence stemming from the work of Bion and from later developments. Several child analysts have become especially interested in the relevance of new developments in technique with adults to work with children and it is likely that this will be a topic for further study.

In the last section concerning the application of Kleinian ideas in other fields of work I suggest that a decline is occurring in the number of Kleinian psychoanalytic commentaries on other fields unless the commentator is also trained in the field concerned, but that this decline is balanced by a gradual spread of knowledge about Klein's ideas to members of the general public and by an increase in interest and use of Kleinian ideas by members of other disciplines.

As in Volume 1, I have confined the discussion almost entirely to the work of Kleinian analysts in Britain, and I have not attempted to examine the interaction between Kleinian work and that of analysts of other theoretical orientations within the British Psycho-Analytical Society.

Note
References for the general introduction and the introductions to the four parts of the book will be found at the end of the volume.

PART ONE

Developments in technique

Introduction

ELIZABETH BOTT SPILLIUS

Although Kleinian analysts take it for granted that a distinctive technique is basic to the Kleinian approach, comparatively little has been written about this technique in its own right until very recently. This dearth of papers on technique has occurred partly because Kleinian analysts were preoccupied with other areas of research, but perhaps also because it was thought for some time that it was novelty of content rather than novelty of method that makes Kleinian work distinctive. Thus, for example, in a paper specifically entitled 'Melanie Klein's technique' (1967) Segal describes the essentials of Klein's technique in less than one page and then spends the rest of the paper describing the effect of Klein's novel theories. The impression one gets from this paper is that the distinctive features of technique are so enmeshed with the distinctive features of clinical content that they cannot be usefully disentangled. Recently, however, there has been increased discussion among Kleinian analysts of problems specifically concerning technique, even though comparatively little of this discussion has been published as yet.

Most of the basic features of Kleinian technique, as Segal notes, are closely derived from Freud: rigorous maintenance of the psychoanalytic setting so as to keep the transference as pure and uncontaminated as possible; an expectation of sessions five times a week; emphasis on the transference as the central focus of analyst-patient interaction; a belief that the transference situation is active from the very beginning of the analysis; an attitude of active receptivity rather than passivity and silence; interpretation of anxiety and defence together rather than either on its own; emphasis on interpretation, especially the transference interpretation, as the agent of therapeutic change. In Kleinian thought there is a particular emphasis on the totality of transference. The concept is not restricted to the expression in the session towards the analyst of attitudes towards specific persons and/or incidents of the historical past. Rather the term is used to mean the expression in the analytic situation of the forces and relationships of the internal world. The internal world itself is regarded as the result of an ongoing process of development, the product of continuing interaction between unconscious phantasy, defences, and experiences with external reality both in the past and in the present. The emphasis of Klein and her successors on the pervasiveness of transference is derived from Klein's use of the concept of unconscious phantasy, which is conceived as underlying all thought, rational as well as irrational, rather than there being a special category of thought and feeling which is rational and appropriate and therefore does not need analysing and a second kind of thought and feeling which is irrational and unreasonable and therefore expresses transference and needs analysing.

Klein and her successors strongly disagree with the idea of encouraging regression and reliving infantile experiences in the consulting room through non-interpretive activities. Analytic care, in her view, should take the form of a stable analytic setting containing within it a correct interpretive process. Even in the development of play technique with children she adhered to these principles, except that play as well as talk was the medium of expression. Similarly, work with psychotic patients has been carried out with only minor changes in technique such as not insisting that the patient use the couch and seeing the patient in hospital if necessary.

Because so little has been written about Kleinian technique until comparatively recently, I have tried to read all the clinical papers by Kleinian analysts that I could find, many of them unpublished; most of these papers were written early on in their authors' careers and were intended only to be informal presentations of clinical work; the authors were not trying to make a contribution to theory. Because these papers include detailed clinical descriptions, they provide source material for drawing conclusions about the principles of technique that their authors were using. Over the period from the late 1940s to the 1980s certain trends of change in technique are evident.

There are certain strikingly original exceptions, but most of the papers of the 1950s and 1960s, especially those by young and relatively inexperienced analysts, tend to emphasize the patient's destructiveness in a way that we would now assume might have felt persecuting to the patient. A second feature of these early papers is that unconscious phantasies were evidently interpreted to the patient immediately and very directly in part-object language (breast, nipple, penis, etc.). In the earliest papers there were very few references to counter-transference or to

6

projective identification, especially to projection of aspects of the patient into the analyst.

Gradually, though rather unevenly, several trends of change emerged in the papers of the 1960s and 1970s. First, destructiveness began to be interpreted in a more balanced way. Second, the immediate use of part-object language diminished. Third, the concept of projective identification began to be used more directly and explicitly in analysing the transference; similarly ideas on counter-transference began to be used more systematically, though counter-transference was not discussed in the papers as explicitly as projective identification. Fourth, there began to be increasing emphasis on acting-in, meaning living out experiences in the transference rather than thinking and talking about them, and more emphasis also on the patient unconsciously putting pressure on the analyst to join in. And finally, though this is as yet less evident in clinical papers than in verbal discussions, there is at the present time much interest in reconstruction and in alternative ways of interpreting the way past experiences express themselves in the patient–analyst interaction.

Most of these trends of change have developed piecemeal and gradually without anyone being very much aware of them until some time after they had happened. They were 'in the air' rather than being the product of conscious striving by any particular analyst. The influence of Bion, however, is apparent throughout. His work on normal projective identification has had a very specific influence in changing analysts' handling of transference and counter-transference, but his influence has also been more general and pervasive. As I have described in the Introduction to the section of the first volume called 'On thinking', Bion insisted throughout his working life that analysts should try to focus on the immediate emotional reality of their experience with the patient so that something new would have a chance of happening. He urged analysts to forget in the session what they knew, including psychoanalytic theories, and to forget what they hoped for either for themselves or for the patient; this meant, among other things, being prepared to face the possibility that no new understanding might emerge. His first presentation of these ideas in 'Notes on memory and desire' in 1967, reprinted here, met with the usual mixture of bewilderment, rejection, and idealization that Bion's statements tend to provoke. The ideas are now better accepted, and indeed recognized to be essentially similar to the attitude of mind recommended by Freud (1912).

I wish to discuss in more detail the trends of change in Kleinian clinical work. First, the question of interpreting destructiveness and self-destructiveness. Both Klein and her followers have often been accused of overemphasizing the negative. Perhaps a reason for this apparent overemphasis was that there had been little focusing on aggression in psychoanalytic theory before the 1920s, even though Freud's case histories give ample illustration of his interpreting rivalry and aggressiveness as well as unconscious sexual wishes. Certainly Klein was very much aware of destructiveness and of the anxiety it arouses, which was one of her earliest areas of research, but she also stressed, both in theory and practice, the importance of love, the patient's concern for his objects, of guilt, and of reparation. Further, in her later work especially, she conveys a strong feeling of support to the patient when negative feelings were being uncovered; this is especially clear in *Envy and Gratitude* (1957). It is my impression that she was experienced by her patients not as an adversary but as an ally in their struggles to accept feelings they hated in themselves and were therefore trying to deny and obliterate. I think it is this attitude that gave the feeling of 'balance' that Segal says was so important in her experience of Klein as an analyst (Segal 1982). Certainly that sort of balance is something that present Kleinian analysts are consciously striving for. In this respect, then, some of the authors of early clinical papers took a step backwards from the work of Klein herself, especially from her later work. Since that time there has been a change, not in the emphasis on death instinct and destructiveness, but in the way it is analysed, with less confrontation and more awareness of subtleties of conflict among different parts of the personality over it. This change has been influenced not only by the work of Bion but also by Rosenfeld's continued stress on the communicative aspect of projective identification and by Joseph's emphasis on the need for the analyst to become aware of subtleties of the patient's internal conflict over destructiveness and thus to avoid joining the patient in sado-masochistic and other forms of acting-out.

Second, changes in the language of interpretation. Klein developed her very concrete, vivid language of part objects and bodily functions in work with small children for whom it was meaningful and appropriate. Extrapolating backwards, she assumed that infants feel and think in the same way, and, further, that this is the language of thinking and feeling in everyone's unconscious. Work since Klein's day has amply demonstrated that vivid bodily-based phantasies often become conscious in the analysis of adults, especially readily in the case of psychotic and borderline psychotic patients. No one who has read the accounts of Klein's work with children or the clinical reports of her more talented students and followers can fail to be impressed by their clinical imagination and their grasp of unconscious phantasy. In less skilled hands, however, this approach lost its freshness and became routinized. As I have described above, some of her more youthful and enthusiastic followers made interpretations in terms of verbal and behavioural content seen in a rigidly symbolic form which now seems likely to have been detrimental to the recognition of alive moments of emotional contact. Such interpretations are based not on the analyst's receptiveness to the patient but on the analyst's wish to find in the patient's material evidence for the analyst's already formed conceptions. 'Memory' and 'desire', in Bion's terms, replace hypothesis and receptivity. This prejudiced attitude can of course operate with any set of analytic concepts.

A number of Kleinian analysts, perhaps especially Donald Meltzer, find it appropriate to interpret unconscious phantasy directly and immediately in part-object bodily language, but the general tendency, as I have described in the General Introduction to Volume 1, is to talk to the patient, especially the non-psychotic patient, less in terms of anatomical structures (breast, penis) and more in terms of psychological functions (seeing, hearing, thinking, evacuating, etc.). Together with this emphasis on function, concentration on the patient's immediate experience in the transference often leads to discovery of deeper layers of meaning, some of which may be seen to be based on infantile bodily experience. Talking about unconscious phantasy in bodily and part-object terms too soon is likely to lead to analyst and patient talking about the patient as if he were a third person (Joseph 1975, Riesenberg Malcolm 1981). But there is a danger also that if the analyst concentrates too exclusively on the immediate present, the here and now, he will lose sight of the infantile levels of experience that the immediate expression in the here and now is based on, that the baby will get thrown out with the bath water so to speak. Both levels of expression need to be listened for together and linked with experience.

Third: changes in the use of the concept of projective identification in analysing the transference. Although Klein herself introduced the concept of projective identification, she does not seem to have envisaged its use in the analysis of the transference in the form which rapidly developed among her close colleagues. Indeed, we now regard transference as based on projective identification, using that term in the widest sense, as I have suggested in Volume 1. According to Segal, Klein frequently used the concept of projective identification in her own work, but phrased her interpretations about it as statements about the patient's wishes, percep-tions, and defences. If, for example, a patient reported a dream in which a screaming baby had the face of the analyst, Klein would have said, 'You can't tolerate your own infantile feeling of screaming, so that you wish to get rid of those feelings into me and therefore see me in your dream as a screaming baby'. If an analyst reported to her in supervision that he had actually felt like screaming, Klein's view would have been that the analyst needed a little self-analysis. Her emphasis was always on the patient's material, not on the analyst's feelings, which, she thought, were only aroused in a way that interfered with his analytic work if he was not functioning properly. Her view is illustrated in the now classic story about a young analyst who told her he felt confused and therefore interpreted to his patient that the patient had projected confusion into him, to which she replied, 'No, dear, *you* are confused', (Segal 1982), meaning that the analyst had not understood his patient's material and was interpreting his own lack of understanding as if it had been caused by the patient's projection.

This example, however, is a case of a wrong or inadequate use of the idea of projective identification; the analyst was not seeing his own problem and was therefore blaming his own deficiencies on the patient. Bion, however, made use of exactly the same process but based it on a brilliant grasp of the way his patients were attempting to arouse in him feelings that they could not tolerate in themselves but which they unconsciously wished to express, and which could be understood by the analyst as a communication. I summarized an example of this process in Volume 1 in the section called 'Projective identification' in which Bion felt frightened in a session with a psychotic patient and then interpreted to his patient that the patient was pushing into Bion his fear that he would murder Bion; the atmosphere in the session then became less tense but the patient clenched his fists, whereupon Bion said that the patient had taken the fear back into himself and now was (consciously) feeling afraid that he would make a murderous attack (Bion 1955). Bion was thus using the idea that a patient can behave in such a way as to get the analyst to feel what the patient unconsciously feels. Unlike Klein, he was explicitly prepared to use his own feelings as a source of information about what the patient was doing.

Our view now is that what matters is not whether the analyst's own feelings should be used as a source of information but whether they are used well or badly. In spite of Klein's doubts, her colleagues continued to use her idea of projective identification as an important factor in counter-transference and indeed it is hard to see how the analyses of psychotic patients reported by Segal, Rosenfeld, Bion, and others could have proceeded without it. Certainly it is now part of the standard approach of every Kleinian analyst. At the same time, most Kleinian analysts are aware of a tendency, especially in inexperienced analysts attempting to use their feelings constructively, to become overpreoccupied with monitoring their own feelings as their primary clue to what is going on in the session, to the detriment of their direct contact with their patient's material.

Klein was uneasy not only about possible misuse of the concept of projective identification but also about the closely related issue of widening the concept of counter-transference, as described by Heimann, to mean use of the analyst's feelings as a source of information about the patient (Heimann 1950). Nearly all Kleinian analysts, however, now use the concept of counter-transference in this wider sense, that is, as a state of mind induced in the analyst as a result of verbal and non-verbal action by the patient, thus giving effect to the patient's phantasy of projective identification. Bion himself, however, uses the literal word 'counter-transference' to mean the analyst's unconscious pathological feelings, his 'transference' in the restricted sense, towards the patient, which indicates a need for more analysis for the analyst. This is of course confusing, since, as I have described above, Bion constantly uses the *idea* of counter-transference in the widened sense; it is only when he uses the actual term that he means counter-transference in the more restricted pathology-in-the-analyst sense. In practice, however, the two types of counter-transference are not invariably separable, since arousing the pathology-in-the-analyst is often the means by which the patient effects his projective identification.

More papers have been written by Kleinian and kindred analysts on counter-transference than on any other technical concept. In addition to Heimann's original paper in 1950, there is one by Money-Kyrle in 1956 (which is reprinted here), a book by Racker (1968, but written in the 1950s), and papers by Grinberg (1962), Segal (1977a), and Brenman Pick in 1985 (also reprinted here). All these authors advocate use of the counter-transference as a source of information about the patient; most also discuss the way the analyst can be thrown off his therapeutic balance by the patient but can sometimes use his own loss of composure to understand the therapeutic situation better.

Money-Kyrle's 1956 paper 'Normal counter-transference and some of its deviations' (reprinted here) describes what he calls 'normal counter-transference', a combination of curiosity and reparative wishes towards himself and his own internal objects whom the patient in part represents. This 'normal counter-transference' corresponds to the idea of the analyst's usual capacity to take in, contain, and transform the patient's feelings described by Segal (1977a) using Bion's container/contained formulation. All goes well with the transference/counter-transference fit, according to Money-Kyrle, so long as the patient produces material which the analyst knows about and can accept in himself because it is familiar from his own personal analytic experience. But when the analyst cannot understand and/or accept what the patient is putting pressure on him to take in, this normal counter-transference is disrupted. The patient is likely to respond to this disruption of the analyst's capacity by increased projection of whatever it is in himself that he cannot stand. The process Money-Kyrle describes is now familiar from Bion's work though this paper of Money-Kyrle's was written before Bion's main contribution on container/contained (1962). Money-Kyrle goes on to add other dimensions; in part he anticipates Grinberg's idea of 'projective counter-identification' as a process in which the analyst identifies with and is emotionally taken over, at least temporarily, by the aspects that the patient is projecting into him, though Grinberg stresses particularly that patients who do this have themselves been subjected to powerful projections from their own primary objects (Grinberg 1962, Segal 1977a). The emotional task for the analyst, according to Money-Kyrle, is to disentangle his own unconscious phantasies from those of his patient so that he is able to interpret his patient's anxiety and the reasons for his increased projection. If the analyst cannot do this, he resorts to 'positive counter-transference', that is, some form of reassurance or placation of the patient, or 'negative counter-transference', that is, some form of attack on the patient. In either case his intuition is gone so that his interpretations are based on theory alone. Racker (1968) develops very similar ideas though with different terminology and much fuller exemplification.

Like Money-Kyrle, both Racker (1968) and Segal (1977a) and more recently Rosenfeld (1987) emphasize the need for the analyst to be susceptible and open to being influenced by the patient but also to be detached and analytic about himself as well as his patient. Otherwise, as Racker puts it, the analyst will either have to repress his counter-transference or drown in it, neither of which helps his patient.

In 'Working through in the counter-transference' (reprinted here) Brenman Pick (1985) emphasizes the need for the analyst to be emotionally open to the patient, for the analyst not to attempt a false detachment that will allow 'the so-called pursuit of truth to be governed by hatred'. She uses the term 'working through' to describe the process which the analyst needs to go through to achieve containment of the patient's projections, which she assumes to be going on in every analytic exchange. It is her view (expressed in the paper but also in further personal communication) that the analyst, like the patient, has a primitive part of himself that wishes not to know, not to think, that wants to get rid of the new thing, the noxious element that the patient has introduced into the analyst's mind. This primitive part of the analyst's mind is in identification with the primitive parts of the patient or the patient's internal objects, and is in conflict with the more mature part of the analyst's mind which wants to know and to understand. This conflict has to be resolved within the analyst before he can mobilize his own capacity to accept psychic truth and thus help the patient to develop a similar capacity to accept the unwanted idea or feeling he is trying to get rid of. If the analyst does not go through the process of conflict resolution within himself, he acts like an 'as if' mother who can cope with everything, and this is likely to be achieved by projecting the non-coping parts of himself (the analyst) into the patient.

In Brenman Pick's view she is trying to describe in more detail what Bion means by the mother's (or analyst's) containing function, and what Money-Kyrle means by the analyst disentangling his own unconscious phantasies from those of his patient. Like Money-Kyrle, she thinks this process goes on all the time, sometimes so easily that the analyst is hardly aware of it, sometimes with considerable difficulty requiring conscious mental effort. But she wants to draw particular attention to the universality of the process, to the fact that all communications have some projective element so that the analyst is always being acted upon; and there is always some mating between what the patient projects and some part of the analyst or his internal objects.

This paper has stimulated discussion among Kleinian analysts though the various views have not been resolved. Some agree; others think, perhaps partly because of Brenman Pick's use of the term 'working through', that she believes in symmetry between analyst and patient, which they find misleading; in their view the reciprocity between patient and analyst is complementary not symmetrical, and, in the specific context of an analysis, the analyst's regression and recovery, when necessary, are necessary for the patient, not the analyst. Other analysts go along with the idea of symmetry between patient and analyst (even though symmetry is not what Brenman Pick thinks her paper is about) because they think analysts need reminding that they are not morally or mentally superior to their patients and that belief in such superiority will colour their interpretive work.

All the writers on counter-transference indicate explicitly or implicitly that far more is involved in transference and counter-transference than explicit verbal communication, that there is a constant non-verbal interaction, sometimes gross, sometimes very subtle, in which the patient acts on the analyst's mind. Many Kleinian analysts have discussed the importance of what the patient does in contrast to the content of what he says, but Betty Joseph has particularly emphasized this contrast as a starting point for her understanding of the way patients very early on in their lives and in the analytic situation adapt to their objects and attempt to control them through projective identification. Her method of work is apparent in all her papers but is perhaps most directly expounded in 'The patient who is difficult to reach' (1975, reprinted here), 'Different types of anxiety and their handling in the analytic situation' (1978), 'On understanding and not understanding: some technical issues' (1983), and 'Transference: the total situation' (1985) which is also reprinted here.

Joseph's basic aim is to discover where the alive, immediate emotional contact between patient and analyst is, this being a prerequisite of true understanding. I am not sure whether the alive immediate emotional contact is only the prerequisite; it seems more likely that it actually *is* the understanding, providing it can be made conscious. Certainly Joseph does not present material in the form of first finding the emotional contact and then proceeding to make an explanatory interpretation. Rather it takes the form of finding the point of contact and understanding momentarily, making it conscious as much as possible, and then analysing the process by which it deepens, shifts to other content, or is lost.

She stresses that much of what patients communicate in a session is not expressed in the representational content of words but through the use of words to carry out actions, to do something to the analyst or to put subtle pressure on the analyst to do something to the patient. The analytic task is to accept the pressure to do or feel some particular thing, hold on to it, reflect on the fact that one is being subjected to it, and then make a limited and precise interpretation only about the immediate action. She avoids what she calls 'double-barrelled interpretations', interpretations with two or more contrasting statements, because one cannot then be sure which part of the interpretation the patient is responding to. She avoids premature links with bodily expressions and conceptualizations of unconscious phantasy and with known facts of the patient's history, which she calls 'the plausible interpretation', because she thinks both patient and analyst then lose the immediate emotional reality and have what is in effect a safe theoretical discussion about a third person, the patient.

Joseph's approach builds on and extends the usual psychoanalytic view that the patient relives and repeats in the transference his infantile experiences, his particular patterns of anxiety and defence, the conflicts between different parts of the personality. Her method particularly stresses the repetition of infantile defences, the attempt to draw the analyst into behaviour that will evade painful emotional confrontations by attempting to maintain or restore an age-old system of psychic balance.

Her method of work has aroused the interest of all Kleinian analysts. All agree with the importance of emotional contact, but many feel that one can make more comprehensive, holistic interpretations and more immediate links with the patient's history without losing emotional contact in the immediate analytic situation. Some feel the method to be too limiting and restrictive, but no one doubts that she has developed a new and very important emphasis in Kleinian technique. Two papers are here reprinted to illustrate her method of work. The first, 'The patient who is difficult to reach' (1975) has become a landmark as the first major statement of her views on technique. It shows how her approach grew from experience and acceptance of therapeutic limitation, from learning to contain and to use constructively feelings of therapeutic discouragement. The second,

'Transference: the total situation' (1985) extends and develops the ideas initiated in the earlier paper.

Finally, in recent years there has been much discussion among Kleinian analysts of the way past experience emerges in the analytic situation, especially of whether and when the patient's account of the historical past should be explicitly linked with interpretations of the transference/ counter-transference situation in the session. There is a considerable range of views which do not fall into neatly demarcated sets.

Reconstruction, remembering, and repeating have always been considered important ever since Freud first drew attention to them, but I think the renewed interest in the topic of the past in the present among Kleinian analysts has come about at least partly because of the emphasis of Joseph and her colleagues on acting-in, that is, on 'repeating' as the central process that analysts should address themselves to. The hope is that through thoroughgoing analysis of 'repeating', 'remembering' will occur, not only in the form of remembering forgotten historical events but in the sense of making conscious anxieties, defences, and internal object relationships that are being kept unconscious in the present.

According to one view this is all that is necessary. If links are to be made with actual events of the past, which can in any case be known only through the filter of the patient's projections, the patient will make these links for himself. Reconstruction by the analyst in the form of making explicit links with the historical past is both unnecessary and misleading. It distracts the patient from the emotional experience in the session.

Most Kleinian analysts, however, think that explicit linking with the historical past is a crucial part of the psychoanalytic process which greatly enriches the meaningfulness of the psychoanalytic experience and gives the patient a sense of the continuity of his experience. There is some disagreement over when and how explicit linking with the past should be done. There is one set of analysts who think that although the first objective should be to clarify and make conscious the past in the present through analysis of the patient's 'repeating', his acting-in. Once that has become emotionally real one can make links with the patient's current view of his historical past. Premature links with the past, like premature links with bodily expressions of unconscious phantasy, are likely to lead to talking about emotional reality instead of experiencing it. But once the emotional experience has become real in the present, reconstructions and links with the past can consolidate it. This is the view expressed in Joseph's paper 'Transference: the total situation' (1985, reprinted here) and in Riesenberg Malcolm's paper 'Interpretation: the past in the present' (1986, also reprinted here). In a somewhat different form the same view is expressed in Brenman's paper 'The value of reconstruction in adult analysis' (1980). Brenman emphasizes the joint exploration, 'new beginning' aspect of exploring the past that analyst and patient can do together once understanding has been achieved in the immediacy of the transference. Common to all three papers is a view that talk about the past is distant, more intellectual, than experience in the immediacy of the here and now of the transference/counter-transference, but all agree that it can be extremely useful provided it is not used defensively.

Segal, however, does not agree that interpretations about the past are necessarily more intellectual and distant than interpretations about the immediate analyst-patient interaction. In this she is joined by Rosenfeld, who thinks that useful reconstructive interpretations and observations can be brought in whenever they seem relevant and are indeed thought of as an essential component of transference (Rosenfeld 1987).

But in some of his later work Rosenfeld goes further. In the case of traumatized patients he thinks that interpretations in the immediate transference/counter-transference situation are likely to be positively harmful because the patient experiences them as the analyst repeating the behaviour of a self-centred primary object, always demanding to be the centre of the patient's attention and concern (Rosenfeld 1986). He thinks the analyst should concentrate, at least initially, on a sympathetic elucidation of the traumatic events of the past in all their ramifications. Critics of Rosenfeld's view think that the problem of repeating the behaviour of a self-centred parent can be dealt with by interpretation rather than by behaving differently from the parent, and are further concerned that concentrating mainly on elucidation of past traumas may lead to splitting between an idealized analyst and denigrated primary objects, and to a belief by the analyst that he can know what the external reality of the historical past actually was.

Thus after many years of very little explicit discussion about technique it now seems likely that these and similar exchanges among Kleinian analysts will lead to more explicit statements of their various views.

Notes on memory and desire

WILFRED BION

These notes were first published in 1967 in *The Psychoanalytic Forum*, 2: 272–3, 279–80. Several analysts took part in the discussion but only Bion's contribution is reprinted here.

Memory is always misleading as a record of fact since it is distorted by the influence of unconscious forces. Desires interfere, by absence of mind when observation is essential, with the operation of judgement. Desires distort judgement by selection and suppression of material to be judged.

Memory and desire exercise and intensify those aspects of the mind that derive from sensuous experience. They thus promote capacity derived from sense impressions and designed to serve impressions of sense. They deal respectively with sense impressions of what is supposed to have happened and sense impressions of what has not yet happened.

Psychoanalytic 'observation' is concerned neither with what has happened nor with what is going to happen but with what *is* happening. Furthermore it is not concerned with sense impressions or objects of sense. Any psychoanalyst knows depression, anxiety, fear and other aspects of psychic reality whether those aspects have been or can be successfully named or not. These are the psychoanalyst's real world. Of its reality he has no doubt. Yet anxiety, to take one example, has no shape, no smell, no taste; awareness of the sensuous accompaniments of emotional experience are a hindrance to the psychoanalyst's intuition of the reality with which he must be at one.

Every session attended by the psychoanalyst must have no history and no future.

What is 'known' about the patient is of no further consequence: it is either false or irrelevant. If it is 'known' by patient and analyst, it is obsolete. If it is 'known' by the one but not the other, a defence or grid category 2 element (Bion 1963, 1965) is operating. The only point of importance in any session is the unknown. Nothing must be allowed to distract from intuiting that.

In any session, evolution takes place. Out of the darkness and formlessness something evolves. That evolution can bear a superficial resemblance to memory, but once it has been experienced it can never be confounded with memory. It shares with dreams the quality of being wholly present or unaccountably and suddenly absent. This evolution is what the psychoanalyst must be ready to interpret.

To do this he needs to discipline his thoughts. First and foremost, as every psychoanalyst knows, he must have had as thorough an analysis as possible; nothing said here must be taken as casting doubt on that. Second, he must cultivate a watchful avoidance of memory. Notes should be confined to matters which *can* be recorded — the programme of appointments is an obvious example.

Obey the following rules:

1. *Memory*: do not remember past sessions. The greater the impulse to 'remember' what has been said or done, the more the need to resist it. This impulse can present itself as a wish to remember something that has happened because it appears to have precipitated an emotional crisis: *no* crisis should be allowed to breach this rule. The supposed events must not be allowed to occupy the mind. Otherwise the evolution of the session will not be observed at the only time when it can be observed — while it is taking place.
2. *Desires*: the psychoanalyst can start by avoiding any desires for the approaching end of the session (or week, or term). Desires for results, 'cure' or even understanding must not be allowed to proliferate.

These rules must be obeyed *all* the time and not simply during the sessions. In time the psychoanalyst will become more aware of the pressure of memories and desires and more skilled at eschewing them.

If this discipline is followed there will be an increase of anxiety in the psychoanalyst at first, but it must not interfere with preservation of the rules. The procedure should be started at once and not abandoned on any pretext whatever.

The pattern of analysis will change. Roughly speaking, the patient will not appear to develop over a period of time but each session will be complete in itself. 'Progress' will be measured by the increased number and variety of moods, ideas and attitudes seen in any given session. There will be less clogging of the sessions by the repetition of material which should have disappeared and, consequently, a quickened tempo within each session every session.

The psychoanalyst should aim at achieving a state of mind so that at every session he feels he has not seen the patient before. If he feels he has, he is treating the wrong patient.

This procedure is extremely penetrating. Therefore the psychoanalyst must aim at a steady exclusion of memory and desire and not be too disturbed if the results appear alarming at first. He will become used to it and he will have the consolation of building his psychoanalytic technique on a firm basis of intuiting evolution and *not* on the shifting sand of slight experience imperfectly remembered which rapidly gives way not to experience but to neurologically certain decay of mental faculty. The evolving session is unmistakable and the intuiting of it does not deteriorate. If given a chance it starts early and decays late.

The foregoing is a brief account distilled from putting the precepts advocated into practice. The theoretical implications can be worked out by each psychoanalyst for himself. His interpretations should gain in force and conviction — both for himself and his patient — because they derive from the emotional experience with a unique individual and not from generalized theories imperfectly 'remembered'.

Author's response

The discussants of my 'Notes on memory and desire' help to make it clear that some of the confusion arises through the ambiguity of the terms 'memory' and 'desire'. I realize that it would be helpful if I could distinguish between two different phenomena which are both usually and indifferently called 'memory'. This I have tried to do by speaking of one as 'evolution', by which I mean the experience where some idea or pictorial impression floats into the mind unbidden and as a whole. From this I wish to distinguish ideas which present themselves in response to a deliberate and conscious attempt at recall; for this last I reserve the term 'memory'. 'Memory' I keep for experience related predominantly to sensuous impressions: 'evolution' I regard as based on experience which has no sensuous background but is expressed in terms which are derived from the language of sensuous experience. For example, I '*see*', meaning I 'intuit through the medium of a visual impression'.

'Desire' should not be distinguished from 'memory', as I prefer that the terms should represent one phenomenon which is a suffusion of both. I have tried to express this by saying 'memory' is the past tense of 'desire', 'anticipation' being its future tense.

These definitory hypotheses have a limited value, and I suggest that every psychoanalyst should make up his mind for himself by simple experimentation as to what these terms represent. For example, he should school himself to avoid thinking of the end of the session, week or term (having made previous provision for terminating the session at the correct time as a matter of administration), and when he has done this for a sufficient period without trying to hurry himself, make up his mind about what *he* would call 'memory' and 'desire'. When he has done this he can proceed to the next stage of extending his suppressions of the experience he has discovered in this way. I must warn psychoanalysts that I do not think they should extend this procedure hurriedly or without discussion with other psychoanalysts with a view to consolidating each step before taking another.

This procedure seems to me to approximate a state which Freud described in a letter to Lou Andreas-Salomé, 25 May 1916: 'I know that I have artificially blinded myself at my work in order to concentrate all the light on the one dark passage.' In my experience this procedure makes it possible to intuit a present 'evolution' and lay the foundations for future 'evolutions'. The more firmly this is done, the less the psychoanalyst has to bother about remembering.

I hope this makes clear some of the points to which Dr French objects, though I am doubtful whether this method should be used if he really feels that he is 'completely unable' to understand. Indeed, I would not 'desire' anyone to employ this approach unless, like Dr Lindon, he feels it has some meaning for him.

The experience which Dr Lindon describes appears to me to afford the foundation for exploring the whole question of psychoanalytic observation. I agree with his feeling that 'memory' and 'desire' are obstacles intervening between the psychoanalyst and the emotional experience of the session. When it is considered how little opportunity even five sessions a week affords the psychoanalyst, any obstacle to appreciation becomes serious.

Dr González draws attention to a defect of which I am very conscious. My own feeling is that my views have 'evolved', and although this must mean they have changed, I think the 'change' less significant than the 'evolution'. I think the expressions he rightly quotes from *Elements of Psycho-Analysis* are wrongly framed, but wrong though the formulations now seem to me to be, they were good enough to lead me to my present formulations which I think are better. In particular, I think the use of language based on the experience of the senses led me to fail to recognize that one does not in fact 'see' (feel, touch, smell, etc.) anxiety. I hope that my experience will be repeated by others who have tried to read these earlier formulations. If it is, I shall feel less remorseful.

I hope that my quotation from Freud will convince Dr Brierley that I am attempting to elaborate on the importance of rapport. I feel some unease if it is suggested that I am departing from psychoanalytic technique, not because I have any objection to innovation if it seems to be necessary, but because it is unlikely that the intuitions of experienced psychoanalysts can be lightly laid aside. I do hope, however, that the points I make may help psychoanalysts to think themselves into closer contact with the psychoanalytic experience.

Darwin expressed the view that judgement was inimical to observation, but, as Dr Brierley points out, the psychoanalyst has to formulate judgements while observations are being made. I hope the distinction I have tried to draw between 'evolution' and 'memory' may help to meet her objections. I believe it would go some way towards meeting Dr Herskovitz's objection to 'illogicalities'. I do in any case feel doubts about the value of a logical theory to represent the realizations of psychoanalysis. I think the 'logical' theory and the 'illogicalities' of the psychoanalytic experience should be permitted to coexist until the observed disharmony is resolved by 'evolution'.

References

Bion, W.R. (1963) *Elements of Psycho-Analysis*, London: Heinemann; reprinted in paperback, Maresfield Reprints, London: H. Karnac Books (1984).

—— (1965) *Transformations*, London: Heinemann; reprinted in paperback, Maresfield Reprints, London: H. Karnac Books (1984).

2

Normal counter-transference and some of its deviations

ROGER MONEY-KYRLE

This article was originally a paper read at the 19th Psycho-Analytical Congress, Geneva, 24—8 July 1955. It was first published in the *International Journal of Psycho-Analysis*, 37: 360—6. It was reprinted in *The Collected Papers of Roger Money-Kyrle*, 1978, ed. Donald Meltzer with the assistance of Edna O'Shaughnessy, Strathtay, Perthshire: Clunie Press.

Introductory

Counter-transference is an old psychoanalytic concept which has recently been widened and enriched. We used to think of it mainly as a personal disturbance to be analysed away in ourselves. We now also think of it as having its causes, and effects, in the patient and, therefore, as an indication of something to be analysed in him.[1]

I believe this more recently explored aspect of counter-transference can be used, in the way described, for example, by Paula Heimann (1950), to achieve an important technical advance. But of course the discovery that counter-transference can be usefully employed does not imply that it has ceased ever to be a serious impediment. And as both aspects in fact exist, we may surmise that there may be a problem about their similarities and differences which still deserves investigation. Perhaps this problem may be put in the form of three related questions: What is 'normal' counter-transference? How and under what conditions is it disturbed? And how can disturbances be corrected in the process perhaps used to further an analysis?

Normal counter-transference

As to the analyst's correct or normal attitude to the patient, there are a number of aspects which have been mentioned both in papers and discussions. Freud spoke of a 'benevolent neutrality'. This I take to imply that the analyst is concerned for the welfare of his patient, without becoming emotionally involved in his conflicts. It also implies, I think, that the analyst, in virtue of his understanding of psychic determinism, has a certain kind of tolerance which is the opposite of condemnation, and yet by no means the same as indulgence or indifference.

Many analysts have stressed the element of scientific curiosity, and certainly we should not get far without this sublimation. But, by itself, it seems a little too impersonal. Concern for the patient's welfare comes, I think, from the fusion of two other basic drives: the reparative, which counteracts the latent destructiveness in all of us, and the parental. Of course, if too intense, they betray excessive guilt about inadequately sublimated aggressiveness which can be the cause of very disturbing anxieties. But, in some degree, both are surely normal. The reparative satisfactions of analysis are obvious and often referred to. So, in some degree, the patient must stand for the damaged objects of the analyst's own unconscious phantasy, which are still endangered by aggression and still in need of care and reparation. The parental aspect has been mentioned, in discussions, by Paula Heimann.[2] No one would suggest that the patient stands only for a child, and not sometimes for a sibling, or even for a parent. But it is with the unconscious child in the patient that the analyst is *most* concerned; and because this child so often treats the analyst as parent, the analyst's unconscious can hardly fail to respond in some degree by regarding the patient as his child.

Now, to a parent, a child stands, at least in part, for an early aspect of the self. And this seems to me important. For it is just because the analyst can recognize his early self, which has already been analysed, in the patient, that he can analyse the patient.[3] His empathy and insight, as distinct from his theoretical knowledge, depend on this kind of partial identification.[4]

But identification can take two forms — introjective and projective — a distinction latent in Freud's concept, the significance of which Melanie Klein has recently brought out.[5] We may therefore expect to find both forms in the analyst's partial identification with his patient.

I will try to formulate what seems to be happening when the analysis is going well. I believe there is a fairly rapid oscillation between introjection and projection. As the patient speaks, the analyst will, as it were, become introjectively identified with him, and having understood him inside, will reproject him and interpret. But what I think the analyst is most aware of is the projective phase — that is to say, the phase in which the patient is the representative of a former immature or ill part of himself, including his damaged objects, which he can now understand

23

and therefore treat by interpretation, in the external world.

Meanwhile the patient is receiving effective interpretations, which help him to respond with further associations that can be understood. As long as the analyst understands them, this satisfactory relationship — which I will call the 'normal' one — persists. In particular, the analyst's counter-transference feelings will be confined to that sense of empathy with the patient on which his insight is based.

Periods of non-understanding

Everyone, the analyst no less than the patient, would be happy if the situation I have just described, and called the 'normal' one, would persist throughout the whole course of an analysis. Unfortunately, it is normal only in the sense of being an ideal. It depends for its continuity on the analyst's continuous understanding. But he is not omniscient. In particular, his understanding fails whenever the patient corresponds too closely with some aspect of himself which he has not yet learnt to understand. Moreover, some patients are much less co-operative than others. There are patients with whom the best of analysts find great difficulty in maintaining contact — with whom the 'normal' relationship is the exception rather than the rule. And even with co-operative patients, it is subject to fairly frequent breaks.

We recognize these breaks at once by our feeling that the material has become obscure, and that we have somehow lost the thread. Now what-ever has in fact been missed, the fact of missing it creates a new situation which may be felt as a strain by the analyst as well as by the patient. Of course some analysts — for example, those who most crave the reassurance of continuous success — feel such strains more acutely than others. But, apart from individual differences, there is a peculiarity in the very nature of the analytic technique which must impose some strain on all of us — especially at moments when we cannot help a patient who is in obvious distress. For, if my argument so far is right, we all have some need to satisfy our parental and reparative drives to counteract the death instinct; but we are much more restricted in the ways in which we can do so than a real parent, an educationalist, or any other kind of therapist. We are restricted to the giving of interpretations;[6] and our capacity to give them depends upon our continuing to understand the patient. If this understanding fails, as fail from time to time it must, we have no alternative therapy to fall back on. Here, then, is a situation peculiar to analysis, when lack of understanding is liable to arouse conscious or unconscious anxiety, and anxiety still further to diminish understanding. It is to the onset of this kind of vicious spiral that I am inclined to attribute every deviation in normal counter-transference feeling.

If the analyst is in fact disturbed, it is also likely that the patient has unconsciously contributed to this result, and is in turn disturbed by it. So we have three factors to consider: first, the analyst's emotional disturbance, for he may have to deal with this silently in himself before he can disengage himself sufficiently to understand the other two; then the patient's part in bringing it about; and finally its effect on him. Of course, all three factors may be sorted out in a matter of seconds, and then indeed the counter-transference is functioning as a delicate receiving apparatus. But I will discuss the first stage first, as if it were a lengthy process — as it sometimes is.

The role of the analyst's superego

The extent to which an analyst is emotionally disturbed by periods of non-understanding will probably depend, in the first instance, on another factor: the severity of his own superego. For analysis is also a form of work required of us by this inner figure — which, incidentally, a demanding patient may sometimes come to represent. If our superego is predominantly friendly and helpful, we can tolerate our own limitations without undue distress, and, being undisturbed, will be the more likely soon to regain contact with the patient. But if it is severe, we may become conscious of a sense of failure as the expression of an unconscious persecutory or depressive guilt. Or, as a defence against such feelings, we may blame the patient.

The choice of one or other of these alternatives seems to me to determine something else as well. For when that interplay between introjection and projection, which characterizes the analytic process, breaks down, the analyst may tend to get stuck in one or other of these two positions; and what he does with his guilt may determine the position he gets stuck in. If he accepts the guilt, he is likely to get stuck with an introjected patient. If he projects it, the patient remains an incomprehensible figure in the external world.

Examples of prolonged introjection and projection

An example of the first, that is, the introjective, alternative may be seen when the analyst gets unduly worried, both on his own and his patient's behalf, about a session that has gone badly. He may feel as if he had regained some of his own old troubles and become almost physically

25

burdened with his patient's as well. Only when he separates the two can he see what he has missed and get the patient out of him again.

Often, it is something towards the end of a session, or of a week, which he feels he has missed, and then he has all the patient's supposed frustration in himself. This may look like a self-punishment for having unconsciously intended to hurt the patient. But we may wonder whether the patient has not contributed to the analyst's distress — whether the leaving of his analyst with an unsolved problem about himself is not his way of projecting himself into the analyst both to punish him for, and to avoid, the threatened separation.

In other words, there may be a symbiosis between the analyst's tendency to prolong the introjection of a patient whom he cannot understand or help and the patient's tendency to project parts of himself, in the way described by Melanie Klein, into the analyst who is not helping him. (This may be particularly disturbing if what the patient is most anxious to get rid of is his own destructiveness.)

In such cases the ultimate cause of the analyst's slowness in understanding and reprojecting the patient may be that the patient has come to stand for something which he has not yet learnt to understand quickly in himself. If he still fails to do so, and cannot tolerate the sense of being burdened with the patient as an irreparable or persecuting figure inside him, he is likely to resort to a defensive kind of reprojection which shuts out the patient and creates a further bar to understanding.

If so, a new complication may arise if the analyst, in projecting the patient, projects aspects of himself as well. Then he will have the chance to explore within himself the workings of those mechanisms of projective identification, which under the influence of Melanie Klein (1946), Rosenfeld (1952) and others have so fruitfully explored in schizophrenic patients. Nor need we be surprised at this, for the discovery of pathological mechanisms in mental illness is usually followed by the recognition of their less obvious presence in normal people too. A 'slow-motion' example of the kind of process I have in mind may be seen in another fairly common weekend experience. For a little time after he has finished his week's work, the analyst may be consciously preoccupied with some unsolved problem of his patients. Then he forgets them; but the period of conscious concern is followed by a period of listlessness in which he is depleted of the private interests that usually occupy his leisure. I suggest this is because, in phantasy, he has projected parts of himself together with his patients and must wait, as it were, till these return to him.

When this partial loss of self occurs within a session, it is often experienced as the loss of intellectual potency; the analyst feels stupid. The patient may well have contributed to this result. Perhaps, frustrated by not getting an immediate interpretation, he has unconsciously wished to castrate his analyst, and by treating him as if he were, has helped to make him feel castrated.[7]

A complicated example taken from my own experience would seem to illustrate the simultaneous operation of all these processes. For while the dominant theme was my projection of a patient who wished to project his illness into me, I also experienced a sense of being robbed of my wits by him.

A neurotic patient, in whom paranoid and schizoid mechanisms were prominent, arrived for a session in considerable anxiety because he had not been able to work in his office. He had also felt vague on the way, as if he might get lost or run over; and he despised himself for being useless. Remembering a similar occasion, on which he had felt depersonalized over a weekend and dreamed that he had left his 'radar' set in a shop and would be unable to get it before Monday, I thought he had, in phantasy, left parts of his 'good self' in me. But I was not very sure of this, or of other interpretations I began to give. And he, for his part, soon began to reject them all with a mounting degree of anger; and, at the same time, abused me for not helping. By the end of the session he was no longer depersonalized, but very angry and contemptuous instead. It was I who felt useless and bemused.

When I eventually recognized my state at the end as so similar to that he had described as his at the beginning, I could almost feel the relief of a reprojection. By then the session was over. But he was in the same mood at the beginning of the next one — still very angry and contemptuous. I then told him I thought he felt he had reduced me to the state of useless vagueness he himself had been in; and that he felt he had done this by having me 'on the mat', asking questions and rejecting the answers, in the way his legal father did. His response was striking. For the first time in two days, he became quiet and thoughtful. He then said this explained why he had been so angry with me yesterday: he had felt that all my interpretations referred to my illness and not to his.

I suggest that, as in a slow-motion picture, we can here see several distinct processes which, in an ideal or 'normal' analytic period, should occur extremely quickly. I think I began, as it were, to take my patient in, to identify introjectively with him, as soon as he lay down and spoke about his very acute distress. But I could not at once recognize it as corresponding with anything already understood in myself; and, for this reason, I was slow to get it out of me in the process of explaining, and so relieving it in him. He, for his part, felt frustrated at not getting effective interpretations, and reacted by projecting his sense of mental impotence into me, at the same time behaving as if he had taken from me what he felt he had lost, his father's clear, but aggressive, intellect, with which he attacked his impotent self in me. By this time, of course, it was useless to try to pick up the thread where I had first dropped it. A new situation had arisen which had affected us both. And before my patient's part in bringing it about could be interpreted, I had to do a silent piece of self-analysis involving the discrimination of two things which can be felt as very similar: my own sense of incompetence at having lost the thread, and my patient's contempt for his impotent self, which he felt to be in me. Having made this interpretation to myself, I was eventually able to pass the second half of it on to my patient, and, by so doing, restored the normal analytic situation.

According to Bion,[8] the capacity to make this kind of discrimination, and much more quickly than in the example, is an important part of the capacity to use one's counter-transference in the interests of analysis.

Positive and negative counter-transference

Coming now to counter-transference in the narrow sense of an excess of positive or negative feeling, this too is often an indirect result of the frustrations arising when a distressed patient is not understood, and no effective interpretations can be given. For the analyst whose reparative impulse is thwarted of its analytically normal outlet may be unconsciously inclined either to offer some form of love instead, or to become hostile to his patient. Meanwhile, the patient may be facilitating the process by trying to provoke one or other of these affects in his analyst, who is the more likely to respond *to* his patient's mood just because he has lost his empathy *with* it.

Now, however scrupulously we may suppress an excess of positive or negative feeling of this kind, the patient is likely to sense it unconsciously. Then a new situation arises in which his response to our mood may itself have to be interpreted.

If, for example, the counter-transference is too positive, the patient may respond to our increased emotional concern by complaining that we have no emotional concern. We do not contradict him as he may wish. But it may be appropriate to tell him he believes we are attracted to him and has to deny it in order to avoid the responsibility for a seduction. For an important early pattern may be involved. As a child, he may have been unconsciously aware that his caresses embarrassed one of his parents, for example, his mother, because she was afraid of being aroused by them; and the sense of being rebuffed may have rankled all his life, because it was needed to counteract his guilt for trying to seduce her. If so, the interpretation of the repetition of this pattern in the transference may enable the patient to reassess, not only his analyst's, but his real parent's attitude to him.

28

But if it goes unnoticed, and its effects unobserved, the unconscious offering of love in lieu of effective interpretations may disturb the analysis in many ways. For instance, the analyst may foster the split, directly in his own mind and indirectly in his patient's, between himself as a good parent and the real parents as bad ones. Then the patient may never become aware of his guilt towards them — a guilt which, paradoxically enough, is likely to be all the greater if they were really bad; for it is in proportion to his own ambivalence. If this guilt is not recovered in analysis, the patient cannot work through that early stage described by Melanie Klein as the depressive position, in which the developing infant begins to become aware of, and miserable about, the conflict between his hatred and his love.

As to the negative attitudes to a patient which may also result from a temporary failure to understand him, these would seem especially to arise when the patient becomes a persecution because he is felt to be incurable. Then, as before, the analyst's triple task is first to become aware of this defensive mechanism in himself, then of his patient's part in bringing it about, and lastly of its effect on him.

To take the last point first. The sort of paranoid patient I mentioned earlier, who hated me for years and seemed to make no noticeable progress, can easily come to stand for one's own bad and persecutory objects, which one would like to get rid of. Such feelings betray themselves in one's sigh of relief after the last session of the week, or before a holiday. One's first impulse may be to suppress such hostile feelings; but if one does not allow oneself to become aware of them, one may miss their influence on the patient's unconscious. For instance, I came to feel that the occasions on which this patient repudiated me with more than ordinary violence, followed rather then preceded, moments when I would really have been glad to see the last of him. And then my interpretation that it was he who felt rebuffed met with more success.

I also noticed more clearly that the times when I was aware of disliking him followed moments in which I had despaired of helping him. And I began to wonder whether he, on his side, was not trying to make me despair and, if so, what his motives were. Several seemed to be involved, of which perhaps the most important was that, in his phantasy, getting well was equated with the renunciation of an unacknowledged homosexual component in himself. He unconsciously wished to prove to me that this could not be done. Meanwhile, he attacked me consciously for not curing him, that is, for not removing the impulse; and unconsciously for not satisfying it for him.

Conclusion

If what I have said so far touches only the fringe of an immensely complicated subject, it at least suggests the possibility of approximate answers to the questions I began with: What is normal counter-transference? How and under what conditions is it disturbed? And how can disturbances be corrected and in the process perhaps used to further an analysis?

The analyst's motive is a blend of curiosity with parental and reparative drives. His equipment consists both of his theoretical knowledge about the unconscious, and of his personal acquaintance with its manifestation which he has gained in his own analysis. But it is with his use of the second that we are here concerned; that is, with his insight, for this consists in his ability, by means of a partial identification with his patient, to apply his acquaintance with his own unconscious to the interpretation of his patient's behaviour. When all is going well, this identification seems to oscillate between its introjective and projective forms. The analyst, as it were, absorbs the patient's state of mind through the medium of the associations he hears and the postures he observes, recognizes it as expressing some pattern in his own unconscious world of phantasy, and reprojects the patient in the act of formulating his interpretation. In this phase he may get that sense of helpfully understanding his patient from within which satisfies both his curiosity and his reparative drives. To some degree, his interest is also a parental one; for, to the parent, the child is his early self, and it is with the same child in the patient that the analyst is most concerned. His sense of being in touch with it, his empathy, comprises his 'normal' counter-transference feeling.

What keeps the process going is the analyst's repeated acts of recognition, in the introjective phase, that such and such a pattern of absorbed emotion expresses such and such a phantasy in his own unconscious. And what causes a break in this relationship is a failure in this recognition.

The cause of a failure may be something still feared, because not yet fully understood, within the analyst to which the patient has come too close. But the result need be no more than a retardation in the analytic process, which enables us the better to observe its separate phases. This happens particularly when it is the first or introjective phase which is slowed down. The analyst then feels burdened with the patient and with some of his old immature self as well. He has to do more slowly, what at other times he does at once: become conscious of the phantasies within him, recognize their source, separate the patient's from his own, and so objectify him again.

But the analyst may also have to deal with two other factors, which are much less in evidence when the process is going quickly. These are

30

the patient's contribution — in particular his use of projective identification — to the analyst's disturbed emotions, and the effect which these in turn may be having on the patient.

It may be, however, that the analyst does not succeed in sorting all this out within himself before he reprojects the patient as something not understood, or foreign, in the external world. Then, since his reparative impulses can find no outlet in effective interpretations, he may be tempted to fall back on some form of reassurance instead. Or, if he despairs of his reparative powers, he may defend himself against depression by feeling angry with his patient. In either case, his intuition has temporarily gone so that any interpretations he makes can be based only on his knowledge of theory, which by itself is likely to be a sterile substitute for a fruitful combination of the two.

If we were omniscient analysts, the only counter-transference we should experience would be that belonging to those intuitive periods when all is going well. In fact, the less satisfactory states I have tried to describe, in which our feelings are at least in some degree disturbed, probably take up a lot more analytic time than we readily remember or admit. Yet it is precisely in them, I think, that the analyst, by silently analysing his own reactions, can increase his insight, decrease his difficulties, and learn more about his patient.

Notes

1   The use of counter-transference as an 'instrument of research' has been especially studied by Paula Heimann (1950). That is to say, she has stressed its *causes* in the patient, while Margaret Little (1951) has stressed its *effects* on him. This, too, is clearly an important aspect. But in interpreting the patient's response to our counter-transference, opinions differ about whether, as she thinks, we should occasionally be prepared to admit to him what our counter-transference was — instead of confining ourselves to interpreting what is in his mind, namely, his *beliefs* about our attitude.

2   The sublimation of curiosity and of parental impulses has been stressed respectively by Clifford Scott and Paula Heimann in scientific discussions in the British Psycho-Analytical Society. But I have not found specific references to these points in any of their published papers. In 'Problems of the training analysis' (1954), however, Paula Heimann does implicitly refer to the dangers of an excess of parental sublimation.

3   Conversely, by discovering new patterns in a patient, the analyst can make 'post-graduate' progress in his own analysis.

4   Annie Reich (1951) speaks of a 'short-lived identification', and Paula Heimann of identification in both introjective and projective forms in her 'Problems of the training analysis' quoted above.

5   Melanie Klein (1946). I think the distinction between introjective and projective identification is implicit, though not very clearly brought out, in Freud's *Group Psychology and the Analysis of the Ego* (1921).

6   The extent to which we are in fact restricted to pure interpretations depends, in some degree, upon our school. We are all agreed that our main role is to give interpretations. No one denies that we also arrange a certain framework within which to give them: we provide the physical comfort of a couch; and we preserve a certain courtesy of manner with minor variations according to the requirements of different patients, some wishing to shake hands before or after every session, others not, and so on. But opinions differ about whether the framework, once established, should be deliberately manipulated. Thus, Winnicott, if I understand him rightly, has argued that some psychotic patients can only form a relation to an ideal object which they have never had, and that the analyst may have to play this role before analysis proper can be started; in other words, that it is not alone sufficient to interpret the patient's efforts to force this role on him.

7   If so, the patient is also likely to introject him in this condition and then feel in more desperate need of external help than ever. At such moments, the analyst may become disagreeably aware that the patient is still more urgently demanding that which he is still less able to give — consciously, a good interpretation, unconsciously a breast or penis which now neither feel they have.

8   Bion (1955). 'How exactly a patient does succeed in imposing a phantasy and its corresponding affect upon his analyst in order to deny it in himself is a most interesting problem. I do not think we need assume some form of extrasensory communication; but the communication can be of a pre-verbal and archaic kind — similar perhaps to that used by gregarious animals in which the posture or call of a single member will arouse a corresponding affect in the rest. In the analytic situation, a peculiarity of communication of this kind is that, at first sight, they do not seem as if they had been made by the patient at all. The analyst experiences the affect as being his own response to something. The effort involved is in differentiating the patient's contribution from his own.'

References

Bion, W.R. (1955) 'Language and the schizophrenic', Chapter 9 in M. Klein, P. Heimann, and R.E. Money-Kyrle (eds), *New Directions in Psycho-Analysis*, London Tavistock Publications, 220—39; paperback, Tavistock Publications (1971); also reprinted by Maresfield Reprints, London: H. Karnac Books (1985).

Freud, S. (1921) *Group Psychology and the Analysis of the Ego*, SE 18, 67—143.

Heimann, P. (1950) 'On counter-transference', *International Journal of Psycho-Analysis*, 31: 81—4.

—— (1954) 'Problems of the training analysis', *International Journal of Psycho-Analysis*, 35: 163—8.

Klein, M. (1946) 'Notes on some schizoid mechanisms', in *Developments in Psycho-Analysis*, London: Hogarth Press (1952); reprinted in *The Writings of Melanie Klein*, vol. 3, *Envy and Gratitude and Other Works*, London: Hogarth Press (1975) 1—24.

Little, M. (1951) 'Counter-transference and the patient's response to it', *International Journal of Psycho-Analysis*, 32: 32—40.

Reich, A. (1951) 'On counter-transference', *International Journal of Psycho-Analysis*, 32: 25—31.

Rosenfeld, H. (1952) 'Transference phenomena and transference analysis in an acute catatonic schizophrenic patient', *International Journal of Psycho-Analysis*, 33: 457—64; and in H. Rosenfeld, *Psychotic States*, London: Hogarth Press (1965) 104—16.

Working through in the counter-transference

IRMA BRENMAN PICK

This is a revised version of a paper first published in 1985 in the *International Journal of Psycho-Analysis*, 66: 157—66.

In this paper I hope to explore something about the complex interaction that takes place between analyst and analysand in our everyday work. Bion made the succinct remark that when two people get together they make a relationship whether they like it or not; this applies to all encounters including psychoanalysis.

Strachey (1934), in his now classic paper, spoke of a true transference interpretation being that which the analyst most feared and most wished to avoid, yet later went on to say that in receiving a transference interpretation, the patient has the experience of expressing murderous impulses toward the analyst and of the analyst interpreting these without anxiety or fear. Strachey is clearly implying that the full or deep transference experience is disturbing to the analyst; that which the analyst most fears and most wishes to avoid. He also says that conveying an interpretation in a calm way to the patient is necessary. The area I wish to address is this ambiguous problem, this walking the tightrope between experiencing disturbance and responding with interpretation that does not convey disturbing anxiety.

Whilst earlier understanding regarded counter-transference as something extraneous rather that integral, Heimann (1950) showed the use of the counter-transference as an important tool for psychoanalysis and differentiated this from the pathological counter-transference response. Whilst this differentiation is an essential part of our psychoanalytic endeavour, I wish to show how problematic the clinical reality is. For there is no such absolute separation, only a relative movement within that orbit.

It was Money-Kyrle (1956) who considerably furthered our understanding of this issue by showing how closely the analyst's experience of the patient's projections may be linked with the analyst's own internal reactions to the material. For example, he showed that in a difficult phase of an analysis the projection by the patient into the analyst of his incompetent self became mixed up with the analyst's own feelings of professional incompetence in not understanding the material quickly enough, and these issues had to be disentangled.

Money-Kyrle, investigating this problem in its more ordinary manifestations, said:

'If the analyst is in fact disturbed [and here it is implied that the analyst is inevitably disturbed in the sense of affected], it is also likely that the patient has unconsciously contributed to this result, and is in turn disturbed by this. So we have three factors to consider: first, the analyst's emotional disturbance, for he may have to deal with this silently in himself before he can disengage himself sufficiently to understand the other two; then the patient's part in bringing it about; and finally, its effect on him. Of course, all three factors may be sorted out in a matter of seconds, and then indeed the counter-transference is functioning as a delicate receiving apparatus.' (p. 361)

Indeed, in so far as we take in the experience of the patient, we cannot do so without also having an experience. If there is a mouth that seeks a breast as an inborn potential, there is, I believe, a psychological equivalent, i.e. a state of mind which seeks another state of mind.

The child's or patient's projective identifications are actions in part intended to produce reactions; the first thing that happens inside a living object into whom a projection takes place is a reaction. The analyst may deal with this so quickly as not to become aware of it: yet it is a crucial factor. The encounter is an interaction and, indeed, if it is being dealt with that quickly, we may have to ask whether the deeper experience is in fact being avoided.

A patient reported the following: when she was born, mother was advised to send away her 18-month-old brother, in the event, to relatives far distant, so that mother would be free to take proper care of the new baby. When the boy returned home six weeks later, mother was horrified to find that he did not recognize his parents, and mother said that after that 'wild horses would not keep them apart'.

I am struck by the metaphor and its relation to psychoanalytic practice. I think that the advice contained in Freud's metaphor of the mirror, or the analyst as surgeon, implicitly suggests that in order to take proper care of the patient's unconscious, the analyst's emotionality should be sent as far away as possible. The consequences of this attitude do result

35

in the non-recognition of essential areas and the danger that when the split-off emotionality returns, 'wild horses won't keep it apart' — with all the dangers of acting-out. To imagine that this split-off emotionality won't return is contrary to the very theories we hold in relation to mental life.

Unless we are to say that psychoanalytic function takes place in a conflict-free autonomous zone of the ego, we have to allow for the problems involved not only in digesting the patient's projections, but also in assimilating our own responses so that they can be subjected to scrutiny. The analyst, like the patient, desires to eliminate discomfort as well as to communicate and share experience; ordinary human reactions. In part, the patient seeks an enacting response, and in part, the analyst has an impulse to enact, and some of this will be expressed in the interpretation. This may range from an implicit indulgence, caressing the patient with words, to responses so hostile or distant or frozen that they seem to imply that the deprivation of the experience the patient yearns for is of no matter; a contention that a part-object mechanical experience is all that is necessary.

Yet an interpretation, and the act of giving an interpretation, is not a part-object selection of a number of words, but an integrative creative act on the part of the analyst. It will include unspoken and, in part, unconscious communication about what has been taken in, and how it has been taken in, as well as information about what has not been taken in.

The patient receiving an interpretation will 'hear' not only words or their consciously intended meaning. Some patients indeed only listen to the 'mood' and do not seem to hear the words at all. Joseph (1975) has shown vividly that we may be misled by the patient's words; the mood and atmosphere of the communication may be more important. The patient may operate with the same accent, listen to the analyst's speech in the same manner. His perceptions may be considerably dominated by his internal configurations and phantasies, but, I believe, following Klein's account in 1952, that: 'In the young infant's mind every external experience is interwoven with his phantasies and ... every phantasy contains elements of actual experience, and it is only by analysing the transference situation to its depth that we are able to discover the past both in its realistic and phantastic aspects' (p. 437).

Inevitably, the patient too will take in, consciously and unconsciously, some idea of the analyst as a real person. When we speak of a mother giving the baby the nipple, we do not consider a simple nipple-mouth relationship; we recognize that the baby takes in a penumbra of experience. There is always something in excess of the actual process. We see reported: 'The patient said ... and the analyst interpreted', yet the complexities are enormous. To address the question of how the analyst features in the internal world of the patient, we need not only to move into the paranoid/schizoid internal world of the patient; we also require some flexibility in tolerating and working through the tensions between our own conscious and unconscious impulses and feelings toward the patient.

Constant projecting by the patient into the analyst is the essence of analysis; every interpretation aims at a move from the paranoid/schizoid to the depressive position. This is true not only for the patient, but for the analyst who needs again and again to regress and work through. I wonder whether the real issue of truly deep versus superficial interpretation resides not so much in terms of which level has been addressed, but to what extent the analyst has worked the process through internally in the act of giving the interpretation.

A patient, Mr A, had recently come to live in London, his first analysis had taken place abroad. He arrived for his session a few hours after having been involved in a car accident in which his stationary car was hit and badly damaged; he himself just missed being severely injured. He was clearly still in a state of some shock, yet he did not speak of shock or fear. Instead he explained with excessive care what had taken place, and the correct steps taken by him before and after the collision. He went on to say that by chance his mother (who lives in the same country as the previous analyst) phoned soon after the accident, and when told about it responded with 'I wouldn't have phoned if I'd known you'd have such awful news. I don't want to hear about it'. He said that thanks to his previous analysis, he knew that he needed to understand that his mother could not do otherwise, and he accepted that. He was, however, very angry with the other driver, and was belligerent in his contention that he would pursue, if necessary to court, his conviction that he would have to pay for the damage.

I believe that he conveyed very vividly his belief that he would have to bear alone or be above the immediate shock, fear and rage generated both by the accident and the mother's response to it. Not only did he believe that his mother did not want to hear the awful news, but that the analyst did not want to hear the awful news of there being a mother-analyst who does not listen to or share pain with him. Instead, he felt he had been taught to 'understand' the mother or listen to the analyst with an angry underlying conviction that the mother/analyst will not listen to his distress. He went along with this, pulled himself together, made a display of behaving correctly, became a so-called 'understanding' person. He replaced the distress of bearing pain with competence in doing the right thing, but let us know that unconsciously he will pursue his grievances to the bitter end.

Although he moved quickly from vulnerable victim to perpetrator of competent cruelty (consciously against the other driver, unconsciously against the mother and previous, and current, analyst), I also experienced an atmosphere that led me to believe that there was space for a more genuinely creative relationship to develop. In the counter-transference I felt that what I was asked to bear was not excessive, and that whilst there was a patient who does not want to know, I might also rely on there being a patient who shared wanting to know with me.

Now let us consider what took place in the session. The patient made an impact in his 'competent' way of dealing with his feelings, yet he also conveyed a wish for there to be an analyst/mother who would take in his fear and his rage. I interpreted the yearning for someone who will not put down the phone, but instead will take in and understand what this unexpected impact feels like; this supposes the transference on to the analyst of a more understanding maternal figure. I believe, though, that this 'mates' with some part of the analyst that may wish to 'mother' the patient in such a situation. If we cannot take in and think about such a reaction in ourselves, we either act out by indulging the patient with actual mothering (this may be done in verbal or other sympathetic gestures) or we may become so frightened of doing this, that we freeze and do not reach the patient's wish to be mothered.

Yet already I had been lured into either admiring the sensible, competent approach, or appearing to condemn it. I found that I was having the experience of feeling superior to and judging the mother, previous analyst and his own 'competence'. Was I being party to taking them all to court? I then needed to reflect about the parts of himself and his internal objects that did not want to know. These too were projected into the analyst, and also, in my view, 'mated' with parts of the analyst that might not wish to know about human vulnerability (ultimately death) either in external reality, or currently in feeling 'tossed about' by the patient in the session.

I then needed to show him that he believed that in presenting me with such an awful picture of mother/analyst, he persuaded me to believe that I was different from and better than them. Yet he also believed (and that was how he had behaved toward me at the beginning of the session) that I too did not want to know about the fear engendered either by unexpected accidents or by the impact which he believed he had upon me.

If we feel at the mercy of an analytic superego that does not support us in knowing about these internal buffetings, we are, like the patient, in danger of 'wrapping it all up' competently. We may act out by becoming excessively sympathetic to the patient, taking the others to court in a superior or angry way, or becoming excessively sympathetic to the others, taking the patient to court in a superior or angry way.

The process of meeting and working through our own experience of both wanting to know and fearing knowing (in Bion's terms +K and −K) facilitates, I believe, a deeper and more empathic contact with these parts of the patient and his internal objects. If we fail to take into account *in statu nascendi* our own conflictual responses, we risk enacting that which we should be interpreting, i.e. the hijacking of all the good propensities and the projection into the other 'driver' of all the evil; we may behave as though we could meet with accidents or the vicissitudes of life with impunity.

In taking the case to court, the patient's belief in the superiority of competently keeping out passions and ostensibly pursuing 'pure' truth, needs to be examined. What looks like truth-seeking is suffused with hatred. There is an underlying menace that if I make a wrong move, my name will be blackened, as he has already blackened the other driver, mother and the previous analyst. My experience leads me to believe in the patient's terror that if he makes a wrong move, he will be taken to court, judged by a merciless superego.

I think that this raises a question for the analyst. If we keep emotions out, are we in danger of keeping out the love which mitigates the hatred, thus allowing the so-called pursuit of truth to be governed by hatred? What appears as dispassionate, may contain the murder of love and concern.

Bion (1962), referring to psychotically disturbed patients, writes

'The attempts to evade experience with *live objects* [my italics] by destroying alpha function leaves the personality unable to have a relationship with any aspect of itself that does not resemble an automaton'. Later he says: 'The scientist whose investigations include the stuff of life itself finds himself in a situation that has a parallel in that of the patients ... Confronted with the complexities of the human mind the analyst must be circumspect in following even accepted scientific method; its weakness may be closer to the weakness of psychotic thinking than superficial scrutiny would admit.'

One great difficulty in our work is in this dual area of remaining in contact with the importance of our own experience as well as our allegiance to the profound value of our technique; this forms part of the impossibility and the value of our endeavours. I think that this problem applies, for instance, to the controversial issue of interpretation versus response; in a way a false argument and in a way a very real one. Yet the issue becomes polarized, as though one was all good, the other all bad. Consider a patient bringing particularly good or particularly bad news; say, the birth of a new baby or a death in the family. Whilst such an event may raise complex issues requiring careful analysis, in the first instance the patient may not want an interpretation, but a response; the sharing of pleasure or of grief. And this may be what the analyst intuitively wishes for too. Unless we can properly acknowledge this *in* our interpretation, interpretation itself either becomes a frozen rejection, or is abandoned and we feel compelled to act non-interpretively and be 'human'. We then do not help the patient to share with the analyst the experience that interpretation itself is not an ideal object, i.e. a depressive position sharing within the analytic framework, rather than a frozen response or non-interpretive aside.

On a later occasion, this hitherto rather propitiating patient began a session the day before a General Election, telling me with pleasure and excitement that he was thrilled at the prospect of the Tory victory. It then emerged that he had picked up either from my careful enquiry or from previous knowledge that I was probably a Labour supporter. I interpreted that I thought he was anticipating with triumphant excitement watching whether in the heat of the moment I would address myself to his reactions or mine.

He associated to a visit to a cousin with a new baby, and the story of his mother's labour with him. (He was not aware of the link labour/Labour Party.) As she was going into labour, she first offered to do all the family washing.

The patient not only reported a past family myth, but relived in the transference this relationship with an internal mother. My counter-transference problem was that either I was programmed to react angrily at this assault in the negation of my 'labour' pains or to be a saintly mother, who would selflessly deal with his 'dirty washing' without a thought for my disturbance.

But beyond that I believe the patient mocked me as a mother who he believed was above all concerned to keep her hands clean. Was I getting caught up with being technically correct, because I could not bear to take in how awful it feels to be a loser, and to be filled with hatred when someone else flaunts his or her success - the cousin with the new baby?

Like the young child, the patient, I believe, is consciously and unconsciously acutely sensitive to the way we interpret his difficulties in confronting the important issues, his labour in getting in touch with his infantile self — his propensities to become sadistic when he feels neglected or jealous or envious, when he feels mother/analyst is engaged with a new baby, and he feels himself to be the unwanted party. The patient raises very deep issues of rivalry between mother and child as to which 'party' is best equipped to deal with the issues, all of which may stir up reactions or excessive defensiveness on the part of analyst as well as patient. It is our professional task to subject these reactions to scrutiny.

I think that the extent to which we succeed or fail in this task will be reflected not only in the words we choose, but in our voice and other demeanour in the act of giving an interpretation; this will include the whole spectrum from frank self-righteous sadism to impeccable masochistic or hypocritical 'patience' in enduring the cruelties to which patients subject us. The point is that we have to cope with feelings, and subject them to thought; as Segal (1977) stresses, we are not neutral in the sense of having no reaction.

Money-Kyrle, in speaking of the analytic function, stresses not only sublimated curiosity on the part of the analyst, but the analyst's reparative and parental function. In his view, in the moment of the projective phase of the interpretation, the analyst is also taking care of an immature part of the self, which needs to be protected from the sadistic part. When we show the patient that he becomes sadistic when he feels neglected or that he identifies himself with the neglecting object and fails to take note of the needy infantile self, I think whether we know it or not, the interpretation will contain some projection of our own wish to protect the baby from the sadistic part. The maintenance of a careful setting is in some way a demonstration of this care.

In developmental terms the infant who is able to begin more genuinely to feel for the mother's hurt and wishes to protect her from it, is an infant who has taken in and identified with a mother who feels for his hurt and wishes to protect him from unnecessary hurt, as well as supporting him to bear pain. This experience does not come from a saintly mother, but a flesh and blood mother who knows about her own wishes to be rid of troublesome problems.

I have been trying to show that the issue is not a simple one; the patient does not just project into an analyst, but instead patients are quite skilled at projecting into particular aspects of the analyst. Thus, I have tried to show, for example, that the patient projects into the analyst's wish to be a mother, the wish to be all-knowing or to deny unpleasant knowledge, into the analyst's instinctual sadism, or into his defences against it. And above all, he projects into the analyst's guilt, or into the analyst's internal objects.

Thus, patients touch off in the analyst deep issues and anxieties related to the need to be loved and the fear of catastrophic consequence in the face of defects, i.e. primitive persecutory or superego anxiety. I shall try to show this with a final example from this patient.

This patient began a Friday session, a week before the holidays, announcing that he felt ill. He did not know what it was; he had the same symptoms as his little girl. But, said fiercely, 'I was determined to come, even if that risks you [the analyst] getting my illness'.

He was clearly frightened by illness and its potential threat. In the

41

counter-transference I found I was worrying about being infected and becoming unable to cope with work next week, i.e. having his symptoms. I interpreted his fear and referred to the part of him that wished me to 'catch the illness' of that fear.

He then told me about his small child's school play the day before. His wife had had a pressing work commitment and could not attend. He had given up his session to be there. He described the delight of watching the children; they would recognize parents and relatives and interrupt the performance to call, 'Hello Mummy', etc. He was hurt and angry that his wife was not present: it was plain that he felt lonely, unsupported by a family. I interpreted the loneliness; the wish for me to have been there as a 'family'. I related this to anger with *my* work commitments (I had not been able to change his hour), as well as my weekend and holiday commitments.

He acknowledged this, then remembered an occasion when he had seen me at a public lecture where psychoanalysis was under attack for not providing patients with sufficient support. He said that he had observed how well I had dealt with this.

I felt flattered and then needed to think about this. I interpreted that I was being flattered into a belief about how well I coped with this charge, whilst in fact I was being watched to see how I manage when I feel alone, unsupported and assailed by persecutors, external or internal.

He said he had woken in the night with a fear that he could die; previously with such a feeling he had experienced utter panic; now it was more with a feeling of terrible sadness to take in that one day he just won't be there. He had had a dream.

In the dream Freud was undergoing an operation for shoulder lesions. There was a worry that the operation was not fully successful; when Freud tried to lift his arm he could not do so. A group of people, including the patient, were trying to protect Freud in various ways, including sedation, so that he would not have to bear the pain.

He told me that I, and indeed Freud, the father of all psychoanalysts, needed group support; part of this support lies in sedation. Whilst he claimed to be part of a group supporting Freud, he had also said at the beginning of the session, that he needed my help even if that meant not protecting me.

There was a seductive, spurious quality to the sedative support. I thought of the operations on Freud, not for shoulder lesions, but for cancer associated with smoking. My patient had seen me smoking at that meeting. I felt a strong urge to avoid this area.

I pointed out that he seemed to be protecting me from this issue; as though that would be too much to put on my shoulders. He admitted this and now said that in the dream the lesions seemed to be a consequence of cancer. He spoke of his aged father and the fear of his death. Now he protected my by placing the problem with an aged father.

We could say that the patient projects into the analyst parts of himself and his internal objects, as indeed he does. He presents two models; the one copes impeccably, the other is broken down. In the course of such projection, he affects me. In the session I found that I was lured into having experiences in both directions. ('I'm terrific' or 'I'm awful'.) I have to remind myself that I was neither. In part, I do share, or am infected, by the child's symptoms, idealization or persecutory fear, in which the depressive position mother gets lost. This has to be recovered so that I and also the patient can be helped to realize that in assailing the mother or father with these pressures, including guilt (putting it all on Freud's shoulders), the child's need to be protected and cared for gets lost. In part the patient projects anxieties about, and rivalrous triumph over, unable parents; he also fears an analyst triumphant over a patient unable to cope with feeling ill or abandoned.

I believe that there is evidence of movement in the patient from the impeccable coping after the accident (as reported earlier) to something that feels more hopeful about anxieties about not coping (more feelings of sadness, rather than feeling overwhelmed by panic). Whilst there is pain and rage about missing parents, or what was missing in the parents, this is interrupted now by child parts delighted to recognize good aspects of parental and analytic support. The need for an impeccable performance has given way to the possibility of more spontaneous interaction.

My stress is that, within the analyst as well, spontaneous emotional interaction with the patient's projections takes place, and that if we fully respect this and are not too dominated by the demand for impeccable neutrality, we can make better use of the experience for interpretation.

The patient's projection of his experience into the analyst may be felt by both as an unwarranted intrusion and touches on issues in mental life where boundaries between internal and external, phantasy and reality, self and object become problematic in various ways. I shall give a brief illustration.

A young married woman had been exposed to a series of unpleasant burglaries. Now their apartment is secured like a fortress. She arrives on a Monday saying that the weekend has been awful, taken over by an event on the Friday night, a burglary, not to their apartment (which is now so well secured), but to the apartment above where the people are always away. 'We were just going to sleep. We could hear the footsteps because the partitions are so thin. We called the police but by the time they got there, the bastards had got away.' Meanwhile they tried to reach the owners at their country house. First they got the Ansafone, and when eventually they reached them, they explained they'd been in the garden clearing up the aftermath of a huge party — 'the discrepancy of our experience and theirs seemed crazy'. The rest of the weekend she felt depressed, upset, exposed and vulnerable and in no state to look after her baby.

The patient reports an actual event at the weekend; an intrusion into her home. In the transference there are already hints linking the 'upstairs owners' with me (I have an Ansafone; I work in an upstairs room in a tall house, and I am also 'always unavailable' at the weekend). She tells me that the discrepancy between the experience of those people who are away having a party and her experience is enormous, implying that I will be distanced from taking in her experience. But am I? On the contrary, as she continues to describe the detail of how the burglars climbed up the drainpipe to the third floor, and says that what was so specially disturbing is that 'we really thought we had got the apartment secured; whilst it's happening, it feels so sinister'. I find that my thoughts have turned, naturally enough, to my house, to thinking with some anxiety — 'a burglary like this could happen to me; I'm not so secure either'.

The patient continues — 'in fact, when the police arrived, they came with vicious sniffer dogs — as I opened the door — the dogs — although held on a tight rein, jumped! I felt terrified and for a moment I felt sorry for the burglar'.

In my view this patient was not only describing the events of the weekend; she was also engaged in intruding into me certain sinister fears, both of being intruded into in reality, but also about being 'sniffed out' and 'jumped on'. She alerts me to her fear of being intruded into and sniffed out and jumped on (suggesting also certain sexual anxieties in the face of a frightening superego). But I would suggest that I am also being sniffed out as to how I take in her experience, and that secretly she will be ready to 'jump on' me.

I would suggest that one view she holds of me as the mother in the transference, is that I so fear being intruded into by a burglar/husband or by the patient/child's projections that I secure or defend myself as though I were living in an analytic fortress. In that way I would be impenetrable by a partner at the weekend, but would also then be impenetrable to the patient's experience. An interpretation of the patient's experience of robbery at the weekend, or the internal experience of feeling robbed of the analyst/mother by the intrusive 'bastard' of a father would be experienced as given by impenetrable or unreachable parents — those parents whose experience is so discrepant from hers, engaged as they are in clearing up the aftermath of their sexual party.

Yet the patient has also intruded into me a wish not to be distanced in that way. On the contrary, I believe that I was invited to feel that I was in the same 'boat' or the same exposed house as the patient. Thus

I am invited to feel that the 'partitions are so thin' that there is no separateness. Then she is the sniffer dog, not only sniffing the parents out at the weekend, but entering my mind as though we were 'one'. What I wish to convey is that the 'partition' between what we tend to call normal projective identification (or empathic sharing) and intrusion is very fine.

In the counter-transference in such situations we may find that we either become 'lulled' into such states of mind by the patient, or so sensitized to that danger that we behave like an impersonation of the police sniffer dogs, ready to pounce the moment the door is opened.

Thus one gains access to the patient's view of her internal objects, felt to be either overidentified with her or so distant and harsh that they are not able to take in her experience.

These issues are very real and we may become particularly vulnerable to them in these areas where the patient touches on our 'shared' external or internal world. Making space to work through these issues internally will much affect the way in which we give our interpretations in both taking care of the exposed baby in the patient, and 'sniffing out' and dealing with the nasty intrusive parts as well.

These issues I have been trying to illustrate become more rather than less problematic when we are dealing with borderline and psychotic patients. These patients may become more or less impervious to ordinary analytic co-operation and may act out in ways that present the analyst with serious management problems. They may make demands, say for an extra session at the weekend, where, for the analyst to acquiesce, may be to feed and reinforce tyrannical narcissistic parts of the patient; to refuse may be to indulge and reinforce sometimes profound grievances. In cases of suicidal patients, anorexia, or malignant hysterics, for example, such management issues may carry life and death implications.

Of course in these situations the patient massively projects parts of the self and internal objects into the analyst; such patients also arouse in the analyst feelings of being helpless and at the mercy of vengeful exploitative behaviour whilst the patient indulges in imperviousness to the analyst's needs. The task of experiencing and bearing these feelings whilst at the same time not becoming alienated from those parts of the patient that are genuinely defective and in need of support is a considerable one. In those cases where the situation becomes unmanageable it is easy to feel that the patient is 'unanalysable' (and sometimes this may be so). The very intensity of how unmanageable the situation becomes, may be the evidence of how unmanageable the internal dilemma is for the patient. In these cases the patient actually makes the analyst feel helpless and at the mercy of a ruthless persecuting object that goes on relentlessly and will not be modified by human understanding — the archetypal primitive superego.

I wish to emphasize that faced with such serious managerial problems, the analyst is also involved in a massive effort not only to contain the patient's projections but to manage his or her own feelings, subjected as they are to such intense pressure. And even in the case of, or perhaps most especially in the case of, such disturbed patients, the patient, either consciously or unconsciously, makes enquiry into the question of how the analyst deals with such feelings.

When analysis proceeds well, the analyst has the luxury of being able to manage the combination of some involvement and some distance. In the case of these very ill patients the power of the patient's predicament, and the capacity to intrude into the analyst's mind and disturb him, may put the analyst in the position, at least for some time, of being taken over and unable to function as a separate thinking person.

The analyst needs to work through the experience of feeling like an overwhelmed mother threatened with disintegration by an interaction with the overwhelmed baby. The analyst may need to be able to turn to an outside person, a 'father' to provide support; for example, a hospital or colleague may be needed for support not only in the management of such a case, but also to encourage the analyst to have the strength to hold the feelings of hatred for the impervious, exploitative, parasitic patient/baby together with the love and concern for the needy or defective baby in the patient. This, in my view, enables the analyst to help the patient to feel that these intense, contradictory feelings can be endured, so that the patient may be helped to begin to meet the issues in relation to parts of the self and internal objects.

Whilst these patients intrude problems relating to actual management, my contention is that these problems form an essential part of the management of any analysis; were it not so, working through would be a smooth, uninterrupted process; it never is for the patient, and my stress is that it cannot be so for the analyst either. Analytic thinking must then include a recognition of, and a struggle with, our desire to enact, in order to be able to think about and decide what to do in the circumstances.

I have tried to show that the experience for the analyst is a powerful one. To suggest that we are not affected by the destructiveness of the patient or by the patient's painful efforts to reach us would represent not neutrality but falseness or imperviousness. It is the issue of how the analyst allows himself to have the experience, digest it, formulate it, and communicate it as an interpretation that I address.

Summary

This paper is intended as a development of Strachey's classic paper, 'The nature of the therapeutic action of psychoanalysis' (1934). Strachey states that the full or deep transference experience is disturbing to the analyst; that which the analyst most fears and most wishes to avoid. He also stresses that conveying an interpretation in a calm way is necessary. The area addressed is the task of coping with these strong counter-transference experiences and maintaining the analytic technique of interpretation. The clinical illustrations attempt to show something of the process of transformation or working through in the analyst, as well as showing that the patient is consciously or unconsciously mindful as to whether the analyst evades or meets the issues.

The contention that the analyst is not affected by these experiences is both false and would convey to the patient that his plight, pain and behaviour are emotionally ignored by the analyst. It is suggested that if we keep emotions out, we are in danger of keeping out the love which mitigates the hatred, allowing the so-called pursuit of truth to be governed by hatred. What appears as dispassionate may contain the murder of love and concern. How the analyst allows himself to have the experiences, work through and transform them into a useful interpretation is the issue studied in this paper.

References

Bion, W.R. (1962) *Learning from Experience*, London: Heinemann; reprinted in paperback, Maresfield Reprints, London: H. Karnac Books (1984).

Heimann, P. (1950) 'On counter-transference', *International Journal of Psycho-Analysis*, 31: 81—4.

Joseph, B. (1975) 'The patient who is difficult to reach', in P. Giovacchini (ed.), *Tactics and Techniques in Psychoanalytic Therapy*, vol. 2: *Countertransference*, New York: Jason Aronson, 205—16, also 48—60 of this volume.

Klein, M. (1952) 'The origin of transference', *International Journal of Psycho-Analysis*, 33: 433—8; reprinted in *The Writings of Melanie Klein*, vol. 3, London: Hogarth Press (1975), 48—56.

Money-Kyrle, R. (1956) 'Normal counter-transference and some of its deviations', *International Journal of Psycho-Analysis*, 37: 360—6; reprinted in *The Collected Papers of Roger Money-Kyrle* (ed. D. Meltzer with the assistance of E. O'Shaughnessy), Strathtay, Perthshire: Clunie Press (1978) 330—42; also pp. 22—33 of this volume.

Segal, H. (1977) 'Countertransference', *International Journal of Psycho-Analytic Psychotherapy*, 6: 31—7; also in *The Work of Hanna Segal*, New York: Jason Aronson (1981) 81—7; also reprinted in paperback, London: Free Association Books (1986).

Strachey, J. (1934) 'The nature of the therapeutic action of psychoanalysis, *International Journal of Psycho-Analysis*, 15: 275—93.

———————————— 4 ————————————

The patient who is difficult to reach

BETTY JOSEPH

This paper was first published in 1975 in P.L. Giovacchini (ed.), *Tactics and Techniques in Psychoanalytic Therapy*, vol. 2: *Countertransference*, New York: Jason Aronson.

In this chapter I intend to concentrate on some problems of technique, focusing around a particular group of patients, very diverse in their psychopathology, but presenting in analysis one main point in common. It is very difficult to reach them with interpretations and therefore to give them real emotional understanding. My aim is to discuss some manifestations of the problem and some technical issues that arise in handling this type of case. I shall not attempt to make a study of the psychopathology of these patients.

In the treatment of such cases I believe we can observe a splitting within the personality, so that one part of the ego is kept at a distance from the analyst and the analytic work. Sometimes this is difficult to see since the patient may appear to be working and co-operating with the analyst but the part of the personality that is available is actually keeping another more needy or potentially responsive and receptive part split off. Sometimes the split takes the form of one part of the ego standing aside as if observing all that is going on between the analyst and the other part of the patient and destructively preventing real contact being made, using various methods of avoidance and evasion. Sometimes large parts of the ego temporarily seem to disappear in the analysis with resultant apathy or extreme passivity — often associated with the powerful use of projective identification.

It follows from what I am discussing that for long periods in the treatment of these patients the main aim of the analysis is to find a way of getting in touch with the patient's needs and anxiety in such a way as to make more of the personality available and eventually to bring about a greater integration of the ego. I find that with these rather unreachable patients it is often more important to focus one's attention on the patient's method of communication, the actual way that he speaks and the way that he reacts to the analyst's interpretations rather than to concentrate primarily on the content of what he says. In other words, I am going to suggest that we have to recognize that these patients, even when they are quite verbal, are in fact doing a great deal of acting, sometimes in speech itself, and our technique has constantly to take account of this.

I want first to examine this problem of the unreachable patient by considering the nature of the splitting in those patients who seem apparently highly co-operative and adult — but in whom this co-operation is a pseudo-co-operation aimed at keeping the analyst away from the really unknown and more needy infantile parts of the self. In the literature this problem has been discussed by such people as Deutsch (1942), with the as-if personality, Winnicott (1960), with the false self, Meltzer (1966), with his work on pseudo-maturity, and Rosenfeld (1964), with the splitting off of the dependent parts of the self in narcissistic patients.

In psychoanalytic discussions on technique stress has frequently been laid on the importance of a working or therapeutic alliance between analyst and patient. What impresses one early in the treatment of this group of unreachable patients is that what looks like a therapeutic alliance turns out to be inimical to a real alliance and that what is termed understanding is actually anti-understanding. Many of these patients tend to respond quickly to interpretations or to discuss in a very sensible way previous interpretations, using such expressions as 'do you mean', referring to previous dreams and the like and seeming eminently co-operative and helpful. One finds oneself in a situation that looks exactly like an ongoing analysis with understanding, apparent contact, appreciation, and even reported improvement. And yet, one has a feeling of hollowness. If one considers one's counter-transference it may seem all a bit too easy, pleasant, and unconflicted, or signs of conflict emerge but are somehow quickly dissipated.

One may find oneself presented with specific problems that a patient wishes to consider: why did he respond in such and such a way to such and such a situation? The patient makes suggestions, but free associations are conspicuously absent. The analyst finds him or herself working very hard intellectually to understand what is being asked of him, and may begin to feel he is involved in some kind of analytic guessing game. Here we can see one of the types of splitting of the ego I am discussing. The patient talks in an adult way, but relates to the analyst only as an equal, or a near-equal disciple. Sometimes he relates more as a slightly superior ally who tries to help the analyst in his work, with suggestions or minor corrections or references to personal history. If one observes carefully one begins to feel that one is talking to this ally *about* a patient — but never talking *to* the patient. The 'patient' part of the patient seems to remain split off and it is this part which seems more immediately to need help, to be more infantlike, more dependent and vulnerable. One can talk about this part but the problem is to reach it. I believe that in some of our analyses, which appear repetitive and interminable, we have to examine whether we are not being drawn into colluding with the pseudo-adult or pseudo-co-operative part of the patient.

This type of split can be found in different kinds of patients and may be maintained for different reasons, connected, for example, with unconscious anxiety about infantile feelings, or feelings of dependence, intense, but usually warded off, rivalry and envy of parental figures, difficulties concerning separateness, and so on. As I have mentioned, I do not want to discuss this aspect of the work, since my principal aim is to look at the technical side.

I shall start with brief material from a patient with a rigid, controlled, and anxious personality, who consciously wants help, but unconsciously struggled against getting it by the use of the kind of splitting I am describing, and whose communications could, in part, be viewed as acting-out in the transference. It is, of course, extremely difficult in reporting fragments of case material to convey this acting-out, which after all one mainly intuits from the effect that the patient's words produce on oneself and the atmosphere that is created. This patient, whom I shall call A, was a young teacher. He came into analysis when he was in his early twenties. He was married and had a young baby. He had already read a certain amount of analytic literature. When he had been in analysis over three and a half years and when we had done considerable work on his manic controlling, he started a session saying that he wanted to talk about his problems about clearing out his cupboards. He was spending so much time on them. He described how he had got to clearing things out and how he did not seem to want to stop. This was put forward as if it were a problem with which he needed help. He added that, in fact, he really did not want to go to visit friends in the evening because he wanted to go on with his clearing out.

He paused as if he expected something from me. I had the strong impression that I was expected to say something about his clearing out his mind or something rather pat, so I waited. He added that, anyway, he did not really like going to these people in the evening, because the last time they went the husband was rude. He had turned to watch the TV while my patient and his wife were there and subsequently made dictatorial statements about children's school difficulties. I suggested to him that I got the impression that he had been waiting for me to make some pseudo-Kleinian interpretations about the clearing out of his mind and inner world and when I did not, I became the rude husband who watched my own TV and was somewhat dictatorial in my views as to what his difficulties were, that is to say, I did not refer to his preconceived remarks. In other words, I considered his preoccupation with cupboards a type of acting-out designed to keep our work sterile and to avoid new understanding. At first he was angry and upset, but later in the session he was able to gain some understanding about his touchiness. He also got further insight momentarily into his competitive controlling.

The following day he said that he felt much better and had had a dream. He dreamed that he and his wife were in a holiday cottage. They were about to leave and were packing things in the car but for some reason he was packing the car farther down the lane, as if he were too modest to bring it to the front door or the lane was too muddy and narrow. This was unclear. Then he was in a market getting food to take home, which was odd: why should he take food if he were going home? He was choosing some carrots — either he could take Dutch ones which were twisted or some better French ones which were young and straight, possibly slightly more expensive. He chose the Dutch twisted ones and his wife queried why he did so.

His associations led to plans for the holidays at a house they were thinking of taking, and to his preference for France over Holland. Carrots led to his memory of the advertisements during the war of carrots as good cheap food and a help against night blindness.

Briefly I suggested that his pseudo-modesty about bringing the car to the door was really linked with the fact that he was not too keen that I should see what he packed inside, following the feeling of having been helped the day before. But now we could see that his attempts on the previous day to force me to interpret in a particular way, as well as the understanding he had gained about it, had become linked with attempts to pack my interpretations inside himself, not to use for himself but for other purposes, as, for example, to use for a lecture which he was actually giving that evening. This then becomes food which he himself buys to take home, not food he gets from home-analysis. He chooses carrots which should help his night blindness, which should give him insight, but what he actually selects are the twisted ones. This would suggest that part of him has insight into his tendency to twist and misuse material — the false interpretations he tried to get from me — and avoid the clear, direct contact with firm, straight, fresh, and new carrots, that is, non-textbook interpretations. This insight is not yet felt but is projected into his wife who queries why he has to do things in this wrong way.

The patient tries to manipulate me into making false and useless interpretations which could then keep me away from contacting anything new and unknown and thus from contacting the part that wants real understanding. The pseudo-co-operative part of the patient therefore clearly works against real emotional understanding. When I did not collude, his anger is described in terms of the anger toward the man who watched TV. Then the dream shows partial insight into the work of the day before. It clarifies the way in which he packs the interpretations into himself secretly, the car up the lane, rather than uses them to help the needy part of himself. This needy part is kept at bay, and from the carrot material, we can see it needs feeding.

In this type of situation I like to be certain that each step is clarified with the patient in relation to the immediate material and not left at a symbolic or quasi-symbolic level. Here we clarified the nature of the twist, that is, the falsification of interpretations, the link between inter-pretations and insight — night blindness. The interpretations are clearly felt as potentially good food but food that can be used, taken in wrongly, and then emerge twisted. One might then postulate that the twisted carrots stand for the nipples taken in in a twisted way but I would not wish to take that step until the intermediary material has been worked through.

In considering this type of problem I am stressing how often the pseudo-co-operative part of the patient prevents the really needy part from getting into contact with the analyst and that if we are taken in by this we cannot effect a change in our patients because we do not make contact with the part that needs *the experience of being understood, as opposed to 'getting' understanding*. The transference situation gives us the oppor-tunity to see these different conflicting parts of the personality in action.

I have been stressing, with the unreachable patient, the importance of locating the splitting in the ego and clarifying the activities of the different parts. In many of these patients one part seems to stand aside from the rest of the personality, observing minutely what is going on between the analyst and the rest of the patient, listening to the tone of the voice of the analyst and sensitive to changes real or assumed. The patient is sensitive, for example, to any indication in the analyst of anxiety, pleasure at achievement, frustration at non-progress, and so on.

Thus, it becomes very important to sort out and make contact with these listening and watching parts of the patient; they contain potentially important ego functions of observation, sensitivity and criticism but so long as they are being used to ward off the analyst and keep other parts of the self at bay they cannot be healthily available to the patient. The patient may have felt that he observed something in the analyst and may have, to some extent, exploited it. Thus a patient may think that he spotted anxiety in the analyst's voice, and may become excited and triumphant, using the resultant criticism of the analyst to avoid understanding interpretations. In such situations I find it imperative for the analyst to wait, work slowly, carry the patient's criticism and to avoid any interpretations suggesting that the trouble lies in projections of the patient's anxiety. It is important to show, primarily, the *use* the patient has made of what he believed to be going on in the analyst's mind. Sometimes we can see the listening or observing part of the patient emerging clearly as a perverse part, which uses interpretive work for purposes of perverse excitement. These patients provocatively 'misunderstand' interpretations, take words out of context and attempt to disturb or arouse the analyst.

I think that in all these apparently perverse situations there is some degree of splitting going on and that we have both to be aware of the intense acting-out in the transference to which we are supposed to respond by acting-out toward our patients, and to be aware that somewhere, split off, there is a part of the patient in need. This part may for a long time be beyond reach in the analysis, but if the analyst is aware that it exists, as well as being aware of the violent acting-out of the perverse part, his capacity for tolerating without acting-out in response is likely to be very much increased. I now wish to discuss further this split-off, observing part and the nature of its activities by bringing material from an apparently different type of patient. But I want to show how here, too, one part of the patient acts as an observer, keeps an eye on the relationship between the rest of the patient and the analyst and uses evasive techniques. I have in mind a young woman, whom I shall call B, who was particularly impervious to interpretations. She was touchy, angry and miserable, constantly blamed the world, and felt hopeless about herself. Consciously, she felt very inferior. She seemed hardly able to take in anything I said and frequently became excessively sleepy after I had spoken.

If she retained what I said it seemed to consist of isolated words with little meaning to her. Often she seemed actually to misunderstand or to become confused. Usually she talked with a quiet shout in her voice. It became increasingly clear that it was futile for me to try to interpret the *content* of what she told me. I assumed that fragmentation occurred whenever anxiety was beginning to be felt. I also had the impression that a part of her was *actively* breaking up interpretations and preventing contact with a more sanely receptive part of herself.

Then I began to notice many references to her boyfriend and how she would watch him speaking with interest to another girl. Then she would become consumed with rage. This type of situation began to emerge in dreams. For example, she had dreams of having a row with her boyfriend because of his interest in another girl. I commented that the dream situation was being lived out in the analysis.

If something really got through in a session and she felt I was able in a lively and alert way to talk to a part of herself that was interested and in contact, another part of herself immediately felt left out, not really jealous but terribly envious that I did the talking and part of her had actually been listening. The onlooker part became wild and reacted with fury. I believe it was this latter part that enviously could not bear me to make contact with her. It defensively shouted and kept me at bay and then felt attacked. One day, she brought a dream in which she was watching her mother bathing a baby, but the mother could not cope. The baby kept slipping out of her hands like a slippery fish. Then it was lying face up under the water, almost drowning. My patient then tried to give the mother some help. It was difficult to convey exactly the way the dream was told — but it stressed mother's stupidity and ineptness and her need for my patient's help.

I interpreted her self-destructive slipperiness and how the infant in her kept, like a slippery fish, evading being firmly held and explosively shouted so as to make it impossible to hold an interpretation or a bit of understanding. I pointed out that she wanted to make me a poor, inferior, inadequate mother. As I interpreted her further slipperiness bit by bit she stressed that there was a part of herself that was perfectly capable of helping her mother-analyst to hold her and to hold interpretations in herself. This shift was very important, since the problem with the unreachable patient is that one ordinarily has no proper ally. It also interests me as a point of technique that as a patient gains understanding, aspects of a dream may emerge, a dream which seems to have become part of the current session. If this happens I believe it is an indication of movement within the session, that is to say, a readjustment between different parts of the personality in a more integrated and constructive way.

Although B is in almost every respect different from the young teacher A, from the point of view of the difficulty of reaching him there are important similarities. Thus the observing part in B, which we could see in the dreams of jealousy of the boyfriend, becomes slippery and evasive. In A there is a different type of evasiveness, pseudo-co-operation. However, the slippery fish is not so different from the twisted carrot. In both patients one can sometimes find a part capable of responsiveness and contact. In A this contact can often be quickly established, whereas in B the enviously watchful aspect of the personality prohibits meaningful communication. It is striking how this watchfulness can confuse and disrupt the patient so that B almost seems dull and stupid, which I very much doubt. The watching part shows itself to be very quick and terribly destructive and self-destructive. It has a perverse quality.

I want now to consider another method of achieving unreachability, where again the part of the ego that we need to work with us gets split off, and in addition becomes particularly unavailable because of being projected into objects. This type of projective identification was, of course, described as long ago as 1946 by Melanie Klein in 'Notes on some schizoid mechanisms.' In some cases, when real progress has been made, insight has been gained and, for example, omnipotence has lessened and more warmth and contact have been established, one finds all further progress blocked by a markedly increased, apparently intractable passivity. The patient seems to become apathetic, to lose contact, interest and any involvement in the work which we may believe to be going on. He does not appear to be actively unco-operative, just helplessly passive. One often gets the impression following an interpretation that everything has gone dead and flat and at the same time that nothing will happen unless one does say something. This is often true. The patient remains quiet or subsequently comes up with a very superficial remark. Then slowly one has the sensation of mounting tension, as if the analyst ought to do or say something, or nothing will ever be achieved. It then feels as though one ought to bring pressure to bear on the patient to talk or respond.

These situations I find extremely instructive. If one does talk because of this kind of silent pressure, without realizing what is going on, nearly always the session gets going but becomes superficial or repetitive or acquires a kind of superego flavour. If one then examines the experience one can often find that the patient appears to have *projected the active, interested or concerned part of the self into the analyst, who is then supposed to act out, feeling the pressure, the need to be active and the desire to get something achieved.* Technically I think that the first step is for the analyst to be aware of the projective identification taking place and to be willing to carry it long enough to experience the missing part of the patient. *Then it may become possible to interpret without a sense of pressure, about the process being acted out, rather than about the content of whatever may have been under discussion before.*

I have frequently watched this kind of process going on in a very passive patient with a rubber fetish, whom I shall call C. In him I began to see the continual retreat to a kind of balance that he established, in which a weakly pseudo-co-operative self talked to me, but the emotional part remained unavailable. Repeatedly we experienced a sequence in which within one session he made progress, became deeply involved and moved by what was going on, but the following day it was a mere flat memory. Then I would find him talking in a bland way, very superficially: 'Yes,

55

I remember the session, it is fully in my mind,' then nothing, or perhaps a remark of a slightly provocative type, such as that despite the session things were not going too well with his wife. I then felt as though I really ought to spur him into activity and understanding, and that if I would do so he would be perfectly willing to think and remember and get going again. I believe that he had split off his capacity for activity, concern, and active distress about his condition and projected this into me. As a result of his projection, I felt that he would be able to move and to make contact and use his insight if only I would take the initiative.

However, this is exactly the major part of his problem, that is, his hatred of really making contact with the loving, concerned and very needy part of the self and bringing it into relation to anyone enough to move physically or emotionally toward them from inside himself. If I push him — however analytically discreetly — he has won, and lost. By my pushing I would confirm that no object is good or desirable enough to attract him sufficiently for him to seek it out and involve himself with it, and therefore that part of the self that can take initiative remains unreachable. Next, I want to look at another aspect of this patient's passivity, also based on splitting and projective identification, of a different type, which manifested itself unobtrusively in a type of acting-out in the transference and thus threw light on the way he kept part of himself out of contact.

C was at this time feeling insecure about the progress of the treatment, being very much aware of its length and feeling rather hopeless and impotent. This type of depression and open anxiety was unusual. During a session he was able to understand a point that I had been making. Then he realized that although the understanding seemed helpful to him, he had become quiet. I commented on the feeling of his having made a sudden shift to passivity. C then started to speak and explained that he felt 'pulled inside' and as if I would now expect him to speak, to 'perform', and he felt he could not. I was then able to show him that he had felt understood but this experience of being understood was concretely experienced as if he were being drawn into the understanding, as into my inside, and then frightened that I was going to expect him to pull outside and to talk, 'to perform'.

Subsequently he added that he felt as if he were in a box lying on his side looking outwards, but into the darkness. The box was closed round him. After a few minutes he started to talk about 'something else'. At a dinner party the other night he had met a woman colleague. She was wearing a very lovely dress; he had congratulated her on it; it had three, horizontal eye-shaped slits near the top — if only he had had three eyes and could have looked out of all three at once. It was almost the end of the session, and I commented that what he wanted now was to get completely inside me through the slits with his eyes, with his whole self, totally inside me and remain there, as in the box. I also added that from the way he spoke he was conveying a very urgent need to make me aware of the importance of his desire to be shut away inside.

When he arrived the following day he commented that the end of the previous session had touched him deeply, but afterwards he had felt as though I had caught him in some guilty secret. I suggested that he had experienced my interpretation of his intense desire to be inside via the slits in the dress, as actually encouraging him to project himself into my inside, and that 'understanding' had then been experienced as my doing something exciting and illicit with him. He had therefore been unable to integrate this understanding. It had a concrete quality and had become comparable to his rubber fetish — he could get inside the fetish, nowadays in phantasy only, in such a way as to pull away from relating to me and from maintaining real understanding and communicating with a real person. So one could follow the movement of the session from real understanding and direct contact between analyst and the more responsive parts of the patient to a flight into a concretely experienced inanimate object, which again rendered him passive and withdrawn and largely unable to be reached.

These examples from C illustrate the living-out in the transference of some mechanisms which he uses to achieve unreachability. They have certain similarities with those used by the other patients I have discussed. They are based on a splitting off of the responsive part of the patient, but are more clearly associated with projective identification. In the first example, the actively alert, needy and contacting part is projected into me so that I should bring pressure on him; in the other the responsive part which came very much to the fore in the session was concretely projected into me or my 'understanding' and there became unavailable. Then the situation became sexualized; this made real understanding unavailable.

As a final example of a similar but slightly different mechanism of achieving unreachability and non-understanding, I want to bring material to show a type of splitting and projective identification going on in the session which enabled the patient to get absorbed into, that is to say, project part of himself into, his own thought processes and phantasies, leaving me in contact with only a pseudo-understanding part of the self and therefore unable to give him real understanding. I want to illustrate the technical importance of looking not only at the content but also at the way the material emerges. The patient's behaviour and the movement of the material in the session may reveal which parts of the ego have disappeared and where we might look for them.

This fragment of material comes from patient A, whom I described first in this chapter. He had always tended to become absorbed in daydreams. He came one Monday with a dream about people being stuck in quicksand in a cave. There was some urgency about rescuing them but while the patient was fussing around looking for long boards, another man came and quickly helped. A then went on to talk about having been absorbed in sexual phantasies over the weekend, but nevertheless feeling more in contact with what had been going on in the analysis. I interpreted that the phantasies seemed to be quicksand in which he tended to get stuck. He told about a phantasy of his childhood, of which he had spoken before, of looking at a cow or horse from behind, watching the anus and thinking of getting inside with only his head sticking out. He also spoke about some excitement in watching animals defecate. I, probably mistakenly (I will come back to this), discussed how getting into his phantasies was like getting into the animal's body, and I linked this with his mother's body and with his putting his fingers up his own anus. He then had many phantasies about babies being born. I could show him that he was proliferating phantasies in this session and getting absorbed into them, and this became his stuck state, like quicksand, so that instead of trying to understand and examine what had happened he was getting more and more absorbed and trying to pull me in with him. This he understood.

Next, he talked about the summer holidays. He and his wife were exchanging houses with some people from abroad. The other people had sent photos, but he had no photos of his house taken from the outside. I interpreted that as he gets absorbed in his phantasies, like the quicksand, they enable him not to have to see the outside, not to recognize separateness from me or an actual relationship with me, not to have to visualize me as really existing as an analyst in the room or away over the weekend. As I discussed this he became increasingly uncomfortable, suggesting that interpretations which brought him into contact with the analyst and the outside world were disturbing.

I think that it is probable that I made a technical error in interpreting the cow phantasy too fully, or rather prematurely, in terms of the mother's body, and that this encouraged my patient unconsciously to feel that he was actually succeeding in pulling me into his exciting phantasy world and thus encouraged him to proliferate his phantasies about babies being born. It might have been better to have kept more on the preconscious level until he was really in contact with me and my understanding, and only later to have linked the phantasy about cows and the dream about caves with the pull toward the inside of the mother's body.

It is also interesting to compare this material of A with the previous material quoted about C, since in both the projection of part of the self into an object can be seen: in C, the projection into 'understanding' concretely experienced, and in A, the absorption into phantasies felt as quicksand. In both patients, contact with the external world or with internal reality, and the experience of separateness and relationship with an object are largely avoided and the patients become temporarily unavailable to interpretive work or real understanding. I have brought this material not only to show this aspect of unreachability but to highlight the importance of considering the way the material is presented as opposed to concentrating primarily on its content or symbolism.

Before concluding I should like to expand a few of the technical points that I have touched upon in this chapter. The first concerns the nature of the transference situation. I have been stressing the importance of the way the material comes into the session and how this enables us to understand the subtle nature of the patient's acting-out in the transference and thus to tease out different parts of the ego and their interaction. Throughout the history of psychoanalysis the need for an uncontaminated transference has been stressed. This is, I believe, of particular importance if we are trying to understand the rather unobtrusive type of acting-out that I am describing. I have given examples of a patient unconsciously trying to manipulate me into pressing him into action, or a patient trying to convince me to join him in a pseudo-analytic discussion. *If we allow ourselves to be manipulated in this way, the transference situation becomes blurred and then we are cut off from parts of the ego with which we need to make contact.*

We also then make it extremely difficult to see the shifts and movements of the patient's defences and parts of the personality as they emerge, alter or disappear in our consulting room. In a sense our ability to remain constant and unaltered in the face of these movements has been much emphasized recently, particularly following the work on projective identification of Melanie Klein (1946), and then of Bion (1962), Rosenfeld (1964), and others concerning the need of the analyst to be able to contain the patient's projections. The kind of acting-out and the projective identification of parts of the ego that I am discussing can very easily pass unnoticed and bring a very subtle type of *pressure on the analyst to live out a part of the patient's self instead of analysing it.*

Associated with this type of acting-out in the transference another technical issue arises — that is, the need for the analyst to keep interpretations in constant contact with what is going on in the session, since we are trying, with these unreachable patients, to observe whether our interpretations are really able to make contact or whether they are being held up or in some way evaded. I think we shall only succeed if our interpretations are *immediate* and direct. Except very near a reasonably successful termination, if I find myself giving an interpretation based on events other than those occurring at the moment during the session, I usually assume that I am not in proper contact with the part of the patient that needs to be understood, or that I am talking more to myself than to the patient.

Useful understanding usually comes from an interpretation of events that are immediate. If it is too far from the actual experience going on in the room, it leads only to verbal understanding of theory. Patients capable of considerable ego integration and of good, whole object relationships may at times be able to integrate interpretations based on putting together previous material. But the kind of patients I am concerned with in this chapter are using much more schizoid mechanisms and are communicating much more concretely by acting-out in the transference — even though with apparent verbal sophistication. We must pay constant attention to this in selecting our technique.

References

Bion, W.R. (1962) *Learning From Experience*, London: Heinemann; reprinted in paperback, Maresfield Reprints, London: H. Karnac Books (1984).

Deutsch, H. (1942) 'Some forms of emotional disturbance and their relationship to schizophrenia', in *Neuroses and Character Types*, London: Hogarth Press (1965).

Klein, M. (1946) 'Notes on some schizoid mechanisms', in *Developments in Psycho-Analysis*, London: Hogarth Press (1952); reprinted in *The Writings of Melanie Klein*, London: Hogarth Press (1975), vol. 3, 1—24.

Meltzer, D. (1966) 'The relation of anal masturbation to projective identification', *International Journal of Psycho-Analysis*, 47; 335—42.

Rosenfeld, H. (1964) 'On the psychopathology of narcissism; a clinical approach', *International Journal of Psycho-Analysis*, 45: 332—7; also in *Psychotic States*, London: Hogarth Press, 1965.

Winnicott, D.W. (1960) 'Ego distortion and the true and false self', in *The Maturational Process and the Facilitating Environment*, London: Hogarth Press (1965), 140—52.

5

Transference: the total situation

BETTY JOSEPH

This paper was first published in 1985 in the *International Journal of Psycho-Analysis*, 66: 447—54.

My intention in this paper is to discuss how we are using the concept of transference in our clinical work today. My stress will be on the idea of transference as a framework, in which something is always going on, where there is always movement and activity.

Freud's ideas developed from seeing transference as an obstacle, to seeing it as an essential tool of the analytic process, observing how the patient's relationships to their original objects were transferred, with all their richness, to the person of the analyst. Strachey (1934), using Melanie Klein's discoveries on the way in which projection and introjection colour and build up the individual's inner objects, showed that what is being transferred is not primarily the external objects of the child's past, but the internal objects, and that the way that these objects are constructed help us to understand how the analytic process can produce change.

Melanie Klein, through her continued work on early object relationships and early mental mechanisms, perhaps particularly projective identification, extended our understanding of the nature of transference and the process of transferring. In her (1952) paper 'The origins of transference' she wrote: 'It is my experience that in unravelling the details of the transference it is essential to think in terms of *total situations* transferred from the past into the present, as well as emotions, defences, and object relations.' She went on to describe how for many years transference had been understood in terms of direct references to the analyst, and how only later had it been realized that, for example, such things as reports about everyday life, etc. gave a clue to the unconscious anxieties stirred up in the transference situation. It seems to me that the

61

notion of total situations is fundamental to our understanding and our use of the transference today, and it is this I want to explore further. By definition it must include everything that the patient brings into the relationship. What he brings in can best be gauged by our focusing our attention on what is going on within the relationship, how he is using the analyst, alongside and beyond what he is saying. Much of our understanding of the transference comes through our understanding of how our patients act on us to feel things for many varied reasons; how they try to draw us into their defensive systems; how they unconsciously act out with us in the transference, trying to get us to act out with them; how they convey aspects of their inner world built up from infancy — elaborated in childhood and adulthood, experiences often beyond the use of words, which we can often only capture through the feelings aroused in us, through our counter-transference, used in the broad sense of the word.

Counter-transference, the feelings aroused in the analyst, like transference itself, was originally seen as an obstacle to the analytic work, but now, used in this broader sense, we would see it, too, no longer as an obstacle, but as an essential tool of the analytic process. Further, the notion of our being used and of something constantly going on, if only we can become aware of it, opens up many other aspects of transference, which I shall want to discuss later. For example, that movement and change is an essential aspect of transference — so that no interpretation can be seen as a pure interpretation or explanation but must resonate in the patient in a way which is specific to him and his way of functioning; that the level at which a patient is functioning at any given moment and the nature of his anxieties can best be gauged by trying to be aware of how the transference is actively being used; that shifts that become visible in the transference are an essential part of what should eventually lead to real psychic change. Such points emerge more clearly if we are thinking in terms of total situations being transferred.

I want to exemplify this by bringing a short piece of material in which we can see how the patient's immediate anxieties and the nature of her relationship with her internal figures emerge in the whole situation lived out in the transference, although individual associations and references to many people came up in the material as if asking to be interpreted. This material comes from the discussion of a case at a recent postgraduate seminar of mine. The analyst brought material from a patient who seemed very difficult to help adequately: schizoid, angry, an unhappy childhood with probably emotionally unavailable parents. The analyst was dissatisfied with the work of a particular session which she brought, and with its results. The patient had brought details of individual people and situations.

The seminar felt that many of the interpretations about this were sensitive and seemed very adequate. Then the seminar started to work very hard to understand more. Different points of view about various aspects were put forward, but no one felt quite happy about their own or other people's ideas. Slowly it dawned on us that probably this was the clue, that our problem in the seminar was reflecting the analyst's problem in the transference, and that what was probably going on in the transference was a projection of the patient's inner world, in which she, the patient, could not understand and, more, could not make sense of what was going on. She was demonstrating what it felt like to have a mother who could not tune into the child and, we suspected, could not make sense of the child's feelings either, but behaved as if she could, as we, the seminar, were doing. So the patient had developed defences in which she argued or put forward apparently logical ideas, which really satisfied no one, but which silenced the experience of incomprehensibility and gave her something to hold on to. If the analyst actually struggles in such situations to give detailed interpretations of the meaning of individual associations, then she is living out the patient's own defensive system, making pseudo-sense of the incomprehensible, rather than trying to make contact with the patient's experience of living in an incomprehensible world. The latter can be a very disturbing experience for the analyst, too. It is more comfortable to believe that one understands 'material' than to live out the role of a mother who cannot understand the infant/patient.

I think that the clue to the transference here (assuming that what I am describing is correct) lay in our taking seriously the striking phenomenon in the seminar, of our struggling to understand and our desperate need to understand instead of getting stuck on the individual associations brought up by the patient, which in themselves would appear to make a lot of possible sense. This we got more through our counter-transference of needing to guess, feeling pressurized to understand at all costs, which enabled us, we thought, to sense a projective identification of a part of the patient's inner world and the distress, of which we got a taste in the seminar.

I am assuming that this type of projective identification is deeply unconscious and not verbalized. If we work only with the part that is verbalized, we do not really take into account the object relationships being acted out in the transference; here, for example, the relationship between the uncomprehending mother and the infant who feels unable to be understood, and it is this that forms the bedrock of her personality. If we do not get through to this, we shall, I suspect, achieve areas of understanding, even apparent shifts in the material, but real psychic change, which can last beyond the treatment will, I think, not be possible.

I suspect that what has happened in such cases is that something has gone seriously wrong in the patient's very early relationships, but that on top of this has been built up a character structure of apparent or pseudo-normality, so that the patient has been able to get into adulthood without actually breaking down and apparently functioning more or less well in many areas of her life. Interpretations dealing only with the individual associations would touch only the more adult part of the personality, while the part that is really needing to be understood is communicated through the pressures brought on the analyst. We can sense here the living out in the transference of something of the nature of the patient's early object relationships, her defensive organization, and her method of communicating her whole conflict.

I want now to continue this point by bringing material from a patient of my own, to show first how the transference was being experienced in a partially idealized way conveyed through the atmosphere that he built up, and linked with his own history. Then how, when this broke down, primitive aspects of his early object relationships and defences emerged and were lived out in the transference and he attempted to draw the analyst into the acting-out. Then how work on this led to more movement and some temporary change in his internal objects.

This patient, whom I shall call N, had been in analysis many years and had made some very satisfactory progress, which was, however, never adequately consolidated, and one could never quite see the working through of any particular problem, let alone visualize the termination of treatment. I noticed a vaguely comfortable feeling, as if I quite liked this patient's sessions and as if I found them rather gratifying, despite the fact I always had to work very hard with him. When I started to rethink my counter-transference and his material, I realized that my rather gratified experience must correspond to an inner conviction on the patient's part that whatever I interpreted he was somehow all right. Whatever difficulties, even tormenting qualities in him, the work might show, there was an inner certainty that he had some very special place, that my interpretations were, as it were, 'only interpretations'. His place was assured and he had no need to change. One could, therefore, have gone on and on making quasi-correct and not unuseful interpretations, exploring and explaining things, but if the deeper unconscious conviction remained unexamined, the whole treatment could have become falsified. This conviction of his special place and no need to change had an additional quality because it included the notion that I, the analyst, had a particular attachment to or love for him, and that for my own sake I would not wish to let him go — which I think was basic to my comfortable counter-transference experience.

I want to make a further brief point about this material, concerning the nature of interpretation. If one sees transference and interpretations as basically living, experiencing and shifting — as movement — then our interpretations have to express this. N's insight into his unconscious conviction of his special place, of the vague unreality of much of our work, of my attachment to him and so on, emerged painfully. It would have been more comfortable to link this quickly with his history — the youngest child, the favourite of his mother, who had a very unhappy relationship with his father, a rather cruel man, though the parents remained together throughout their lives. But had I done this, it would have played into my patient's conviction again that interpretations were 'only interpretations' and that I did not really believe what I was saying. To my mind the important thing was first to get the underlying assumptions into the open, so that, however painful, they could be experienced in the transference as his psychic reality, and only later and slowly to link them up with his history. We shall need to return to the issue of linking with history later.

I shall now bring further material from N from a period soon after the time I have just discussed, to show how when the omnipotent, special place phantasies were no longer dominating the transference, early anxieties and, as I said, the living out of further psychic conflict came into the transference, emerged in a dream, and how the stuff of the dream was lived out in the transference. At this period, N, despite insight, was still liable to get caught up in a kind of passive despairing masochism. On a Monday he brought the following dream. (I am only giving the dream and my understanding of it, not the whole session nor his associations.)

The dream was: there was a kind of war going on. My patient was attending a meeting in a room at the seaside. People were sitting round a table when they heard a helicopter outside and knew from the sound that there was something wrong with it. My patient and a major left the table where the meeting was going on and went to the window to look out. The helicopter was in trouble and the pilot had baled out in a parachute. There were two planes, as if watching over the helicopter, but so high up that they looked extremely small and unable to do anything to help. The pilot fell into the water, my patient was wondering whether he would have time to inflate his suit, was he already dead, and so on.

I am not giving the material on which I based my interpretations, but broadly I showed him how we could see the war that is constantly raging between the patient and myself, which is shown by the way in which he tends to turn his back, in the dream, on the meeting going on at the table, on the work going on from session to session here. When he does look out, knowing that something is wrong (as with the helicopter), he sees that there is an analyst, myself, the two planes, the two arms, the breasts, watching over to try to help him, but he is absorbed watching the other aspect, that is the part of himself, the pilot, that is in trouble, is falling out, dying — which is the fascinating world of his masochism. Here I mean that he shows his preference for getting absorbed into situations of painful collapse rather than turning to and enjoying help and progress.

At the time, he seemed, as the session went on, to get well into touch with these interpretations, and to feel the importance of this fascination with his masochism. On the following day he came, saying that he had felt disturbed after the session and the work on the dream. He spoke in various ways about the session and his concern about the fight, how he felt awful, that whatever goes on in the analysis he seemed somehow to get caught up in this rejection and fight; he went on to speak about his awareness of the importance of the excitement when he gets involved in this way. And then he talked about various things that had happened during the day. This sounded like insight, almost concern. In a way it was insight, but I had the impression from the tone of his voice, speaking in a flat, almost boring, way, that all that he was saying was now second-hand, almost as if the apparent insight was being used against progress in the session, as if a particular silent kind of war against me was going on, which I showed him. My patient replied in a gloomy voice: 'There seems to be no part of me that really wants to work, to co-operate' and so on. . . . I heard myself starting to show him that this could not be quite true, since he actually comes to analysis — and then realized, of course, that I was acting as a positive part of himself, as if the part that was capable of knowing and working had been projected into me and so I was trapped into either living out this positive part, so that he was not responsible for it, or for the recognition of it, or I had to agree that there was no part of him that really wanted to co-operate, etc. So either way there was no way out.

My patient saw this, said he could do nothing about it, he quite understood, but he felt depressed, he could see what I meant. . . . More and more the session became locked in the notion of his understanding but not being able to do anything about or with it. (This picture is, I think, in part what the previous day's dream was describing when he became fascinated watching the pilot about to drown, and I myself, as the plane high up, was unable to help, and he was now fascinated with his own words like 'I understand, but it cannot help'. The dream is now lived out in the transference.)

I showed him that he was actively trapping me, by this kind of remark — which was in itself a demonstration of the war going on between us. After some more going to and fro about this, my patient remembered for 'no apparent reason', as he put it, a memory about a cigarette box; how when he was at boarding school and very miserable, he would take a tin, or a cardboard box, and cover it extremely carefully with canvas. Then he would dig out the pages of a book and hide his cigarette box inside the cover. He would then go into the countryside alone, sit, for example, behind an elder bush and smoke; this was the beginning of his smoking. He was lonely, it was very vivid. He subsequently added that there seemed to be no real pleasure in the cigarettes.

I showed him that I thought the difficulty lay in his response to my showing him about how he was trapping me with the remarks such as 'there seems to be no part of me that wants to co-operate', etc. He realized that he felt some kind of excitement in the fight and the trapping, but that what was really significant was that this excitement had very much lessened during the last sessions and indeed the last year; he was much less addicted to it now, but could not give it up, it would mean giving in to the elders, myself (the reference to sitting behind the elder bush), but he was not really getting much pleasure from the smoking, which, however, he silently, secretly, had to do. The problem now, therefore, in the transference, was not so much that he got such pleasure from the excitement, the problem lay in the recognition and the acknowledgement of his improvement, which would also mean his being willing to give up some of the pleasure in defeating me. He was willing to talk about bad things about himself, sadism or excitement, you will remember, at the beginning of the session, but not his improvement, and he was not yet willing to give in on this point and enjoy feeling better (in terms of yesterday's dream to acknowledge and use the helping hands, the planes).

My patient tended to agree with this and then said that things had changed in the last bit of the session, he realized his mood had altered, the locked and blocked sense had gone, now he felt sadness, perhaps resentment, as if I, the analyst, had not given sufficient attention to the actual memory of the cigarette box incident, which seemed to him vivid and important, as if I had gone away from it too quickly. I went back to the cigarette box memory, and had a look at his feelings that I had missed something of its importance; I also reminded him of the stress he had put on his excitement while I felt that a lot of pleasure had really gone out of this now, as in the non-pleasure in the smoking. But I also showed him his resentment at the fact that his feelings had shifted, he had lost the uncomfortable blocked mood.

N agreed, but said: 'Still I think you have gone too fast.' He could accept that part of the resentment might be connected with the shift that the analysis had enabled him to make — to undo the blocked feeling — but 'too fast' he explained was as if I, the analyst, had become a kind of Pied Piper and he had allowed himself to be pulled along with me.

I pointed out that it sounded as if he felt that I had not really analysed his problem about being stuck, but had pulled and seduced him out of his position. It was my initiative that had pulled him out, as he felt seduced by his mother as a child. (You will remember the earlier material in which he was convinced I and his mother had a special feeling for him.) He quickly, very quickly, added that there was also the other fear at that moment, the fear of getting caught up into excited warm feelings, like the feeling he used to call puppyish.

I now showed my patient that these two anxieties, that of my seducing him out of his previous state of mind and his fear of his own positive, excited, infantile or puppyish feelings, might both need further consideration — both were old anxieties that had come up before as important — but I thought they were being used at that moment so that he could project them into me in order not to have to contain and experience and express the actual good feelings and particularly the warmth and gratitude which had been emerging in the latter part of the session (and was linked, I believe, with the awareness in the dream of a helpful quality in the planes overhead). At this point, very near the end of the session, my patient agreed with me and went off, clearly rather moved.

I am bringing this apparently rather straightforward material to stress a number of points that I find of interest in the use of the transference. First, the way in which a dream can reveal its meaning in a fairly precise way by being lived out in the session, where we can see the patient's specific and willing involvement with misery and problems rather than meeting up with his helpful and lively objects, the planes, which are minimized, small. The analysis, interpretations, breasts are turned away from, when they are recognized as nourishing and helpful. The helpfulness is recognized specifically, but old problems are mobilized against it — called excitement, badness, non-co-operation. Positive aspects of the personality are seen, but his own capacity to move warmly towards an object is quickly distorted and projected into me, it is I who pull and seduce. But the whole thing is cleverly hidden, like the cigarette box in the book (probably bookish old interpretations, now no longer so meaningful). But he really knows that he doesn't get pleasure from the activity. We have here the specific meaning of the symbols and we can locate them in the transference. The patient gets insight, I believe, into what is almost a choice between moving towards a helpful object or indulging in despair — his defences are mobilized and he goes the latter way and tries to draw the analyst into criticizing and reproaching — into his masochistic defensive organization. Then followed further work and we can see that these defences lessen until he can actually acknowledge relief and warmth. Further, as he can acknowledge a helpful object, he can relate to it and internalize it, which leads to further internal shifts.

I think in addition we can see here how the transference is full of meaning and history — the story of how the patient turns away, and I suspect always has done, from his good feeding objects. We can get an indication of one way in which, by projecting his loving into his mother and twisting it, he has helped to consolidate the picture of her as so seductive, an anxiety which still to some extent persists about women. Of course we can add that she may well have been a seductive woman towards her youngest son, but we can see how this has been used by him. The question of when and whether to interpret these matters is a technical one that I can only touch on here. My stress throughout this contribution has been on the transference as a relationship in which something is going on all the time, but we know that this something is essentially based on the patient's past and the relationship with his internal objects or his belief about them and what they were like.

I think that we need to make links for our patients from the transference to the past in order to help to build a sense of their own continuity and individuality, to achieve some detachment, and thus to help to free them from their earlier and more distorted sense of the past. About these issues many problems arise, theoretical and technical. For example, is a patient capable of discovering in the transference an object with good qualities if he had never experienced this in his infancy? About this I am doubtful; I suspect that, if the patient has met up with no object in his infancy on whom he can place some, however little, love and trust, he will not come to us in analysis. He will pursue a psychotic path alone. But what we can do, by tracing the movement and conflict within the transference, is bring alive again feelings within a relationship that have been deeply defended against or only fleetingly experienced, and we enable them to get firmer roots in the transference. We are not completely new objects, but, I think, greatly strengthened objects, because stronger and deeper emotions have been worked through in the transference. This type of movement I have tried to demonstrate in N, whose warmth and valuing have, over time, apparently come alive, but I am convinced that they were weakly there before, but much warded off. Now, I think, the emotions have been freed and have been strengthened, and the picture of his objects has shifted accordingly.

There is also the issue as to when and how it is useful to interpret the relation to the past, to reconstruct. I feel that it is important not to make these links if the linking disrupts what is going on in the session and leads to a kind of explanatory discussion or exercise, but rather to wait until the heat is no longer on and the patient has sufficient contact with himself and the situation to want to understand and to help to make links. Even this, of course, can be used in a defensive way. These, however, are technical issues which do not really belong to this contribution.

I want now to return to a point that I mentioned earlier on, when I spoke of the transference as being the place where we can see not only the nature of the defences being used, but the level of psychic organization within which the patient is operating. To demonstrate this, I shall bring a fragment of material from a patient whom I shall call C, who is a somewhat obsessional personality, with severe limitations in his life, the extent of which he had not realized until he started treatment. I began to gain the impression that beneath the obsessional structure, controlling, superior and rigid, there was a basically phobic organization. I shall try to reduce the piece of material that I am bringing to its bare bones.

C had asked during the week to come a quarter of an hour earlier on the Friday, my first session in the day, in order to catch a train, as he had to go to Manchester for work. Then he described in great and obsessional detail on the Friday his worries about catching the train, getting through the traffic, etc., and how he had safeguarded these problems. He also discussed an anxiety about losing his membership in a club because of non-attendance, and spoke about a friend being slightly unfriendly on the phone. Detailed interpretations about his feeling unwanted related to the weekend, feeling shut out, and a need not to go away but rather to remain here or shut inside, did not seem to make real contact or to help him. But in relation to my showing him his need to be inside and safe he started to talk, now in a very different and smooth way, about how similar this problem was to his difficulty in changing jobs, moving his office, getting new clothes, how he stuck to the old ones, although by now he was short of clothes. Then there was the same problem about changing cars. . . .

At this point I think that an interesting thing had occurred. While all that he was saying seemed accurate and important in itself, the thoughts were no longer being thought, they had become words, concrete analytic objects into which he could sink, get drawn in, as if they were the mental concomitant of a physical body into which he was withdrawing in the session. The question of separating off, mentally as physically, could be evaded since our ideas could now be experienced as completely in tune and he had withdrawn into them. When I pointed this out to C, he was shocked, saying: 'When you said that, Manchester came into my mind, it was like sticking a knife into me.' I thought that the knife that goes in was not just my pushing reality back into his mind, but a knife that goes in between himself and me, separating us off and making him aware of being different and outside, and this aroused immediate anxiety.

I bring this material to show how the interpretations about his obsessional control and his reassuring himself and me, then the interpretations about his needing to avoid separation, new things, etc., and to be inside, were not experienced as helpful explanations, but were used as concrete objects, as parts of myself that he could get inside defensively, warding off psychotic anxieties of a more agoraphobic type associated with separation. Thus the two levels of operating — obsessional defending against phobic — could be seen to be lived out in the transference, and when the deeper layer was tackled, when I showed him the smooth defensive use of my words, my interpretations were felt as knife-like, and the anxieties re-emerged in the transference. In one sense this material is comparable with the case we discussed in the seminar. In such situations, if interpretations and understanding remain on the level of the individual associations, as contrasted with the total situation and the way that the analyst and his words are used, we shall find that we are being drawn into a pseudo-mature or more neurotic organization and missing the more psychotic anxieties and defences, which manifest themselves once we take into account the total situation — which is being acted-out in the transference.

In this paper, I am concentrating on what is being lived in the transference and in this last example, as at the beginning, I tried to show how interpretations are rarely heard purely as interpretations, except when the patient is near to the depressive position. Then interpretations and the transference itself becomes more realistic and less loaded with phantasy meaning. Patients operating with more primitive defences of splitting and projective identification tend to 'hear' our interpretations or 'use' them differently and how they 'use' or 'hear' and the difference between these two concepts needs to be distinguished if we are to clarify the transference situation and the state of the patient's ego and the correctness or not of his perceptions. Sometimes our patients hear our interpretations in a more paranoid way, for example, as a criticism or as an attack. C, after getting absorbed in my thoughts, heard my interpretations about Manchester as a knife that cut into him — between us. Sometimes the situation looks similar, the patient seems disturbed by an interpretation, but has, in fact, heard it, understood it, correctly, but unconsciously used it in an active way, thus involving the analyst.

N, I believe, did not hear my interpretations about his dream of the helicopter as cruel or harsh, but he unconsciously used them to reproach, beat and torment himself masochistically, thus in his phantasy using me as the beater. Or, to return to C: having heard certain of my interpretations and their meaning correctly, he used the words and thoughts not to think with, but unconsciously to act with, to get into and try to involve me in this activity, spinning words but not really communicating with them. Such activities not only colour but structure the transference situation and have important implications for technique.

71

Summary

I have tried in this paper to discuss how I think we are tending to use the concept of transference today. I have stressed the importance of seeing transference as a living relationship in which there is constant movement and change. I have indicated how everything of importance in the patient's psychic organization based on his early and habitual ways of functioning, his phantasies, impulses, defences and conflicts, will be lived out in some way in the transference. In addition, everything that the analyst is or says is likely to be responded to according to the patient's own psychic make-up, rather than the analyst's intentions and the meaning he gives to his interpretations. I have thus tried to discuss how the way in which our patients communicate their problems to us is frequently beyond their individual associations and beyond their words, and can often only be gauged by means of the counter-transference. These are some of the points that I think we need to consider under the rubric of the total situations which are transferred from the past.

References

Klein, M. (1952) 'The origin of transference', *International Journal of Psycho-Analysis*, 33; 433—8; reprinted in *The Writings of Melanie Klein*, vol. 3, London: Hogarth Press (1975), 48—56.
Strachey, J. (1934) 'The nature of the therapeutic action of psycho-analysis', *International Journal of Psycho-Analysis*, 15: 275—93.

—————————— 6 ——————————

Interpretation: the past in the present

RUTH RIESENBERG MALCOLM

This paper was read at the 6th Conference of the European Psycho-analytic Federation in 1985 and was published in 1986 in the *International Review of Psycho-Analysis*, 13: 433—43.

The analytic process is a process of communication. The patient communicates his psychic world to the analyst by experiencing it and reliving in the transference. The analyst communicates to the patient his understanding of this relationship — that is, he interprets the relationship itself with the aim of bringing about psychic change. The transference is an emotional relationship of the patient with the analyst which is experienced in the present, in what is generally called 'the here-and-now' of the analytic situation. It is the expression of the patient's past in its multiple transformations.

In this paper I want to make the following points: (1) that by interpreting the transference the analyst is interpreting simultaneously past and present, (2) that the genesis and resolution of the patient's conflicts can only be reached and achieved by interpreting the patient's relationship to the analyst and (3) that the so-called 'genetic interpretations', that is, interpretations that refer to the patient's past history, are not the aim of analytic work, but they do have the function of providing the patient with a sense of continuity in his life.

What transference is, its place in analysis and how to understand it, has concerned analysts continually. Sandler (1983) reviews the concept of transference. Isaacs (1939) and Klein (1952) emphasize that transference should be looked at as a total situation, encompassing all the patient's communications. Recently Gill (1982) argues for the centrality of the transference in the psychoanalytic process and he also conceives of transference as an amalgam of past and present. His views are discussed in great detail, and argued for and against by writers such as J. and A.-M. Sandler (1984), Steiner (1984), Wallerstein (1984), and others.

Let me first focus briefly on what is being 'transferred' in the transference. Strachey (1934) has described lucidly how 'the neurotic' tends to repeat with each person his old patterns of relating to objects and how the analytic situation, by virtue of the specific behaviour of the analyst, facilitates this repetition as well as the understanding of it.

Internal object relationships — that is, the internal world of the patient — consist predominantly in relations to archaic objects which, for different reasons, have not developed. These archaic objects are objects into which, in infancy and childhood, the child has projected great parts of itself, and has introjected them. Therefore they do not necessarily correspond to or much resemble the original external objects. Because of these projections the internal objects are distorted. The patient goes on relating to them in ways similar to those in infancy — that is, they are often perceived as dangerous and hostile. The patient experiences anxiety, against which he uses defensive patterns, and the analyst will be perceived by the patient in the very way he perceived his objects, and will react to the analyst accordingly.

Joseph (1985) enlarges and refines our understanding of the transference. She says:

'transference ... by definition must include everything that the patient brings into the relationship. What he brings in can best be gauged by our focusing our attention on what is going on within the relationship, and how he is using the analyst, alongside and beyond what he is saying' (p. 447).

I have chosen this quotation from Joseph's paper because it expresses, in my opinion, what should be the centre of the interpretation — that is, the immediate relationship between analyst and patient, with its verbal and non-verbal expressions. This means that the knowledge of 'projective identification' is central to the understanding of the analytical material. Projective identification is an unconscious phantasy through which the person projects parts of himself into his object, which is then perceived as affected by that which was projected. The reasons for projective identification are multiple and beyond the scope of this paper. But whatever the reason for this mechanism, it does not always contain some elements of communication, and sometimes its use is specifically to communicate something that cannot be expressed in any other way, perhaps because it occurred before language had been established, or perhaps because it refers to nameless feelings, or perhaps because it repeats a very early infantile experience.

By focusing on what goes on in a relationship one is, of course, referring to both sides of this relationship. The analyst's reactions to the patient's communications play a part in his understanding of the patient. Bion's researches (1962) on the impact on the mother of the baby's projections, and her capacity to transform those feelings projected into her by the process which he called 'reverie', opened great insight into the understanding of the counter-transference and the analyst's role of containing the patient — that is, being emotionally affected by the patient and transforming his own reactions into an understanding of the patient.

The patient does not only express himself through words. He also uses actions, and sometimes words and actions. The analyst listens, observes and feels the patient's communications. He scrutinizes his own responses to the patient, trying to understand the effect the patient's behaviour has on himself, and he understands this as a communication from the patient (while being aware of those responses which come from his own personality). It is this, comprehended in its totality, that is presented to the patient as an interpretation.

This interpretation should be verbalized directly and concisely in terms of the present. We describe to the patient what is going on, and we explain why we think it is going on; we allow the relationship to evolve and we try to draw the patient into looking at the relationship.

Generally the patient perceives what we say in (at least) two ways. If it makes sense to him, he may feel relief and think about it. But, at the same time, the interpretation interferes with his usual way of reacting, and this can either loosen the defences or bring out further defensive behaviour. This continuous shift in the contact of the patient with the analyst — shifts that are provoked by our interpretations — reveals in the analysis, bit by bit, the patient's defensive structure, and we, analyst and patient, can learn how these defences were built up and affected his reactions to his objects.

The analyst understands the patient's present relationship to him as a function of the past. Therefore his understanding of the present is the understanding of the patient's past as alive and actual.

The changes brought about through interpretations of the transference result in changes in the patient's relationship to his internal objects and his view of his early family often emerges with greater clarity and realism.

By so interpreting, we try to reach towards an emotional awareness in the patient, to resonate in such a way that he can feel and understand our account of what is going on. Only when this has taken place does the linking to the past become meaningful and important. I am speaking of interpreting the past in the present, and of integrating this alive past of the transference with the inferred historical past.

In the discussion of the clinical material which follows I hope to show how by interpreting the transference we are interpreting at one and the same time past and present, and that we do so mainly in the 'here-and-now' of the analytic situation. I will discuss the effect of the interpretations and the movements in the patient that occur in session, and the reasons why the linking with the inferred past is necessary. I will also speak about modes of verbalization and refer briefly to the problem of reconstruction.

I will now offer a vignette from an analysis, primarily to show the patient's method of communication and how alive those communications are in the transference. I will also try to show how the interpretation helped the patient to move from repetition towards understanding.

The patient is a very ill young man. Early in his analysis I became aware that very often after I spoke he said 'yes'. Slowly I came to realize that these 'yeses' had a mechanical quality. I also noticed that I myself had spoken, after his 'yeses', as if nothing had been said. This puzzled me and I became more attentive when he said 'yes'. I had already been somewhat aware that he punctuated his own discourse with 'yes'. For instance, he would say, 'I was reading in the paper — yes — while I was travelling here in the underground'. He would expand on the worrying quality of the news he was reading about, say 'yes', and proceed to his own views on the news.

When he said 'yes' after something I had said to him, it bore no relation whatsoever to what he thought, made of, or felt in relation to what I had said. This would appear in further associations or in occasional direct references. This way of saying yes, which might have been considered a verbal mannerism, impressed itself on my mind. Curiously, at first it made me feel a sense of isolation. Slowly the picture emerged in my mind of a baby crying or trying to communicate something, and being met with a mild, 'Yes, yes, dear', which was an automatic response. From his behaviour and my own reaction, the thought came of a very early relationship with his mother, who though physically present (and from his account, very devoted to him), seemed mentally to be either absent or incapable of resonating to her baby.

I called his attention to his saying 'yes', to the way he did so after either of us had said something; and I pointed out the unrelatedness of those 'yeses' to what had been spoken. He looked alert, said 'Yes' in his usual way, stopped himself, and smiled. Consequently I was able to show him that by those 'yeses' he might without knowing it be trying to reassure me, but that his saying 'yes' to me had no relation to what he felt or thought about what I had said. He was thoughtful, looked responsive, and said 'Strange'. I added that he probably felt me to be vulnerable. He said 'Mmmm' — neither doubting nor agreeing. I went on to say that this behaviour towards me seemed also to be taking place inside himself, as if a bit of him were trying to talk about something and another apparently unconnected bit of him, not listening, was soothing him. Later on I told him that there seemed to be in him simultaneously two parallel relationships. In one he had split a part of himself into me and was perceiving me as being in need of reassurance, and himself as having to provide this assurance; and that also inside him, together with what was going on between us, a part of himself was behaving towards another part in the way I have just described. I ended by saying that his lodging a bit of himself in me was done both to get rid of the part of him that felt so unhappy and lonely (a frequent and intense complaint of his) and also to make me know how it feels when not listened to or understood properly. He looked relaxed and a very broad smile came to his face — a mixture of pleasure and some surprise.

I shall now consider the implications of what I said to the patient. The projective identification process I was describing in him was, in my view, used by him at that moment both as a defence and a communication. He had partially projected into me an infantile aspect of himself, while at the same time he was identified with an unresponsive internal object. I suspected that this was an early relationship to his mother, the quality of which had remained frozen in him and separated from other parts of his personality.

I will continue with the session. After my interpretations, he spoke with more warmth in his voice about his hope of being accepted by the university, where he had applied for postgraduate work. He expanded a little on what he expected from the course of study, and said that maybe this time he would be able to carry it through, due to his being in analysis. This was stated directly and firmly. He returned to talking about the anxiety he had felt when he had attempted to do similar studies in the past. He went into detail, talking both about the coming year and his past problems in the university. (Twice he had had to drop out of a similar course.)

While speaking he was becoming progressively more anxious. His way of speaking grew vaguer, the yeses reappeared. He looked dejected and what he said was less coherent than when he had begun to speak.

I said it seemed to me that at first he had felt understood and hopeful about gaining more insight into the strange things in himself, and thus becoming able to cope with the university, but that this hope seemed to provoke a conflict in him. Following this, I was able to show him what was going on, the infant in him who perceived mother as unresponsive, and how sometimes he felt this infant to be in me, sometimes in him.

I have presented this material because I think it gives a picture of how alive is the past in the present and how it affects the analyst. It shows how I was able to use the way it affected me to enhance my understanding of the whole communication, and how I focused the interpretation on the situation immediately present between the patient and myself. In this way I could see the patient's anxieties, the defences that were mobilized, and how the interaction between him and me produced shifts which permitted a view of how his defences operated, and probably how they had originally been built up.

I think that maintaining the focus on the patient's relationship to the analyst permits one to explore in detail the patient's unconscious phantasies. This also forces the analyst to examine closely every issue in relation to himself, which in turn forces the analyst to be emotionally more active, while at the same time remaining, in his behaviour, constant and neutral for the patient. This emotional closeness to the patient, as we all know, can often be very uncomfortable and the analyst has to be careful not to avoid the discomfort by too quickly explaining the present situation in relation to its probable origin in the past, or by reducing the description to language based on infantile experience.

From what I have been saying, and the brief example, one can see that analysis is an active dialogue. In this dialogue the analyst should, ideally, only communicate verbally to his patient; but we also know that this ideal is never completely achieved, since the analyst's tone of voice changes, he moves his body, or he speaks in ways that might communicate more to the patient than he would wish to do. Still, we know that this is inevitable. The analyst, in my opinion, should try as far as possible to be alert to such events, or be ready to see them through the patient's reactions or associations, and should try to understand the meaning of his own behaviour, as well as the effect it might have had on the patient, and the patient's reaction to it.

The analyst needs to distinguish in his reactions what comes from himself and what is provoked by the patient. This should also affect the interpretation. To avoid misunderstanding, I should like to stress that I do not mean that the analyst's involuntary actions are therapeutic in the analysis. On the contrary, they add difficulties to the analytic work, and one should be aware of these so as further to understand and contain the patient.

To summarize: in order for the interpretations to be alive and to bring emotional conviction to the patient, they have to be expressed in terms of the immediacy of the relationship to the analyst. On the other hand, the analyst, when formulating them, should keep in mind the notion that it is the patient's past that is expressed in his unconscious phantasies. For instance, in the case I have presented, when I started interpreting the yeses, I was examining in my mind the patient's feeling and thinking as an indication of his early relation to his mother. At some point this part should be made explicit for the patient and linked to his actual present experience. I shall return to this later.

I should like to mention here a problem that has occupied analysts for decades — that is, the so-called 'too deep' interpretation.[1] If we agree that interpretations should be made in the emotional heat of the transference situation — as understood by the analyst with the help of the counter-transference, his theoretical background, and his knowledge of the patient — we would also agree that each correct interpretation is a deep interpretation, since it aims at touching the depths of the patient's feelings. I do not think that the mind of a person is formed of structured layers, which we should try to reach one after another. What are repeated in the transference are conflicts in relation to internal objects. Those conflicts, as experienced with the analyst, come to light through the patient's shifts in the session, from one mode of reacting to another. In these shifts he portrays his anxieties, and the defences he puts into action against them. It is this conflict which we interpret when it appears. It is my belief that what has often been described, and feared, as interpretations which are 'too deep', are probably wrong interpretations, that have failed to capture what is alive and available in the transference.

Now I shall present clinical material and discuss in its light different aspects and problems of interpretation. I will present a complete session from the analysis of the patient I have just been discussing.

Mr A is a young man in his early twenties, exceptionally intelligent and very ill. He is of average height, rather slim, with blond hair and blue eyes. He could be quite handsome, but his appearance and expression change from day to day. He can have an open look and a bright, warm smile. He can also look and dress as a menacing 'punk'. Sometimes he comes to the sessions looking remote and expressionless, but more often he will show anxiety. These striking changes appear from day to day, but are usually not so marked within a session. His immediate reason for seeking analysis was that during the past two years intense anxieties (which he had suffered all his life) had finally prevented him continuing his university studies. He had graduated with one of the best degrees from a prestigious university. Twice he had been accepted for postgraduate work and both times he broke down, suffering from intense anxiety attacks, and ideas of reference. If it were not for the devotion of his family in looking after him, he would have been hospitalized.

Among his complaints, a feeling of numbness and of being cut off is a very central one. He thinks that people can read his mind and that they are talking about him. He oscillates between a grandiose view of himself and a sense of uselessness. Sometimes he fears that he stinks, that he is ugly, and that people are looking at him and thinking, 'What is he doing here?' He has never had a relationship with a woman, this being another explicit reason for coming to analysis. His ideal in life is to find the perfect girl. She should be like the heroine of a soap opera, beautiful, intelligent, somehow independent; she should think like he does and be with him always, in the country, where he could work on research with no need to mix socially with other people. He has some friends who appear to like him and seek him out, but he very rarely contacts anybody himself; and often when phoned he feels intruded and imposed upon. From the beginning, in spite of the severity of his problems, I found him amenable to analysis.

Mr A is the elder of two boys. The information about his mother is that she is a very fragile, immature person. His maternal grandmother suffers from a severe psychopathology. In the father's family, there are several cases of psychosis. Father himself seems to be the strongest and most stable person in the family, and he is a great support to the patient.

The session I wish to present took place in the fourth month of Mr A's analysis. Before starting the analysis he had to wait a term for a vacancy. In the meantime, strongly pushed by his father, he had started a course in education, which he hates. The practical aspect fills him with unbearable anxiety. The training itself bores him. But he likes meeting other students there. At the time of this session he was seriously considering interrupting the training, especially as he would shortly have to start practical work. Also, this practice would probably prevent him from attending analysis.

Mr A is a person of unusual culture, considering his background. He is well read and has for some time been interested in philosophy. Before his analysis he mainly read existential philosophy, but since coming into analysis he has been compulsively buying and reading books on the philosophy of mind. This has been a central theme in the analysis, and has occasionally been spoken of as continuing and substituting for the analysis in my absence. Also, the books and ideas he mentions often make me wonder whether he knows my personal connexion with that type of philosophy. Before starting the analysis he knew that I had known a relative of his, and that I was South American. In his first session, and often subsequently, he spoke of having 'a Nazi' in himself, and daily he speaks of his fear and hatred of President Reagan and Mrs Thatcher. He also hates his maternal grandparents, who are mentioned almost every day, and who seem to have no redeeming qualities.

On the Wednesday of the week preceding the session to be presented, there was a strike of workers on the underground, and he phoned me early in the day to tell me he was not coming. That was the first time he had missed a session. When he came the following day, the reason he gave for not having attempted some other means of transport was that this would have proved that analysis was an addiction. He reported on the Thursday that he had been very withdrawn the day before, and, indeed, he was very withdrawn both in the Thursday and Friday session.

80

In the latter part of Friday's session he spoke mainly of his desire to go and buy more philosophy books, and that he planned to spend the whole weekend reading philosophy.

Monday's session[2]

Mr A came in, looking livelier than he had looked the previous week, and he showed some eagerness in his expression when he greeted me at the door. No sooner was he on the couch than he said he had had three dreams, and immediately proceeded to tell me the dreams, one after the other.

First Dream. He dreamed that I, the analyst, was in his house, in his parents' bedroom. I was wearing a nightie and was being very cruel to him. I was teasing him by saying to him that his mother had cancer of the mouth and I was laughing at this. Apparently, it seemed all the time that this was just a tease, that what I said wasn't true. He said that after a short while I left the room and went to the bathroom where I started chatting with his father. The way he said this last bit had a peculiarly insinuating ring to it that made me think more of 'chatting up' than chatting with.

Second Dream. He was in the United States. There was a horrible woman with two girls. He added that the girls had very long hair and ice-cold eyes. Those girls were wicked and cruel and they had psychic powers: for instance, power to cut a cake with their minds. Later on he added that for some reason the cake seemed to be suspended in the air. 'Quite peculiar,' he said. The dream went on. Those girls were also rounding up the children in the playground. This was awfully grim; and he went on repeating and emphasizing that they were awful, evil and wicked.

Third Dream. Dave, a friend of his (who is doing the education course with him), phoned to ask the patient if they were still friends. The dream grew vague. Other people were present. The whole scene was happening in an underground train. But instead of going to Chelsea, where he lives, the train turned towards somewhere else. This last was very frightening.

When Mr A had finished narrating the dreams, he said that the previous night he had woken up at 4 a.m. and had written the dreams down. He feared that he would forget them. Then, without a pause, he began talking in a thoughtful way. On Friday he had received a letter from the university informing him that he had been accepted for the postgraduate studies that he had applied for, starting in the next academic year. As soon as he read the letter he began to question whether he wanted it or not. It might have been easier had they rejected him, but at the same time, this would have made him extremely unhappy.

On Friday he went out to dinner with his parents. His father was worried, and did not want him to stop his present studies. His friend Dave had asked him to come on a trip to Europe during the summer vacation. Somewhere at this point he said that the nightgown I was wearing in the dream was like one that his mother had, but not the one she was actually wearing during the weekend. He then said that on Saturday night he had gone out with some people from his old university. It was boring. They were, as usual, just drinking beer. He didn't drink too much — only five pints!

He went back to the subject of his education course, his father's attitude to him, and to the fact that he does not want to do the next term's practice. He continued along this familiar line. He does not see himself as a teacher. He referred again to the problem of the timetable conflicting with his analysis. And, sounding very upset, he said that teaching bothered him, and he then added that if he did not teach he did not know what he would do all day long.

Still speaking about the teaching, he said that to teach felt to him like supporting the social system of which he disapproves. He then remembered that his friends had said on Saturday that he was an 'armchair socialist'. He added that in a way they were right, since he lives off his father. He felt guilty because of this. And then he remembered that he was feeling guilty, on and off, over the whole weekend. Finally he mumbled something about his not seeing himself doing a 9 to 5 job. Then after a brief pause he said that the train in the dream reminded him of a film called *Train to Hell*.

Here I intervened. I said that he felt I was being very cruel in stopping for the weekend. In his mind, I felt to him like a cake that was out of reach, and it felt as though I were teasing him, as in my 'chatting up' his father in the first dream. I said that he hated wanting something, especially if it was not immediately available. And I linked this with his wish for the place at the university to do a doctoral degree and his reaction to the letter. I spoke about the way he dealt with those painful feelings and with his menacing anger, by cutting them off and pushing them out of his mind and lodging them in me. And that, as a consequence of this lodging, his perception of me as someone like the woman with the girls in the dream — powerful and menacing; and that on coming back from the weekend, he did not know if there was any friendliness left between us or if this would just be a hellish place. At these last remarks, he smiled slightly.

After a short silence he responded warmly to my interpretation. He said that the letter from the tutor at the university was very friendly. He had written that he had enjoyed meeting Mr A at the selection interview and that he was looking forward to their working together. Mr A spoke a bit more about the content of the letter in the same direct way in which he had spoken after my interpretation. But now his tone changed. It became slightly haughty, rather provocative and mocking — almost as if he were teasing me. He continued to speak about the letter, saying, 'Oh, you know the typical things people say in this kind of letter'. In a still more provocative way he said that his father had suggested that he should miss two months of analysis, saying that 'this could not possibly matter since the analyst also took holidays'. These provocative remarks went on a bit longer and then I said I thought that what I had previously said had made sense to him. He responded by saying, 'That is true'. I continued, that my having made sense to him was perceived as a friendly contact between us. But that as soon as he felt better, a bit of him felt very hostile and started undermining, mocking me, and probably himself. This act of undermining feels like the cancer that cuts into the analysis and into his own feelings; and also, by lodging his feelings in me, he experiences me as having this cancer. That is, he fears that I will not be able to assess properly his need for analysis, as indicated by his remark about his father's comment on the possibility of his skipping two months' analysis.

I will pause here to consider in a rather schematic way the meaning of this material: what I chose to interpret; why I chose it; and the effect of the interpretation on the patient.

I think the three dreams are interconnected and were triggered by the immediate stimuli of the weekend separation, reinforced by the interruption in the previous week. In the first dream he feels his object split between a damaged feeding object and a sexual object. He is taunted by my weekend and responds with a destructive biting which is projected into his object, that is now said to have a cancer of the mouth. The object's separate existence is felt as tantalizing to him. And because of his own reaction to this, he feels threatened by a total loss of the good object. A cancer is a fatal illness. Cruelty seems to prevail, and violence is a possibility.

The second dream portrays neatly the, for him, tormenting quality of an unavailable object, with increasing conflict between loving and sadistic feelings. As I suggested before, he deals with his problem by cutting. He either cuts off by his withdrawal or he cuts into me with his mockery, and then he projects his actions into the object. In the dream the suspended cake is the target of his cutting, but the psychic power to cut is felt as belonging to the girls. This is similar to what happened in the first dream, where it was the mother who was said to have cancer of the mouth while in the session he mocked me bitingly.

I think that the third dream points towards the possibility of a more

83

benign response. Thoughts about friendliness re-emerged. He became aware of having turned the wrong way — that is, against the object. And he is aware of the frightening consequences of this action, which I think connects with guilt as well as the hellish situation that he has to face.

The interpretation that I have given brought a shift in the material. He felt relieved and better. His relief brought an upsurge of envy expressed by sadism. His teasing held a rather veiled sarcasm (he finds it difficult to be directly sarcastic or openly hostile to me, but he can be extensively so in a slightly muted way). In this session the sarcasm had a biting, excited quality, and a greedy feeling associated with it.

In interpreting this last shift, I reminded him that my previous interpretation had made sense to him, and that because it made sense to him it had stimulated his hostility. I also mentioned that he had been pleased by his tutor's letter.

Mr A then spoke of his friend Dave's suggestion that they have a holiday together in the summer. He said that Dave was poor and that travelling with him in Europe would mean having to rough it. He described how exposed he feels in such circumstances, and that having to be social with all kinds of people frightened him very much, adding, 'like what happened to me that time I told you about in Holland'. He then reminded me of how on that occasion his brother had protected him. He talked about those holidays on the Continent some years ago which he had taken with his brother and some friends (all students at the same university). But at some point he had parted from them and had returned home while they had gone on to Greece. He finished by saying that Italy, and more especially France, felt 'almost civilized' to him, but the rest he could not face.

I asked him if he spoke French. He looked surprised and said 'Yes'. I said to him that in the analysis we have a common language, when he felt that I understood him and that he could take in what I said. Then we were — almost — 'civilized'. Whenever, as occurred early in the session, some cruel, hostile bit of him steps in, or something else happens, then he is exposed to incomprehensible feelings which he perceives as dangerous, and he panics.

He said, 'It's like the panic attacks in Holland I have been telling you about. It happened when I was in the Red Light district and it was not the sex that frightened me. It was the violence.' I linked this with the first dream in which I was in the nightgown, and teasing him. I said that when he is faced by sex (me as the couple in the first dream) he feels hatred and he perceives me as menacing. He replied, with an expression of puzzlement, 'What you said feels right, but I don't understand why'. I said, 'Because you feel excluded'. He said, 'Yah', and relaxed with a big sigh. After a pause, I did say that perhaps this was how he had felt as a baby, and later on as a child, left in his cot or a play room: miserable, angry, feeling violent towards his mother, whom he might have felt to be doing something cruelly evil to him by being with his father. I told him that probably when he was an infant this had been felt as the loss of an exclusive relationship with mother, an exclusiveness in which he felt protected. I stressed his need to be protected by these good feelings with mother. I said that he needed to have those old good feelings from when he was very little to protect him when he felt assaulted by 'uncivilized feelings' — that is, hatred, which made him attack when he was not in an exclusive relation, at one with the object. He was thoughtful and silent for a little while, then said that he wondered why the dream had taken place in America.

After a brief pause he returned to the theme of having to rough it, and then in a slightly self-mocking tone said that he is such a socialist but he likes good, comfortable hotels — nice places. Here he made a funny noise that he had made on a few previous occasions in the analysis. In a rather guttural voice — not at all his usual one — he uttered 'Ach', and then went on for a short while on the subject of roughing it and hotels.

His saying 'Ach' had a strong impact on my mind. I sensed that it was central to his communication. I also fleetingly experienced him as someone unknown to me. I asked him if someone in his family said 'Ach'. He reddened a bit and said, 'Yes, my horrible rich grandmother. Why?' (By then I had also remembered an experience he had had when he was in the United States. He had felt utterly helpless, even physically paralysed, so that he had been unable to walk for a while. He had been in a great panic.) I said to him that when he felt limited in the analysis, whether by time (it was nearing the end of the session) or by other people arriving, he finds it rough and feels very powerless, so he quickly turns himself into his grandmother whom he has often described as being anorexic and a kleptomaniac. In this way he does not have to receive from me, but can steal his way into me and have all he wants — a good place, and no socialism; that is, total possession without sharing. However, he then feels himself to be horrible — that is, guilty. He laughed and said, 'Strange', and started talking about Dave. I interrupted and stopped the session.

I hope that I have been able to show from the clinical material that the analytic session is an active dialogue about a relationship of which this dialogue itself is a part.

As I said earlier in this paper, it is the immediacy of the relationship with the analyst which is the focal point of the interpretation. The careful scrutiny of the details of the patient's responses to the interpretation is of central importance. We see from the session how, once he felt understood, he reacted both with hope and with envy towards myself as the object. The analysis of that reaction unravelled further anxieties connected to incomprehensible states of confusion that resulted probably from his attacks. This in turn permitted us a clearer view of his possessiveness and of the mechanisms he used to avoid both the awareness of his possessiveness and the conflict he experiences by wanting an object, feeling separate from it, and having to share it. His solution to this conflict is to become the object, which at that moment is a rich, anorexic kleptomaniac — and thus, someone who has everything and needs nothing. This solution made him feel guilty, and then the analysis began to focus on those guilt feelings.

I will now turn to the interpretations. As the material shows, in most of these I focused on myself. The person of the analyst comes to stand for the internal object through whom the conflicts are experienced. Throughout this session, I thought myself to be in a maternal role. When the interpretation was heard and felt by the patient, I could branch out into explorations of other aspects of the material. Some of these can be seen in the material, but for the sake of brevity I have had to condense much of what went on. It can still be seen, however, that not everything was interpretation. I made comments, and asked direct questions. In this last, of course, I depended on my judgement of the nature of the contact with him.

The way I spoke was direct and ordinary. Some of the patient's material, especially his dreams, had a powerfully evocative quality, bringing to my mind imagery of early infantile relationships; but, as can be seen, I did not express my interpretations in terms of the archaic experience. I think that using a language derived from the archaic experience (that which has sometimes been called 'symbolic language'), creates a number of problems. First, it employs repetitive words, on the meaning of which both patient and analyst believe there is mutual understanding but which in fact lose the quality of specificity which should belong to each element of the session. Therefore, these terms stand in the way of further exploration of the material in the transference. Second, it is an artificial language that hinders ordinary communication and renders itself open to idealization. Third (and most importantly), it relates to my earlier remarks on so-called 'too deep' interpretations. Using symbolic language bypasses the depths of the transference experience. It destroys the live contact between analyst and patient, and turns the analysis into *talking about* unconscious phantasies, rather than experiencing them in their crude impact.

My last point concerns the linking of the interpretation of the present to the historical past. I think that the main reason for doing this is that, by connecting the historical past with the past as it appears in the transference, we enable the patients to gain a sense of the continuity of their lives. By analysing the past in the present, the ego of the patient becomes more integrated and therefore stronger.

By linking the interpretations to the historical past we also allow the patient to distance himself both from the immediacy of his experience and from the closeness to the analyst. The distancing from his own immediate experience helps the patient to gain perspective on his problems and stimulates his thinking about his own ways of viewing the past. The distancing from the immediacy of the relationship to the analyst allows the patient at moments to view his analyst as separate and different from his internal object, as someone with whom he is working out his problems. But in order for the links to the inferred historical past to be useful, they can be made only when the patient has experienced and understood the past situation in the present.

It will be noticed that I have mainly used the expression 'linking to the past' rather than 'reconstruction'.[3] I think that the real work of reconstruction goes on in the transference. The patient, by repeating with us again and again his problems with his internal objects, portrays in the analysis the way that his relationship with those objects evolved. The interpretations mobilize defences which correspond to the old defences used in infancy and childhood. The understanding of those defences is formulated in new interpretations. Those interpretations form the actual reconstruction. It is only here that the patient understands his own past and his relation to his real external objects.

When interpreting the present the patient will often remember scenes from the past, incidents that occurred with different people, or he will narrate episodes of the past. The interpretations of the present are more definite and precise than the linking to the patient's history, which I think should be done in a way that is loose enough to allow the patient himself to provide more precise connexions with his own past. As we interpret the present, the patient's relationships to his internal objects change, revealing bit by bit under our very eyes how those relationships were built up. And as I have been emphasizing, those changes are achieved by interpreting past and present at one and the same time.

Summary

In this paper I maintain, and illustrate clinically, the point that the analyst, by analysing the transference, is analysing past and present at the same time.

Following the Kleinian understanding of the internal object relationships, and using case material to illustrate my point, I support the view that the past is alive in the present, and that transference is an alloy of past and present. By understanding and interpreting the transference the analyst is dealing with the patient's early conflicts, which can only be understood and resolved when lived through in the present with the analyst.

I maintain that the work of reconstruction is done in the analysis of the transference and that references to the past have an important linking value for the patient, in that they help him to get a sense of continuity in his life which helps him toward integration.

I also discuss the level of interpretations and the language in which I think they should be expressed.

N.B. My psychoanalytic thought is rooted in Freud and Melanie Klein. I have been greatly influenced also by Betty Joseph's papers and thoughts on technique.

Notes

1   Sandler and Sandler (1984) address themselves to the problem of at which level the conflict should be interpreted. They say: 'This problem disappears if we direct our interpretations of conflict to the here-and-now, guided by what we assess to be the predominant affect as shown in the material (and also often in one way or another in the countertransference). Because the patient's conflicts are always related to the present, it is the current form that is important; their origin in the past unconscious is of secondary concern, a matter to be dealt with as evidence for reconstruction accumulates' (p. 384). As can be seen I am very much in agreement with their viewpoint, though I think we place different importance on the role of the internal objects in the conflict and in its expression.
2   Because of the need to condense the presentation, the interpretations appear to be longer than they really were.
3   Reconstruction and its place in analytical work has been a recurrent theme in analytic literature; for example, Sandler et al. (1973), Blum (1980), Brenman (1980).

References

Bion, B.W. (1962) *Learning from Experience*, London: Heinemann; reprinted in paperback, Maresfield Reprints, London: H. Karnac Books (1984).

Blum, H. (1980) 'The value of reconstruction in adult psychoanalysis', *International Journal of Psycho-Analysis*, 61: 39–52.

Brenman, E. (1980) 'The value of reconstruction in adult psychoanalysis', *International Journal of Psycho-Analysis*, 61: 53–60.

Gill, M. (1982) *Analysis of Transference*, vol. 1, New York: International University Press.

Isaacs, S. (1939) 'Criteria for interpretation', *International Journal of Psycho-Analysis*, 20: 148–60.

Joseph, B. (1985) 'Transference: the total situation', *International Journal of Psycho-Analysis*, 66: 447–54; also 61–72 of this volume.

Klein, M. (1952) 'The origin of transference', *International Journal of Psycho-Analysis*, 35: 433–8; reprinted in *The Writings of Melanie Klein*, vol. 3, London: Hogarth Press (1975), 48–56.

Sandler, J. (1983) 'Reflections on some relations between psychoanalytic concepts and psychoanalytic practice', *International Journal of Psycho-Analysis*, 64: 35–45.

—— and Sandler, A.-M. (1984) 'The past unconscious, the present unconscious, and interpretation of transference', *Psychoanalytic Inquiry*, 4: 367–99.

—— Dare, C. and Holder, A. (1973) *The Patient and the Analyst*, Maresfield Reprints, London: H. Karnac Books.

Steiner, J. (1984) 'Some reflections on the analysis of transference: a Kleinian view, *Psychoanalytic Inquiry*, 4: 443–63.

Strachey, J. (1934) 'The nature of the therapeutic action of psychoanalysis', *International Journal of Psycho-Analysis*, 15: 127–59.

Wallerstein, R. (1984) 'The analysis of the transference: a matter of emphasis or of theory reformulation?' *Psychoanalytic Inquiry*, 4: 325–54.

Clinical papers on adult psychoanalysis

PART TWO

Clinical papers on adult psychoanalysis

Introduction

ELIZABETH BOTT SPILLIUS

From the very large number of Kleinian clinical papers, I have chosen three to give the reader an impression of how Kleinian analysts work clinically. All three have much in common, but, in addition, each gives an example of work at a different time period, Segal's in 1950, Riesenberg Malcolm's in 1970, and O'Shaughnessy's in 1983. The first two were intended to be purely clinical papers whereas the third was contributed to a symposium on communication so that the ideas were central and the clinical material, though detailed, was intended primarily to illustrate them.

All three papers show features I consider to be the hallmarks of Kleinian work whatever the time period and the individual differences in temperament and style. First, they give a vivid sense of their patients' unconscious thoughts and feelings, a legacy of Klein's emphasis on unconscious phantasy. Second, the descriptions of all three analysts make it clear that they made very detailed observations of the patient, of the analyst, and of the connexions between the two, including, most importantly, the connexions established by projective identification. And third, all three authors use Klein's basic theoretical framework of the paranoid-schizoid and the depressive positions.

The three papers are only partly useful as examples of the trends of change I have discussed in the previous section on technique because I have tried to choose papers that make a more original contribution to practice and to theory than the typical clinical paper of their respective periods.

Segal's (1950) paper, as I have remarked above, is of special interest because it is the earliest account of the psychoanalytic treatment of an acute psychotic patient without basic alterations in technique. In it she gives vivid illustration of her schizophrenic patient's use of primitive defences, especially splitting and denial. She evidently made interpretations of unconscious phantasies to him very freely in part-object bodily language, which were meaningful to her patient in spite of his frequent denials; what he repressed and resisted were the links Segal tried to establish between different trends of thought. It is clear too that Segal was interpreting the patient's projective identification both with herself and with external figures, though the concept is not explicitly mentioned. In her postscript of 1980 she notes that she did not pay enough attention to the processes of ego fragmentation and pathological projective identification described by Bion in 'Differentiation of the psychotic from the non-psychotic personalities' (1957). (This paper is reprinted in Volume I of the present work.)

Segal's interest in symbolism is already evident in this paper, for she points out that her patient had developed symbols but that they remained 'equivalent' to the thing symbolized, work which was soon to develop into her differentiation between symbolic equations and symbols proper (Segal 1957).

In 'The mirror: a perverse sexual phantasy in a woman seen as a defence against a psychotic breakdown' (1970), Riesenberg Malcolm describes an analytic process in which she became aware of a patient's perverse phantasy through the patient's unconscious attempts to draw her analyst into collusive acting-out of it in the sessions. A second feature is the analysis of a perverse phantasy as a defence against ego disintegration and psychosis. The most dangerous aspects of the patient's internal world were encapsulated in the phantasy and there controlled.

In Riesenberg Malcolm's paper the concept of projective identification is much more explicitly used and discussed than in Segal's paper of twenty years earlier, and similarly Riesenberg Malcolm explicitly uses her counter-transference, especially her feelings of curiosity and potential excitement, to understand the psychic situation of her patient.

One gets the impression that the language of interpretation used by Riesenberg Malcolm was very similar to that used by Segal twenty years earlier, that is, that unconscious phantasies were described in bodily terms, though not in a manner that would have encouraged the patient to distance herself from the very disturbing forces in herself that she was uncovering and expressing.

In O'Shaughnessy's paper 'Words and working through' (1983) the clinical material is presented to expound and explain the thesis that patients communicate not only by words used symbolically but also by the more primitive mode of projective identification. The paper develops from Money-Kyrle's idea that there is a sequence from concrete thinking, to the dream, to symbolic thinking in words (Money-Kyrle 1968). Mutative interpretations by the analyst may slowly help the patient to become aware of his primitive forms of communication until he is able to use words creatively to express his own understanding of himself not only in words but also in his own way, his own words, rather than according to the conceptions of the analyst.

In O'Shaughnessy's paper the discussion of projective identification is even more explicit and conceptualized than in Riesenberg Malcolm's of thirteen years before. O'Shaughnessy's use of bodily and anatomical part-object language was also much more cautiously applied and less immediately used. As I have described in the Introduction to the previous section on technique, part functions rather than part structures are nowadays the usual initial focus of interpretation.

Thus, although these three papers have much in common — a shared body of concepts and basically similar ideas on technique — trends of change are apparent in the increasingly explicit use of the concepts of projective identification and counter-transference, in the focus on acting-in, and in the language of interpretation.

—————————— 1 ——————————

Some aspects of the analysis of a schizophrenic

HANNA SEGAL

This article was first published in 1950 in the *International Journal of Psycho-Analysis*, 31: 268—78 and subsequently in *The Work of Hanna Segal*, New York: Jason Aronson (1981), 101—20.

In recent years an increasing number of psychoanalysts have begun to treat schizophrenic patients psychoanalytically, using various modifications of technique. I think that the case I describe will be of interest since I have attempted to analyse a typical schizophrenic — with no doubt about his diagnosis — with only minor deviations from strict analytic technique. I took special care not to step out of the role of the analyst who interprets into that of an ally or an educator.

Edward was a diffident, over-sensitive child and adolescent. Very intellectual and over-ambitious, he was superficially well adapted to his surroundings but, in fact, completely withdrawn and secretive to the point of obsession. As a child, he was already interested in biology and centered on it all his infantile sexual curiosity and his intellectual interests. He found another outlet for his emotions in daydreams, usually about idealized girls, the princesses whom he was going to win over from a terrible father or rival. At school he got along quite well. Somehow his personality seemed to fit the requirements of the old-fashioned public school. His difficulties went unnoticed by himself as well as by his teachers and schoolfellows. Within the limited field of his interests he was quite brilliant and won a scholarship to a famous college, first among hundreds.

When at the age of eighteen and a half he was called up, things became much more difficult. He was sent to India and went to an Engineers' OCTU but could not cope with the training. He said he was very good at blowing mines, but no good at all at building bridges. He failed to get his commission and was referred for six months. Then he started to worry obsessionally about whether he should remain at the OCTU or resign in the hope of getting released sooner and being able to resume his studies. He became anxious, brooding, and showed signs of an approaching breakdown. Eventually, he resigned impulsively when an officer called him a fool. But he could not bear being a private. He felt that he had lost control and was imprisoned. He admitted to an overt sexual jealousy of officers; he felt that a private did not stand a chance with girls. He became hypochondriacal and suspicious.

After a few months he was asked to work in a photographic laboratory, in a darkroom, and that seems to have precipitated a complete breakdown. The breakdown began with worry about his eyes going wrong. Then ever-growing delusions appeared. These concerned Chinese plots to take power in India, a biologist wanting to destroy the whole world and so on. He had his first aural hallucinations. At last he wrote a letter to his Colonel denouncing the biologist who wanted to destroy the world, and this led to his being put in a mental hospital.

There he seems to have gone to pieces completely. In his memories, the six months he spent in the various military hospitals were a horrifying jumble of delusions, nightmares, hallucinations, complete loss of feeling of identity, sense of time and place or any continuity in himself or in the world.

In the hospital notes, I found little beyond brief descriptions of his being hallucinated, deluded, irrelevant, impulsive, etc. I know that he had two series of phrenosol injections which brought no improvement and that he had been diagnosed at different stages as either a hebephrenic or paranoid schizophrenic. When he returned to England he had been examined by an eminent psychoanalytic psychiatrist who diagnosed a rapidly deteriorating schizophrenia. All psychiatric reports noted a poor prognosis.

Since my emphasis is not on the differential diagnosis I should like to stress that no diagnosis other than that of schizophrenia was ever suggested. Further, my account of this analysis may be misleading. It is most important, especially when dealing with a schizophrenic, to link up phantasies with real events present and past, but I have had to avoid many references which might have revealed too much of the patient's background. Also, as a result of the necessary compression of material, it may seem that the patient was very talkative, when, in fact, he was generally silent, except early in the treatment when he would occasionally become over-excited.

I saw Edward for the first time at a short interview in the military hospital. He was completely withdrawn, apathetic, with retarded movements and a half-placating, half-foolish smile that was out of keeping with what he spoke about. He was kept in bed because of aimless wandering and impulsiveness while in the ward. His only spontaneous contribution to the conversation was to ask me if London was all right, because India had become completely altered. I did not answer the question, but suggested that he felt that he himself had changed and the world was changing with him. 'Yes,' he said, adding with emphasis, 'I have been changed.'

These two sentences gave me the first intimation of some of his problems. (1) He was afraid that the world was being destroyed. (2) He put a persecutory interpretation on what had befallen him (he had not changed, he had been changed). (3) He seemed unable to distinguish between himself and the world; his own destruction was felt to be equivalent to the destruction of the whole world. The lack of distinction between himself and 'everybody' or 'everything,' together with the emphasis on change, remained characteristic of his attitude throughout the acute stage of his illness. Edward would say to me one day, 'Everything is being changed around. The hospital is quite changed,' and I would find out from his medical officer that some small alteration had been made in his room. Or he would come into the room coughing and say, 'Everybody is coughing today,' on a day when another patient was taken to the sanatorium with T.B. When he had hallucinations, he felt that the voices he heard were ubiquitous. He would say 'All prisoners hear voices,' or, speaking of shock treatment, 'The doctors were so maddened by voices that they tried to stop them by killing the poor patients.' Obviously, Edward felt that his own hallucinations were in everybody's mind. At times the boundary between the internal and external world seemed completely obliterated.

After a few days in the military hospital Edward's parents obtained his transfer to a private nursing home where I started a regular analysis of five hours a week. In the first session Edward showed no surprise at seeing me. He was excited, elated and showed flight of ideas. He told me, in a disconnected way, about the terrifying things done to him in the hospitals by the mad doctors and about the necessity of his being allowed out of this prison immediately. He hoped I would help him to get out. There was no question, at this point, of asking him to lie down on the couch or of explaining to him the nature of the treatment.

I did not interpret any of his delusions or hallucinations then but pointed out how cut off and misunderstood he felt. I selected this interpretation because it was obvious that, though Edward was talking to me, I meant no more to him than a piece of furniture; his isolation was complete. Then he looked at me in a different way and said that all the prisoners felt like that and that prisoners in Germany sent him voices.

On my suggesting that being in the hospital was like being a prisoner, and being like a prisoner meant to him being actually imprisoned, he seemed relieved and said it was so, but would I please keep it a secret.

The significant point which emerged in this session was Edward's equating the notion of 'being like something' and 'being something'. There was no distinction between the symbol and the thing symbolized. At a later session, he blushed, stammered, giggled and apologized after bringing a canvas stool. He behaved as if he had offered me an actual faecal stool. It was not merely a symbolic expression of his wish to bring me his stool. He felt that he had actually offered it to me. His inability to use symbols, which I interpreted to him repeatedly, was probably the greatest single difficulty throughout his analysis.

Melanie Klein (1930) has described the failure of symbol formation in schizophrenia; but her patient's difficulty was not exactly the same as Edward's. Dick, a boy of four, failed to form symbols and therefore could not use speech, and generally failed to develop. Edward did form symbols but he could not use them as mere symbols. Unlike Dick, he could transfer his interest from the object to the substitute symbol, for instance, from faeces to the canvas stool. Once formed, however, the symbol did not function as a symbol but became in all respects equivalent to the object itself. Thus, the canvas stool was to him an object of shame and embarrassment since he thought it really was a faecal stool. In this he resembled another schizophrenic who, when I asked him why he did not want to play the violin any more, answered with a shrug, 'Fancy masturbating in public.'

The difficulty of forming or using symbols is, I think, one of the basic elements in schizophrenic thinking. This certainly is at the root of the concrete thinking described in schizophrenics. It accounts, probably, for much of the difficulty in understanding schizophrenic speech. When one says, 'I don't understand what he is talking about,' this may be literally true. The schizophrenic holds in his hand a violin but his speech refers to the penis with which the violin is equated in his mind.

Another frequent symptom, which is largely dependent on the failure of symbol formation, is the poverty of thought so often displayed by the schizophrenic. As I see it the mechanism here can be twofold: either symbols are not formed, as in the case of Melanie Klein's patient, and therefore interests do not develop; or, having been formed, symbols become equivalents instead. Then, endowed with all the anxiety belonging to the original object, these symbols have to be repressed or denied. The result is the same in either case: deprived of the use of symbols, the intellect cannot develop and function adequately. Before his illness, Edward must have repressed extensively many of the symbols already formed, and he confined his interests mainly to biology — substituting the plant and the animal for the human body. During the acute stage of his illness, the repressed returned with its characteristic equivalence of symbols and original objects.

After this digression I shall have to leave the subject of symbol formation, for it deserves a paper to itself, and return to my patient.

It is extremely difficult to give a coherent summary of the sessions we had at the nursing home. The material was disconnected; I often did not understand the patient's behavior, reactions and speech. Gradually, however, the picture became clearer. It seemed that the apparently disconnected material centered mainly around the two phantasies expressed already in his first hour with me: the phantasy that he was in prison and the phantasy that he and other people were changed.

Of course, the prison theme was not altogether a phantasy. One could hardly be more a prisoner than the mental patient in an old-fashioned military psychiatric hospital especially if, like Edward, the patient has to suffer days or weeks of solitary confinement. But in addition to this important element of reality, there was, in this case, a deeply ingrained, spontaneous delusion of being imprisoned.

In his own view, Edward's illness started when he was given work in the darkroom, the darkroom being the equivalent of a prison. To Edward, being imprisoned meant being treated like a criminal or like a child. Or rather, he felt imprisonment turned him into a child or a criminal. Through the failure to distinguish between that which was thought of and that which was, being treated like a child meant actually being a child; and child was equated with criminal.

These two main themes — imprisonment and changing — were often interconnected. For instance, in the nursing home, where Edward was treated well, he complained of being given nothing to do or to think about, of being supervised or fed too much. He felt as though he was nothing but a huge stomach, the limbs and head being irrelevant little appendages. He felt that all his thinking was done by his stomach, and that all this was due to his being imprisoned.

These phantasies were immediately followed by terrible anxiety that the world's food supply would disappear because everybody thought only of eating, and no one took the trouble to cultivate the earth and to plant new crops. Thus, imprisonment led to a change in him: he became a greedy child. His greediness, in turn, led to the world's food supply being exhausted and to the world changing. This phantasy was depressive in its contents: the baby greedily empties the mother of food and babies but is incapable of a reparative genital relation. The feeling accompanying it, however, was persecutory. He did not feel guilty or responsible in any way, because his greed was forced on him by those who imprisoned him.

His anger, like his greed, could change and destroy the world around him. Imprisonment led to anger; anger then made him into the child-criminal, and led to imprisonment. The vicious circle was established.

Another important phantasy in which imprisonment and changing were connected was the phantasy of pregnancy. Usually when he spoke of changes he described destruction, damage, ruin. Occasionally, however, he would present a different picture. Things were growing out of all proportion, becoming distorted in a mysterious and terrifying way. The vegetation of India had changed, he said; it seemed to become enormous, luxurious, awe-inspiring. Clearly this referred to the mysterious changes in his mother's body during pregnancy.

A few months later, when I was analysing him in his home, these anxieties became much clearer. He told me that he did not remember the birth of his next sibling, but he had been told that he was very jealous. He remembered the birth of the next baby when he was four, and he remembered feeling very angry and jealous. His first impression of the baby was that it was very greedy and very naughty. Gradually it became clear that he had felt envious of both the mother and the baby, and that he identified himself with both. Whenever I interpreted that, he would try to shift his ground and speak of his jealousy of either the father or of the older brother. Earlier on, in the nursing home, he had reacted by an increase in his feeling of persecution by male doctors.

My interpretations were felt to be actual castrations. For the wish to be a pregnant woman or a baby made him become a pregnant woman or a baby and that implied his not being a man. To interpret such a wish to him also meant castrating him.

In the pregnancy phantasy, the change in the external world, the mother, led to a change in himself. He was both the pregnant mother, the big tummy full of babies (full of voices) and the embryo imprisoned in her womb, castrated, helpless, all tummy and no limbs.

Of course, these phantasies and the links between them became clear only after months of analysis. From the start, however, some of his delusions could be recognized as phantasies familiar to every analyst. But I found that there was no point in interpreting them out of context. Edward's emotional life centred on the wish to be let out right away and on the fear of change and persecution. I had to bring these feelings into the transference, connect them with his phantasies and delusions and, finally, with his past. In trying to do that I met defence mechanisms of the most primitive kind: magic denial, splitting, and a series of rapid defensive introjections and projections.

In his changing world full of fear, he needed one unchanging good figure, and he tried to believe that I was this figure. But, to preserve this belief, he had to use all his defences. In the first place, he had to deny that I had anything to do with his being kept in the hospital. If I frustrated him, he would deny the frustration and split me in to a good and a bad figure. The bad figure would be introjected as hostile voices or reprojected onto the hospital doctors. In effect, he felt acutely persecuted from within and from without.

Even the good figure was a very insecure possession. He could not love me any more than he could hate me, for love would lead to dependence and dependence to hatred. Love itself was often felt to be wholly bad. Giving me his love could give me his illness. As a result, I could be good and safe only if he withheld both hatred and love. He often expressed this by saying he wished I did not come to the nursing home where the voices would change me. I was much safer outside. The nursing home represented himself, and I could not be safe near to his madness. He could keep me good, but my goodness was of no avail, and his isolation was complete. His narcissism was a way of saving me from madness.

Whenever he gave me a chance, I interpreted to him his fear of involving me in his madness and the feeling of complete isolation when he successfully kept me out. His conscious fear of any change in me enabled me to bring into the transference some of his important phantasies. And though he rejected most of these interpretations, subsequent work convinced me that they had been effective.

After three months in the nursing home he was sufficiently improved to go home. At our first session in his parent's home, Edward was full of rage and despair. He spoke bitterly of his parents, reproaching them with their lack of warmth and their cruelty. But the real cause of his despair lay elsewhere. Having equated imprisonment in the hospital with his illness, he had hoped to leave the illness behind in the hospital where it belonged. He found that the delusions, the hallucinations, all his illness in fact, had followed him to his own home. And he was in despair.

Edward wanted reassurance. He wanted me to tell him that whatever was wrong was the fault of his parents and of the hospital. He wanted me to become his ally against the persecutors. I pointed out to him that he needed the reassurance so much because he was afraid that he was mad and that I was not an ally but the enemy — the doctor. Now that he was home I remained the only obvious link with the hospital. In his unconscious I was equated with all the hospital doctors. In a way, we were alone with madness: it was either in him or in me. If anyone was driving him mad it could only be I.

I had to bring this situation into consciousness, to substitute a conscious suspicion of me for blind acting-out. Had I not done so, Edward's unconscious identification of me with the hospital might have led him to break off the treatment. Though he did not agree with my interpretations, he did not reject them altogether.

This raises a technical problem about which there is considerable controversy: should the analyst reassure a very ill patient at a moment of crisis and when the patient is craving reassurance? I have not done so, and I feel strongly that it would have been a mistake to give in to the patient's wishes. By giving sympathy and reassurance, the analyst becomes, for the time being, the good object, but only at the cost of furthering the split between good and bad objects and reinforcing the patient's pathological defences. The unconscious suspicion of the analyst is then not analysed but is acted out, and sudden reversals may occur when God turns into the Devil and the negative transference may become unmanageable. And even while the 'good' phase lasts, the progress of analysis is interfered with by the repression of phantasies about the 'bad' analyst. Furthermore, whenever the analyst is artificially kept 'good' someone else is chosen by the patient as the persecutor. Usually this is a member of his own family, someone obviously less adequately equipped than the analyst to cope with the patient's hostility.

After about three months' treatment at home, we decided that he should start coming to me for the analytic sessions. On his first visit he walked anxiously round the room investigating various objects and asking questions. When I interpreted his anxiety and distrust, Edward for the first time did not deny them. He admitted that he was afraid that I might imprison him again. He thought for a moment, and said, that a bottle on my table contained poison and that the little ivory skulls on my mantlepiece might be the skulls of patients I had killed. But he also said that he knew it was not, in fact, true. I had never before seen him distinguish between delusion and reality.

A few days later he lay on the couch for the first time. He was extremely anxious and his body looked quite rigid, but he did go on associating. Lying down reminded him of the hospital where he was kept in bed, and of his childhood, when being put to bed was a punishment. In his mind, bed and bad were equated; one was put to bed for having been bad and being in bed, in turn, made one bad. The humiliation and the frustration produced a rage which made him feel helpless against both the world and his own instincts. He remembered himself as a child in bed screaming in utter rage and despair. He freely acknowledged his fear that the same feelings might be reawakened on the analytic couch.

After that session, some of the particular difficulties of this analysis disappeared. In the first six months of treatment, my main concern was to establish an analytical situation. At the beginning of the analysis, the patient was detached from reality and unable to grasp the nature of the treatment. He appealed to me repeatedly to let him out of the hospital and would follow my footsteps when I was on my way out. He kept asking me to take him to the pictures or for walks, to arrange a means of escape for him. He was constantly demanding reassurance and, except at times when he was treating me ceremoniously like a neutral visitor, he was extremely curious and inquisitive.

My aim then was to retain the attitude of the analyst even without the co-operation of the patient. To achieve this, I had, first of all, to make him accept interpretations instead of the various gratifications he wanted, and to do it without appearing needlessly rude or cruel. I tried to show him in every interpretation that I understood what he wanted from me, why he wanted it at any particular moment, and why he wanted it so desperately. And I followed most interpretations of that kind with an interpretation of what my refusal had meant to him.

At that time, Edward was a deeply regressed psychotic with a disintegrated ego and his behavior was very infantile. When he went home later, he became more like a child in the latency period. He modelled in clay, remembered toys which his father used to make for him and tried to make similar ones. He wanted to make a flying machine with which prisoners could escape, knowing, yet somehow oblivious of the fact, that planes had already been invented. Finally, he developed a great cunning in concealing his delusions and hallucinations.

That, in itself, was partly a sign of progress. He recognized that delusions and hallucinations were not shared by everybody, and that he would be considered mad if he did not hide them. But it made a new difficulty in the analysis: he began hiding things from me consciously and deliberately. At the same time, he would fail to bring out material because of a lack of connection in his mind. He could tolerate ideas which naturally belonged together without either repressing or linking them, and I was not always able to discover if he was genuinely unaware of any particular omission.

On one occasion I remember, Edward became obsessed with the evil of money. He spent an entire hour speaking about it bitterly and vehemently. During this and the next hour I made several interpretations about his relation to money. But it soon became clear to me that there must have been an actual external cause which produced this outburst, and I told him that. He said he could not remember anything which would have made him think about money matters. I learned subsequently, and not from him, that he had received a letter from the Army authorities concerning his pay — a letter which he considered very humiliating. I am quite sure that he did not consciously conceal from me the existence of the letter but that he really failed to make a connection between the letter and his anger about money.

In the sixth month of treatment the formal analytic situation was finally established. The patient lay on the couch, associated and, at least consciously, expected nothing from me beyond analysis. From that time on, my problems were the same as those of the analysis of a neurotic, that is, the analysis of the patient's system of phantasies and defences.

Edward's principal mechanisms of defence changed little. Splitting into an idealized and a persecuting object and magic denial continued. For weeks he would co-operate in the analysis of some important phantasies and then say happily, 'Oh well, I don't think this can have anything to do with psychological reasons.' Unconsciously, he felt certain that by saying 'No' he could completely abolish any unpleasant experience. An interpretation could always be either split off and isolated, so that it was tolerated in consciousness but useless, or magically abolished by a conscious or unconscious 'No.' I always had to follow carefully his internal response to my interpretation to discover how far he was trying to invalidate it or do away with it.

The denial was often determined by a failure of symbolization which, at this stage, took a different form than it did at the beginning of the treatment. Then, consciously and unconsciously, the symbol and the thing symbolized were equated. Now the unconscious equation remained unchanged but consciously the symbolism had to be completely denied. A cigarette was a cigarette, and he would not accept that it might stand for a penis. For if he accepted that, it would mean that he was actually sucking and biting a penis — which would be madness. In effect, nearly every phantasy had to be totally denied.

With time, however, the rigidity of his defences lessened and he gradually became capable of tolerating in his consciousness some phantasy and conflict.

Along with the analytic progress, a marked clinical improvement took place. Toward the end of the first year of treatment, all conscious delusions disappeared. Edward was in touch with reality, leading an apparently normal life, following a course at the university, working on some minor inventions and making himself useful in his country home. He was still preoccupied with phantasies about soil erosion, but now they give rise to sublimations. He planted some very tall trees which had never before been successfully planted in this country. The planting and his later work on these trees (which he is still carrying on) was so successful that eminent biologists and experts in forestry wrote to him for information and advice. In this sphere, he tried realistically to become the father with the biggest penis (the tallest trees) returning to mother earth the food taken from the breast and the destroyed babies.

His relationships were better, he felt, than before his illness. He complained only of a recurring noise in his left ear which he called a 'buzz' and of some difficulty of concentration. The improvement was in part genuine; but some of it seemed due to a magic denial of madness and to a splitting off and 'encapsulating' of his illness in the insignificant little buzz, strictly localized in his ear.

His sex life remained unsatisfactory. He started having sexual relations for the first time during the analysis and it was a great relief to him to find that he was potent. He became a great flirt, always trying to have many girls whom he could make love to and trying not to be dependent on anyone in particular. But he confined his sexual relations to prostitutes. In his mind he divided women into three categories: prostitutes, with whom to have intercourse, girls of his own social sphere to flirt with and to tantalize, and the ideal woman whom he would marry one day.

I shall now describe two incidents which happened approximately eighteen months after the beginning of the treatment. They show some of the schizophrenic mechanisms still operating, and the way in which these mechanisms were modified by analysis.

The first of these incidents led to the only recurrence of 'voices' and, I think, might easily have brought a complete breakdown had the patient then not been in analysis. I have chosen this particular incident because it throws a light on some of the mechanisms of hallucinations. At the time when the patient was heavily hallucinated, it was impossible to follow these mechanisms in detail. In his temporary relapse he reproduced them in a mild and manageable form.

Two male relatives of Edward's mother died in quick succession. One, who had been ill for some time, died at the beginning of a week. Two days later, the other died suddenly in the street, on the way to an appointment with Edward's mother. Though he was very fond of both, he repressed all strong feelings and said that he was very sorry but not overwhelmingly so. His associations showed, however, that he identified himself with both of them.

The first relative had already come into the analysis in connection with his illness, and Edward admitted then to a strong identification and fears for his own health. When the relative died, Edward omitted telling me that it was the same man, obviously defending himself against the identification. He tolerated the thought of identification with his uncle's illness and of the latter's death, without making any connection between the two. Edward was not going to mourn the uncle, he said, because the man had been a cheerful person and would not wish to be mourned. About the second relative, he said that it had been a kind death and he himself would wish for a similar one.

Underneath the superficial detachment there was the identification, brought about partly through guilt and fear of retaliation, partly in order to influence the dead by sympathetic magic. He was saying, in fact, 'If I had such a quick, kind death, I would not be angry; I would not persecute people with regrets and mourning. Therefore I am safe. The dead are not going to be angry with me and persecute me.' When I pointed this out to him, he rejected the interpretation. Nor could he admit that he was afraid that the death of the two men — rivals in relation to his mother — proved his own omnipotence: that is, proved that at any moment now, his foremost rival, his father, might die.

During the weekend after his relatives' deaths, he attended an official function at his old school. He returned exultant. In contrast with his first visit, a year earlier, this time he had felt quite confident, free and happy. In the evening he had been out with a girl and was very pleased with himself. I interpreted his triumph in being young, strong and potent, while the fathers were old and dead. I pointed out to him his feeling that I, too, had died during the weekend which he had found so enjoyable.

On the following day, he lay on the couch silent for a long while and then said violently, 'I wish that buzzing would stop.' At first he denied that the 'buzz' was worse than usual; he was merely expressing a general wish, he said. But after a while he admitted that, as he put it, the buzzing had become articulate. Slowly, and with many hesitations, he told me that he had been doing eye exercises the day before and, while he was counting them, an echo in his head counted together with him. To illustrate this point in the session, he counted aloud a number of times.

I shall not go into the details of the various defences and evasions, associations and interpretations. The picture which emerged was this: the counting stood for competition with his older brother, in childhood, for control — keeping a check — killing as in the childish 'counting out'. It could also be used as a reassurance that all the relatives were still alive, and that all the limbs and members of his body were all right. Eye exercises stood for the wish to acquire omnipotent eyesight, so as to be able to see across the streets, which separated our houses, and to watch me in sexual intercourse. We were here on the very familiar ground of sexual curiosity; that much he eventually agreed to.

As he went on to describe the echo, it struck me that the echo had a mocking quality. Edward accepted this interpretation with unusual alacrity and seemed to find great relief in becoming aware of the pervasive persecution of this voice. Then I made a more complete interpretation. I reminded him of the death of his two relatives, his identification with them, his refusal to mourn them, and the triumph over them during the weekend. I suggested that, in performing eye exercises, he was watching the intercourse between his parents, and that he was killing the father or both parents, represented by the two relatives, by magic looking and magic counting. Finally he introjected the dead and triumphed over them. But apparently, they were not defeated; they came back to life inside him and mocked him, mocked particularly his magic looking and counting — the means by which, he thought, he had secured his triumph. Edward rejected this interpretation.

In the following session, Edward said that the articulate buzz was still there and had said 'dreams, dreams.' When I told him that it was I who had become the internal voice and was nagging him for dreams, he recounted a dream of the preceding night. He dreamed that he saw four people playing a very fast game of which he did not know the rules. This game was something halfway between tennis and squash. Then he saw two men, one black and one white, advancing in the distance. As they came nearer, the white man became more and more brown and he grew a stubble on his face.

Edward's first association was that he could not play squash. But what intrigued him most was the white man turning brown. It made him think of two things: (1) that in a film he had seen, a white man looked brown because of the way he had been photographed, and (2) of India, being brown with the sun and not shaving. The first reading of the dream made him accept the interpretations I gave in the preceding session. Watching the very fast game of which he did not know the rules, or knew them only in part (he could play tennis but not squash) meant watching intercourse. In his jealousy, he felt he had killed and introjected the parents, thereby changing them into faeces, i.e. the approaching figures of a man who is brown and one who turns brown. These men were also the two dead relatives now representing the two parents. He made them brown by looking, that is, by photographing.

But the meaning of the dream does not end here. The white man turning brown was also himself; India always stood for his illness. The man turning brown represented the threat of an approaching breakdown. But the man was brown because of the way he had been photographed, which means that by showing Edward to himself in a bad light, by making him aware of his illness, I was magically making him ill. My evil eye changed him into faeces, just as his own evil eye changed the copulating parents into faeces.

This aspect of the dream gave us a link with the transference. As he tried to watch me in intercourse, while doing eye exercises, he swallowed me up in anger with his eyes and changed me into faeces. (He watches; they turn brown.) Then, as the internal voice, I started persecuting him from the inside: 'dreams, dreams.' But reprojection occurs almost simultaneously. By looking, Edward also filled me with faeces; then, in retaliation, my looking both swallowed him up and changed him into faeces (by introjection) and filled him with faeces (by projection). So that, by looking at each other, we put the excrements — illness and death — into each other.

This was the last session of the week. On the following Monday, he came to me with a very swollen face and immediately started assuring me that he had only been stung by a bee. When I said that he must have thought me very anxious to have to reassure me like that, he admitted that he did think I was anxious. He himself had had an excellent weekend. The buzz had disappeared and he felt very well. Obviously, he felt that he had projected the illness into me, so that he was free, but I became both the anxious and ill person and the external persecutor – the bee which had stung him and filled him with poison.

In Freud's view (1917), analysis meant essentially the analysis and resolution of a transference neurosis. Therefore, he saw in the schizophrenic narcissism a factor precluding analysis. Speaking in the *Introductory Lectures* of patients suffering from the narcissistic neuroses, Freud said, 'They manifest no transference and for that reason are inaccessible to our efforts, not to be cured by us.' The later work of Melanie Klein on internal objects has shown that narcissism is a complex phenomenon. There is in every case a relationship to phantasied internalized objects; and a state of narcissistic withdrawal can be approached in terms of a relation to internal objects.

In Edward's case, the object-relationship to the dead relatives broke down under the stress of anxiety and guilt. There came the splitting and introjection of injured and bad objects with the subsequent hallucinations and narcissistic withdrawal. But in the analytic situation, the patient experienced the internal persecution in the transference. My voice, asking for dreams, appeared in the hallucination. Canalized into the transference situation, the process became accessible to analysis.

I have chosen the second incident to illustrate how the splitting mechanisms lead to idealization and persecution, and how the analysis of these mechanisms reduces the split and makes possible a more realistic attitude.

During a holiday Edward was interested in two things. He milked cows in his country home, and he practised sketching very quickly various items of botanical interest. He was very pleased with himself as he used to be very bad at drawing and had never tried milking cows before. He felt that when milking he was doing good; he was relieving the cow, providing milk for others and assuring himself of fresh milk every morning. Sketching represented to him an attempt at keeping things inside him unchanged – a new achievement.

But his attempt to get the milk inside him and keep it good there was not wholly successful. A day or two after his return to London, he developed a rash on his face. He found this embarrassing and extremely annoying. Simultaneously, he started working on the idea of sterilizing milk by ultraviolet rays, since he felt that it was impossible to keep the cowsheds clean enough to satisfy the requirements of health inspectors.

Obviously he felt unconsciously that there was something hopelessly wrong with the milk, something that called for magic measures. When I interpreted this to him, he admitted that he had thought for a minute that he got the rash by infection, while milking a cow with a sore udder. The happy picture of his milking gave place to a persecutory one: the breast was sore, the milk dirty and infected, his own inside poisoned, and the poison coming out in the rash.

After the situation had become clear to him, Edward had a short but extremely violent dream in which he felt that he was torn open and possibly devoured — he did not know by whom or by what. He associated it with the fact that in India, he had used a goat as a decoy for a panther. The panther tore the goat's belly open and devoured it while he photographed the scene. He felt that in the dream he was like the goat. But the goat, which he threw to be devoured for the satisfaction of his own greed and ambition, represented the mother. Two things were telescoped here: his attack on the mother's breast — the cow's udder — and his later attacks on her body, caused mainly by curiosity and phallic ambition. He was identified with the attacked and incorporated mother (the goat).

After this analysis the rash cleared up. Two nights later he dreamed that he was imprisoned by the Russians and a young woman helped him to escape. They travelled together, changing trains frequently because if they stayed too long on any single train they would be caught. He immediately associated the young woman with me and the Russians with any kind of persecution. I was helping him to escape from it. But when he spoke of Russia, it became clear that the Russians also represented me. The trains he had to change represented trends of thought. If he followed a trend of thought long enough he would be caught, that is, he would realize that his ideal object is also the object which he had injured and the persecutor.

The dream also directly connected with his current sexual problems. The journey on the train represented sexual intercourse with me, but he could not go the whole way with me — the longed-for vagina would turn into the dangerous and persecuting one. He could not go the whole way with me, the ideal love object, and he had to sleep with prostitutes, changing trains often for fear they would become dangerous.

Thinking about the cow led Edward to see that the milk he tried to obtain and keep inside had poisoned him. Thinking about the Russians made him see that I, who was to help him, had become the persecutor from whom he was escaping. This recurring situation in which the very best object turns out to be the most injured one and the worst persecutor was the deepest tragedy in his internal world. Throughout his life he had to 'change trains quickly,' never to go deeply into things or relationships, to remain superficial, cold and detached, for fear the tragic situation would become conscious. Here, again, we see the long history behind the narcissistic withdrawal.

In the following session Edward was sad. He thought it might be because he was losing the ideal picture of the woman. But it appeared that his feeling of persecution was giving way to depression. He told me that an old servant was leaving on the same day. She had been kind to him when he was a child and he was sorry to lose her and sorry that he had not always been good to her. Toward the end of the hour, he brought up the first happy memory of his childhood which he ever produced in analysis. At the age of two he had been transferred from the washbasin to a real bath, and he had been thrilled by the experience. These associations showed that after the analysis of the splitting, the idealization and the persecution, he had become free to accept a real good object, a real good experience and a real hope of growing out of babyhood.

The continued analysis of the splitting led to a gradual bridging of the gap between the persecuting and the idealized object. The process manifested itself in many ways. It showed in his dreams. The first dream he had in his analysis was of a panther in the central room of his home and of his terror. A year later, he dreamed that there was a bullock in the hall; it was behind bars, but the bars could easily be removed. And Edward was more sorry for the bullock than frightened of it. Clearly the internal persecutor (in the last analysis, identified with his own instincts) became more genital and more manageable. Another effect was the general improvement of his relationships, including the transference. While he became freer to admit that in his phantasies I appeared in various persecutory figures, his relationship to me became incomparably more confident and warmer. I think he felt that he had found in me a friend, and if that is so, this was the first intimate relationship that he had ever experienced in his conscious memory.

There is, I think, no doubt that the diagnosis of schizophrenia has been confirmed by the analysis. The patient, though apparently recovered, is still psychotic in his defenses.

The prognosis was relatively bad, in view of Edward's schizoid personality before the illness and of his rapid deterioration. In his favor was his youth (he was just twenty years old when the analysis started), and the short duration of his illness and of the psychiatric treatment (in this case, ill-treatment) which preceded analysis.

It will be seen that the analytic technique I used was different in many important respects from the technique used and described by the American analysts, particularly Frieda Fromm-Reichmann and Paul

Federn. They hold that the analyst must not give interpretations that would introduce into consciousness any new unconscious material, as the ego of the psychotic is anyway submerged by it. Federn (1943) has written, 'The question as to whether one should use for further analysis the unconscious material produced by psychotics is answered. It is dangerous to call for still deeper layers and to introduce problems into the patient's mind.'

I proceeded differently and I brought into consciousness new unconscious material whenever it was warranted. For instance, at the beginning of the treatment, Edward was very much under the sway of castration fears, which were much less repressed than is usually the case with neurotics. These fears did not diminish until I introduced new material into his consciousness. I had to interpret to him the underlying and entirely unconscious phantasy in which he identified himself with both his pregnant mother and her unborn child. His castration fear was partly a result of this phantasy in which he ceased to be a man and which his masculine self felt as a castration. The castration fear also acted partly as a blind; he forcibly drew my attention to his masculinity and the rivalry with his father and brothers to cover up his rivalry with me, the woman.

I found that in Edward's analysis, as in any other analysis, understanding and progress were achieved only by making the patient aware of what hitherto had been unconscious. The fact that many things are tolerated in consciousness by the schizophrenic must not blind one to the necessity of interpreting what is repressed. Schizophrenics, more than others, repress the links between different trends of thought. They often tolerate in their ego thoughts and phantasies which would probably be repressed in the neurotic; but on the other hand they repress the links between the various phantasies and between phantasy and reality. Those links have to be interpreted whenever possible. Another important difference between the neurotic and the schizophrenic is in the kind of material which becomes conscious by the return of that which is repressed, although this mechanism occurs in the psychotic and neurotic breakdown alike. The phantasies of the psychotic, especially of the schizophrenic, are far more archaic and primitive. But that does not mean that in the psychotic repression does not operate and does not have to be analysed. For example, my patient produced consciously primitive phantasies of being poisoned, overfed or starved. These were not repressed, but what was repressed was the fact that these phantasies referred to his mother in the past and to me in the present. Secondly, they were believed to be largely the result of his own attacks on his mother, exhausting her breast so that it was empty and he would starve, and poisoning her milk with faeces which would eventually poison him.

Also, all these phantasies were a regression from later depressive phantasies which themselves were entirely repressed.

The delusions about being poisoned cleared up after those other unconscious phantasies were interpreted and connected with the conscious delusions.

The first important difference between the technique advocated by Federn and the one I used in this case is as follows: I tried to analyse in this psychotic all the important resistances and to interpret the unconscious material at the level of the greatest anxiety, much as I would do with a neurotic. The second important difference lies in the handling of the transference situation. Federn (1943) wrote, 'Psychotic patients offer the positive transference to the analyst; the analysts must nourish it as something precious in order to preserve their influence: transference is helpful in the analysis of underlying conflicts of the psychosis but a positive transference itself must never be dissolved by psychoanalysis.' He added in the same paper, 'The general conditions which should be considered in every psychoanalytic treatment: establishment of positive transference, treatment to be interrupted when transference becomes negative.'

I believe that this attitude must deepen the already deep pathogenic split characteristic of schizophrenia. I thought it worthwhile in the analysis of a schizophrenic to attempt that which Freud has shown to be the only way of attacking the roots of a mental illness, that is, not strengthening the defence mechanisms of the patient but bringing them into the transference and analysing them.

In the early stages, Edward's analysis differed from the analysis of a neurotic in that I had to go and see him in the hospital and later at his home and he did not lie on the couch. I never explained the basic rule to him but from the start I maintained the analytic attitude. In other words, I interpreted defences and material with an emphasis on the transference, both positive and negative.

Edward has been in analysis nearly three years. In his case this approach has proved possible and, so far, entirely rewarding.

Postscript (1980)

At the time I started analysing this patient, there was no published account of a treatment of a schizophrenic by a purely psychoanalytic method so that I had very little guidance. Looking back on it, I think I did not pay enough attention to processes of splitting and fragmentation in his ego and, in particular, I did not see enough of the process described later by Bion (1957) as 'pathological projective identification.'

It is maybe, because of this failure, that this analysis has not been entirely successful.

Soon after the time described in the paper, after some four years of analysis, the patient stopped it on a hypomanic swing. This interruption of his analysis, against my advice, was partly due to an internal and external pressure of his family tradition, which required that he attend a university outside London, and partly to the manic resistance to analysis. He remained well for some twenty years. He completed his university studies, married, had a family, and had an adventurous and varied — though not always successful — career in one of the major professions.

In 1968, under strong provocation of external events, he had another schizophrenic breakdown. He retained a sufficient internal link with me to evade rather cleverly the threatened certification and to come to me for help. As I had no vacancy at the time, I referred him to another analyst for further treatment, and he is doing well in his present analysis.

References

Bion, W.R. (1957) 'Differentiation of the psychotic from the non-psychotic personalities', *International Journal of Psycho-Analysis*, 38: 266–75, also in W.R. Bion, *Second Thoughts*, London: Heinemann (1967), 43–64; reprinted in paperback Maresfield Reprints, London: H. Karnac Books (1984) and in *Melanie Klein Today: Volume I*, London: Routledge, (1988).

Federn, P. (1943) 'Psychoanalysis of psychoses', *Psychiatric Quarterly*, 17: 3–19.

Freud, S. (1917) *Introductory lectures on psycho-analysis: Part III*, 'General theory of the neuroses', SE 16.

Klein, M. (1930) 'The importance of symbol formation in the development of the ego', in *The Writings of Melanie Klein*, vol. 1: *Love, Guilt and Reparation*, London: Hogarth Press (1975), 219–32.

2

The mirror: a perverse sexual phantasy in a woman seen as a defence against a psychotic breakdown

RUTH RIESENBERG MALCOLM

This paper was first read to a Scientific Meeting of the British Psycho-Analytical Society in 1970. It was published in Spanish in 1970 as 'El espejo: Una fantasia sexual perversa en una mujer, vista como defensa contra un derrumbe psicotico', *Revista Psicoanalisis*, 27: 793–826. It is published here in English for the first time.

In this paper I intend to discuss the use of a perversion as a defence against psychosis. I have come to recognize in the material of the patient I shall discuss that her personality is divided into psychotic and non-psychotic parts in the manner described by Bion (1957). The psychotic parts are encapsulated within a perverse syndrome which allows the rest of the personality to establish some contact with reality and to maintain at least a modicum of normal functioning.

The psychotic state I shall try to describe consists of a condition in which the internal objects are destroyed and fragmented; the main anxieties are of disintegration. To cope with this situation the perversion has been erected as a protection against breaking in pieces.

The patient on whose analysis I have based this paper was forty-two at the beginning of her treatment. She is the eldest of seven children. The family used to own a shop in a small village in Northern Ireland. The mother attended to the customers while the father manufactured the products which were sold in the shop. When very young the children were expected to help either in the shop or with the housework. The patient describes the mother as weak and very much dominated by her husband and afraid of him. She was concerned about her children's well-being and education but was not very sensitive. The father is said to have been tyrannical, ill-tempered, and rigid. He dominated the mother, who was felt to abandon the children because of the father's demands on her. Father had suffered a mental breakdown in his youth. Life at home was

115

described as very gloomy, restricted, and isolated. The patient's relationships with her next younger sister and brother, four and five-and-a-half years younger than the patient, were characterized by intense jealousy and rivalry. With the sister the patient had a homosexual relationship for five years, from when the patient was ten until she was fifteen. The next sister, seven years her junior, has always been her favourite. She is the person she loves most in life but this is because she feels it to be an exclusive relationship. This sister is unmarried and it sounds as if she is a very isolated person. The remaining three siblings were much younger than the patient and she had almost no contact with them. At school there were innumerable behaviour problems, mainly stealing and lying. She had very few friends at school and remembers it as a very unhappy time. She left school at sixteen against her mother's wishes, got a secretarial training and started work at seventeen. She lasted in the job only for a few weeks and had to leave it because of what appears to have been a paranoid breakdown. Following this she had several jobs and after the war went overseas to work for an international corporation. She had to be brought home after some eighteen months because of a mental breakdown requiring hospitalization.

On leaving hospital she enrolled in a university to read science. In spite of great difficulties and having to go to hospital for a short time from university, she managed to get a good degree. After leaving the university she joined a convent as a postulant, remaining there for some months.

She has been unable to work in her own field and has been working as a secretary in a research laboratory for some years, where she seems to be efficient and capable. During the past twenty years her sexual life has consisted exclusively of masturbation with perverse phantasies. Prior to this she had had a period of intense promiscuity which came to a stop on admission to hospital for the first time.

The masturbation phantasies have a compulsive character. They take up a large part of the patient's time, during which she either practises them directly or is preoccupied by thoughts about them.

'The Fantasy' (she refers to it by this name) consists of a 'mirror with one-way vision' inside which a number of sexual activities take place. These activities generally possess very violent characteristics, including openly sadistic activity. The experiencing of humiliation is fundamental and must be felt by every participant in the action. These participants often form incestuous couples. They are described as a man, a mother, a father, etc., with no individual or personal characteristics. There are often openly grotesque or bizarre couples. The duration of the intercourse is often extremely long; the couples are hindered from reaching a state of satisfaction by frequent interruptions. In general the satisfaction that is allowed to them is very meagre, and cruelty is a prevailing factor throughout. Homosexual activities occur frequently, sometimes parallel with, sometimes simultaneous with, and sometimes consecutive to the heterosexual ones. During The Fantasy the patient feels that she 'is' or she 'is in' each one of the participating characters.

While these events take place inside The Mirror, there are outside The Mirror a number of onlookers. These onlookers can be 'just people', but more often they are specified as photographers, cameramen, or reporters. The presence of the onlookers outside The Mirror is an essential condition for The Fantasy to take place. These spectators are often excited by what they are witnessing inside The Mirror, and they have to put up a struggle against this excitement. If they succumb to it, they become drawn inside The Mirror. Once inside it, a partner has to be provided, as unaccompanied persons are not allowed in The Mirror. The number of people from outside The Mirror who are attracted and drawn into it varies. The temptation to succumb to the excitement is always made great for them.

The thesis of this paper is that The Fantasy represents an attempt to reconstruct the parental couple as a means of reconstruction of the patient's ego which is otherwise felt to be in bits, like the destroyed parental intercourse contained by her.

The Fantasy and promiscuity

As I have mentioned before, The Fantasy 'settled in' in the patient's life some time after a period of intense promiscuity which ended in her first admission to hospital with a breakdown in which she felt unable to cope and had feelings of 'falling to pieces'.

During this promiscuous episode she drifted from man to man for sexual relations, occasionally perverse, characterized by lack of personal contact with them and by an excited childish attitude, very much tinged with cruelty, and followed by a masochistic reaction. The sadism was often expressed in her thoughts towards the men but sometimes also expressed directly in her behaviour in an intense and uncontrollable way. For instance on one occasion when asked by a man to masturbate him manually, she got hold of his penis and started banging it up and down and pulling at it with extreme violence, unable to let go in spite of the man's screams of horror and pain.

The breakdown after this episode could, in my view, be explained as the result of the intense projective identification which went on with her different partners. They always contained 'the desire and wish'. The patient felt cold sexually and had an intense contempt for the partner's

117

excitement. During the sexual relation she felt how humiliating it was for the partner to be prey to such intense desire. Immediately after intercourse she felt humiliated and tried to rationalize this humiliation by the thought that things never worked or developed, or that the man did not love or respect her. The continuous change and drifting from man to man seemed to have been accomplished by intense splitting of herself such that each man came to contain a different part of herself with which she was unable to establish any proper contact, so that in the end she was left in bits — as represented by the different men going off in different directions — she herself being impoverished, lost, and unable to recover or to bring these parts together, feeling that there was not sufficient core in her with which to do this.

The promiscuity was seen by her friends and partners as crazy behaviour leading to madness which, later on in trying to deal with its consequences, became encapsulated in The Mirror. Acting out these phantasies in real life with real people made her break down and feel that she was scattered all over the place.

This tendency to disintegrate, as seen in the promiscuous episodes, seemed often to overwhelm the patient. She tried to use various devices to cope with it. For a time she entered a convent. In other situations when things appeared about to overpower her, particularly when at home by herself, she would lock herself into a cupboard as a means of getting inside a concrete container where she could feel a little safer. By entering the convent she tried to cope with her anxieties not only by finding a safe restricted container but also by cutting out sexuality altogether, trying to become part of an idealized asexual world. It is worth noting that her description of her stay at the convent made it clear that the characteristics of that institution did not differ very much in her mind from the cupboard. Both were expected to be solid, with unchangeable borders, but lifeless.

None of these methods of defending herself from madness seemed to work for any length of time; each just helped her out of the immediate situation for a short time. Only the masturbation phantasy has had more lasting effects, and when she has felt that she was falling to bits it has helped her for a longer period of time.

Work situation and The Fantasy

In spite of having a good training in science the patient has never been able to use it directly in her work. Work is the central aspect of her life, but she is completely unable to take any part in the real scientific life of the laboratory where she works; she cannot participate in discussions or use her knowledge in the creative aspects of the work. In her post as laboratory secretary she is constantly witnessing, listening to, and observing the discussions and experimental work being carried on. She projects parts of herself in phantasy into the different members of the staff, with whom she then feels identified, managing in this way to feel that what they do not only depends on her but is actually carried out by her. From this angle in the work situation there is the same endless repetition of being an onlooker, the secretary who is only on the periphery of the practical aspects, recording them, reporting about them, etc., but really powerless to contribute in such a way as to modify anything.

In this sense she seems to feed on the excitement of what is going on like the excitement of the onlookers about what occurs inside The Mirror. This excitement, as I have said before, is created not only by her being a permanent outside witness, but mainly by getting, in her mind, into the inside of each member and feeling that she makes them act. This excitement is a substitute for the real thing, as she never participates in the real scientific life of the laboratory, and it is excitement like that of the perversion which is substituted for real life. I should like to emphasize the difference between the patient's work as a secretary, in which she is efficient, doing real work for which she is evidently highly assessed by the people with whom she works, and the scientific work of the laboratory which is much more valued by her than her actual tasks.

The role of the eyes and looking

Long before the patient admitted the existence of The Fantasy in the analysis, the role of the eyes for her had caught my attention. The following material is from a session that took place in about the third month of the analysis on a Friday.

The patient came into the room giving me an unusually prolonged, penetrating and sustained look, then she lay down. She said she thought that everything would now be all right, because she had it all under control. She proceeded to tell me that while she was trying on a hat in front of a mirror, a hat that was too big for her and kept falling over one eye, she remembered that she had dreamed about putting on a ski hat which was too small for her. The hat had a dark blue and white pattern.

She associated that the colours reminded her of the blue pullover and white skirt that I had been wearing the previous day. She commented that it was funny that the hat in the dream was too small while hers is in fact too big. It actually reminds her of her sister Maria's hat, which is too small for her. She recalled a skiing holiday that she had had with

119

Maria. While they were abroad Maria met a man she liked. When they came back home Maria and the man started going out together. She spoke here about her feelings about it, how she could not stand seeing them together, neither could she stand the sister touching her while this friendship lasted, not even touching her by chance, as for instance when sitting in a cinema. She had had to go away from Maria with whom she was living at that time, and shortly afterwards had had a breakdown. (These last events were already known in the analysis.)

I interpreted this way of looking at and watching me when she came into the room as her getting into me and then being able to control me, hence her reference that now everything was under control. In this way things are felt to be all right; my weekend, my going out, my relationships with men became controlled by her in her mind. I linked it with the hats, their sizes, and how in the dream she ends by having on a combination of Maria's hat and my clothes so that she does not have to see her phantasies about my weekend. Through this projective identification she was avoiding being aware of having any phantasies about my weekend. If she had become aware of having such phantasies, she would not have been able to avoid attacking and breaking me up inside herself, which would have resulted in her being unable to stay in touch with a more helpful me in her mind.

The patient remembered that the previous day one of the heads of the research department came late to the laboratory had brought his girl-friend with him. The patient felt anxious, agitated, and thought that the lateness was due to their being in bed. She felt that she could not stand having to look at them, and proceeded to lock them out of his laboratory. After doing this she felt much better. My interpretation had referred mainly to the use of her eyes in the session to get into me and control me, but here she was also expressing a feeling and belief that if she feels she cannot look at an interpretation about my relationships over the weekend, she will stop watching, lock me out, expel me from her mind as she expelled the couple from the man's laboratory. While we were working over this, the patient brought two memories:

1. When she was around ten years old, one day standing with her sister Anna (the sister who was four years younger than herself), they witnessed through the window a couple having intercourse in the house next door. A day or two later the two sisters started a homosexual relationship which went on until the patient was fifteen. It consisted of mutual masturbation imitating intercourse.
2. The other memory refers to a period when she was around four years old. She was suffering from eczema. For some days she could not open her eyes on waking. This she remembered with intense horror and acute anxiety.

It appears to me that these two examples help our understanding and illustrate the use the patient makes of her eyes as organs of projection and reintrojection. In the first example, by witnessing the couple she felt that she got into the intercourse and by projective identification she 'became' one of the partners of the intercourse, as she did in the dream by projecting herself into Maria's hat and into myself in the session. The second example shows what would happen should she be deprived of this means of projection; she would be exposed to the terror of being blind, trapped in an insane world with no way out.

It is the eyes that create the visual image in The Mirror, into which she projects herself at the same time and becomes identified with (she 'is' or 'is in') each one of the participants. In The Fantasy the eyes play a similarly central role by 'putting' into The Mirror the participants and their activities.

It seems that the eyes, as well as having an expelling function, play a unifying part in an attempt to keep things together. What the onlookers see they report and warn about.

Aspects of 'acting-out' in the transference

At the beginning of her treatment I knew very little about the patient's history and it was very difficult to obtain information from her. Most of the data that slowly emerged in the course of the analysis was obtained through interpretations in the transference of the feelings that she provoked in me and was only later confirmed by her associations. For months I had no knowledge of The Fantasy or any perverse activities of the patient, and I should like to describe how the gradual understanding of her behaviour towards me within the analysis finally brought this central problem to light.

During the first six months of the treatment there evolved very slowly in the sessions a situation in which I was continually submitted to material more acted-out in the transference than communicated by words. Often the relation between what she was saying verbally and her actions was very slight and her greatest aim seemed to be to make me curious and excited. Her communications were made in such a way as to invite me to witness something very fascinating, but which she did not express verbally. She spoke about work and details of everyday events. Sometimes she would start something and then break off as if she had never mentioned it. If I questioned her, my words were felt as very concrete, driving her into a state of anxiety and confusion.

My questions were also felt to show that I was very curious and that she had succeeded in involving me in whichever situation she seemed to want. For instance, she would announce that she saw Peter (a physicist in the laboratory), he came into her office — already her way of saying this was such that I found myself wondering what was his reason for coming, very unrelated to what she was saying and to the fact that it was absolutely natural for him to go into the secretary's room. After saying that he came into her room, her voice changed; she started to say something else, interrupted herself and started something different yet again. The feeling it gave me was that something was going on and that I was missing important links. I was getting intrigued and confused. The more she said the more confusing it felt to me, but it did not appear that the patient was confused; on the contrary she seemed to be following a clear line of thought. If I made an attempt to question her (which I quickly learned to avoid) on any aspect she was speaking about, her reaction was very excited both in posture and in voice.

Gradually it began to emerge with more clarity in my mind that I was supposed to be very curious about and excited by something that was happening in her. Something in the situation which I was supposed to be witnessing was displayed as having very fascinating qualities which were meant to act as a temptation to me and to compel me to join in. This I interpreted in a rather blind way, since I did not know what the situation was or what was the meaning of the fascination that it was meant to exercise upon me. However, I was well aware that it was there.

By the continual interpretation of this behaviour there gradually evolved a situation in which the patient started to perceive me as an analyst, as trustworthy, as somebody able to contain these problems without being reduced to acting them out or reporting them but able to give her the hope of getting some understanding about them. In this sense I had been, without realizing it, and without any direct information about The Fantasy, one of the onlookers outside The Mirror. Thus she had tried, during all this time, to drag me inside The Mirror, as she did the onlookers, and I was supposed to struggle against it, in spite of the excitement I was meant to feel, but I was unable to do more than that.

To illustrate this I shall bring extracts from sessions that took place around two weekends immediately before she brought the narrative of The Fantasy into the analysis.

On Monday she came looking very strange, a mixture of withdrawn and excited. She started saying, 'All right I tried to write dreams, it is no good . . .' Her language sounded very peculiar with prolonged pauses between syllables. She said, '. . . a dream, Reis–Violet, washed her head, no, it is no good'. My first interpretation, which I cannot recall exactly, referred to her behaviour. She answered it by wringing her hands in a highly theatrical way saying, in a hoarse voice, 'Oh you! — you — what do you want? — why do you speak like that? — why do you make me suffer, it doesn't matter', etc. Her way of speaking is very difficult to transcribe as any way of describing it appears to make more sense grammatically that it really did. But it conveyed very strongly how excited she was. This excitement seemed to be based on very sadistic feelings, as if to tease me, in a way that would make me want to ask questions, a way that would provoke curiosity. I interpreted how her way of speaking was meant to provoke me into questioning her, and that this would be a proof of my being excited by her. I explained that her attitude was meant to make me feel frustrated and curious and that she was getting intense satisfaction from it. I also linked it with the feelings and fears in relation to the meaning she attached to the weekend and the reversal of roles by projective identification which made me into the child. After a while she quietened down and started a repetitive complaining. 'Well ... I can do nothing about it, you say I want to make you curious, I can see that, I feel excited, I see what you mean, but that is all that comes into my mind. I cannot do anything about it.' A bit puzzled, I interpreted how she could not allow me to do anything more than describe her behaviour. That was all she took in from my interpretation, but she did not take any notice of the more dynamic elements of it (as the projective identification with parents in intercourse, related to my weekend, as a reaction to separation, etc.). Then slowly she started to speak in a coherent way.

The following Friday she spoke about a Mr X whom she had met and whom she believes to be a friend of mine. She spoke in a kind of broken way, being, as usual on Fridays, more difficult to establish contact with. She reported a dream in which she was carrying a folder from which bits of corpses were falling out. She associated to a previous dream about hiding corpses wrapped in a red skirt of hers, and her mother standing near and looking very sad. The cupboard was the one where she used to hide her wet panties at home. Her mother in that dream also looked like her piano teacher, the expression being the one she remembered her having had once when the patient urinated on the chair during a piano lesson. In summary, my interpretations referred to her feelings when I came into her mind in connection with Mr X, what she did to me inside her with her urine, and how it seemed to drop out as faeces and water. I linked it with the attack on the parents and with masturbation activities, which I also connected with her behaviour in the session.

In the following session, for the first time, she brought The Fantasy.

By now I had been turned in her mind into a 'sane onlooker' in the sense that not only was I felt to have succeeded in the struggle against the excitement offered for me to succumb to and report about what was going on, but I had also in her mind become different from the onlookers in the sense that I appeared more capable of bringing modification into the situation.

Fragmentation of the object as a result of the attack on sexuality

In a Monday session immediately after a Christmas break (after approx-imately eight months of analysis), she started by saying how horrible she felt the holidays to have been, spoke about her sister Maria spending some days with her and that she had dreamt about her. (Maria had often stood in the analysis for an ideal asexual mother, while the other sister Anna is mainly connected with sexuality.)

In the dream she and Maria were in a garden. Through a fence they could see that preparations were being made for a wedding party in a neighbouring garden. She felt that one of them was not invited, although she was not sure about the other. She started walking towards it, her sister disappeared, and she herself was at the wedding. Her associations to this dream referred first to her grandmother's garden. She remembered weddings at her home town, events to which her parents often had to go as part of their business, where they did not take her. She usually felt very curious and intensely resentful at being left out. She then spoke about her Aunt V, whom she met when she went home for the holidays. Maria's staying with her during the holidays went all right and she was helpful to the patient but it was very bad when she left; she felt like running away and has been running away from herself ever since.

My interpretations of this dream referred first to the holidays and her 'running away' from contact with myself as with Maria on parting. I pointed out how the holidays were felt to be like the wedding in the dream, historically the parental intercourse; when this occurred she felt left out and resentful and rushed to get into it, to go to the wedding and attack it. This made her feel so destructive that the 'helpful' analyst, the asexual Maria in the dream, disappeared and ceased to exist.

The patient, more or less at this point, remembered that when she was about five years old the family went to Aunt V's wedding, which did actually take place in the garden that she was reminded of by the one in the dream. Her mother was wearing her best dress. When trying to open a bottle of milk to give some to the child, she pushed the cardboard lid into the bottle, spilling the milk over her dress, particularly the blouse, and spoiling it forever.

It can be seen from this dream and the associations to it how sex is felt by the patient to spoil the relationship with the mother, not only in the present but in any possible future. It was 'spoilt forever'. The envious attack on the parental union makes her feel this union to be so damaging that it destroyed any hope for her. The blouse, the breast, the mother, all were put out of use.

These feelings, that the mother's sexuality spoiled the patient's relation-ship with her, were re-enacted continually in the transference mainly in relation to holidays and other interruptions. The material she reported on Mondays, both verbally and in her behaviour, could be linked with her feelings that the weekends represented my sexuality; in her mind she made an intense attack on my sexuality and my relationships with others. Because of this attack I was often felt by her at the beginning of the week not only to be no good to her but to be unreal or non-existent.

During such times her general way of speaking was very fragmented: it became cold muttering, sounded distant, was delivered as somehow fluent but made very little sense so that it was very difficult to follow her speech and also to record it convincingly here as it was the tone, general posture, and way of pausing that felt more expressive than the actual words. I directed interpretations mainly to this behaviour in the sessions in an attempt to establish some contact with her.

During periods in which this kind of conflict and its accompanying behaviour were prevalent, the information that I could gather from her about her life outside the analysis pointed to intense anxieties of falling to bits, and a continuous state of terror which made her whole situation very precarious. In working on such material, mainly from her verbal expressions, it became clearer that this type of fragmentation corresponded for the most part to a urinary attack.

In parenthesis here I should like to mention that the patient had suffered all her life from urinary incontinence both by night and by day, the urine being felt by her as very corrosive and used as a weapon. It appeared in her mind, both in memories and in dreams, as very powerful, destructive, and one of the things she had to hide and felt very badly about; this was expressed in the example mentioned earlier, of the dream in which she was hiding the skirt with the bits of corpses in the place where she used to hide her wet pants.

Preoccupation with urine also shows the intense fragmentation of her internal world. This is often felt by the patient as being in a mashed or liquid state. (The terms 'liquefied' and 'liquefying' appear very often in her dreams.)

To illustrate this I should like to refer to a problem that the patient had for some months with her flat: the roof was in a very bad state with the rain coming through all the time. She felt despairing about this but at the same time could not get herself to have it surveyed for repairs. Analysing her reaction to separations, as described before, gradually allowed the material to evolve and be worked through so as to bring some modification. After some weeks of preoccupation with this flat situation, the patient brought the following dream: she was in a room similar to the analytic room, but communicating with another room. A man walked through it into the next room. Then she was alone, and at her side there was a bun of the kind that has cream inside and a top. She pulled the top off and all the contents spilled on to the floor, turning into a mess. She woke up in a state of anxiety.

My interpretations referred to the man as my partner; when we came together she felt left out and alone. In her anger she tried to pull him out like the top of the bun, turning it into a mess. It was seen how this partner's penis was confused in her mind with the nipple in the breast felt as a joined couple; by pulling it out she spills the contents and turns them into a mess. We could then work on her fears of being found out, and the links with the present situation of her difficulties with her flat, and only then could she get herself to communicate with the landlord and get the thing mended.

Fragmented state of her internal object

The following dream is from a session some days before a holiday. She was in Germany. She had to meet a man, Mr Y. Prior to meeting him she went into a big store where she got a 'funny looking' white cream in a glass jar, which she put in her carrier. She thought the cream could be shaving cream, and it was presumably for Mr Y. When she came out of the shop, she found herself taking a tram. Mr Y was in it, but he was neither sitting nor standing, but levitating perpendicularly and she thought perhaps she could hold on to him; she thought he looked like a penis.

On waking up she felt the dream to be terribly funny, and even when reporting it she could not help but laugh. Nevertheless, she said that it also felt as if it had a sinister atmosphere about it.

On associating to the dream she referred to Mr Y as somebody known to have been a Nazi. She considers him good-looking and very attractive, with something in his facial expression that made her wonder how cruel he might be. The cream reminded her of a depilatory that belonged to an aunt of hers with whom she was staying when the news about the first atom bomb came. The cream also reminded her of soaps and other objects made of the remains of people killed in concentration camps. She felt horrified and she recalled that the previous night she had been looking at a book with illustrations of women and children walking into the gas chambers.

My interpretation dealt mainly with her feelings towards my holidays, how holidays immediately gave rise to a deathly war in her which was directed to the extermination of the Jewish woman analyst. I pointed out to her that the attack was done, via the penis, Mr Y, into whom her sadism and destructiveness were projected. Through this projection, it is the penis in the intercourse, the Nazi man, who distorts the mother-analyst and atomizes her into the mashed cream.

Through working on this, it could be seen how this atomized destroyed analyst (the mother) was what the patient contained inside her, like the jar of shaving cream that she put into her bag. This destructiveness was felt to take place because of the sexuality and the penis was blamed for it, but it was she who took hold of it and was felt to attack the mother, via this father, because of the mother's relationship with him.

Secondary fragmentation

Progress in working through material such as the example just presented was very slow, and there was an immediate setback because the horror for the patient of becoming aware of this situation was enormous.

The realization of her sadistic attacks on the analyst made her feel extremely persecuted by guilt and frightened of containing both a very destroyed and destroying internal analyst. She was continually terrified and suffered from intense hypochondriacal symptoms. These consisted mainly of feeling her inside to be 'wrong'; abdominal pains made her believe that she had a very damaging cancer which had already affected most of her organs. The affected organs, though mainly in the abdomen, were sometimes also her throat, lungs, and mouth, depending very much on the type of attack or introjection that took place. For instance, after a particularly ferocious verbal onslaught on me she developed overnight a severe pain in her throat and was convinced that the cancer was there. When her doctor saw her he could not find anything wrong with her, a fact that did not reassure her at all; her fear diminished only after days of interpretive work.

Any little insight achieved could only be held for a very short time, and she would then immediately resort to secondary fragmentation as a defence. During such times, with the increase of her anxieties, her urinary incontinence used to increase too, and she felt that she was 'dripping' all the time. This kind of fragmentation made her feel as if she was in bits and lost, feeling that everything was slipping away from her. The contact with her in the analysis was very tenuous and she felt harassed by anxieties about death.

While analysing this kind of material there occurred a series of dreams, or sensations when half-awake. They were described as looking at newspapers on which the black printing felt like incoherent letters which she was completely unable to relate together so as to form a word, let alone sentences. They also often appeared like film newsreels running very quickly in front of her eyes non-stop. During periods of this type it was difficult for her to differentiate being asleep and being awake.

127

The dreams or sensations terrified her and she remembered that during the times just before her various hospitalizations they used to occur in the same way, very frequently, and they made her feel horrified and in a state of continuous panic because she could not stop them. Sometimes the only way for her to deal with these experiences and the terror of them was by resorting to The Fantasy which she felt helped her to come out of the terror and pull herself together a little.

While we were working on this, mainly in its relation to myself in the transference, the following dream occurred.

She was in the station in B. She feels that from there she has to go somewhere, possibly to her analytic session. B also appears to be Hampstead Tube station (the analysis takes place just two streets from Hampstead station). It is time for her analysis but she cannot move from there. She wants to communicate with me but she cannot remember my name, only some letters come into her mind — 'r — s e?' — they are scattered letters and she feels desperate. Nor can she remember my telephone number; if she recalls some figures then she cannot remember the exchange. She feels she is going to faint and is in a panic. Some very frightening and bizarre-looking buses are there and she wonders whether she should take one. This possible action is regarded with horror.

From this dream it can be seen how trapped she is in this terrible state. To get out of it she has to get in touch with me, but this is prevented by my being turned into unrelated bits inside herself. Should she not be able to contact the analyst — standing for a good object, the breast — she feels she is left to madness, the bizarre bus which she thinks she has to get into, and that horrifies her. But to do something about getting in touch with an object felt to be more whole, she will have to see what she has done to it.

On interpreting this we were reminded of a previous dream some time ago. In this dream she was at Euston station and had lost a child, then seen as a child part of herself. To find the child she had to go to Golders Green, but to get there she had to go through the Chamber of Horrors at Madame Tussaud's. (Between Euston and Golders Green she had to pass through Hampstead.) She was also reminded that some years ago she went on holiday to B. On the day of her arrival she went to a cinema. On going inside she was overtaken by uncontrollable vomiting which lasted for over 24 hours. The physician who saw her could not find any physical reason for this and advised her to consult her psychiatrist, who proceeded to admit her back into hospital.

The link between the dream, the scattered letters, and the above mentioned episode can then be seen. In the dream she seems to have fragmented the internal image of her analyst and expelled it in such a way that she could not at once remember my name. Then she feels she is left in a state of collapse, with nothing to support her and in danger of getting into complete madness, represented by the strange and frightening bus. The newsreels and newspapers represent the expelled fragments of her internal object, now persecuting her from outside, but which she could not bring herself to put together because of the dread of facing what she had done to them, the chamber of horrors, that the newspapers or newsreels will tell about if the letters make any sense. Then she feels that the resource left to her is more fragmentation and only bizarre combinations, as for instance the buses in the dream.

It is worth noting that over a period of time this dream was followed by a series of several dreams on the same lines in which she became progressively more able to remember the analyst's Christian name and surname. In that sense it seems that the pressure from the horror and persecution because of her unconscious attacks on her object must have diminished somewhat, bringing a lessening of this type of fragmentation.

Explanatory attempt

In my view the perverse Fantasy had set in as a means of 'cure' of a state of disintegration due mainly to the internalization of a very destroyed intercourse which led to the destruction of the patient's ego. Before discussing theoretically the phenomena I think take place, I should like to bring some material mainly round a dream which led to masturbating accompanied by The Fantasy.

In the sessions immediately prior to the one I am going to present, the patient's sister Maria came very much into her thoughts. Maria, who lives out of London, had come to visit her and brought her some of her clothes, and by accepting them the patient felt like a beggar.

On the previous day the central theme was a dream in which the sea figured prominently, and by association it came to picture an ideal relation to the mother.

The Wednesday session: she starts by saying she hates herself, and on coming here felt that she would not be able to talk, and that she did not wish to tell me anything. She appears withdrawn and depressed. She goes on to say that this is one of those days when anything she reads, thinks, or does, starting with MA sounds immediately to her like masturbation. She sounds a bit dramatic and says it is terrible, checks herself and says, 'I am being daft.' Then she says that the picture in the waiting room says Chile, she had always read it Cheile. She had a dream, could not get out of it and had to masturbate, started rubbing and this started off The Fantasy.

She was speaking all this in a rather bit-by-bit way, getting as she went on more high-pitched and in a tone that partly suggested anxiety and partly that she was trying to make me curious.

I interpret how curious she feels about my life, the Chile picture, and how she tries through her way of speaking to make me into the curious child. She says it is true; her tone changes and is more direct; she says that she finds it difficult to speak, maybe it is better to start with the dream, as this is what she thinks led to The Fantasy which feels so difficult to talk about.

In the dream she was with Maria, in a place like a cinema. There were empty seats at the back and also further forward. Maria walked to the centre of the cinema and chose seats; the patient resented her doing this without consulting her.

At this point of the dream a story went through her head, it was 'Men make passes at women in places like this.' It felt exciting. Also, it went on, the passes were at women like herself who were likely to respond to them. At this point the scene changed and it looked more like a theatre with a frosted glass screen on stage. Maria has disappeared and she is sitting with John (a physicist who works at the laboratory) in the front row. Something is happening on the stage. She has no idea what it is but can vaguely see some figures. It also feels like something frightening and could be to do with the sea. From the back of the place, fog or smoke is coming. She feels like pushing with her feet against the screen, but here the whole thing feels very confused to her and the scene changes completely and she is in the school hall: it looks as if it is covered with green linoleum. Her family is there, Anna, but she is not sure about Maria. The headmistress is also present. The green floor covering everything grows; she knows in the dream it cannot grow, but it does grow as if proliferating. At this point she woke up in a very anxious state; she felt that she couldn't pull herself out of the dream, especially the green growth, and had to masturbate in order to get out of it all.

The Fantasy in the masturbation consisted of The Mirror inside of which there was a man who was tied on to a bench. A girl came in to have intercourse with him. The man couldn't move and she had to lower herself to get his penis. It was all extremely unsatisfactory for the two of them and very humiliating. But they had to do it so as to make a baby, and the girl was going to stay until she made sure that she was pregnant. Then another man came in; the first one must have been homosexual because he started sucking his penis, but couldn't be left without a partner, so a girl was brought into it. Here it stopped. The patient thinks she was in all of them but was not very sure where by the end. During all the time the onlookers were watching, but she does not think that they were drawn into the excitement. Associating to this material, she started saying that the previous evening she went to the cinema and saw a film with Yul Brynner whom she feels is very attractive because he looks cruel. In relation to Maria choosing the seats, she is reminded that she always wanted Maria to be the one who decided about things, but when she did so the patient resented it bitterly. Sitting next to Maria reminded her also of the time when Maria was going out with her boyfriend and the patient had not been able to stand any contact or proximity to Maria as this made her feel unbearably anxious.

John is a very anti-establishment person. The school hall is a place she hated. It was there that the headmistress admonished her for stealing. It was in the hall that the school dramatic presentations were performed, but she was not allowed to go and watch them because of the stealing for which she had to be punished. The hall was not green, but the lavatory in her flat is, also the colour of envy is green. She did also associate to the story of 'men making passes' to an event that happened when she was fifteen: a man made a pass at her in a cinema; she let him do it.

In interpreting I started by pointing out how Maria (looked at in the light of previous material) was representing the analyst in a very central position and how this aroused intense resentment. When I, as Maria, came into her mind associated with a man, she hated it intensely and turned to stories of men making passes at her. At this point Maria/myself, standing for a feeding/looking-after mother, disappeared. She has the man, John, probably a masculine part of herself, based on a faecal phantasy. They join together in an anti-parents, anti-establishment activity. These are very intense attacks of an anal nature, the fog from behind, and by turning the scene on the stage into something very frightening, which starts by being related to the sea — the expression of an ideal relation to the mother in the previous session — but which ends by growing into a lavatory.

This attack in her mind on the couple, Maria central and connected to a man, the parents together, makes her feel trapped and she has to resort to The Fantasy, which seems to have as its main aim here an attempt to reconstruct intercourse for the 'baby' to be made, and it is only when this is felt to be achieved that she can escape from the feeling of being trapped in horror.

This interpretation was given in parts, and with a bit of dialogue. At the end, the patient was silent for a moment, looked depressed and spoke in a slow sad voice. She said that she sees what I mean about the dream, and the green was awful, like a cancerous growth, The Fantasy was so humiliating for everyone, but with it she could somehow pull herself out

131

of the green and in one piece. Then she said that now when she said the word 'green' what came into her mind was *Viridiana*, a film which she is not able to remember but for one scene. In it the beautiful girl and her cousin had gone out together, and a lot of beggars who had been kindly protected by her invade the dining room. The beautiful table with its white tablecloth, shining silver, china, and food is assaulted; they make a ghastly mess, spilling and breaking everything, and finally when the girl comes back they attempt to rape her. There is also a murder. She said it was awful. She was speaking in a rather anxious voice. She stopped, and said she felt frightened of getting excited.

I summarized the interpretations for her and how this excitement was in my view an attempt to bypass the 'awfulness' she felt about what she does to me in her mind, as she did to her parents when she was little.

Proceeding now to elaborate theoretically what has been presented. I believe that by establishing the division between the onlookers and The Mirror, there becomes possible a delimitation in the structure by which the most disturbing aspects become encapsulated, contained in a firmly delineated area, and only then can an attempt to deal with them take place. The main task seems to be an attempt to reconstruct her internal world as a way of reconstructing her ego by bringing her parents together. The parents, or aspects of them, are represented by the participants in the scenes inside The Mirror.

These unions, as illustrated by the aforementioned example, are attempted under the following conditions. They are allowed to join under intense control and with no freedom whatsoever, as all this is done through mechanisms which allow her either to be, or to be in, each of the participants in The Fantasy. Because of this she is identified with every participant and takes part in each single action that takes place, avoiding thus ever being excluded and feeling left out or stimulated by the parents. The parents are controlled or triumphed over by being made to do what she orders and in the way she decides, and also they are all the time humiliated and treated with the greatest contempt. They are robbed of any satisfaction or pleasure and only allowed to come together just enough to keep the situation (herself, the baby in the example) going. It is of interest to note how in the different variations of The Fantasy no one is ever allowed pleasure of any kind, and the delaying, so much connected with prolonged masturbatory excitement, is used instead of satisfaction.

The central factor prevailing in all this is the cruelty under which these activities in The Fantasy take place. The whole bringing together, though meant to provide for a condition of survival of the patient's ego, which is a minimum requirement for love, is done under such conditions of cruelty, hatred, and humiliation that it appears that her love impulses are suffused by her destructiveness, turning in this way into sadism, which then prevails over all the activities. It is this sadism that never has to be properly modified by love; on the contrary, as can be seen, it is constantly gratified so that a true integration or an approach to integration never occurs.

It seems to me that by this means the problem of having to deal with the diminution and sublimation of sadistic impulses is bypassed and kept static, which in its turn makes for the continued repetitiveness of the symptom because of the continually on-going conflict.

Nevertheless, The Fantasy, I think, contributes also a clear attempt to bring about a cure of the psychotic process, which is achieved to a certain degree by bringing a halt — or pause — to the more fragmenting processes.

I think that in this sense it could be compared with Freud's statements about the relation between delusions and more severe psychotic expressions, and the constructions which are built up in the course of an analysis, referred to by him in his papers on Schreber and Constructions (Freud 1911, 1937).

It is by means of attempting some kind of integration, although in such a bizarre and confined way, that she manages — not to be 'normal' or 'ordinary' by any standard, but somehow not to disintegrate and not to be overtly mad. It would seem that whenever her ego collapses completely, the feeling of it is a total loss of coherence — a falling to pieces — followed probably by a massive projection into her outside world, which will end in a paranoid state without the patient being capable of contact or of any kind of perception of reality. Historically this was the main element of her first breakdown.

Through this encapsulation in The Mirror she manages to keep the destruction within certain limits, preventing it from affecting the whole of her personality and allowing other parts of it to resort to less damaging means, permitting them some degree of development and function.

To bring about a real improvement there should have occurred a modification of her sadism, which would have allowed some proper reparation to her objects. This has never been achieved. The bringing together of the parents under the rigid control, lack of freedom, and continuous intrusion by the patient only allows for a minimum of cohesion so as to prevent her from falling to pieces.

To be able to make real progress from there, she would have to face intense pain and frustration in experiencing love for her objects and the consequence of the attacks to which she has submitted them. But the horror that this situation produces in the patient makes her resort to further fragmentation, this time of a defensive nature which makes for the increase in her state of disintegration, which can only be stopped by resorting to The Fantasy. The Mirror, as a concrete image within which the encapsulation takes place, provides her with borders firmly delineated and stable. In the choice of the device to assist her it is interesting to note that a mirror is an object allowed only to reflect the subject's image and with no other characteristics. It was in this sense the ideal thing into which to project different internal objects, controlling them and allowing them to reflect only what she puts into them.

The Mirror represents a breast, but a dead breast whose only function is to act as a concrete container, with solid borders but nothing more. This breast, in the actual sense, is felt to be hard, cold, and absolutely mechanical, lacking any life of its own to provide the baby with anything in a positive way.

In this way I should like to differentiate this sort of 'containing' from the containing qualities of the breast described by Bion (1962) in that there is no feeling expressed by it or allowed to it; it is meant just to be there, to allow feelings to be put into it and to reflect them, but not to modify them at all, neither by furthering change nor by relieving the intensity of the anxieties.

As I have indicated before, this conception of the breast seems to contain only one positive aspect, the stability or firmness of its frame, which never seems to be affected or threaten to change. This aspect seems to be not only the basis of the breast's functioning but also the means of some development in the phantasy and in the work of the analysis.

Regarding the other aspect of The Fantasy, that is, the outside of The Mirror, the onlookers, they represent the so-called saner parts of the patient. She feels also that she is all the time 'in them'.

It is interesting to note that the patient herself compared them to a 'Greek chorus', as the onlookers very much share their functions; as I had been felt to do at the beginning of the analysis; they appear to know what has happened and its meaning, and its results, catastrophic or otherwise. But they are powerless to modify the events; they can report them but their warning is unheard, and even when, as often happens, they feel threatened in their very existence as onlookers, the only thing they can do is to struggle against the excitement and curiosity to which they are being exposed by way of pressure to make them lose their role.

The number of the onlookers who form The Mirror viewers varies, and gives a measure of greater or lesser availability of sane parts. Should they all be drawn into The Mirror, it would seem to me that the outcome could be an hallucinatory state. However, their existence outside cannot be of any modifying help, as they are powerless to change anything at all.

It seems that the onlookers represent partly the patient's superego functions, the reporters of the moral implications of what is happening, and partly ego functions, in the attempt to report about reality which should be perceived and perhaps accepted. But the expression of both appears to be merely formalistic, devoid of any life, just empty and opaque. In this sense both Mirror and onlookers are representing dead or almost dead objects, being without life which is then replaced by the excitement of the events that take place in The Mirror and which are being reported by the onlookers.

It is excitement which has been glorified and put above any other feeling, and which keeps the perversion in its place instead of any other relationship with real people or objects. Excitement in the analytic situation has taken a central place in the patient's expressions; she feels it most of the time and tries to spill it over the analyst.

In this sense excitement seems to have been a basic defensive response against the envy experienced at the breast and later on towards the parents' intercourse. It seems that for the patient it could be expressed in the following way: 'I am excited and I am alive. Provided they are excited — analyst, breast, parents — they want me, need me, and that's why they come to get it from me.' In the sessions over and over again I was felt to want to know about her laboratory or flat because of my being excited. Here it can then easily be linked with her promiscuous experience; she felt nothing but arrogant superiority and contempt for her partners because they were the prey of such hot desire and excitement.

Through all this, the repetitiveness of the situation and the total impoverishment of the patient's life can, I think, be easily explained.

I would like to add here the role I think her intelligence plays. It seems to me that the complications and sophistications of the mechanisms used by this patient can only be achieved by someone of a very high IQ and by paying the price that the patient paid of being prevented from using her intelligence in a more constructive way.

In speculating on the possible explanations for this state of affairs in which the anxieties were never modified to a degree which would make it possible to progress into a more integrated state, it seems to me that it can be traced to the relationship between internal factors, mainly primary envy, and a mother as she appears in the transference who, although externally concerned about her children, is lacking in real empathy with them. It looks to me as if the need for a breast to contain, hold, and modify the baby's anxieties was never fulfilled in the patient by the mother.

I think it is worth noting here that the patient has often mentioned the feeling of remembering her mother feeding her siblings and interrupting the sucking, putting the baby down for some moments to attend to customers coming into the shop and resuming the feeding only after she had finished with the customers. The patient feels that this was done under the orders of or intimidation by her father who always played a main and dominating role at home. She believes that the same procedure must have taken place with her. This feeling only came into her mind after continuous interpretation in the transference of reactions to what she felt to be interruptions, either real or taken as such, as for instance my coughing and similar things; while working on such events and the subsequent excitement, the memories mentioned above came into her mind.

This impossible situation, plus the patient's intense envious impulses, seem to have played an important part in preventing the establishment of a relationship with the breast with any degree of security. The combination of these factors must have made the patient perceive the breast as an unreliable object, desirable, exciting, and tantalizing.

On this basis, with such a precarious relationship to the breast, and when faced with an early awareness of the parental relationship, her reaction of intense hatred led her to attack this relationship and also to put the blame upon it for her deprivation and lack of satisfaction at the breast. It is this very early Oedipal situation and her response to it — the hatred and attack on the parental intercourse — in which she seems mainly to have become fixated. In my view the father's domination of the mother confirmed and reinforced this pattern. It is interesting to note that this type of pattern has been carried into all the patient's relationships.

As previously mentioned, the attempt to enclose the most disturbing conditions inside The Mirror is made through projective identification. This omnipotent phantasy is doomed to fail with the return of that which she tried to eliminate or 'imprison' in The Mirror. Projective identification or any other omnipotent mechanism cannot successfully be used to get rid of bits or part of the self, as these cannot be disposed of. The return of what has been projected in this way is felt as an invasion or an intrusion by the rest of the personality, which has then to resort again to violent splitting and projection to deal with the newly created situation and thus perpetuates the vicious circle which undermines more and more the integration process and brings about such a considerable impoverishment.

Also, the spectators, with their functions of sanity, are felt as intruders and are resented by the more ill parts of the patient. These more ill parts then try to get rid of the healthier spectators by tempting them and turning them into inside participants.

Summary

In this paper I have described a perversion and its function as a defence against psychosis. The aim of this perversion is to encapsulate the most severely psychotic parts of the patient's personality, and once this has been done, to allow certain modifications to occur but without any real alteration of sadism. There is no real reparation and only with great cruelty are such modifications allowed to occur, intended only to prevent the ego from breaking completely into bits.

I have presented some material to illustrate the type of relationship to the breast, how this has been carried as a basis into an early Oedipal situation, and which under the pressure of intense envious and jealous attack is being destroyed, introjected in that state, and blamed for the difficulties of the breast relationship.

I have also brought material to show how these aspects are perceived by the patient, the anxieties which they arouse, and the defences used against them.

Finally, I have tried to provide an elaboration and explanation of the underlying meanings of The Fantasy and have discussed the role of intrapsychic and possible external factors in contributing to the patient's state.

References

Bion, W.R. (1957) 'Differentiation of the psychotic from the non-psychotic personalities', International Journal of Psycho-Analysis, 38: 266–75; W.R. Bim, Second Thoughts, London: Heinemann (1967), 43–64; and also in Melanie Klein Today, volume 1, London: Routledge (1988).
—— (1962) Learning from Experience, London: Heinemann; reprinted in paperback, Maresfield Reprints, London: H. Karnac Books (1984).
Freud, S. (1911) 'Psycho-analytic notes on an autobiographical account of a case of paranoia (dementia paranoides)', SE 12.
—— (1937) 'Constructions in analysis', SE 23: 255–69.
Klein, M. (1946) 'Notes on some schizoid mechanisms', in M. Klein, P. Heimann, S. Isaacs and J. Riviere, Developments in Psycho-Analysis, London: Hogarth Press (1952), 292–30 also in The Writings of Melanie Klein, vol. 3, 1–24.

3

Words and working through

EDNA O'SHAUGHNESSY

This paper is an enlarged version of the paper read at the London Weekend Conference of English-Speaking Psychoanalytical Societies on 3 October 1982. It was first published in the *International Journal of Psycho-Analysis*, 64: 281–9.

This paper discusses communication, its modes and its changes, between analyst and patient, and, more particularly, within the patient himself in the course of a psychoanalysis. In the form of spoken dialogue, communication has always been at the centre of the psychoanalytic method and there have always been puzzles and complexities about it.

A patient's talk is not simple. It is multiple in function as Freud showed when he differentiated three related processes — repeating, remembering, and working through (Freud 1914). Nor is an analyst's talk a simple conveying of information. James Strachey, in his classic paper 'The nature of the therapeutic action of psycho-analysis' (1934) was among the first to review the work on, and himself notably advance the problem of, what a therapeutic interpretation is. An interpretation becomes the agency of change, according to Strachey, when it is specific about the point of urgency in the transference, i.e. the patient's impulses and anxieties at that moment active towards the analyst. Then it is a mutative interpretation, as Strachey called it, which enables the patient to change his archaic internal figures by introjecting the interpreting analyst.

Since Strachey's time there has been a vast discussion about analysts' interpretations and patients' communications. The investigations and controversies in the literature have recently been summarized and reviewed by Langs (1976). From Langs' two volumes it emerges that, while some analysts endorse active, non-interpretive techniques for special pathology or situations of impasse, currently there is still agreement that interpretations play the key role, and that a mutative interpretation is a verbalization of the immediate emotional transference.

Analysts still agree, too, that their patients' communications involve Freud's basic three of remembering, repeating and working through.

Over the past fifty years, however, psychoanalysts have changed their view of their own method. It is now widely held that, instead of being about the patient's intrapsychic dynamics, interpretations should be about the *interaction* of patient and analyst *at an intrapsychic level*. It is timely to note in this issue of the *International Journal of Psycho-Analysis*, which commemorates the centenary of Melanie Klein's birth, that her work has been the most powerful single influence for this shift of perspective. Her view, that object relations and also an inner world of objects start at birth, precludes pre-object and objectless phenomena in development, and leads clinically to an object-directed, interactional view of the transference. From her first papers of the 1920s, Melanie Klein advocated a technique of interpreting positive and negative object relations between analyst and patient from the start of every analysis, adult and child alike.

It is also timely to recall our indebtedness to Melanie Klein for our much increased understanding of primitive defences and modes of communication. It is now generally accepted that the interchange between analyst and patient is wider than verbal; as well as words there are other transmissions by projection: feelings like anxiety, sexual excitement, hatred; mental images; sensations of drowsiness or rigidity; and so on. These processes remain mysterious, but an understanding of their defensive function was made possible by Melanie Klein's (1946) discovery of projective identification — her name for a group of early defence mechanisms in which the infant in omnipotent phantasy projects parts, sometimes even the whole of himself, into his objects, for his own safety or to control or to stimulate his objects, etc. Through highly original research, W.R. Bion (1962) extended Melanie Klein's work. He found that projective identification is not only a defence mechanism, but is also simultaneously an infant's first way of communicating with his objects. Bion's theory is that projective identification is the earliest mode of defence and communication which needs to be understood by the nurturing object. From this primitive form of communication and understanding there develops, in his view, more sophisticated forms — ultimately language and verbal thought.

Clinically these are important findings. They explain and conceptualize the familiar transference in which words and what words unconsciously express are not all that is happening, when important events are also occurring beyond words, communicated in more primitive modes. In diverse modes of communication — verbal and more primitive — a patient can bring his unevenly developed personality into analysis. In the service of the less developed part of himself, a patient may also use words not as words to express meaning, but along with the other non-verbal aspects of the encounter to engender his projections in the analyst. In this paper I discuss two patients who need to communicate both by words and more primitive means.

My first patient, Mr B, illustrates one type of psychic predicament that unfolds in the transference in a dual way, divided between words and communications 'beyond words'. A man of 36, an only child, by profession a manager in a construction industry, he wanted an analysis after his girlfriend of several years left him suddenly. At the preliminary interview he seemed lonely and withdrawn. He told me he was depressed after his girlfriend's departure and unable to work properly, which surprised him because he had to admit he had not been that fond of her — not enough to marry her. A few days before starting treatment Mr B broke his arm.

At the start of his analysis he talked flatly about his ex-girlfriend, problems on sites, his state of mind, and so on. His talk did not arise from intensely felt experience nor convey much of an experience to me. In a minimal way it informed me of his life and his responses to starting a psychoanalysis. When I related his worries about the soundness of the builders to suspicions about myself, or when he told me how his girlfriend broke it up so suddenly, and I interpreted his fear that I, his new analyst, might suddenly get fed up with him, such interpretations relieved the real doubts and fears his talk expressed, but these were somehow minor. I sensed an area of latent anxiety and agitation far from his words and his awareness, which I did not understand at all. Moreover, during his sessions I often had an experience for which there was no evidence in his talk. There were no derivatives in his verbal material of an enormous hatred (I could not say of what or whom) which entered me during his sessions.

I began to notice that Mr B paid great attention to why I said what I said. He tried to find out how I looked at, and what I looked at, in his material that made me interpret in the way I did. He was very relieved when an interpretation was as he expected. I noticed, too, that Mr B was acquiring what he called 'new interests' like going to concerts, which were activities he believed his new analyst engaged in. As I tried to work, I felt almost as if Mr B was physically pushing into me: I felt watched in my head, uncomfortable, restricted in what I could say — only obvious familiar interpretations seemed to exist as possibilities. These experiences were my reception of Mr B's primitive communications and defences, the interaction between patient and analyst conceptualized and explained by Klein and Bion in terms of projective identification. I tried to put these experiences into words to Mr B. I spoke about his need to get into my mind, his feeling of being located there, his manoeuvring of me to give him familiar interpretations, and his relief at interpretations he knew would come. When he got these at first quite new and unexpected interpretations from me, Mr B made agitated endeavours to make them into old, deadened, 'familiar lines' as I called them.

Gradually Mr B's split-off activities became less dissociated, and his latent anxiety, inaccessible earlier, now erupted into his awareness. His material became entirely taken up with anxieties about a problem on a building site to do with joins. He spoke agitatedly, repeatedly asking the question 'What are the joins?' and saying 'I have to get the joins settled'. On the building site he countermanded the 'joins' he had ordered for the assembling of material and ordered different ones. I interpreted the joins on the building site as his representation of his problem of joins between him and me. Starting a psychoanalysis — now some six months under way — meant to him he had to find a whole new set of 'joins' for him and me to escape his acute anxiety when he got unexpected interpretations, which made him feel the joins between us were not settled and we were separate. Mr B kept distancing the problem away from the analysis back to the building site, needing not to know that he ever felt unjoined and separate from me. From my repeated experience of hatred arising in me during his sessions, I thought it was above all hatred that he feared and needed to split off and project into me. We began to see how he and I had a meagre, human, whole person contact through out talk, which was certainly without hatred, and how most of Mr B was still a frightened infant constructing and maintaining a unity of himself and myself, in his phantasy so joined, restricted and rigid that there was nothing to fear from it.

I say 'We began to see', meaning I *and* Mr B began to see. Over the months, as I tried to experience his verbal and also his more primitive transmissions and formulated these in words to him, I think Mr B gained some feeling of being known by me. He definitely looked less lonely. That he was also himself gaining awareness was shown in a session to which he brought one of his rare dreams. Mr B began by speaking about one or two familiar themes and then fell silent. On this day his flat words conveyed so little of an experience to me that I said nothing. As I waited an enormous feeling of hatred washed into me. Then he spoke, saying he was pleased, he had had a dream.

He dreamt there were two houses on adjacent sites, placed so that one was to the front and the other was further back. The most prominent feature was a gleaming white concrete strip between the two houses. The strip ran along the side of the front house and continued until it reached and ran along the side of the house set back, making a narrow path joining them.

Mr B's association was that the concrete strip was incredibly level.

I said to Mr B that we were the houses of his dream placed as we are placed in his sessions — he in front and I behind him, a little to the side. I said the dream brought his recognition of the familiar lines he tries to establish between us being a narrow path joining us concretely. In a quite alive way Mr B agreed. I then talked about his first association that the concrete strip was 'incredibly level'. I thought he meant what he said — he didn't believe it. I am not supposed to get higher by interpreting what he doesn't know, but of course I do. He gets higher, too; I reminded him I had sometimes caught a gleam of sexual excitement about his experiences of penetration and conquest of me. I went on to suggest, because of my experience earlier in the session of Mr B's split-off, projected hatred, that he feared there would be hatred between us if we were not kept apparently level. Mr B said 'Yes, possibly', still sounding thoughtful, but now also anxious. After a silence, he said he didn't know, but the concrete strip in his dream reminded him of a long thin bone. He then remembered the bone in his arm which was now mended, and then said a feeling of cold horror had just swept over him. I thought his horror came from the sensation of him and me internally as one long thin dead bone inside himself. Later, I pointed out that in his horror that he could only make 'dead bones' with people, it didn't exist for him that he could do anything alive — such as dream, or have an alive session with me as he was in fact doing on this day.

This was an important session and his dream was one of those dreams that becomes a reference point in an analysis. Starting analysis had meant to Mr B mending the break he suffered with his girlfriend, a break he had experienced as the snapping of a bone. Mr B's existence with me thus repeats his existence with his girlfriend, as she in her turn would have repeated his relations with previous objects. Mr B has been unable to develop; he exists in repeated ossifying unions with the minimum of human contact.

By this time he had been in analysis for nearly a year. A new phenomenon now emerged. Mr B would talk about something, and then say 'I presume that means such-and-such', 'such-and-such' being a stereotyped version of an old interpretation. These 'presumings' occurred more and more in his talk and began to persecute him, as I suspected, from one or two remarks about 'boring concerts', did the 'new' interests he had acquired after starting analysis. Mr B was able to see how his 'presumings' came from a dead bone object inside him, which he could not stop from intruding with its repetitive unthinking bonehead speech, a meaningless echolalia, out of touch with itself and others. As to my talk, sometimes when he listened and wanted to know what I said, he was deeply disappointed. He would say 'Yes, that must but right. But what you say doesn't do anything for me'. He felt an increasing despair that talk could neither express nor convey meaningful experience. I think it is always the case in a transference with a preponderance of events 'beyond words' that at certain phases of the analysis the communicative properties of words are impaired as the talk increasingly reflects the entire primitive defensive organization. To the patient's despair, interpretations cease to be mutative. This is the transference version of his deep anxiety that his objects are powerless to help him.

I have not considered the origin of Mr B's difficulties — the nature of his objects or his own endowment. I present his case to show how his primitive non-verbal communications brought into the transference a controlling, deadening form of projective identification, a defensive organization by which he repeatedly and concretely evaded his infantile fear of any but the most minimal object relations which he expressed in his talk. In so far as I was able to experience, understand and put his emotional predicament into words that reached Mr B, it unfolded in the transference not as an 'acting-in', a mere repeating between patient and analyst, but as part of a new process in which in successive stages Mr B was gaining increasing contact with himself. In the beginning, Mr B's joining was mentally dissociated, an event completely beyond not only words but all awareness, internally a somatic event. Later, he was able to find a first concrete representation in the joins on his building site, and experience his anxiety about joining in his sessions. His dream of two houses joined by a concrete path was his first mental representation, the beginnings of true awareness. However, though Mr B dreamt and understood the transference meaning of his dream, the words about it were mine; at this stage he himself has not yet talked about 'joins' — a much later and crucial developmental step. The progression during a psychoanalysis from somatic event, to concrete representation, to a dream, and ultimately to verbal thought, has been described by R.E. Money-Kyrle (1968) as the frequent path of 'cognitive development' in his paper of that name.

A second patient, Mr E, shows the psychic change which results as work progresses to the stage when the patient himself can express in words his former primitive communications and defences 'beyond words'. Mr E illustrates a different form — almost a polar opposite — of a transference divided between talk and activity detached from talk. Mr E, a sensitive man in his late forties, started analysis in an acute state of suffering — sexually impotent, confused whether his jealous suspicions of his wife were delusional or real, afraid of her and his own cruelty, afraid also of turning to homosexuality or even going mad. As a boy he had been seduced by an older boy, and later he had in his turn seduced younger boys. Still later, he married and had children, who meant much to him. In his sessions he talked narcissistically, with a patronizing attitude that denied his need to be understood and to understand himself, and his desperate dependence on me to relieve him of his acute anxieties and confusions. His words were ambiguous, confusing, even contradictory, making it impossible for me to be sure of anything. Not during, but after, his sessions I was invaded for hours by feelings relating to Mr E of anxiety, confusion, guilt, and need; since these occurred only after his sessions, as regards immediacy of interpretation and effective containment, I was rendered impotent. Mr E split off and projected his impotent, confused and anxious self into me, while he himself was identified with sadistic superego persecutors.

After about a year's work, when I suspected rather than knew — since he gave me no information — that Mr E felt much less mentally threatened, he developed an erotized homosexual transference to me, quite detached from his talk. That is to say, two different things were now happening beyond words: there was still the depositing into me in a destructive way of acutely painful states of mind, and, in addition, there was now Mr E's increasing state of erotization, with a voyeuristic invasiveness, projection of excitement and stimulation of phantasy. Mr E was a strong personality, with more areas of illness, trickier, more omnipotent and difficult than Mr B, not least because too much happened too fast. From the first it had been a struggle not to seem to Mr E to have 'become' his projected, impotent self, and to find a way of interpreting so as to give Mr E the experience of being understood and contained. It now became also a struggle not to 'become' his excited partner. Sometimes, under pressure of his projections, I found I was expressing myself in a wrongly jokey way. Often he formulated his material with tricky, built-in presuppositions to get me to talk to him with some subtle difference that meant to him I was his intimate friend, a contemporary or junior, not a parent-analyst. Sometimes I would be tricked into participating unknowingly in private jokes, and experienced as an exciting seducing older boy, or young boy, or bisexual lover he had seduced. Mr E put enormous pressure on me to 'act in' — a subject explored by Joseph (1978, 1983) — and increasingly found ways of substantiating his phantasy that his analysis was a sophisticated affair with a collusive agreement between us not to get off our respective chair and couch and 'do' anything about it. Certain words and all kinds of non-verbal events, e.g. my necklace happening to match the colour of his tie, became exciting 'signs'. He was uncaring of his marital difficulties and used the analysis to stimulate his wife's jealousy. In any session, if Mr E believed he had seduced me into acting out erotic phantasies with him, his excitement and sense of omnipotence mounted; be believed he had entered me, and seen my corrupt erotic nature. He felt physically enlarged, the room itself, the entire neighbourhood, became the debased mother's body which he occupied and owned. His sense of omnipotence was enormous, as was his feeling of omniscience. He responded swiftly to what I said, talked profusely with a proliferation of analytic and other ideas he believed me to have, with a sense of knowing their source and direction completely.

144

Though alarmingly excited and feeling dangerously omnipotent (it was I, however, who felt the alarm and the danger), apart from brief delusional states in some sessions, he retained an awareness that we were patient and analyst alongside what had become a consuming passion, dangerous because it was so omnipotent and concrete and also because it was so confused a mixture of communication, action, identification, defence, hatred and love, adult and infantile sexuality. It brought into the transference his identification with a series of persecuting over-stimulating objects — notably older seducing boy, mother and, on the part-object level, the breast which I think he had experienced as (and which very likely was) narcissistic and invasive and not containing. His excitement expressed his hatred through the destruction of the analyst as a sustaining parental object. It gratified his narcissism. But it was also for him a finding — in the wrong place on the wrong basis — of an object he felt he had never had, to which he would be able to offer happiness and tenderness that would be returned, as formerly in a confused way he had hoped to find an ideal object in the buttocks of boyfriends. Even though my talk at times was so stimulating and exciting to Mr E as to be useless analytically, I continued to put into words his feelings of excitedly invading me and knowing me, and my equally excitedly trying to penetrate him with interpretations. I talked about the code 'signs', etc. Gradually Mr E felt safer with me, was less wild, and concrete representations of various bits of his psychic state began to appear in his sessions. His excitement began to decline, ushering in a new phase, which I want now to describe in more detail. Above all, it was a phase in which words became paramount.

Less erotized and more hopeful, Mr E wanted to communicate. His proliferated talk, which until then he had narcissistically admired, he now began to hate. He had an outburst one day: 'Words are useless. They're very slippery. They're nothing. If I had to write with broken fingers they would be worthwhile, but they're two a penny', he said with disgust and hatred. The next day he spoke about breaking through the 'language barrier' and, in spite of some wild fragments and sundry ambiguities and contradictions to nullify me, Mr E was really trying now to talk to me, and break through the language that had almost ceased, with its code words, intimacies and contradictions, to be an instrument for communication.

Arriving for his next session, he took out a cheque to pay me, holding up for a moment as he did so two theatre tickets. On the couch he said, 'The couch felt the right size today. It was big enough. It fitted'. Then he paused and said: 'I could give that all a twist — it could sound like bureaucracy, everything fitted, everything in the right pigeonholes, and then there's the bed of Procrustes. . .' but just as his speech was gathering momentum he made an effort and stopped himself. Equally I think he needed to test me to make sure that when he flashed his tickets at me I would remain the right size and would not with precipitate — to him excited — interpretations change into a 'boy lover'. Internally and externally he still had only a fragile feeling of a firm object. He then spoke calmly about paying his bill, showing me his theatre tickets, mentioning the play he was going to that evening. Then the thought of a 'real conversation' occurred to him. I think Mr E was at that moment having a real conversation with me. But it could easily cease either because prevented by Mr E out of meanness, or anxiety about being mocked, or a conviction that I was manipulating him, or, above all, because homosexual phantasies supervened again. His conviction of a homosexual affair could still be swiftly stimulated by a chance 'sign'. But whereas before his erotization would be lived concretely and excitedly in the session, it was now for the first time communicated verbally. I want to report two consecutive sessions to show the changes that occur when a patient is himself able to put into words what before was enacted and communicated in primitive modes. Melanie Klein remarks that words are the bridge to reality. I think Mr E's material shows how his ego changes as his omnipotence goes, as his sense of reality arrives once he can use verbal thought.

In the first session Mr E put into words, for the first time, his realization that he is drawn into phantasies which he mistakes for reality. As I fetched him from the waiting room he got visibly excited. On the couch he talked fast, saying he had had three dreams. In the first he was a teacher taking the register. He called a name and three boys put up their hands. They didn't do it to be disruptive; they just did it. In the second dream he was in a room which had water in it and he pushed off from one side, zooming and swimming across to the other side. In the third dream a tree had grown through the floor of a room. Mr E's second and third dreams gave me a weird mad feeling. I interpreted that he was conveying to me his weird and mad experience on meeting me that day: he felt he zoomed across the room and swam into me, and that I, like the tree, shoved myself up into him. After a moment Mr E said: 'That's right.' He then talked more slowly and quietly about other matters, but increasingly sounded anxious and insecure. I thought he was anxious that I would be critical of his initial excited response and accuse him of being disruptive, which I said to him. I then interpreted the three boys who put up their hands as him responding eagerly with outstretched arms and an excited penis, and said he wanted me to recognize how the boy in him can be instantly stimulated and zoom into others and feel they zoom into him, and that he didn't mean to be disruptive, he is just like that. Though his anxiety subsided, Mr E made no direct reply this time. He talked on, becoming

146

elaborate and ambiguous. He remarked on how he and his wife have a code. Eventually he said in a different and sincere tone that sometimes they don't mention that something is a dream but behave about it as though it were real. In his whole complex communication Mr E was trickily trying both to twist into a code our undoubted real contact at the beginning of the session, when he told me his 'dreams' — his instant phantasies, really, and I interpreted them and he felt understood, and at the same time Mr E was still also really talking. I said I thought he was now doing two opposed things: trying both to get him and me twisted together, claiming it is only codes between us, and also genuinely wanting to tell me that he realizes he sometimes believes his very vivid phantasies — like his dreams of today — are real. Mr E responded warmly and straightforwardly: 'Yes. I know that.'

The next day was an important session. He began by saying he had a dream the night before from which he had woken in terror. It had taken him a long while to realize that he was safe in his bed and that his wife was there safe in hers, which was a great relief.

In this dream he and L (his wife) were first in a school, waiting to see some list or other of some examination, perhaps results, it wasn't clear. He knew he and L had something to talk about, but it wasn't clear what. Then he and L were seated on the edge of a high mossy hill overlooking a precipitous drop. Far down below he could see a small pool, so far down the abyss it made him shudder. He was holding on to a slender pine tree which was not firmly rooted. It was coming away from the ground, and he was terrified. Even worse, his wife L was nearer the edge than he was. He suddenly realized he cared for her and that he must somehow slide forward and get hold of her and stop her falling.

After relating the dream he said again how terrified he was, adding 'It's my situation really'. Mr E is right. The dream, even the way it is in two parts, is his situation really. He talked about how he and L were really on the brink of disaster, describing their current dangerous situation. Then he said: 'The pine tree must be you I have been holding on to — in the terms we'd been speaking yesterday, my taking it for real, I mean.' I pointed out that in his dream he recognizes how dangerous it is when he believes he has really pulled me off the ground into his phantasy; then he has nothing to hold on to, and could go crashing down — could mentally crash, which I interpreted was part of his terror on waking. Mr E agreed.

The contact between us was straightforward and real. The session then changed in a similar way to the day before. Mr E became elaborate and ambiguous. His statements got vaguer. I reminded him then of the first part of his dream, so different in its vagueness from the second part, in which he knows he is terrified about crashing, and about himself and L.

In the first part of his dream he apparently does not know any results of his examination in the analysis, as apparently he does not know what he and L should talk about. I interpreted that now there was another him to the fore, busy with vagueness getting rid of what he knows. There was a prolonged silence. Mr E said: 'I shall have to have what is vulgarly', he sneered, 'called a heart to heart talk with L'. He was again silent. He suddenly said 'I saw a programme on T.V. about refugees'. His voice broke as he went on 'I began to think that's all there's been in this century, ever since the thirties. Refugees, refugees. Pathetic. Evicted from their cities, leaving with their paraphernalia on their backs'. His words expressed and conveyed pain, distress and despair, this time reaching me *in* the session. Mr E cried brokenly for several minutes. He was crying for his lost omnipotence; its loss evicts him from his city, myself as mother's body. He was crying about his marriage. And he was crying with a deep realization about himself as a paederast with his paraphernalia on his back, a pathetic refugee from a frightening world who has been so all his life since his birth in the thirties.

In these two sessions Mr E is changing. He uses language for thinking and for communicating to me. He understands he is a refugee — 'refugee' is *his* word — and he feels the pathos of it. In the richly compressed way only language can achieve, he remembers his past, understands his current predicament in analysis and in his life and internally integrates himself. He is working through in words.

It is interesting to contrast Mr B and Mr E, so different, yet similar. Where Mr B (B is for Bone) is minimal, controlling and controlled, Mr E (E is for Erotized) is maximal and almost out of control. Each needs to unfold his predicament in a mixture of words and primitive communications. In a dry way Mr B's talk informs me of the facts of his daily existence as he also by projective identification constructs and maintains a relation of narrow unity with me, to protect himself from a fuller libidinal life with its feared consequences of anxiety and hatred. Mr E's talk expresses his identification with a sadistic superego, conceals as it reveals, and is used to evacuate fear, impotence and mental confusion into me. Meanwhile, in omnipotent phantasy, he also zooms into me to make an erotized intimacy — multiple in function — to escape the fear and guilt of mutual cruelty and to evade also his despair about loving and being loved in real object relations. Both try to actualize with the analyst as partner these primitive defensive phantasies of symmetrical relations (Matte-Blanco 1975), 'incredibly level' relations, as Mr B calls them. The ossification and erotization are repetitive, concrete and omnipotent — with Mr E omnipotence is paramount. Until Mr B's wordless ossifying and resulting impairment of the words themselves are

148

analysed he will keep the analytic process so minimal that talk will be useless to bring about real change. He will stagnate, existing in a restricted state of projective identification with the analyst, repeating what he has always done with his objects. With Mr E the situation is more dangerous. The talk and entire analytic setting are in danger of becoming so erotized as not only to repeat his former homosexual relations to boys, but to run the risk, because *au fond* the analyst represents a primary sustaining object, of precipitating Mr E into a psychotic state.

The chief clinical problem in a dual transference of words and activities beyond words is to enable the patient's predicament to unfold by experiencing both what he conveys by talk and what he conveys by projective identification, while at the same time preventing him from living out his defensive phantasies with the analyst and so using the analysis as a refuge from life instead of a process which leads him to a fuller resumption of his own life. His predicament will unfold as part of an alive analytical process that lessens the underlying anxiety which drives him to omnipotent defensive phantasies only if the analyst avoids becoming identified with his projections and enacting them — a task not always easy — and instead contains and expresses them in interpretations. Then like Mr B he may in stages — from a dissociated somatic event of a broken and mended bone, progress to felt anxiety about a symbolic equivalent, and then to dreaming and working his dream through with his analyst — develop awareness of what he is doing and why he needs to. This is psychic movement though not yet structural change. At this stage Mr B still needed mostly to 'join' with me. I think change only comes, as Mr E's material illustrates, with the active functioning of the patient's ego in working through in words. This is the mutative moment, even though one only among the many needed.

In conclusion briefly: Why do words have a special importance in working through? Above all, the use of language is an activity of the ego. A patient hears interpretations, sees his dreams, etc., but he stays a passive subject of the analysis *until his ego engages actively* — as it does when he uses his own language for thinking and communicating. And, secondly, words break omnipotence. In the omnipotent mind of the infant, an impulse is the experience of its fulfilment. Omnipotence is always hostile to verbalization because the moment a patient expresses himself in words he is restricting his omnipotence — words rest on a recognition of a gap between impulse and fulfilment, and an acknowledgement of the separateness of subject and object. (The connection between the recognition of separateness and the formation of symbols has been extensively explored by Segal 1957.) Thirdly, words have multi-faceted meanings uniquely suited — this is no surprise since they are formed for it — to psychic awareness. In a few brief sentences, a patient, as did Mr E, can link in depth, connecting the past with the present, the transference and his life, as he tells his analyst his understanding of himself.

Summary

The paper discusses communication — its modes and its changes — between analyst and patient, and, more particularly, within the patient himself in the course of a psychoanalysis. Clinical material from two cases illustrates how patients may need to communicate to the analyst both in words and also — in order to bring their less developed self — by more primitive modes, which can be understood and conceptualized by Melanie Klein's notion of projective identification. As the patient feels understood by the analyst's words (the mutative interpretations) he may slowly become more aware of his primitive modes of relating, until, ultimately, his method of communication changes and he is himself able to express his understanding of himself in his own words. This brings structural change and a resumption of ego development, and is a mutative moment. In brief: mutative interpretations are not by themselves the agency of change. They put the patient in a position to change. He himself must do the active, mutative working through in his own words.

References

Bion, W.R. (1962) *Learning from Experience*, London: Heinemann; reprinted in paperback, Maresfield Reprints, London: H. Karnac Books (1984).

Freud, S. (1914) 'Remembering, repeating and working through', SE 12.

Joseph, B. (1978) 'Different types of anxiety and their handling in the analytic situation', *International Journal of Psycho-Analysis*, 59: 223—8.

—— (1983) 'On understanding and not understanding: some technical issues', *International Journal of Psycho-Analysis*, 64: 291—8.

Klein, M. (1946) 'Notes on some schizoid mechanisms' in *Developments in Psycho-Analysis*, London: Hogarth Press (1952); also in *The Writings of Melanie Klein*, London: Hogarth Press (1975), vol. 3, 1—24.

Langs, R. (1976) *The Therapeutic Interaction* (2 vols), New York: Jason Aronson.

Matte-Blanco, I. (1975) *The Unconscious as Infinite Sets*, London: Duckworth.

Money-Kyrle, R.E. (1968) 'Cognitive development', *International Journal of*

Psycho-Analysis, 49: 691—8; also in *The Collected Papers of Robert Money-Kyrle*, (ed. D. Meltzer with the assistance of E. O'Shaughnessy), Strathtay, Perthshire: Clunie Press, 1978, 416—33.

Segal, H. (1957) 'Notes on symbol formation', *International Journal of Psycho-Analysis*, 38: 391—7; also in *The Work of Hanna Segal*, New York: Jason Aronson (1981), 48—65, reprinted in paperback London: Free Association Books (1986) and in *Melanie Klein Today: volume 1*, London: Routledge (1988).

Strachey, J. (1934) 'The nature of the therapeutic action of psycho-analysis', *International Journal of Psycho-Analysis*, 15: 127—59.

PART THREE

The analysis of children

Introduction

ELIZABETH BOTT SPILLIUS

Kleinian analysis began through the analysis of children, which is a major focus of Klein's writings; indeed it is *the* focus of her earlier writing. A brief historical account of the development and of the central ideas of Kleinian child analysis can be found in Brenman Pick and Segal's 'Melanie Klein's contribution to child analysis: theory and technique' (1978).

The analysis of children continued to be the main area of research and development through the 1920s, the 1930s, and the 1940s, though by the 1940s the impetus was diminishing as the analysis of psychotics became the prime area of development and research. Since the 1950s there has been a decline in the amount of five times a week psychoanalytic work with children, and, for a time too, with the exception of work by Meltzer, a decline in the amount of Kleinian writing about children and child analysis (Meltzer 1967, 1973, Meltzer, Bremner, Hoxter, Weddell and Wittenberg 1975). Since the mid-1970s there has been a renewal of interest in training in child analysis and alongside it an increased interest in the relation of work with children to work with adults.

Esther Bick's paper 'Child analysis today' (1962, reprinted here) notes the declining interest in child analysis, though her brief paper describes the rewards of it so vividly that she arouses more enthusiasm for undertaking it than understanding of its decline.

In spite of the decline in the volume of child analysis, the field has not been totally without innovation. One important development, not in child analysis but in a related field, has been Esther Bick's development of psychoanalytic observation of infants and mothers described in her paper 'Notes on infant observation in psychoanalytic training' (1964). As

155

the title indicates such observation was developed primarily to help students learn how to observe psychoanalytically, but it also provided a rich fund of data for use in seeing whether Kleinian theory is visibly consistent with the behaviour of babies and mothers. Infant observation has now become an accepted part of the training of students of adult as well as child analysis, not only in the British Psycho-Analytical Society but in many other psychoanalytic societies as well. Bick herself used her observations of infants and mothers not only to train students but also to provide information additional to that afforded by the analysis of children and adults in the development of her theory of the 'second skin' and 'adhesive identification'. (See Bick 1968, reprinted in Volume 1.)

Change in the technique of child analysis is another important development. There was a tendency for a considerable time for child analysts and child psychotherapists to focus mainly on that aspect of Klein's approach that concerns the elucidation of unconscious phantasy. In skilled hands this approach has an imaginative grasp that compels admiration, as expressed, for example, in Martha Harris's paper 'Depression and the depressive position in an adolescent boy' (1965 and reprinted here).

As in the case of the clinical papers described above in the section on technique, however, concentration on unconscious phantasy has sometimes led to routinized 'symbolic' interpretations that can be true of anyone's unconscious and miss out the particular child's nuances of expression. Klein's own mode of interpretation may have changed in this respect, for the way she used part-object language when she was analysing 'Richard' in 1941 seems to have been succeeded, by the time she wrote *Envy and Gratitude* in 1957, by a language of interpretation based first on the patient's present experience in the session with a less immediate use of symbolic interpretation (Klein 1961, 1957). By 1957 she was no longer working with children so that it is difficult to tell whether her technique with children would have changed in a similar manner. It is not something she drew attention to in her later notes on 'Richard's' analysis, but it is a development in technique that has proved important to some of her followers. Some Kleinian child analysts, notably O'Shaughnessy, Joseph, and Robin Anderson, are especially interested in exploring whether recent developments in technique with adults are also appropriate to work with children. Edna O'Shaughnessy's 1981 paper 'A commemorative essay on W.R. Bion's theory of thinking', reprinted here, gives a lucid exposition of the use of some of these later developments in the Kleinian approach, especially the technical implications of Bion's ideas on 'knowing' (K) being as fundamental as the instincts of love (L) and hate (H) for work with children.

In 'The invisible Oedipus complex' (printed here) O'Shaughnessy describes a similar theme in a child and in an adult patient, giving a vivid sense of the different ways in which the problem was expressed. She gives a particularly detailed sense, at once careful and imaginative, of the way her child patient used the analytic situation, including the physical environment of the consulting room, to disclose the object relationships he was seeking but also avoiding.

Terttu Folch's paper 'Communication and containing in child analysis: towards terminability' (1988a and reprinted here) describes how a child's capacity to face difficult internal and external situations is affected by the analyst's capacity for containment in the analysis. Comparing this and Folch's other papers on child analysis (1983, 1988b) with Martha Harris's paper written twenty years earlier one can see a change in the language of interpretation but the underlying conceptions are similar.

A considerable amount of other work with children is going on. O'Shaughnessy has described (1986) problems of melancholic identification that emerged in the brief analysis of a three-year-old boy. In work with a young child, Patricia Daniel has studied problems in a child's sexual development that may lay the basis for the development of a perversion (Daniel 1984, 1985). Sandra Piontelli is conducting research that correlates intra-uterine and post-uterine behaviour (1986a, 1987) and has recently suggested in an interesting but controversial paper that features which have emerged in the treatment of a very young psychotic child may have originated, at least in part, in intra-uterine and birth experience (Piontelli 1986b). Athol Hughes has discussed a child's use of the manic defence (Hughes 1988). Several other Kleinian analysts are working in the field of child analysis though without as yet having published their work on it.

Thus the volume of child analysis is increasing, so that this field is recovering at least something of the importance in theory and technique that it held in the days of Klein's early work.

1

Depression and the depressive position in an adolescent boy

MARTHA HARRIS

This paper was first published in 1965 in the *Journal of Child Psychotherapy*, 1, 3: 33—40.

Introduction

The clinical material in this paper will be centred around a dream, which was dreamt and reported by a boy of fifteen-and-a-half after some three-and-a-half years of analysis. In its context the dream, which was an important and vivid experience for him, typically conveys, I think, the picture of a patient struggling against those aspects of himself that perpetuate depression and inanition. He struggles to be able to face the conflict of ambivalence and the guilt it entails, and to maintain the depressive position, i.e. a state of integration, of responsibility for the conflicting emotions and parts of himself in relation to valued objects.

I am assuming that pathological depression ensues from an inability to face pain and to work through the depressive anxiety occasioned by some experience of loss or disappointment. This inability then leads to failure to rehabilitate the lost object or the object which has betrayed one, within the personality. In the course of treatment, early anxieties about loss and defences against experiencing these, come to be relived in the transference relationship at every break, and in the case of patients who are seen four or five times a week, at every weekend. The material which I would like to discuss in detail was stimulated by a forthcoming holiday.

First, however, I shall give a very brief account of Malcolm, although I do not propose to go into details of his history and of possible environmental factors in the aetiology of his depression. He is a highly intelligent boy with considerable artistic gifts, who has been able to use his intellect and talents fairly well. He was referred for analysis by unusually perceptive parents because of recurrent bronchial and catarrhal colds, behaviour that was a little too good, and a certain flatness of affect that convinced them he was not able to enjoy life as fully as he should have done.

In his analysis, he was from the start reliable and meticulously co-operative. He appeared to be appreciative and he provided interesting material, though somehow never so interesting in actuality as it could have been. We came to realize that his associations were less spontaneous and less responsive to my interpretations than they seemed to be, that they were carefully edited and controlled, or appreciated by him as much more important than anything I could say about them. They were regarded as works of art to which I made little contribution. I was necessary to him as a repository for his worries, a place in which to examine and to sort out his own thoughts. His analysis was seldom appreciated at the time, although he took away and made use of my interpretations in later sessions to understand himself — they were all grist to his mill.

He gradually became more aware that he was missing something, in his analysis and in life generally. He felt that his parents were able and willing to offer him more than he was able to accept. Of his mother he said he had always known that she was a good mother, but somehow not for him, something always stood between them. He watched his young brother's friendly confiding relationship with her and envied its spontaneity. He became more aware of his own subliminal depression as it began to thaw, as the world outside his narcissistic preoccupations was a warmer and more exciting place. As in the analysis I became more of a person and less of a repository, he began to feel badly about his boringness, his lack of generosity in giving himself. He said he now realized what a help analysis could be if he could only learn how to keep contact with me. When a more enjoyable working/feeding relationship with me had been established, it was soon again attacked and destroyed in order to avoid Oedipal jealousy, which was stimulated by any signs of my private life or other professional commitments, and recurrently by breaks in the analysis. In earlier stages, his adolescent self had usually managed to split off any experience of infantile jealousy of the parental intercourse by maintaining that his parents, like myself, were now passé and dull, whereas all the glamour of life was before him. As he became more aware of, and therefore more able to contain, his infantile jealousy and attacks upon me as the parental couple, his psychosomatic symptoms, resulting from the intrusion of objects attacked and damaged by his projections, diminished. He became worried at realizing his dependence on the analysis. As he was learning more, he became afraid that if he had to stop, all the benefit he had received would disappear. At weekends he became depressed and resentful about this reluctant dependence, as he

159

once put it, feeling that he was so small and I was so important. His infantile resentment which when projected, created paranoid fear of me as a self-important father who kept mother and her breasts for himself, recurrently interfered with a learning/feeding relationship with me as the mother in the sessions.

After some months of working on this, he became much more confident that he was able to keep inside himself as a permanent possession what he had learned about himself from analysis. He thought he should stop shortly. He felt badly about being such an expense to his parents; also, no doubt, I had other patients waiting for me.

A little investigation revealed the unconscious hypocrisy in this apparently reparative urge, deflected as it was from the object to which it should primarily have been directed, from myself as the analyst, the breast that had fed him, to whom gratitude and reparation were due. His improvement was seized upon by an omnipotent part of himself which wanted to make off with it to enjoy it on its own.

The dream gives us some information about this part of himself. He dreamed it shortly before a holiday which he was facing with mixed feelings. He was depressed about the break from analysis, but he also wanted to use it as an occasion to test out his progress, to see whether he could engage upon some fruitful enterprise with his friends. He said he was aware that his parents were allowing him freedom. They were not insisting that he should go with them and do what they did, but inwardly he did not feel free to choose.

He came to the Thursday session saying that he had had a vivid dream the night before. It remained as a bad taste in his mouth but he hesitated to tell me in case he was just trying to get rid of it all. It was a long dream.

Dream

He was going to a farm with Rhoda to buy a barn or a building. The farm belonged to a man who was terribly hard-up, and rather horrible, perhaps a madman. This man told them about a scheme he had for getting more money to make his fortune. This was to do with injecting stuff into girls to give them bigger busts, and he was anxious to know how he could advertise this. He asked Malcolm if any of the girls he went out with would be interested in the idea. Malcolm was going to say that all the girls he knew were well-developed. He thought that the idea was disgusting and unsafe, and he told the man that the hormone pills which were used for this were unsafe, so his idea must be even more dangerous. Rhoda was very taken aback by the man and withdrew.

Malcolm went with her to protect her. The man suddenly became wild and rushed down his little hill shouting 'Everything that I can see is mine!' Malcolm thought this terribly pathetic, he had so little, just a measly few fields and a small little hill. He went away with Rhoda leaving him to his poverty. Later on, however, the man followed them to town with a cartload of old coats to sell.

Rhoda is a young married friend of his mother's and of the family in general, who was expecting a baby and looking for a house. She had frequently appeared in the analysis as a somewhat idealized version of his mother and myself, but a really good person, the kind of girl whom he would like to marry.

Malcolm's first association to this dream was that the crazy man was distinct and familiar, he could not say just who he was like. As he elaborated his description, it was clearly that of Malcolm himself, but with a sallow jaundiced complexion. He described the few fields in the dream as somewhat sickly looking too, muddy and waterlogged. The little hill on which the man was sitting was muddy too.

I suggested to him that his initial hesitation in telling me the dream was due to anxiety lest it came from the crazy man, the mad part of himself which maintained that by injecting me with its flatus it was thereby filling my breasts. By blowing it all into me he would get rid of the bad taste in his mouth caused by awareness of this crazy part and the food it poisoned. He said that in the dream he had enormously resented this man's implications that girls needed to have their breasts made bigger; they were all right as they were. Agreeing to my interpretation that this man was a part of himself, Malcolm said that he seemed to be timeless, to have no regard for time, as if this were some aspect of himself that had been with him always and would never change.

Malcolm himself in the dream had felt that the things this man was satisfied with, that he called 'all mine', were so basically bad because they were puffed up to be more than they were. It seemed absurd that he was not repairing his barn and cultivating his fields which were really a potential source of wealth, instead of indulging in this crazy scheme of expanding breasts. There was such a distinct division between the crazy man and himself with his friend that he felt it was no wonder the man was so furious and susceptible to being got rid of, because he must feel so isolated, although when he ran down the hill he seemed to be going to a wife in the valley. She was not an active person or helpful but someone just like himself and content to do as he did. Malcolm himself, the 'I' in the dream as he said, knew the difference between good and bad but he was too weak to do anything about it; he did not know how to talk to the crazy man who did have the power and the ability to improve his poverty if he could only see it for what it was. There was no one to tell him; his wife was as blind as he was.

This madman is the most complete delineation we have had in the analysis so far of a homosexual part of himself that attempts to acquire power and wealth by omnipotently entering and controlling the breasts with his own flatus and using them as sexually enticing objects. It operates in his relations with girls, where the girls are sometimes evaluated as desirable in so far as they increase his status with other boys. Similarly in his analysis, he has in the past often collected sessions and interpretations to puff up secretly into works of his own designing in order to enlarge his self-importance. Malcolm indicates that it is madness to use the breasts thus, as masturbatory objects into which to enter to void his sexual envy and jealousy thereby making them unpalatable to a saner baby part of himself which needs to feed from them and to develop, to really learn from his analysis. This baby part is represented in the dream by the pregnancy of Rhoda, the mother whom he protects from the dangerous seducer. It is his omnipotent infantile masturbatory self which has a wife in the bottom of the valley, which seeks comfort from its own bottom when frustrated. Thus in his analysis he has often sat upon my interpretations, made them his own, playing with them and cogitating upon them privately, while withholding from me his spontaneous reactions, which could have enabled me to feed him with subtler understanding.

This masturbatory part is without insight and difficult to talk to because it is cut off from the Malcolm who knows the difference between good and bad. It becomes wild when it feels rejected and isolated but he cannot finally get rid of it. It follows him with a cartload of old coats, the worn-out objects that have been used to clothe its projections, the recipients of its masturbation, and with which it persists in trying to eke out a living for itself. It is nevertheless a part of himself which has strength and potential real wealth if the strength can be employed in reparation, in rebuilding the barns and planting the fields. Malcolm said that he knew in the dream that the barn and buildings had to be restored first before the fields could be dug and planted; that is, that the internal containing breast mother, who has been damaged by masturbation, must be restored before he has a secure basis for genital potency. But the problem is to bring the Malcolm with insight into contact with the real strength which is obscured by the omnipotence. In his analysis reparation can be consolidated and omnipotence diminished by acknowledgement of what he does learn from me and by recognition that it is harmful and unnecessary to blow it up into something bigger than life.

When the dream had been interpreted in these terms, Malcolm said that on further thought when the madman said 'All that I can see is mine' he was really implying that his possessions were restricted by his vision. If he could only see more he could have more. This reminded him of the previous weekend, when at a party he had a long talk with a friend's father who is a great opponent of psychoanalysis. Malcolm had been telling this man how much he himself had benefited from analysis. He thought that he was making quite an impression on him, but later he was terribly hurt to overhear him passing derogatory remarks both about himself and about psychoanalysis. He now realized that he must have been behaving in a subtly superior way, like the man on his little hill, smug about himself and his possessions, without realizing how much he was antagonizing his friend's father. He thought it must be this disguised superiority that prevents him at times from getting on easily with people, rather than shyness. He agreed to my suggestion that this was a way of invoking envy in others, by flaunting his possession of esoteric knowledge, or symbolically, the idealized analytic breast which he had appropriated in order to avoid experiencing envy in himself at having to leave it behind with me at the weekend, for me to share with my party, my husband and children.

Some time later in the session he said that the ramshackle buildings on the farm had not in fact been sordid, that they were lighter and warmer inside than outside. He had noticed this when he stood inside them at one point. I took this as yet another indication — we had had many others before this — that he felt there were reserves of warmth and understanding inside himself, a lifegiving breast at the core of his being, which could not yet be fully utilized because his omnipotent self-importance was impeding the work of reparation.

Discussion

This brief but richly condensed material of Malcolm's throws some light on the forces that cause and perpetuate his depression. He had said he knew his mother was a good mother but something came between them, i.e. he realized he had a good object although he could not always reach it. He saw that his young brother could appreciate his mother. He knew from the occasions when the appreciative baby part of himself was able to accept the understanding I could offer him that there was a good analytic breast available when it could be approached in the right way. The madman in the dream is the destructive part of himself which threatens his good object — Rhoda representing the mother — the baby part of himself that needs to be fed from an uncontaminated breast.

163

This madman can also be seen as a father who holds domain over mother, who spoils the breast for Malcolm by injecting poisonous sexuality, and who is a threat to the maturer protecting relationship which he tries to have with women. The madman is not the real father whom Malcolm currently experiences as encouraging him to enjoy his friends and to have a life of his own and whom he now visualizes as having an interesting and worthwhile relationship with his mother. It is a lofty archaic superego figure, formed from his own projections, in alliance with his id (the wife in the valley) and equally out of touch with his ego.

Malcolm himself, his ego, is in between. He tries in the dream to recover something from this possessive crushing superego, but is defeated. On former occasions when for instance I seemed so big to him and he so small, this superego had been projected into me in the transference, had made him feel persecuted by me so that he had to go away, to retreat from contact. In this session he was, however, able to ally himself with me as a support to his ego and to acknowledge the crazy superego as part of himself. He was also able to link it with his superior behaviour, an idealizing and possessive way of using the analysis, which does disservice both to himself and to his good object, apparently puffing it up to be so marvellous, but in fact sitting on it as the man does on his muddy little hill, the pot full of faeces.

On the other hand, we have seen that this superego controls potentially valuable objects — Malcolm goes to the farmer to buy a barn, and this barn though ramshackle has light and warmth inside. He needs the co-operation of the farmer, this controlling paternal superego, to recover good life-giving parts of himself which through projection remain unavailable to him, in order to have a rehabilitated internal object as a basis for developing, making a happy marriage and a home for himself and his future family. (Rhoda, if you remember, was looking for a house.) His ego needs to recover the power of the aggression which is encapsulated in the superego, reintrojected there after it has been split off and projected into the father's penis. Without that power he remains relatively impotent though not entirely, because he does protect Rhoda. His superego, deprived of insight, is grandiose, restrictive, and liable to degenerate into a blind expression of id impulses — the rushing downhill. (The games field had hitherto provided for him one of the few constructive channels for the expression of this violent instinctual force. This was, however, to a large extent an expression of a split off part of himself, rather than an insightful experience of this part of his nature. The fear of this force caused inhibition in other spheres, as for example in his relationship with girls.)

I would suggest that it is the crushing weight of this blind omnipotent superior superego which is causing the weakening, the depressing, and the general impoverishment of his personality. Formed by the projection into the father's penis of an envious omnipotent part of himself which is felt to be threatening to his primary good object, the breast mother, it thereby creates for him an internal mother who is constantly menaced by a bad intercourse. In identification with the oppressed and denigrated internal mother, the passive wife in the valley, he is depressed and impotent; he is also depressed about his inability to make full use of himself, of his potential strength which becomes unavailable through projection and encapsulation within this superior paternal part of himself. In the dream, however, and in the working through of the dream, Malcolm is making an effort to integrate this destructive and powerful figure as a part of himself, although he does not like to swallow it, it leaves a bad taste in his mouth. In trying to take responsibility for it and for the harm it has caused and to use it in the service of repairing his good objects, to further the analysis, he is attempting to use depressive anxieties in a creative way. He attempts to maintain and work through the depressive position as fully as possible. That this must be a gradual process one can see from Malcolm's statement that this mad part is timeless, has always been with him, and from his fear that it will never change.

There were in his earlier history certain situations of actual deprivation and loss, which were, however, well within the ordinary range of children's experiences. His family circumstances and relationships are more than averagely good, and to a great extent he has been able to benefit from them and to develop on favourable lines, as he has always been able to benefit from his analysis to a certain degree. He cannot, however, fully realize the richness of his personality and of his creative capacity until he is able to consolidate insight into this mad and destructive part of himself, and the devious ways in which it expresses itself, how it interferes with good relationships with people outside and with his internal objects. By this interference it recurrently brings about experience of loss.

Malcolm may be right that there is an unalterable core to this aspect of himself. If, however, he can accept this as belonging to himself — remember that the man in the dream became so wild because he was so isolated — if his saner self can learn how to talk to his mad part, to direct it better, to limit its distortion of good objects, then he will have a lesser load of unconscious guilt to carry, be less identified with destroyed objects, and therefore less incapacitated by depression.

Conclusion

In conclusion, a few comments on some of the features which have been mentioned by a number of psychoanalytical writers on depression (Abraham 1911, 1924; Rosenfeld 1959).

Malcolm shows impoverishment of the ego due to the introjection of and identification with a denigrated object (Freud 1917) as a result of the overemployment of the mechanism described by Melanie Klein (1946) as projective identification. She uses this term to describe a process whereby parts of the self are split off and projected into objects which become identified with the projected self. The denigrated object is thus created by the projection of destructive and spoiling parts of the self.

Malcolm also shows marked idealization, which derives from a narcissistic overvaluation of his own products, but this narcissistic aspect exists in him alongside a more normal object-oriented self (Rosenfeld 1964). There is in him awareness not only of idealization with concomitant anxiety about the persecution which is being defended against, but of a really good object and good parts of the self which are not fully repaired and maintained because of his ambivalent attitude to them.

The feeling of superiority, which together with that of inferiority, Abraham noted as characteristic of melancholics, is clearly illustrated in Malcolm's dream. This derives from the severe superego mentioned by so many analysts from Freud onwards. We can see how in Malcolm, under the meticulous superego that kept him up to the mark, underlies the early archaic superego formed from the projection of primitive destructive emotions and parts of the self (Klein 1933). In Malcolm's case where the depression manifested itself as a dampening of affect rather than as a flagrant illness, there were no signs of a particular precipitating factor. His depression was perpetuated rather by the omnipotent possessive part of himself which could not face the envy entailed in feeling dependent on a good object and allowing it to keep its integrity. Through resorting to its own self-created idealized objects and self-image, this narcissistic part of himself made him recurrently lose contact with good objects, both external and internal.

References

Abraham, K. (1911) 'Notes on the psycho-analytic investigation and treatment of manic-depressive insanity and allied conditions', *Selected Papers on Psycho-Analysis*, translated by Douglas Bryan and Alix Strachey, London: Hogarth Press (1942), 137–56.

—— (1924) 'A short study of the development of the libido', *Selected*

Papers on Psycho-Analysis, London: Hogarth Press, 418—501.

Freud, S. (1917) 'Mourning and melancholia', SE 14, London: Hogarth Press.

Klein, M. (1933) 'The early development of conscience in the child' in *The Writings of Melanie Klein*, vol. 1, *Love, Guilt and Reparation*, London: Hogarth Press (1976), 248—57.

—— (1935) 'A contribution to the psychogenesis of manic depressive states' in *The Writings of Melanie Klein*, vol. 1, 262—89.

—— (1946) 'Notes on some schizoid mechanisms' in *Developments in Psycho-Analysis*, London: Hogarth Press (1952) also in *The Writings of Melanie Klein*, London: Hogarth Press (1975), vol. 3, 1—24.

Rosenfeld, H. (1959) 'An investigation into the psycho-analytic theory of depression', *International Journal of Psycho-Analysis*, 40: 105—29.

—— (1964) 'On the psychopathology of narcissism: a clinical approach', *International Journal of Psycho-Analysis*, 45: 332—7; also in *Psychotic States*, London: Hogarth Press (1965), 169—79.

2

Child analysis today

ESTHER BICK

This paper was first read at the 22nd International Psycho-Analytical Congress in Edinburgh, in 1961, and was published in 1962 in the *International Journal of Psycho-Analysis*, 43: 328–32.

This Symposium is in the nature of an historical event — it is the first symposium on child analysis at an International Congress of Psycho-Analysis. In May 1927, such a symposium was held before the British Psycho-Analytical Society. On that occasion Melanie Klein contrasted the development of child analysis with that of adult analysis, discussing the striking fact that although child analysis had a history of about eighteen years, its fundamental principles had not yet been clearly enunciated, whereas, after a similar period in the history of adult analysis, the basic principles had been laid down, empirically tested, and the fundamental principles of technique firmly established. She went on to discuss why the analysis of children had been so much less fortunate in its development.

I am well aware that progress has been made during the last thirty-four years, both in actual child analysis and in its allied fields, such as in child guidance clinics, progress which has been deeply and variously influenced by the work of Melanie Klein and Anna Freud. To give examples, the range of children who are felt to be suitable for treatment has been extended: play technique is now in general use, though often in a modified form; the importance of interpretations has been widely accepted, and there is a greater recognition of the psychoanalytic approach in the training of child psychotherapists and child psychiatrists.

However, if we examine the position of child analysis in relation to the whole field of psychoanalysis, we see what a small place it occupies, in terms of practice of child analysis, of training, of scientific discussions and publications. Very few people trained in adult analysis go on to train as child analysts, and very few institutes of psychoanalysis are able to offer systematic training in child analysis, the British Society of Psycho-

Analysis being the only one, I believe, to give an actual qualification. Even this training is recognized to be inadequate. Contributions from child analysts to scientific discussions are numerically very low — for example, less than 5 per cent of the papers at International Congresses are on child cases.

This neglect of child analysis is the more striking when we consider the vital interest of analysts in the psychology of children as a source of understanding of emotional development and our concern about the prophylactic aspects of child analysis. The position of psychoanalysis in the community must also to a great extent depend on its offering help to children and its understanding of their emotional problems.

There must, therefore, be specific difficulties interfering with the development of child analysis which do not apply to the same extent to adult analysis. In this paper I shall attempt to contribute to the understanding of this problem. In order to do so, I shall discuss some of the differences between analysing adults and analysing children, from the point of view both of the student and of the practising analyst. I shall discuss the stresses and gratifications, both external and internal.

First, to consider some of the external stresses: the student who is embarking on child analysis may be restricted owing to commitments related to his training in adult analysis, both financially and with regard to the times he has available, which may not suit the child's parents. There is also the difficulty for the student that the ordinary parent will only undertake to bring the child five times a week over a period of years if the child is severely ill, and such cases are not suitable for the beginner in child analysis.

An analyst wanting to restrict himself to child analysis would find it unrewarding financially. Certain aspects of child analysis, such as keeping in contact with the parents and caring for the play room, can be very time-consuming. These are real difficulties, but they can be used as rationalizations to cover up the emotional problems of studying and practising child analysis.

Before discussing the emotional stresses, however, it is important to remember the pleasures and gratifications arising out of child analysis, such as the unique opportunity for intimate contact with primitive layers of the child's unconscious mind; the sense of privilege in being entrusted by the parents with their child; the awareness that one is dealing with a human being who has almost all his life ahead of him and who is still in the early stages of developing his potentialities.

I want now to turn to the internal stresses, and shall divide these into two categories: first, those which are in the nature of pre-formed anxieties related to the treatment of children as such, and second, the specific counter-transference problems. In the first category there are the student's general anxieties about his ability to communicate with children, especially if he has had little or no previous experience with young children. There are also the anxieties about taking responsibility. These are much greater with children than with adults, not only because it is a dual responsibility — to the child as well as to his parents — but also because the less mature the patient's ego, the greater is the responsibility resting on the analyst.

The student has to be clear about what his responsibility is in analysing the child, although this may clash with what he feels the parents really want of him. Here belongs, for example, the responsibility of analysing such problems as the child's hostility and his sexual wishes towards the parents. This may provoke anxiety in the student concerning his relation with the parents. Closely associated with this is the question of setting independently, on the basis of one's clinical judgement, aims for the analysis, as distinct from aiming to cure the presenting symptoms for which the child was originally brought for treatment. There are also anxieties related to becoming excessively attached to, or hurtful to, the child. The former anxiety may lead to greater strictness, to a type of behaviour which interferes with the unfolding of the positive transference. The latter anxiety may lead to reassurance, to a denial of the child's hostile feelings and persecutory anxiety, or to such behaviour as appealing to the child's reason — suggesting that the analyst has been unable to accept painful analytical responsibility and has assumed the role of parent substitute.

Such anxieties, related to the painful aspects of responsibility, may be kept within bounds and often diminished through the help of a supervisor who shares the responsibility. But if they are too severe, they can impose such grave limitations on therapeutic effectiveness that supervision can be of little or no help and only further analysis can enable the student to overcome the inhibiting unconscious conflicts. Such anxieties approximate to those of the second category, the stresses arising out of counter-transference phenomena.

As Freud stated in 1910: 'We have become aware of the counter-transference, which arises in him [the physician] as a result of the patient's influence on his unconscious feelings ... We have noticed that no psycho-analyst goes further than his own complexes and internal resistances permit.' I have suggested that the counter-transference stresses on the child analyst are more severe than those on the analyst of adults, at any rate of non-psychotic adults. This is due, I think, to two specific factors: first, the unconscious conflicts which arise in relation to the child's parents; and second, the nature of the child's material.

With regard to the first factor, the child analyst has the constant problem of his unconscious identifications. He may identify with the child against the parents, or with the parents against the child, or with a protective parental attitude towards the child. These conflicts often lead to a persecutory and guilty attitude towards the parents, making the analyst over-critical of them and over-dependent on their approval. In addition, there is the student's difficulty in understanding the twofold nature of the child's relationship to his parents: his normal and healthy dependence on them, relative to his age, and the infantile elements in the relationship, due to his internal difficulties. The more this is recognized and accepted by the student, the more the infantile parts of the child can come into the transference, with a resulting improvement in his relationship to his parents, even in the early months of analysis. The student can then foresee and be prepared for the risk that the parents will lose sight of the child's illness and want to stop treatment, and for an intensification of difficulties at home during analytic holidays.

I cannot go into the many vicissitudes of the analyst's difficulties in his relationship with the parents. It is an integral part of his work, intricate and delicate to handle, needing flexibility and considerable confidence in child analysis in general and one's own work in particular. If one can take these things for granted, the relationship with many parents can become an added source of gratification.

The second specific factor in child analysis concerns the strain imposed on the mental apparatus of the analyst, both by the content of the child's material and its mode of expression. The intensity of the child's dependence, of his positive and negative transference, the primitive nature of his phantasies, tend to arouse the analyst's own unconscious anxieties. The violent and concrete projections of the child into the analyst may be difficult to contain. Also the child's suffering tends to evoke the analyst's parental feelings, which have to be controlled so that the proper analytic role can be maintained. All these problems tend to obscure the analyst's understanding and to increase in turn his anxiety and guilt about his work.

Moreover, the child's material may be more difficult to understand than the adult's, since it is more primitive in its sources as well as in its mode of expression, and requires a deeper knowledge of the primitive levels of the unconscious. One may have to sit with children for a long time completely in the dark about what is going on, until suddenly something comes up from the depth that illuminates it, and one interprets without always being able to see how one reached that conclusion. It imposes on the child analyst a greater dependence on his unconscious to provide him with clues to the meaning of the child's play and non-verbal communications.

I will bring two clinical examples to illustrate some of the points I have made. The first concerns a case of my own, the second, one of an analyst supervised by me. I am giving an instance from a first session of a nine-year-old boy, referred on account of bedwetting, shyness, and clinging to his mother. He came into the treatment room with me and stood twisting his cap and blushing. I pointed out that he might feel awkward because he might not know what we were going to do here. There was no response. I showed him his box with play material and said that was for his use in the sessions. He made no movement but stood there as if dazed. I said that he had been told that he would be coming to see me five times a week, and that I would try to help him with his worries; but it seemed to me that he expected something quite different which he was not able to tell me or might not even know himself. He continued his silence and immobility, but looked tense and troubled. Then he glanced towards the paper on the table. I said that he indicated he would find it easier to tell me something on paper than to talk. He nodded, sat down, and drew a hut on the mountains, a path, and a tree. When I asked him about this, he told me that it was about a young man who lived alone in a log cabin in the mountains. He had a deer who kept him company. One night a man came and stole the deer. When the young man woke in the morning, he could not find the deer. He went out of the cabin and saw the tracks of a man and of his deer in the snow. He followed the tracks. He was afraid that the man might kill him, but he went on. He told me this story in a solemn, dull way. I said that there was a Christmas tree in the drawing, and that in this way he was telling me one of the things he expected from me: that I should be like Father Christmas who would make everything wonderful, and that perhaps he had waited for the analysis as he had waited for Father Christmas as a small boy. He smiled, his whole face lit up, and he said: 'Fancy you should say that! This morning a boy at school asked me if a fairy told me I could have three wishes what would I want.'

I interpreted that we could now understand why he could not speak at the beginning of the session. On the one hand he hoped that he would find in me a fairy capable of fulfilling all his wishes in a magic way; at the same time he was afraid that I might be a witch who would cast a spell on him and immobilize him; it seemed that he had felt this when he could neither move nor speak at the beginning of the session. In the story there were two male figures; one was Father Christmas, and the other the man who stole his deer and might kill him. So as with the fairy and the witch he also hoped that I might be a father who, like Father Christmas, would give him what he wanted most — to keep his deer forever. But he was also afraid that I might be like the man who would steal it from him. Such were his hopes and fears before he came, and when he met me, he did not know which of the figures I was. Although he was very frightened, he came with me into the room, perhaps thinking that if he did what I wanted, I would not harm him; and also because he so much wanted help in tracking down his worries and becoming cured.

He said, 'Yes, I didn't tell the boy that my wish would be to be cured from bedwetting. I can't do anything, I can't go camping with the Scouts. I can't stop it.' We then went on to the other important meanings of the deer.

What can be seen in this boy, as in many other young patients, is that, together with the hope of finding a solution to his internal problems, there is also a deep pessimism about being understood by the adult world. This can be seen clearly in the boy's excitement when he exclaimed, 'Fancy you should say that!'

My second example is taken from the first session of a three-year-old girl. She followed the analyst stiffly but easily into the play room. He told her that the toys on the table and in the drawer were for her to play with. She looked into the drawer, took out a toy sheep, sat down and began to handle the pencil. The analyst asked whether it was a mummy, a daddy, or a baby sheep; but this made her increasingly withdrawn. She began to rock and suck a sweet she had in her mouth. The analyst interpreted her feeling of being alone and frightened and her wish to be with her Mummy, and linked it with her feeling at night and a wish to snuggle up and have her bottle with Mummy. Her head dropped, there was some play with her fingers of the 'little piggy' type. The analyst indicated to her her wish for Mummy's soft breast to sleep on. Her head drooped and hit the table. The analyst put a pillow there. Her head drooped backwards, and he put the pillow behind her; but she systematically avoided it. He interpreted that the pillow was unable to replace Mummy's breast, and her similar discomfort and dissatisfaction with the analyst. There was some rubbing of eyes, scratching of the face, and picking of the nose. The analyst interpreted her disappointment in having a man as an analyst and suggested she had hoped to have a woman, like her brother who was also in analysis. He also indicated it was about time to stop. She gave the sheep back to him, looked at him, and seemed in fair contact with him before leaving. In the following session there was a marked change in the nature of the contact with the analyst. She produced rich detailed material in which her anxieties about the transference to him as the brother came to the fore.

We see in the opening session with the little girl how what seemed to be very sparse material became richer and more detailed following interpretations; whereas in the case of the older boy, material rich in detail but impoverished of emotion became flooded with feeling and contact through interpretation. In both cases the interpretations were based initially on the analyst's intuitive response to the situation growing out of the pre-verbal projective process from the child's unconscious into the analyst. In the case of the little girl, the sleeping and the near falling had the effect of projecting into the analyst considerable anxiety for her safety, which he actually dealt with by providing her with a real pillow. Her systematic avoidance of the pillow increased his feeling of hopelessness to protect her. These two projections worked together: 'I cannot help this child; in fact I will damage her because I have not got the right kind of pillow.' It was not until the interpretation of her disappointment in the analyst as a man, without real breasts, that she came into contact with the analyst on leaving and produced the enriched material of the next day, expressing her anxiety of repeating with the analyst her sexual involvement with her brother.

In the case of the boy, he conveyed from the beginning his distress through his non-verbal behaviour. The analyst's anxiety led her to give explanations about the analytic procedure. In this situation, these were tantamount to reassurance and therefore made no contact with the child. Following his glance, the analyst invited him to draw. The picture and the story were produced flatly, lifelessly, although the story in itself seemed vital and filled with anxiety. The analyst felt that the hopelessness which he projected into her, both at the beginning of the session and through his lifeless dull way of telling the story, came from a more primitive level than the Oedipal material. She reacted to the Christmas tree as representing a far deeper process of splitting his objects into ideally good and dreadfully persecuting ones, with their magic powers for good or evil. She was able to make contact with his primitive internal world of witches and fairies, and in this way to reach the split-off affects of hope for an omnipotent good object.

Thus with both children, following leads from the depths arising from the taking in of projected distress, the analysts were able to interpret into the deeper strata. In the case of the little girl, with regard to her expectations of a real breast to sleep on and suck; in the case of the boy, the hope for an omnipotent fairy to protect him against persecutors.

In addition to the ability to deal with the kind of material that the child spontaneously produces and to bear his concrete projections, there is the difficulty of allowing the child to experience pain without intruding in a non-analytic way. The strain in bearing the child's suffering is greater than with adults, not only because of the child's weaker ego, but because of his appeal to one's parental feelings. This is painful when the child is persecuted or crying, but particularly so when he is trying to be good and repair, but cannot manage it because of internal conflicts. A little girl broke most of the toy figures following the first holiday in the analysis. After some working through of her holiday feelings, she decided to mend the mother figure of which she had broken the head and an arm. She managed with difficulty to stick on the head with Plasticine, but was very clumsy in fixing the arm. It kept falling off. She was very distressed, but persevered for a long time. Eventually she said, pointing to the figure, 'She is tired', and gave up. In such a situation the child analyst may find great difficulty in resisting the mute appeal of the child for direct help.

My comments on the internal stresses of the child analyst can perhaps be best summarized by a quotation from Gitelson's paper 'The emotional position of the analyst in the psychoanalytic situation' (1949). After quoting Freud's original definition of transference, he goes on to say: 'If the transference is to be a truly irrational recapitulation of childhood relationships subject to psychoanalytic interpretation, then nothing in the current reality must intervene to give it concurrent validity. These are still the guiding principles of classical psychoanalytic technique.' This quotation refers to adult analysis. Klein was guided by the same principle of classical psychoanalytic technique in her work with children. She showed that in order to do this the child analyst has to provide an analytic setting, both external and within himself, to enable the child to re-experience the irrational infantile and childhood relationships. I have tried to show that it is easier to accept the external setting which Klein evolved in her play technique than to accept and tolerate the stress produced by adhering to the fundamental psychoanalytic attitude in work with child patients.

The student of child analysis is thus exposed to great anxieties. It is, therefore, important that he should do the child training while he is himself in analysis; and, indeed, the working over of these anxieties will help to deepen his analysis. I have found that analysis of children brings a greater conviction to the student about the reality of unconscious phantasy than his work with adults. To see this concretely presented in the child's play and in his spontaneous communications, and to see the immediacy of relief from, or change in the nature of, anxiety following prompt interpretations, constitutes in itself an unending source of wonder and delight to many child analysts.

In conclusion, the aim of this paper is to draw attention to the grave neglect of child analysis. I have singled out two factors responsible for its slow development: the external stresses associated with financial and time difficulties, constantly exacerbated by the lack of adequate training, and the manifold internal stresses which are an integral part of the nature of child analysis. I have also indicated the gratifications inherent in analysing children and have stressed the importance of further developing this work, both in terms of its value to psychoanalytic understanding in general and in its contribution to the community.

References

Freud, S. (1910) 'The future prospects of psycho-analytic therapy', SE 11.

Gitelson, M. (1949) 'The emotional position of the analyst in the psycho-analytic situation', *International Journal of Psycho-Analysis*, 33: 328—32.

Klein, M. (1927) 'Symposium on child analysis' in *Contributions to Psycho-Analysis 1921–1945*, London: Hogarth Press (1948) and in *The Writings of Melanie Klein*, vol. 1, London: Hogarth Press (1975), 139—69.

—— (1932) *The Psycho-Analysis of Children*, London: Hogarth Press and in *The Writings of Melanie Klein*, vol. 2, London: Hogarth Press (1975).

3

W.R. Bion's theory of thinking and new techniques in child analysis

EDNA O'SHAUGHNESSY

This paper was first published in 1981 in the *Journal of Child Psychotherapy*, 7, 2: 181—9, under the title 'A commemorative essay on W.R. Bion's theory on thinking'.

When W.R. Bion died in 1979 his own work, in his lifetime, had changed psychoanalysis. He made clinical discoveries which led him to formulate new concepts and original theories over a wide spectrum of fundamental psychoanalytic problems. Because of its close connection to new ways of working with patients, I have chosen as the topic of this commemorative essay Bion's work on *thinking*.

Bion formulated a theory of the origins of thinking. He posited an early first form of thinking, different from, but the basis for the development of, later forms. The first form of thinking strives to know psychic qualities, and is the outcome of early emotional events between a mother and her infant which are decisive for the establishment — or not — of the capacity to think in the infant. Bion's theory, which carries the interesting implication that knowledge of the psychological precedes knowledge of the physical world, represents a new understanding of thinking as one of the fundamental links between human beings, a link which is fundamental also for the forming and functioning of a normal mind. Throughout, Bion connected his work on thinking to analytic technique and so made possible clinical advances with patients of all ages.

It is not easy to convey the rare originality of Bion's thought. He expressed himself in austere propositions with a high yield of exact meaning. They repay the reader's repeated return, as, for diversion, do his occasional and lastingly funny jokes. My plan is first to summarize some of the main aspects of his work on thinking and then give clinical illustrations of its use in child analysis.

What does Bion mean by 'thinking'? He does not mean some abstract mental process. His concern is with thinking as a human link — the endeavour to understand, comprehend the reality of, get insight into the nature of, etc., oneself or another. Thinking is an emotional experience of trying to know oneself or someone else. Bion designates this fundamental type of thinking — thinking in the sense of trying to know — by the symbol K. If xKy, then 'x is in the state of getting to know y and y is in a state of getting to be known by x'.

Bion's work on thinking began in a series of brilliant clinical papers delivered and published in the 1950s (Bion 1954, 1955, 1956, 1957, 1958a, 1958b, 1959). These papers record his investigations of thought disorders in psychotic patients who illuminated for him the nature of normal and abnormal thinking. In 1962 he formulated these discoveries theoretically in a paper called 'A theory of thinking' and published his book *Learning from Experience*, in which he developed his ideas further, expounding them in terms of the symbol K. He never tired of acknowledging his debt both to Freud and to Melanie Klein, particularly to Freud's 'Formulations on the two principles of mental functioning' (1911) and to Melanie Klein's theory of early object relations and anxieties, and her concept of projective identification. Bion developed their ideas and also combined them in a new way which formed then the foundation for his own discoveries.

In 'Formulations on the two principles of mental functioning' Freud described the aim of the pleasure principle as the avoidance and discharge of unpleasurable tensions and stimuli (Freud 1911). In 'Notes on some schizoid mechanisms' (1946) Melanie Klein described something similar to the pleasure principle from a different perspective — an early mechanism of defence which she named projective identification. In her view the young infant defends his ego from intolerable anxiety by splitting off and projecting unwanted impulses, feelings, etc., into his object. This is an object relations perspective on the discharge of unpleasurable tensions and stimuli. In the course of exploring the nature of projective identification, Melanie Klein noted how its use varied in degree from one patient to another; more disturbed patients made what she termed 'excessive' use of this mechanism. Bion, from his work with psychotic patients, recognized that more than a quantitative factor was involved. He came to the conclusion that psychotic patients employ a different abnormal type of projective identification. Bion made another discovery. Projective identification, in addition to being a mechanism of defence, was the very first mode of communication between mother and infant — it is the origin of thinking. The very young infant communicates his feelings, his fears, etc. to his mother by projecting them into her for her to receive and know them. During a psychoanalysis projective identification as a mode of communication is an important and distinctive occurrence in a session. A nine-year-old girl, for example, while going swiftly and systematically from one activity to the next, at times projected into me a feeling of isolation. I felt the isolation intensely in myself, i.e. I contained and became momentarily identified with her projection. After thinking about what I had received, I interpreted that she wanted me to know her feeling of isolation. Such an event in a session is a primitive transmission from patient to analyst by means of projective identification, the transference version of the type of early event between mother and baby which forms a K link between them and which allows thinking to develop.

This is a very important finding. According to Bion, the infant discharges unpleasure by splitting off and projecting anxiety-arousing perceptions, sensations, feelings, etc. — such as in our example the feeling of isolation — into the mother for her to contain them in what Bion calls her 'reverie'. This is her capacity with love to think about her infant — to pay attention, to try to understand, i.e. to K. Her thinking transforms the infant's feelings into a known and tolerated experience. If the infant is not too persecuted or too envious, he will introject and identify with a mother who is able to think, and he will introject also his own now modified feelings.

Each such projective-introjective cycle between infant and mother is part of a momentous process which gradually transforms the infant's entire mental situation. Instead of a pleasure ego evacuating unpleasure, a new structure is slowly achieved: a reality ego which has unconsciously internalized at its core an object with the capacity to think, i.e. to know psychic qualities in itself and others. In such an ego there is a differentiation between conscious and unconscious, and the potential also to differentiate between seeing, imagining, phantasizing, dreaming, being awake, being asleep. This is the normal mind, the achievement of which depends on both mother and infant.

Failure to develop a reality ego may be due to the mother's failure to K her infant's communications to her by his first method of projective identification. If she fails, she deprives him of a fundamental need for an object unlike himself which does not evacuate the unpleasurable, but instead retains it and thinks about it. Failure may also be due to the infant's hatred of reality or his excessive envy of his mother's capacity to tolerate what he cannot. These lead him to continued and increased evacuation, both of the modified more tolerable elements returned to him by his mother and also of the containing mother herself, and, in extreme cases, to an aggressive attack on his own mental capacities. It is this last which brings about psychosis.

In Bion's view, psychosis comes with the destruction of those parts of the mind potentially capable of knowing. His classic paper 'Differentiation of the psychotic from the non-psychotic personalities' (1957) characterizes the divergence of psychotic from normal functioning thus. 'The differentiation of the psychotic from the non-psychotic personality depends on the minute splitting of all that part of the personality that is concerned with the awareness of internal and external reality, and the expulsion of these fragments so that they enter into or engulf their objects.' This is a disaster for mental life, which is then not established in the normal mode. Instead of thinking based on the reality principle and symbolic communication within the self and with other objects, an anomalous enlargement of the pleasure ego occurs, with excessive use of splitting and projective identification as its concrete mode of relating to hated and hating objects. Omnipotence replaces thinking and omniscience replaces learning from experience in a disastrously confused, undeveloped and fragile ego. Bion has described the grievous result of the psychotic's attack on his mind. The psychotic feels 'he cannot restore his object or his ego. As a result of these splitting attacks, all those features of the personality which would one day provide the foundation for intuitive understanding of himself and others are jeopardized at the outset' (p. 46). And further: 'in the patient's phantasy the expelled particles of ego lead an independent uncontrolled existence, either contained by or containing the external object; they continue to exercise their function as if the ordeal to which they have been subjected had served only to increase their number and provoke their hostility to the psyche that ejected them. In consequence the patient feels himself surrounded by bizarre objects' (p. 47).

The psychotic is in despair, imprisoned in his bizarre universe. In analysis psychotic patients discharge a barrage out of terror of contact with either themselves or the analyst, who is experienced as a murderously punitive object. Their frail grasp of the normally distinct states of being awake, dreaming, hallucinating, perceiving, phantasy and reality makes for a confused, confusing and sometimes delusional transference. By continual use of projective identification, which may invade the analyst long outside the therapeutic hour, they attempt to evoke involvement and action from him, rather then K. Bion's hypotheses disagree with theories which view thinking as merely the emergence of maturation or as an autonomous ego function. According to him, K is hard-won by the infant ego from emotional experiences with a nurturing object, functioning normally on the reality principle.

But even when achieved, K is subject to hazard; it may become minus K through being stripped of significance. Minus K is understanding denuded until only misunderstanding remains. Among its chief causes are excessive envy and inadequate nurture. Excessive envy changes the way projections are given. Bion writes: '. . . the infant splits off and projects its feelings of fear into the breast together with envy and hate of the undisturbed breast', and goes on to describe in his chapter on minus K in *Learning from Experience* the infant's progressive denudation of his psyche which becomes permeated by nameless dread. From the mother's side, a failure to accept projections forces her infant to assail her and project increasingly, and he experiences her as denuding him. He then internalizes 'a greedy vaginalized "breast" that strips of its goodness all that the infant receives leaving only degenerate objects. This internal object starves its host of all understanding'. ('A theory of thinking', p. 115). Continuing mutual denudation and misunderstanding between mother and infant will leave only minus K between them, a cruel, empty, degenerative link of superiority/inferiority.

So far I have summarized Bion's exploration of three phenomena: K, the emotional experience of trying to know the self and others; *no K*, the psychotic state with no mind able to know the self or others — the patient, in the psychotic part of his mind, exists in an unreal universe of bizarre objects about which he cannot think; and minus K, the cruel and denuding link of misunderstanding the self and others. I want now to illustrate their application to the understanding and interpretation of clinical material in child analysis.

Bion places the capacity to know at the very centre of mental life. His work puts the pleasure principle and the reality principle on a par with the life instinct and the death instinct as the fundamental governors of psychic life. In Bion's symbols, K is as fundamental as L (love) or H (hatred). He links his theoretical regrouping to clinical practice. According to Bion, there is a key to each session. The key is L or H or K. When the analyst decides that L or H or K should be the subject of his main opening interpretations he has decided the key of the session, which can then 'act as a standard to which he can refer all the other statements he proposes to make' (*Learning from Experience*, p. 45). If Bion is right, K, or any of its forms of minus K, or no K, is as likely as any of the forms of L or H to be the pivot of a session. The implication for clinical practice is that we must often work with our patients about K and that our attention should float as freely to the K link within the patient and between ourselves and our patients as it does to the L or H links.

This could be put by saying (although it would be quite foreign to Bion's view of analytic work to make rigid use of the idea): ask of clinical material the question: Is the material in this session emerging as an expression of, or anxiety about, or a defence against, etc. . . . L or H or K? (I shall omit L and H from further consideration as not the subject of this paper, and anyway more familiar.) If K is most urgent in the material there is a next question: What form of K? Is the child trying to know or is the child, e.g. too anxious to think about his internal or external object? In these cases the key is K. Alternatively, is the child misunderstanding or denuding his experience? If so, the key is no longer K, but minus K. Or, is the child expressing in his material a psychotic condition in which he exists without the capacity to think? In this case the key is no K.

Suppose a girl of nine begins her session by drawing a house. The house is unexceptional; it has a conventional roof, a pair of windows with curtains, a central door. The neat drawing conveys order and emptiness. What, if anything with respect to K, does the drawing communicate? Is the child attempting with her picture of the house to tell her therapist that she knows her internalized mother is orderly but empty? And is she expressing also her feeling and her fear that the therapist who gives her regular appointments, has the same setting each session, and so on, is like that, too? If so, then the key to the session is K. The child is thinking about her internal object and strives in this session as against other times (she is, in fact, the child mentioned briefly on pages 178—9 who projected feelings of isolation; she was at that time too anxious to think about the nature of her object and was instead being it) to know also the current and immediate external object, the therapist in the maternal transference.

But the communication might be different. Such a drawing may express a child's feeling that ordinary relations — and, in fact, this second child attends regularly, comports herself in an unexceptional way with the therapist — are empty of meaning to her. If so, and the total context of her other communications and the therapist's counter-transference feelings will decide, she is communicating that the session has no significance for her and that she will learn nothing from it, though she is there and does and says the 'right' things. The key to the session is minus K, and an opening interpretation might be that she feels being with the therapist, like the house drawing, is empty and means nothing to her. The session will develop in one of many possible ways from there. The child may be relieved to be understood, perhaps her anxiety about the pervasiveness of such futile object relations at home and at school may emerge, or her fear that she cannot feel differently. More minus K will almost certainly occur in the session, now in relation to the new K events of the hour (with some children it will occur at once in relation to the first interpretation) and the process of denudation can be caught in the immediacy of its happening.

There is a third possible category of communication in K. The child's drawing of the house may be orderly but empty because it is merely an inoffensive item to engage the therapist while the child is really engaged elsewhere. One such child produced neat conventional drawings and models for me while engaged in watching a hostile 'eye' watching him from the lock on the window — a terrifying bizarre object in Bion's sense. This third child had not the mental equipment to think thoughts about a house or draw a symbolic house, as could the first child — the drawing of a house was for him something quite different. He always took his drawings and models with him at the end of each session. Once, early in the analysis, he made an attempt to leave a drawing. An hour later I found him standing outside the play room, panic-stricken, unable to go without his drawing, which he believed was a piece of himself he had extruded via his pencil on to the paper. To leave it was a self-mutilation. I was experienced as a terrifying object who must be appeased by drawings, models, etc. and from whom he must conceal his bizarre world about which he could not think; both because it would overwhelm him with terror and also because he had not the mind with which to think a thought. There was no K in his session. The key to his session, notwithstanding its apparent quiet and the patient's overt conventional activity of drawing an unexceptional house, is his state of being without K and his consequent despair about help with or rescue from the hate of the objects by which he felt surrounded — the hatred of the watching eye on the window, and the hatred of the therapist.

'The smile of the psychotic means something different from the smile of the non-psychotic', thus Bion, and the same can be said of children's play. In these illustrations, somewhat stylized for presentation though from three analyses each a type familiar to child psychotherapists, the drawing of a house means something different for each child. For the first it is a symbolic communication which expresses K. For the second in Segal's (1957) sense it is a symbolic equivalent of emptiness and meaninglessness, i.e. of minus K, and another drawing or another sort of play would do as much or as little, just as at this stage analysis was an experience no different from anything else. For the third child, the drawing is a concrete extrusion of a piece of himself in a house-like shape to appease the therapist, without K in fear of H.

Bion's clinical insights have made possible quite new work with patients in each of the three areas of K, minus K and the psychotic condition of no K. Consider, for example, the connection between K and splitting and integrating the ego. When K of her mother aroused too much anxiety in the first of the three children described above, she split off her memory and her judgement that her mother was orderly but empty. She defended herself from knowing by splitting and by being the object moving quickly, systematically from one activity to another. When she became less afraid to K, she was able to draw, and drew the orderly, empty house, integrating her knowledge of her internalized mother, and striving to know also her therapist/mother. Later in this session she communicated an intense feeling of isolation — which before used to be projected into the analyst as an unconnected event. This was a further movement of integration, bringing her the painful emotional realization

183

that it is her orderly but empty mother who makes her feel so isolated. It is important, I think, to analyse both the relief due to integration as well as the pain K brings.

In regard to minus K, Bion's work enables us to understand how delusional areas persist in children who nonetheless 'know' what the reality is, the clue being that such knowing is not K but minus K. The second child knows in the sense of minus K that she comes to an analyst and has drawn a house as she 'knows' she has a father and a mother. But it means nothing to her. She suffers from meaninglessness and futility. Split off, as Bion's work prepares us to find, is an alarming omnipotence and superiority to objects whom she does not know to be parents. There are no adults in her world; only objects who have pretensions to being 'grown-up' but who misunderstand, as she herself does. Between the child and her object, as Bion expressed it, 'the process of denudation continues till . . . [there is] . . . hardly less than an empty superiority/inferiority that in turn degenerates to nullity' (*Learning from Experience*, p. 97).

Perhaps the most original of Bion's contributions to psychoanalysis is his exploration of previously little-known processes in the mind of the psychotic: his concrete experiences of invasion and manipulation in the head, his evacuations from all organs, the strange trajectories of his projections, and the bizarre objects which furnish his inner and his external worlds. Bion's understanding of what it is to exist without K has greatly helped analysts in their endeavours to reach children like the third one described above, who exist — it is not too much to say — in a horror chamber both internally and externally. Bion's papers illuminate in depth and with precision the nature and the difficulty of the analytic task for the psychotic patient and his analyst.

As well as advancing clinical understanding of K, minus K and no K, Bion illuminates the interconnections between them. Understanding these interconnections can help the analyst with two situations of psychic movement as they occur in the play room: the movement from emotional understanding to loss of that experience — the movement from K to minus K, and the movement from being sane to being psychotic or vice versa — the oscillation between K and no K.

To take first the movement from emotional understanding to loss of the experience. The shift from K to minus K is a problem of varying seriousness in different analyses. Sometimes all work done is denuded and minus K spreads like a cancer over every link between patient and analyst. Sometimes the stripping of K until it is minus K occurs only in pockets. Bion's work demonstrates the necessity for tracing the fate of meaningful interpretations, to see whether they retain vitality and their connection with the analyst. If they do they will be developed unconsciously; but if they become disconnected they will lose meaning and go dead. It is necessary to trace the particular processes which reverse the achievement of K, to ascertain whether the child believes they come from his object or from himself, for whatever reason of anxiety, perversity, pain or envy.

A brief example will illustrate what I have in mind. At a certain period of her analysis when real contact was made with an intelligent sixteen-year-old girl her relief and gratitude at this were evident. This was her initial response. Sessions later, however, there was a sequel. The very interpretations which had given her relief and made her grateful to the therapist were now produced as her own clever understanding without any knowledge of the fact that she had got them from her therapist. This was the emergence in the transference of a perverse process of phallic exhibitionism which was changing K into minus K. That she was not keeping but losing what she gained crystallized for her when, following an unusually moving hour, she came the next day very late. She felt, as she said, bleak and flat. Just before the end of the session she remembered the previous night's dream. She had dreamt she was in her mother's house and her mother had died. She was wondering how to dispose of the old furniture. My patient needed no help from me. She said: 'That's how it is. Yesterday's session is old furniture.' Her moving experience of the day before had become useless minus K. Such losses during treatment foreshadow the impermanence of therapeutic gains after the analysis is over. Clinically, in the hope of at least to an extent averting such ultimate loss, it is important that patient and analyst discover why the mother/analyst dies and the patient is left with interpretations which are merely useless furniture in her mind; in this particular case the pathological process was the patient's perversion of knowledge by her exhibitionism.

To discuss now the other movement — the oscillation between sane and psychotic states. To some children this is familiar and frightening: they know they 'change'. For example, a thirteen-year-old boy under threat of expulsion from school was provocative and violent to his therapist to a degree almost unmanageable. The therapist was frightened and felt impotent. Each onslaught forbidden was resumed at once with no sign of fear — exactly his escalating situation at school. He shouted at his therapist: 'I'll wipe you out.' In this state the child was not psychotic but using primitive defences of projective identification and splitting against massive anxieties. He was in a state of projective iden-tification with frightening adult figures, like the headmaster threatening to expel him and so 'wipe him out'. Into the therapist he had projected himself — a child at the mercy of punitive grown-ups. Interpretations needed to focus on his terror of hostile grown-ups who drove him to split off from himself and project himself into them, with ever increasing fear and violence. The key to the session was H — above all, his terror of the H of the object, and his own H, and how H made all L vanish between him and his object.

At other times, however, as he violently broke each successive limit on the expression of H, his triumph and with it his sexual excitement escalated. Then he felt changed. His huge irresistible excitement destroyed his capacity to think and he had no K of who or where he was really. His penis became stiff — he undid his trousers to show his therapist. He had cut the link with reality, could not think, and was in a delusion of omnipotence. No K was then the key to the session, instead of, as before, H. The facts which now needed to be understood and interpreted were how his huge sexual excitement made him feel changed, how he did not know what he was doing, and the pleasure and the excitement of the change in which he knew no fear including the fear he was being mad, and how all his K was gone from him and existed now to be mocked at in the therapist. Though his excited psychotic states were often impossible to penetrate, there were times when such interpretations reached him and enabled him to move back into sanity; then he would know intolerable despair and fear which would almost overwhelm him and he would try with renewed aggression to raise his sexual excitement to attack his sanity and thinking again.

Bion has two central contentions. To develop a normal mind with a sense of reality an infant must learn from experience, i.e. he must use his emotional experiences with the object to try to know them. This means to notice them, assess them, understand their nature, remember them, i.e. to think. As well, the infant needs to be loved and known by his nurturing object. Of an infant's knowledge of the reality of his emotional life Bion writes as follows: 'a sense of reality matters to the individual in the way that food, drink, air and excretion of waste products matter. Failure to eat, drink or breathe properly has disastrous consequences for life itself. Failure to use the emotional experience produces a comparable disaster in the development of the personality; I include among these disasters degrees of psychotic deterioration that could be described as death of the personality' (*Learning from Experience*, p. 42). Of the mother's reverie in which she knows the reality of her infant's feelings Bion writes: 'Reverie is that state of mind which is open to the reception of any "object" from the loved object and is therefore capable of the reception of the infant's projective identifications whether they are felt to be good or bad' (p. 36).

Often our patients are anxious about their ability to learn from the experience of analysis. This is the transference emergence of their anxiety about not learning from their experience with their early objects. They feel pessimistic, and worry that their analyst is obliviously optimistic.

186

Consciously or unconsciously they know they do not think about and keep a truthful and real record of their relationships. In so far as it is themselves they fear, they fear K may become perversely twisted, or denuded into minus K, or even get totally lost through an attack on their perceptions and memories: in this regard it is their own envy they fear the most. Envy leads them also to withhold information. Patients know knowledge is the analyst's lifeline as much as it is theirs. By withholding information about happenings in the session or current events in their lives they know they can make the analyst useless. Just as refusal of K often arises from an intense envious hatred, so conversely, the giving of K often expresses love and gratitude.

Patients are likewise anxious about the analyst's capacity to understand them. At depth this is anxiety about the analyst's capacity for 'reverie', in Bion's sense. A patient wants understanding based on actual events of emotional containment, he wants his analyst to be open to his first mode of thinking — viz, to communication by projective identification. Can the analyst receive primitive projected states and know what they are? Children do research on the analyst's capacity for reverie and bring material for the purpose of testing whether he can think, notice, remember, tell the difference between truth and lies, and emotionally understand — as opposed to verbally, mechanically, or from books. Especially those children whose internal objects cannot K will have deep uncertainty about the therapist. Can he know me? And how does he do it? Anxiety-ridden research into the analyst's mind rather then into his own may be the focus of the analysis for a long time. The patient knows if the analyst cannot K he has no hope at all.

Each patient has a point beyond which he does not extend his K. Scanning an analysis for what K is present and absent gives a broad indication of the patient's level of development. Whole areas of knowledge may be absent from the analysis because the child does not emotionally K them. Sometimes the central pivot of the analysis becomes a disagreement between the patient, who believes it is better to be without further K, even at the price of deterioration or 'death of the personality', than to follow the analyst whom the patient believes to advocate more K. The patient fears that more K will bring not benefit, but intolerable conflict or uncontrollable emotion, psychotic states of persecution, mania, depression, or even total disintegration. In such analyses the patient's fear of, and antagonism to, the analyst and the analytic work is an antagonism to K.

This source of resistance and hostility may be missed, as I missed it in a thirteen-year-old girl. She was a sullen, heavy girl, the eldest of four children. Her parents were seriously caring of their children, but had also considerable psychological difficulties of their own. Her father had had

187

two psychotic episodes since her birth, and her mother dramatized daily events and attitudes in a way that was at once foolish, frightening and exasperating. My patient was brought to analysis on account of her surliness and intractability at home, poor schoolwork, and unhappiness. Notwithstanding her suspicion and anxiety, in the first phase of the analysis she had communicated clearly and well, making it possible for me to understand her. This was evident from her response in the sessions and some betterment in her life.

In the middle period of her analysis, however, she became increasingly difficult to make contact with. Her sullen hostility, which had abated, returned increased. Session after session she set out farm scenes of figures and animals in a dull and surly way. These she fenced off in silence. Sometimes she sealed her mouth with a strip of sellotape. A pall fell over the sessions and I had to struggle to stay awake. She gave no response to interpretations I attempted, there was no shift of play, nor could I satisfactorily locate myself in the transference. Her material persisted with minimal variation and I became very worried that it was repetitious because not understood. Broadly speaking, I had taken the key to her material to be hate (H). I had understood her sullenness and silence as hostility, the emergence of H towards a persecuting object, myself, from whom she fenced herself away, and on an oral level, sealed her mouth to stop anything entering her from me. Bion's work provided an illumination: the key was not H, but K.

I approached her material differently. Her sullen resistance, which I had taken to be hostility, I now understood to be a dulling and deadening of her mind. The pall which fell over the sessions was a deadening of awareness in us both. I tried to show her she felt a need not to be aware, to make us both unthinking — she should not know me and I should not know her. Within a few sessions she stopped the farm play and brought new material. She sealed her mouth with sellotape. Then she drew two knobbly misshapen figures, writing underneath 'Old Age Pensioners'. She raised her hand and lifted the sellotape off her mouth for a moment. I got a glimpse of a horrifying twisted smile before she covered her mouth again. The smile was her twisted excitement about her parents, old-age-pensioner-parents, knobbly, psychologically misshapen. I think she was terrified of a twisted, rampant, manic state seizing her if she let herself know her object's shortcomings. I think she also wished to spare her objects the pain of knowing that she knew them. Her dulling of her faculties and her deadening of any link between us was in order not to know, or be known to know — as I now tried to show her in an analysis that was moving again.

From the founding of psychoanalysis Freud held that K, knowledge, was at the centre of the therapeutic process. He wrote, for instance: 'we have formulated our tasks as physicians thus: to bring to the patient's *knowledge* the unconscious, repressed impulses existing in him, and, for that purpose, to uncover the resistances that oppose *this extension of his knowledge about himself* ' (1971, p. 159, my italics). Bion's work returns us to Freud with a deepened understanding of what such knowledge is — both for the patient and for the analyst. The insight the patient gains in analysis rests on primitive introjections which are emotional experiences of psychic reality linked to his analyst. Equally, the analyst's understanding rests on emotional experiences of knowing his patient in the original and deepest mode, i.e. through reception, containment and thought about his patient's projective identification. Bion's conception of thinking, his work on the conditions of the achievement of K, its lapse into minus K, and the psychotic's disordered 'thinking' with no K, will continue, I am sure, to be a rich source and a potent catalyst for developing work with patients for many years to come.

References

Bion, W.R. (1954) 'Notes on the theory of schizophrenia', *International Journal of Psycho-Analysis*, 35: 113—18; also in *Second Thoughts*, London: Heinemann (1967), 23—5; reprinted in paperback, Maresfield Reprints, London: H. Karnac Books (1984).

—— (1955) 'Language and the schizophrenic' in *New Directions in Psycho-Analysis*; reprinted in paperback, London: Tavistock Publications (1971) and by Maresfield reprints, London: H. Karnac (1985).

—— (1956) 'Development of schizophrenic thought', *International Journal of Psycho-Analysis*, 37: 344—6; also in *Second Thoughts*, 36—42.

—— (1957) 'Differentiation of the psychotic from the non-psychotic personalities', *International Journal of Psycho-Analysis*, 38: 266—75; also in *Second Thoughts*, 43—64 and in *Melanie Klein Today: Volume 1*, London: Routledge (1988).

—— (1958a) 'On hallucination', *International Journal of Psycho-Analysis*, 39: 341—9; also in *Second Thoughts*, 65—85.

—— (1958b) 'On arrogance', *International Journal of Psycho-Analysis*, 39: 144—6; also in *Second Thoughts*, 86—92.

—— (1959) 'Attacks on linking', *International Journal of Psycho-Analysis*, 40: 308—15; also in *Second Thoughts*, 93—109 and in *Melanie Klein Today: Volume 1*, London, Routledge (1988).

—— (1962a) 'A theory of thinking', *International Journal of Psycho-Analysis*, 43, 306—10; also in *Second Thoughts*, 110—19; and in *Melanie Klein Today: Volume 1*, London: Routledge (1988).

—— (1962b) *Learning from Experience*, London: Heinemann; reprinted in paperback, Maresfield Reprints, London: H. Karnac Books (1984).

Freud, S. (1911) 'Formulations on the two principles of mental functioning', SE 12.

———— (1917) 'Lines of advance in psycho-analytic therapy', SE 17.

Klein, M. (1946) 'Notes on some schizoid mechanisms' in *Developments in Psycho-Analysis*, London: Hogarth Press (1952); also in *The Writings of Melanie Klein*, vol. 3, London: Hogarth Press (1975), 1—24.

Segal, H. (1957) 'Notes on symbol formation', *International Journal of Psycho-Analysis*, 38: 391—7; also in *The Work of Hanna Segal*, New York: Jason Aronson (1981), 49—65, and in *Melanie Klein Today: Volume 1*, London: Routledge (1988).

4

The invisible Oedipus complex

EDNA O'SHAUGHNESSY

This paper was first given at a Melanie Klein conference on 'The Oedipus complex today: clinical implications', at the Psychoanalysis Unit of University College, London on 19 September 1987. It is being published simultaneously here and in R. Britton, M. Feldman and E. O'Shaughnessy, *The Oedipus Complex Today: Clinical Implications*, London: H. Karnac Books.

A current controversy about the Oedipus complex is whether it is indeed universal and of central importance, still to be regarded as 'the nuclear complex of development'. It is a clinical fact that there are long periods of analysis, possibly, some have suggested, even whole analyses in which there seems to be little or even no Oedipal material. In trying to account for this fact analysts have taken different ways. One way, taken by Kohut and his followers, is to set the Oedipus complex aside, posit a theory of self-psychology and advise a new clinical technique which focuses on deficit and offers restoration. Kleinians take an opposite way. Their approach, when the Oedipus complex is what I am calling 'invisible', is that this is so, not because it is unimportant, but because it is so important, and felt by the patient (from whatever causes) to be so unnegotiable, that he employs psychic means to make and keep it invisible.

In this paper I focus on one small area of the Oedipus complex: its first stages when these are reached after a disturbed early development. When Klein added early stages to Freud's nuclear complex, and later linked the depressive position on which, in her view, mental health depends, she expanded the emotional constellation from which the Oedipus complex of each patient will take its very individual form. The patients I describe are struggling to obliterate an early Oedipal situation which feels continually to be threatening. As will become apparent, feelings of exclusion, problems of separateness and being single in the presence of an Oedipal pair, and a distinctive type of sexual splitting, are foremost in these patients.

I begin with a detailed account of Leon, who at eleven years old is nearing puberty, but whose mental life is still largely occupied by defences against his disturbed relations to his primary objects and a traumatic early Oedipal constellation. His presenting problem was panic at any new prospect. A move to secondary school was looming when he began his analysis and his parents thought he would never manage it. Otherwise, they told me, though father seemed not quite convinced, there were 'no problems'. He was 'just an ordinary boy'. Leon was their first child, followed closely by a second, another boy, conceived when Leon was four months old. Leon's younger brother is a head taller, rowdy and active, while Leon stays in his room with a book, though he will go out to play if a friend takes the initiative. Only with difficulty could his mother bring herself to talk about Leon's infancy, which she said was 'terrible'. He cried for hours: she could not bear that or the feeding. 'Not what I expected', she kept repeating. This limited, and particularly on the mother's side, uninsightful picture of Leon — intolerable as an infant, and now, his anxieties unrecognized, with parents not expecting him to want or to be able to manage life — foretold accurately part of what unfolded in the analysis.

On the first day Leon placed himself near and opposite me, seating himself with a sort of screwing-in movement on a little bench in between two cushions. Except for two sessions, during the first eighteen months of analysis, he has left his bench only to go to the toilet. He watches me through two different pairs of glasses, one like his mother's, the other like his father's, checking the room or myself for the smallest movement or change. Any change makes him acutely anxious. He seems younger than his years, a depressed, lumpy, soft boy, who conveys that he has almost no hope of being understood. His appearance can change astonishingly. He can 'become' and look like some version of his father, or 'become' and look like his mother; he also 'becomes' a small sick infant and at times he looks strangely enlarged. These changing appearances are due, I think, to this projection into an almost total iden-tification with his objects on an early feeling level. The figures he lets into, or which he feels force themselves into his inner world, he experiences in a similarly physical and concrete way; they possess him and he personifies them. Leon experiences analysis as a disturbance which he is both against, and also for, sometimes gratefully so. He said once, 'I don't want you . . . I need you . . .'

In the beginning after inserting himself between his cushions and checking the room quickly for change, he spent his sessions staring silently at the floor below or the door opposite him. I elicited that he saw dots on the floor, that they 'pulled him in', 'made him dizzy', but by looking away he could get out. About the door he said he 'saw patterns'.

He pointed out what he called a 'pattern': distinctly a penis with testicles. He described how the door moved nearer and nearer, but if he left the room and came back the door would be again at its proper distance. He reported these events in a matter-of-fact voice in answer to questions over many sessions, the anxiety which underlies these near hallucinations and his fascination with them totally split off. He seemed to be fragmenting into dots and patterns two terrifying internal objects and emptying them out of his mind on to the floor and the door. There he watched them, withdrawn from contact with myself or the play room, trying to stay in control and remain free of anxiety and emotional content. He could never succeed in staying mentally void and withdrawn for long. Momentarily, terror pushed into him and a flash of hatred of me, or acute depression, or a sudden tenderness. He would quickly rid himself of these intense contradictory feelings which pushed and pulled him about. He had an ongoing conflict whether to withdraw or whether to allow contact, a conflict indicated by his feet which retreated under his bench, came out towards me and then retreated again. Sometimes he blocked his ears, more often he listened intently. After the first few months his enormous latent anxiety was greatly lessened which brought him much relief. And to his parents' astonishment he managed the move to secondary school without panic.

This brings me now to the subject of Leon's Oedipus complex. It was possible and necessary to continue to interpret his fear of the smallest change, his need of an empty mind, his wish to keep me always curious and closely attentive, his chronic anxiety that I would not understand him, but come too close, or force his feelings back into him, etc. But between whom and what were these processes occurring? What was the symbolic significance or equivalence of Leon's inserting himself in between two cushions on the bench? What was the meaning of the movement and change he dreaded? What or who was I in the transference? In Leon's denuded universe I found it difficult to speak of meaning: it sounded artificial, and if I persisted it also aroused his anxiety and hatred.

To consider this more closely. If I interpreted that he did not expect me to understand him, he sometimes acknowledged such an interpretation with relief, and, I came to notice, with more than a hint of a gloat. However, if I went a step further and spoke of myself as being like an inadequate parent he became anxious. 'No! You're not like my *Mum*'. One issue which emerged was that he heard me as disparaging his mother and father and narcissistically implying that I was superior to them. This aroused his loyalty to his parents, and in addition, a fear of forming a nasty collusion with me against them. Beyond this, however, was something more important. If I referred to myself as a parent in the transference Leon became enraged and anxious, but in contrast, if I interpreted his projection into me of a confused watching child while he felt he was being a cruelly indifferent father or mother (often I thought one of the dynamics in his sessions) Leon liked especially that bit of the interpretation in which I referred to myself as the child. He received it with satisfaction, as if to say, 'Ah, you admit it. You *are* a child'. Thus, while seeming to comply with the view that he has parents who supposedly have arranged for him to have something called psychoanalysis, a part of him privately held another view of the proceedings. He was big, his parents and I were little, and he had attractive superior activities — the dizzy pull of the floor and the nearing of the door, and from on high he watched our little goings on, sometimes even protecting us. In one of his rare spontaneous remarks he said to me loftily 'I know all your little habits. I know the way your watch on your arm slips around. I know the way your shoe slips off'. These two selected observations are accurate. I thought their meaning was that he knows how my watch, that is, his mother's eye, has the habit of slipping round him and not really seeing him. And he knows also father's habit of not staying in himself and slipping off, i.e. projecting himself into and getting too close and involved with Leon. But Leon did not want these 'little habits' to be transference phenomena with a dimension of meaning such as my watch to be linked to an eye. He cut the links between his inner world and his analysis, which he stripped of meaning, and he wanted me to accept and to adopt his disconnections, and also to endorse his omnipotent phantasy of reversal — he was big and I was little — to join him in this as in other things.

I was also at this period drawing Leon's attention to how he mostly spoke softly, to draw me near to him to hear and how I had also to come to him with questions as he rarely spoke voluntarily. I interpreted that he felt that he pulled me so near that I became like the cushions next to him. I pointed out how he wanted me to stay very close, never disturb him, not make any connections or expect him to change, while he sat and looked on from on high, unmoving. Leon agreed this was what he wanted. He also amplified with further freely given accounts of himself when I related what he let me see in the play room to his daydreaming at school and his liking to stay in his room at home. But when I tried to explore the meaning (almost always there seemed to be some part of his ego for which meaning remained a possibility in spite of his continual stripping) of his high observatory, interpreting, however gradually, that with the movements he made when he sat down he imagined he inserted himself into a home in mother's body, there to be the baby inside, or that he felt he held mother and father down on either side of him and so prevented their moving and coming together, or that sometimes he felt

194

altered and big and saw me from far as small . . . Leon was both enraged and disturbed. Often he rushed out of the room to the toilet, blocked his ears on return, and told me, 'I hate your talking'.

At such moments instead of being his cushions — he once explained he didn't mind other little changes in the room, so long as the cushions didn't move — he saw me exercising my analytic function. I then became parents who move and so destroy his phantasy of being inside. His rush out of the room expressed a momentary ejection from his seat on the bench, a change which made him hate me.

It is interesting to return for a moment to the beginning of his analysis to the time when a change first occurred. By checking the room and knowing the fixed routine of his sessions, Leon was maintaining an overall phantasy world of no change, no separateness, and no separations — the gap between sessions or at weekends did not exist for him. His routine was first altered when I did not work on a Bank Holiday Monday. He failed to arrive for the last session of the preceding week; during his hour his father telephoned in a panic saying he had arranged to meet his wife and son at the Underground and then bring Leon to me, but they were not there.

On the Tuesday Leon arrived wearing no spectacles. At first he was terrified of being punished and pushed out of his home on his bench or even out of analysis altogether for missing a session, and was relieved when I interpreted his acute anxiety. Then he tried to re-establish me as his cushion close to him, staying silent, making little movements to get me attentive and around him. After which he told me he had dropped his glasses at the weekend and they had smashed. He then stared short-sightedly at the door on which he said there were 'waves', and at the floor on which he said there were 'bits not as nice'. I think Leon had found the changed routine unbearable, could not come, had smashed his sight and smashed also the objects of which 'waves' and 'not nice bits' were the residues but so residual that it was impossible to know what he had fragmented and expelled.

After eight or so months of analysis, Leon was more able to bear contact with the content of his psychic life, and then the nature of the change he dreaded became clear as over widely spaced sessions bits of his early Oedipal situation returned. First there was his move from the bench to sit for the first time at the table. He took out a pack of cards and we played a game. He was secretly enormously pleased to have moved. The next day he again sat at the table. He took out a different pack of cards. During the game he said, 'These cards are someone else's. They are nicer than mine', speaking as if stating a fact accepted by him and me. He never brought cards again and for ten months more never again moved from his bench. Through this painful episode he gave me a glimpse of the trauma that the birth of his brother was and still is to him, and of his belief in a family presumption that his brother is nicer than he is. Leon showed me that he surrenders and does not compete; he never tries again in the play room, just as he does not try at home or at school.

Following the two sessions with the cards he resorted to various manoeuvres to find out the next holiday dates without actually *asking*. When I told him the dates he gave one of his rare smiles, said 'OK', nodding his head happily. And then with the approach of the break, several early Oedipal feelings pressed into consciousness.

On the last day of the week Leon brought a roll of sweets. He asked me if I would *like one*, slightly emphasizing 'like' and 'one'. I interpreted that he wished to know if I liked what he was offering, really, if I liked him. I went on to say he was expressing his longing for me as a mother who has only him, rather than the mother who has his brother too. Leon was furious. He pushed and pulled the knobs on his electronic wrist-watch very fast saying angrily 'I'm getting the time right'. I said he felt I had mentioned his brother at the wrong time, just when he was longing to have me to himself, and rage and disappointment were now pushing and pulling him about. I linked these feelings to his infancy and how the baby that is still there in him feels his mother by becoming pregnant when he was four months old filled herself with his brother at the wrong time because he still needed to have her for himself. Leon continued to push and pull furiously at his watch, all his sweetness gone. He rushed out to the toilet, returned looking empty, and became very sleepy. However, when he said goodbye he nodded his head as if to say 'OK'.

On the Monday he was burdened and instead of cursorily checking that the room was the same he kept looking curiously about. He spoke longingly of 'the chair with the cushion' at the far end of the room. This 'chair with the cushion' is more capacious and he would be more comfortable, and as it is not opposite me he would not be closely watched or watching me. He said with great pain that it was 'far'. I am not certain what this 'chair with a cushion' meant to him, but it was the first time Leon had seen a place he wanted to get to and realized he could not, that it was at the moment too far for him. With insight into himself it was a widening of horizons.

He did not look at the 'far' chair in the next few sessions. He restricted the area on which he used his eyes to the small patch of the floor beneath him. Each time he was about to speak he put his hand over his mouth and stopped himself. He became withdrawn and then despondent. When I spoke to him about the strong force in him which stopped him talking and moving, and how he feels hopeless about ever being able to reach what he longs for, he was very moved.

The last session of the week was again different. Leon came in without looking at me, not even when I opened the front door to him, and in the play room he kept me entirely out of his vision. I interpreted that he didn't want to see me because at the end of the week I was his going-away analyst. As if a shock wave was passing through him Leon's whole body shook. Then he kicked violently in my direction and made a rude gesture of 'up you'. He split off his feelings and became aloof. He said coldly 'I am looking forward to the holidays'. I agreed that he was, that he wanted to be free of me, now a hateful disturbance to him. 'Yes', he answered with a cruel smile. I remarked on his cruel satisfaction and he was instantly anxious, rushing out to the toilet, and when he returned he listened intently to my voice to assess my state of mind. When I next looked at him I had a shock. Quite unconsciously he had bulged his jacket out like a pregnant woman and his face had changed and become his mother's. He sat looking more and more suffering and unloved. I think he had incorporated and was totally identified with, an analyst/mother whom he had cruelly called 'a hateful disturbance'. When I said he seemed to be feeling the suffering inside of him of his unloved pregnant mother, Leon's face worked in distress. For a moment it was real grief. Then he looked angry and anxious. Somewhere in the house a noise sounded. The word 'man' was drawn unwillingly from him: 'M—A—N' he said. It was his recognition of father's presence when mother is pregnant with his brother.

When the session ended he was both trying desperately to pull me closely round him by his usual methods, and also repeatedly making three taps in a very menacing way, indicating how again and again there is a hateful threatening three. As he was going he prodded the wall as if feeling its solidity and sensing the barring quality of a baby or perhaps a father who closes mother to him.

The end of this sequence was on the Monday. Leon looked different, for the first time like a boy nearing puberty, in smart trousers, such as a twelve-year-old might choose. At first he was more communicative and active than usual, but as the session went on he was in increasing conflict, his feet coming out and going back under his bench, whether to continue to go forward or retreat.

In the last week he became a high onlooker from his position between the cushions. The sessions were immobilized and there were no significant elements, dyadic or Oedipal. The coming holiday was idealized. He said he was glad to get away because here it was 'empty' and 'boring'.

His Oedipus complex is not the kind where sexual desire for mother and sexual rivalry with father are foremost. Leon starts not with a parental pair, but with a menacing three — mother pregnant with a new baby and father. There is no rivalry; instead, as he showed in the sessions with the playing cards, there is surrender. Leon competes neither with his sibling nor with his father — he retreats. The onset of the Oedipal situation is so intolerable to him that he expels his own and his parents' sexuality. When he started analysis his internal sexual objects were ejected on to the floor and the door, and he looked sexless. On the floor was a confused vagina and mouth, minutely fragmented into dots which suck him in or make him dizzy which he sees as 'not as nice'. On the door was a more intact father's penis, alarmingly invasive, reduced to pattern, which is what it is for Leon — his predominant identification is with his father.

In the earliest stages of the Oedipus complex the infant has phantasies of mother containing father's penis or the whole father, and of father combining with mother's breasts and vagina, all in a state of perpetual gratification. Leon's feelings of exclusion and frustration would have been enormously increased by a new baby in reality inside mother enjoying all that he phantasizes is granted in mother's insides.

Foremost for Leon is the problem of separateness. At four months mother's pregnancy came at the wrong time in his development when he still needed an exclusive relationship for the reception of his projections, all the more so because of his disastrous start. He was still in the paranoid-schizoid position, on the brink of the depressive position, old relations to part-objects overlapping with emerging relations to whole objects. The perception of a 'going-away' analyst sends a shock wave through him. He feels ejected and instantly makes a two-pronged attacking entry of 'up you' on the pregnant mother. The sweetness there is in him on the one-to-one basis he longs for with his mother is gone, and his hatred turns cruel. Pregnant she is unloved by him, and when Leon senses her suffering he feels a grief more than he can bear, and then is angry and anxious. His ego cannot cope: it is pushed and pulled about by a succession of unmanageable emotions. At the first cancelled session near the start of his analysis he had even to smash his glasses and stay away. Now that his ego is a little stronger he can allow elements of his Oedipus complex to return, see mother, new baby and father, which affects his own identity. Instead of sexlessness and seeing the world through mother's and father's glasses because of being in a state of projective identification with one or other of them, he had a proper boyishness about him for the first time, even though he did not maintain it for long. He was soon again in conflict whether to go forward or retreat. As the break drew near he dispersed his Oedipal experiences which were invisible as he inserted himself in omnipotent phantasy into and between objects with whom he stays and which are his cushions.

Leon's cushions are desexualized parents whom he holds apart and around himself, the comfortable remainders from which frightening components have been expelled on to the floor and the door. Because

198

these expelled objects are so minutely fragmented or denuded into a mere pattern the nature of the sexual splitting that has taken place is difficult to see. In other patients like Leon for whom the earliest stages of the Oedipus complex constitute a fixation point this is more possible. Melanie Klein writes 'this [the combined parent figure] is one of the phantasy formations characteristic of the earliest stages of the Oedipus complex and which, if maintained in strength, is detrimental both to object relations and sexual development', (1952, p. 55).

In my view, a most important feature of this constellation is that the projective identification which aims to separate and attack the sexual parents, *fractures a combination*. Because the emotional level is early the objects of the fracture are anyway already distorted by unretrieved projections, but through their fracture and further projections their heterosexual procreative qualities are destroyed, and the patient has instead pathological sexual objects — distorted, incomplete, and broken open. Often the father is seen not as father or husband but as a sadistic, phallic male, and the mother becomes a weak, open, masochistic female, both felt to be open to homosexual alliances against the other sex. These phantasies are so omnipotent that the patient believes he has achieved a separation of the sexes, and will, for instance, have dreams about, and make references to women, but always with women or girls, and men are again always with other men or boys.

For instance, one of my other patients, an adult, saw the analyst who fetched him from the waiting room as female, oversensitive and too eager to be empathic and nice to him. Once he was on the couch, he felt I changed. I was male, high, aloof, and condescending, and he immediately projected himself into this figure becoming totally like it. A patient I analysed many years ago brought his fractured images in a dream. He was in a foreign country. There were two houses apart from each other, each with a tennis court. In one house, though there was no sign of it on the outside, he knew there was a woman inside with a corset and stockings wanting to have sex; the surface of the tennis court of this house cracked. The surface of the tennis court of the other house was all right. There, two men were facing each other playing very competitive tennis without a net. This patient has split apart the early Oedipal couple and maintains separate relations to each. His dream illustrates how profoundly affected both his sexual life and his object relations are. For him, the mother is an evidently cracked and seductive female, wanting sex from him, one half of his predominant perception of me in the transference for a long time. At the start of analysis he was himself highly erotized, feeling almost totally identified with a mad, promiscuous female — promiscuous sex with promiscuous women is one of his problems. During adolescence this patient had felt he was in a feminine body with breasts, a transsexual feeling so near to delusion that he had been unable to undress in the changing rooms at school or swim without a vest to conceal his chest. The seductive woman in the house in his dream is thus also himself inside his mother. Apart, meanwhile, males play a watchful, competitive face to face game, with no way of knowing the true score. This was the other half of his transference which corresponded to the area of his life, his career, which on the surface is all right, although he was enormously envious and competitive with me (as he is with his business associates), and believed me to be so with him, both of us cheating to win. Often, in these cases, the analyst is made into a watcher, while the patient repeatedly acts out sexually with unsuitable partners in painful triangles, where possession of one excludes and makes hostile another of the combination.

Leon fractured the combined parent in a rather similar way to the patient who split me between waiting and consulting room. As we were able to see later in the analysis, as mother I was to be drawn away from father, come closer round him, coax him with questions, not only when he was anxious and needed me to, but also when he was hostile and chose not to relate to me. His feeling then was that I was no more a mother but a little girl, too soft, who does not confront his hostility but cushions it, with abasement and pleading that turns into a horrific masochistic sucking him in. The cushion on his other side was a caricature of father, stupidly idealizing the practical and ordinary, cruelly aloof from meaning and marriage, and instead wanting to come too close and pair with Leon.

I want now to take up again my main theme of the early Oedipus complex following on faulty early development and to focus on two aspects which drive the patient to fracture and obliterate out of sight the combined Oedipal parents. The first is the stimulation of this primitive primal scene. Leon, for instance, felt pushed and pulled about by an onslaught of feelings beyond the limited capacity of his ego to tolerate. The second comes from the fundamental fact that the primal scene excludes the patient. At this early stage and especially when there has been an excessive use of projective identification to compensate for disturbed object relations exclusion is experienced as ejection from the object. The patient feels not only impossibly stimulated, but also outside and alone, twin aspects I hope to illustrate with some brief material from Mr A.

Mr A, an intelligent and sensitive man, is married and a father. Earlier in his life he had several homosexual relationships, and under pressure he still has strong homosexual inclinations. Among his reasons for coming to me for an analysis was tormenting jealousy of his wife. He thought she was betraying him sexually; but he was not sure if she really was or if he was only tormenting himself with phantasies. If he saw her speak on the telephone or make herself ready to go out, he saw her planning, almost having, sex with someone else.

There were many strands in Mr A's analysis which I must ignore to focus on what is relevant to this paper. In some respects Mr A was like Leon. He was affectionate, had a strong death instinct, and at depth a conviction of fundamental non-acceptance by a narcissistic and otherwise preoccupied mother. Mr. A lacked a securely internalized good object and used projective identification and omnipotent control as his main methods of operating with his objects. Unlike Leon, an early pregnancy played no part in shaping his Oedipus complex, for Mr A is the youngest. The adverse external circumstance in his family is the degree of overt sexual relationships. Father and mother seem to have had some homosexual relationships, and from the age of thirteen an elder brother had sexual relations with my patient. Since debased sexual figures are both the result of Mr A's projections and fracture of the Oedipal pair, but also really correspond to his actual parents to some extent (and later to other real objects) Mr A is often confused and suffers a loss of reality sense; he then becomes terrified that there are no objects with whom reality testing is possible.

Unlike Leon, Mr A is psychically highly mobile and during the analysis was highly erotized. He aimed for instant penetration and possession to take him away from confusion and anxiety. The need to feel inside his object, not to be out and single, to be instantly recognized and form an excited pair was paramount in Mr A and (in addition to identifications) was the driving force behind his homosexuality. In the beginning he stripped the relation between patient and analyst of transference meaning — it was he and I, personal. I was an idealized 'new' object who would give him what he had failed to find before, and give it to him in a way he could tolerate, with no exclusion, no waiting, without stimulating anxiety or guilt or envy or jealousy, or wounding his narcissism. Mostly he was excited by homosexual phantasy in which he was inside a high phallus looking down on and in control of me, a boy who would admire and serve him. But if I disturbed him in some way he turned cold and cruel. Sometimes he was in a state of projective identification with an effeminate figure, softer, more corrupt. The sexes were always split. This erotized homosexual transference and a conviction of perverse erotized relations obtaining everywhere, was for a long time an enclave disconnected from his Oedipal situation. Oedipal figures were nowhere in view, in or out of analysis, and nor was the child in Mr A.

As his excitement lessened he grew watchful. He started to see 'signs' in the room, or my clothes, speech, or intimacies, parties, sex, etc., which invited him or excluded him — he could not tell which. Confused

201

Oedipal delusions and doubts about my sexuality were hidden in his material. Had I been, was I perhaps still, actually excited and over-involved with him, as he was with me? It was so painful a period of his analysis that I would say Mr A was in anguish as his deep Oedipal suspicions, delusions and confusions emerged. His paranoid feelings decreased gradually, and he allowed me more contact with his shame, disappointment, anxiety, and depression about his objects and himself.

As his sexual delusions faded in the transference, he began sometimes to feel painfully exposed to an Oedipal pair who do not consummate his phantasies, but exclude him. There were very considerable difficulties in his life at this time and Mr A was more easily disturbed by 'signs' than was usual at this stage. An important detail is that on the day of the session I report I was more formally dressed than usual.

The instant he saw me when I fetched him from the waiting room he looked anxious and dark in the face. On the couch he was silent for a long time. Then he said he had had a dream, and speaking fast, sounding both desperate and excited, he said he was in France, and he had gone to a restaurant, and he had ordered '*tête de veau*' and when the waiter brought it, it was on the plate without its eyes, black eye sockets, vacant mouth, black stuff, mushrooms, neck standing up ... He went on and on. He paused, waiting, I thought, for me to interpret something about a chopped-off head or unseeing eyes. However, the effect of his rapid relating of what he was calling a dream, which I think was really a swift flight into psychotic phantasy, had been to project chaos and disturbance into me. Mr A continued. He said: 'Then there was some string, do you say *ficelle*? This is what I ordered. Or was it *cervelle* ...' He paused again.

After a while he spoke about a frill on a chamber pot, or a cake oozing out over the edge, and so on. When he stopped, I interpreted that he had gone into the world of his dream and wished me to join him there, to get away from the chaos and disturbance that the sight of my suit had caused him. He answered: 'I had my eyes shut. I'm thinking of analysis, anal Isis. Suit? What suit? Oh, you mean your *suit* ...' Mr A continued mocking me and falsely pretending not to know what I was talking about. I suggested that when he saw me and now when I spoke to him he felt controlled, ordered to notice my suit and talk about it, on top of being made to feel so disturbed and chaotic by it, and that this was so offensive to him that it drove him to mockery and pretence.

At slower speed Mr A continued with his French 'dream' or theme with more variations but his excitement was lessening. He ended saying in a bitter voice: 'Proust's Charlus ordered some rough trade and all he saw was his parents "doing it".' I said I thought he was describing his experiences in the session. The rough trade he wanted was having me join him in his world of homosexual phantasy, but what he became aware of instead was me at my job, that is, parents 'doing it', which made him feel bitter and sneering. After a long silence Mr A said 'But why?' He paused, and said 'We are not there together. I'm alone'. He began to cry saying, 'It's ridiculous to feel like this'.

Melanie Klein writes 'Sometimes the analyst appears simultaneously to represent both parents — in that case often in a hostile alliance against the patient, whereby the negative transference acquires great intensity' (1952, p. 55). My suit is the 'sign' of a hostile primal pair who are so enormously disturbing to Mr A that he is impelled to perverse defensive and destructive phantasies. Before, Mr A would have immersed himself in homosexual phantasies for sessions, become increasingly aloof and persecuted and end with a masochistic depression. In this session, he and I can get through his fast, massive defences against Oedipal disturbance and stimulation and he recovers his contact with me and himself. He then is aware of his parents' doing it, his hostility to their intercourse and his bitter feelings of betrayal. The boy in the man is suddenly on the couch, and he feels alone, cast out, and cries.

Before I conclude, a brief word on technique. Mr A pressures the analyst to join him in rough homosexual trade, as Leon pressures the analyst to be a cushion in unchangingness and meaninglessness. Part of the pressure to 'act in' with the patient is the pressure to formulate interpretations that accept that rough trade or unchangingness and meaninglessness are all there is. The patient invites the analyst to ignore the mental work he has done, and which he is still doing in the session, to keep invisible an early Oedipal situation he is endeavouring to control and obliterate.

To give one small example from Leon's material. When he brought sweets and asked if I would *like one*, in this session simply to interpret his longing to be my only one would not take into account the full situation, viz., that he is trying to make invisible and induce me too to annihilate the fact of a weekend break which means that I as mother shut him out because I have another baby. The fuller interpretation of his longing for a mother who was not also the mother of his brother enabled him to express rather than keep split off his rage at a mother forcing a brother on him at the wrong time. With Mr A there is the opposite problem in the session reported. His pressure is not as with Leon to go too slowly or not go at all, but to go too fast, to rush to interpret the content of his dream. Had I done so, I think he would have felt that he fractured the combined parents and annexed me to himself homosexually in 'rough trade'. As it was, he felt the parents stayed firm, were 'doing it', i.e. that I had stayed at my job of understanding the emotional chaos and disturbance the Oedipal combination causes him. Naturally, an analyst has to try to sense afresh in every session what is urgent and near enough to be potentially dynamic. In other sessions, the exploration of Leon's primal need for a one-to-one relationship, or the meaning of the details of Mr A's swift phantasies may be where the emotional dynamic is.

Summary

Leon and Mr A belong to a group of patients whose Oedipus complex is not part of a normal developmental thrust with sexual desire, and jealous rivalry foremost. For them, awareness of an Oedipal pair, because of their ongoing defences against their continuing early impairment, is forced upon them. It is almost intolerable and they use further defences to make and keep it invisible. I thus disagree with the Kohutian view of deficit with no Oedipus complex in these cases.

Above all, because projective identification into the object has become their mode of coping with their disturbed relations to their original object, awareness of a combined figure ejects them from their projective home inside the object. In addition the combined parents — a cruel structure in these cases — demand sexual watching, threaten invasion or suction into their perpetual intercourse, stimulate envy, increase enormous anxiety and depression. Because the patient lacks an internalized figure which can contain and modify this nearly overwhelming state of mind he feels alone with an intolerable psychic load and threatening chaos. To disburden his psyche and re-enter his object the patient in phantasy inserts himself between the combined figure, pulls the couple apart, and projects himself into one or other of the separated pair. These exclusive relations, however, differ significantly from earlier pre-Oedipal ones. His objects, distorted already by unretrieved projections now bear the marks of the defensive and attacking fracture of their sexual combination so that the patient feels himself to be in a world not of Oedipal figures but of debased and damaged sexual objects. This form of splitting an object in the early stages of the Oedipus complex is so distinctive in its effect that it should I think be known by the special name of fracturing an object. Leon's sexless immobilization and Mr A's homosexuality, both with at times near delusional confusion, are two of the many forms this constellation takes: pathological sexual relations in a triangular framework are also characteristic.

Finally, because of their lack of an internal good object, these patients feel little capable of bearing singleness. They must be in a state of projective identification with another object. In Leon's analysis singleness is not yet even a dynamic, and Mr A, well on in his analysis, is still in distress when he perceives the parental couple and feels alone. For them the Oedipal story begins there — cast out. After all, this is where the original myth began: Laius cast out Oedipus.

Reference

Klein, Melanie (1952) 'The origin of transference', *International Journal of Psycho-Analysis*, 33: 433–8; reprinted in *The Writings of Melanie Klein*, vol. 3, London: Hogarth Press (1975), 48–56.

5

Communication and containing in child analysis: towards terminability

TERTTU ESKALINEN DE FOLCH

This paper was first published in the *International Journal of Psycho-Analysis*, 69: 105–12.

In 'Analysis terminable and interminable' Freud (1937) discusses the different obstacles against change in the analytical process — focusing his thinking on the balance of the ego and the drives. He describes various alterations in the ego which weaken it and consequently make difficult its dealing with both internal and external dangers and problems. On page 237 he gives one of his extraordinarily penetrating descriptions of the damaging consequences of the ego's defence mechanisms: how 'they are condemned to falsify one's internal perception and to give one only an imperfect and distorted picture of one's id. In its relations to id, therefore, the ego is paralysed by its restrictions or blinded by its errors; and the result of this in the sphere of psychical events can only be compared to being out walking in a country one does not know and without having a good pair of legs'.

Our task in the analysis is 'to secure the best possible psychological conditions for the functioning of the ego' (p. 250) to help it perceive, think, speak, and thus to re-establish communication with both the external and the internal world. This then strengthens the ego sufficiently to enable it to deal with the ordinary adversities of life. When we think of a strong ego, and are considering the possibility of successfully terminating an analysis, we are thinking in terms of the internal safety produced by the internalization of a solid object which then becomes part of the individual's own ego, enabling it to stand on its own feet and to contain and deal with its own problems.

Bion, following Klein's ideas, described an archaic, early form of communication through projective identification. He described how the child projects into the mother and her breast distressing unknown emotions. If things go well the mother is then able to metabolize these and give them back to the child in a more familiar, known, and tolerable form (Klein 1946; Bion 1962).

When the mother is unable for whatever reason to contain and metabolize the child's emotions, the child experiences them as even more unbearable and terrifying. He feels that he cannot face them and frenetically tries to cut out all contact with them by reprojecting them. By doing this the individual destroys his own capacity both for introspection and for the perception of others, who become contaminated and distorted by these projections. This is, in other words, what Freud probably meant by his comparison of inadequate ego functioning with the individual walking in an unknown place — his own mind.

In this paper I aim to show the relationship between certain qualities of communication and containment, and how these lead to change either in the direction of greater integration or in the direction of increased splitting and regression. When the child patient feels his communication is understood by the analyst, the child introjects an analyst who can tolerate, look, think, and speak of the most unbearable feelings. In the opposite situation, when the child feels not understood in his particular form of anxiety, he consequently cuts off and destroys his capacity to perceive, communicate, and feel. I shall attempt to describe the process of one particular child's ego functions becoming 'paralysed' and 'blind' in the session, and the reverse procedure, how she becomes more capable of relating, knowing, and dealing with conflicts.

Ann was six when her parents brought her to analysis because of difficulties at school and at home. Her teachers considered her 'a child of bad instincts' and at home she was touchy, possessive, and domineering. She had been asthmatic since her parents separated when she was three. The parents had already been on bad terms since before she was born and she is their only child. She lives with her mother but regularly spends time with her father who has a new partner. Both parents love this child and do their best to educate her. There is also evidence to suggest that mother was very depressed whilst Ann was small.

Ann is pretty and outstandingly intelligent. She often openly expresses deep hopelessness about her situation and herself, but this can then quickly shift into a cold self-punitive attitude.

I will describe two series of sessions which took place in the first year of Ann's analysis when she was then aged seven. In the first series I could not understand the dramatic dilemma Ann so insistently tried to communicate to me. My lack of understanding seemed to release a violent response in her. She destroyed part of the work we had done together (drawings); she behaved in such a way that it became impossible for me to think or speak; and she appeared to cut herself off from her own perceptions and grew cold and cynical. She lost the possibility of communicating with either her internal world or with me.

This was however partly masked by the split between her feelings and her intellectual functions. These latter seemed able to continue and could give a false impression of integration.

Ten months later the situation was just the opposite. Ann was very disturbed at having just been informed of a long trip her mother was to make. She was caught up in a rejecting, provocative attitude and initially it seemed almost impossible to make contact with her, to communicate with her. However, by standing her provocations and by understanding up to a certain point her different attempts to communicate with me I was able to establish sufficient contact with her to enable her to feel differently. She could then begin to speak of her feelings and even to relate them to her childhood history.

The first series of sessions took place just after the Christmas holiday, after four months of analysis, when, for the first time, Ann met another child patient of mine, a very small boy. Before describing these sessions I want briefly to give information about a pregnancy phantasy Ann had expressed since her first consultation session; the collapse of this phantasy, at the sight of my other child patient, was the central theme in the session I am going to describe. In the first session Ann had drawn a pregnant woman, which I took for a wish for her mother to have a new baby and be happy again. But in many sessions Ann pushed out her own stomach indicating that it was she who was pregnant. Just before the Christmas break she had been drawing something she called 'Christmas story'. In it she drew the birth of a baby in great detail. Then she also drew different situations in which a young child took care of this baby. She seemed to oscillate between her omnipotent phantasy that she was the mother of the baby and that she was only taking care of the baby.

After meeting the little boy at the door, Ann comes into the play room with a serious expression and remarks that there is a new heater. I draw her attention to the fact that something else new had happened today, she had met somebody. She smiles and says, 'Yes, the little boy'. She then gives me an old drawing of a butterfly and asks me to colour it, saying 'Do it well though!' She makes the outlines of the butterfly clearer with the black pencil and warns me not to draw over them saying, 'One tends to do it when one is tired'. She is being kind and protective towards me. She gives me a yellow pencil which she then immediately takes away, saying now more severely, 'Not like that! Can't you see the outlines!' I speak to her about how I am the person who is unable to control herself and that she has to show me how I should behave. 'I have to go to wee', she says and goes to the bathroom.

When she comes back she begins to draw with great intensity and says,

'You don't know what happened to me. You have to understand it from my drawing'. She draws a girl with red spots on her skirt, something red in the 'air' above her head. She shows something on the right of the drawing and says, 'This is the lavatory'. I ask about the girl and about what is falling in between her legs. Ann answers, 'Look, look! the result is here', showing on the left of the drawing a circle and something in it. I tell her that seeing the boy struck her like lightning (the red line above the girl's head) and hurt her whole body and now she tells me that it was blood which came from between her legs, like mother who has her periods. Ann answers, 'Yes, I know about the periods. But you haven't yet seen what's the matter, what *happened* to me!' I continue saying how hurt she had been. Ann is more and more upset. She begins to take toys out of her drawers and throws them around, sometimes at me. She grows more and more cold and begins to sing coldly 'Sweet Christmas'. The room is now in a mess. She sings aloud 'Joy, jou, sweet Christmas'. At this point I realized something else was going on which was causing her rage so I interpreted the breakdown of her Christmas phantasy. She had drawn a baby she had treated as if hers. Now it was I who expressly hurt her by showing her that it was I, not she, who had a new baby here. But my understanding came too late and Ann was shouting and singing so she could not hear. In rage against me she reduces everything into a mess and expresses that she does not care about anything, her feelings or anything else.

Clearly in this session I was not on the same wavelength as Ann. She had been struck by the sight of the other child but then in a flash she had projected her disturbing and uncontrollable feelings into me. She was then at first protectively advising me, later more severely admonishing me. This I could convey to her well enough, I think. Her responses showed that she now understood that it was not I but she who could not contain her feelings; she had to go and wee. After she came back from the toilet, she insistently tried to make me understand her dramatic dilemma. The omnipotent phantasy of herself being the mother of the baby was smashed by the sight of the small boy with me and yet still she tried to cling to this phantasy. When I did not pick up soon enough the point she had been making so insistently and what it meant to her, Ann grew more upset and began to destroy all possibility of communicating. By singing loudly and throwing toys around she created a situation in which it was impossible to think, speak, or be heard.

In the following session I still continued to put the stress in the wrong place, speaking mainly of her jealousy of the other child. Ann began to throw away into the dustbin the Christmas drawings (which I subsequently rescued). Then she made a face of the pencils:

Baldness

Hair

Eyes

Mouth

baldness, hair, eyes, and mouth. Then she took away the pencils representing the hair and baldness saying with a cruel expression, 'Now I cut the hair and the baldness patch'. Then she takes the eyes into her hand saying, 'Now it is blind'. Then with ascending cruelty in her expression she says, 'Now an illness comes and rots the mouth and nothing is left'. I tell her that she is now hurting herself and me. She is not going to see or think or say anything and this serves me right for having had a new child here.

Ann now takes the drawing of the Christmas story which represents the birth of the baby (Drawings 1 and 2). She cuts out the baby from between its mother's legs. Then she cuts out the dogs and what she had called 'the grandmother's jewellery'. I show her that in her anger she cuts into me and takes away all my good things so that nothing is left to be given for the new baby, for the boy she saw. I show her moreover her destruction of her own capacity to see, to think, and to speak, thus cutting the possibility of our relating to each other. Ann looks at me very coldly and says, 'I steal them', indicating defiantly that no affectionate, warm tie exists any longer between us.

In the following sessions Ann organized 'sets' of all the objects she had cut out: 'animals', 'babies of different ages', 'jewellery'. These sets were made up perfectly logically, e.g. all the babies together, but seemed unrelated to human beings and their feelings. For example, the baby was not with her mother, the jewels were not those of the grandmother, and the dogs did not belong to anybody.

When Ann destroyed the face, the eyes, hair, and the mouth, she showed what she had acted out in the previous session, how she actively cut out, split off, her organs of perception and her feelings. Communication became impossible, nor could she have any contact with her own self. Her internal world had become icy. Moreover, when she was cutting so cruelly she showed that she had begun to derive a secondary sado-masochistic pleasure from destroying both her own feelings and

Drawing 1

Drawing 2

perceptions and also destroying any possibility of my understanding her, of my having her as my analytical child.

I shall now describe a different kind of session in which the movement was just the opposite and I had the impression that I could understand the deep despair which seemed to fuel Ann's provocative attitude. Ann's mood then changed and she was able to become communicative.

Ann's mother was going on a three-week business trip and apparently Ann was informed of this just before the session. I did not know anything about the trip until the following week. It was Thursday, the last session of the week: I see Ann four times a week. Ann rings the bell and when I open the door she is sitting on the stairs, head in hands, looking very miserable. I ask her what's the matter. She does not answer or move. Her coming into the flat and then into the consulting room takes more than fifteen minutes, and I shall summarize it. After having entered the flat Ann lies on the floor with an angry and withdrawn expression, she does not answer any of my questions or follow me into the play room. She begins to kick the walls and provocatively pulls at the wall-hanging, which she knows she is not allowed to do. She looks at me sideways to see my reaction. I say that she cannot do this and ask her to come upstairs into the play room. She asks me to carry her up in my arms. As a compromise I push her from behind.

Once in the play room, she lies on the couch and says in a very commanding tone, 'I am hungry, give me some food'. When I query this she indicates some Plasticine cakes and chicken she had made the previous day. When I give them to her she throws them away in a tantrum.

I speak to her about her distress. She wants me to give something to her, to feed her, but cannot bear to take anything. I question whether this is related to something about the weekend. This was only a tentative interpretation of Ann's behaviour, as I had the impression from the violence of her reaction, that there might be something special happening outside of the session about which she was not informing me.

'Shut up, I don't want you to speak!' With the pencil-box Ann threatens my eyes. I stop her hand with mine. It seems that this is something that she wanted. We struggle now, body against body. I sense that all this is not simply a fight, but that there is also some desire for contact. I wonder whether she is so angry that only by fighting can she allow herself to come near me. I say this to her and I also interpret her threatening behaviour as an attempt to arouse anxiety in me about something that is threatening and hurting and yet unknown, in order to communicate her own anxiety and sense of threat.

She now climbs on to the couch and hangs from a pipe near the ceiling. She screams with anxiety and watches my reaction. This type of behaviour is frequent with her. As there is a real danger I go to catch her. I interpret her need to provoke extreme anxiety and fear of loss in me and at the same time to test whether I will really want to rescue her.

She now goes to her drawer and takes out two balls, asks me whether or not they bounce (they are made out of cloth), and throws them against the wall as if beginning a throwing and catching game. When she cannot catch them easily because they only bounce slightly, she throws them angrily away and lets herself slide down against the wall and sits on the floor. She seems very, very desperate. 'I am hungry, they have not given me anything to eat. I want macaroni and cannelloni. I cannot stand it any more'. (Macaroni and cannelloni are Ann's favourite dishes.) I speak here of her desperate wish to be close and to be fed and her disappointed feeling that I am not giving anything, when I am not giving it in an exact, perfect form.

All the time I had the impression that there was something very disturbing going on that I did not know about and although I linked her upset with the weekend I had the feeling that it was not only that. I knew that she had been separated from her mother very early on when she had been taken to a nursery, when she was three or four months old. I spoke of that experience saying that in the nursery she had probably felt that her mother would never come back and she had been so desperate. I asked whether or not she knew something about it. She said that she was one when she was taken to the nursery school and then she corrected herself. 'No, I was much smaller, I was only four months old and I was crying all the time'. I say that her mother, by leaving her crying in the nursery, had turned into a bad and menacing person, almost like that pencil-box with which she had threatened my eyes. That was why she could not bear to have me near her although that was also what she wanted. Now Ann becomes much more open and comments that her parents had told her that she had been very angry about the nursery school. She also says that when she was one and she was in the nursery school, she knew how to say 'Mum', 'Dad' and 'peach'. She so much loved peaches, she says. From this moment on there is vivid communication between us. I speak to her of her change of mood and attitude with me. Now she could actively use words and specifically ask for things from me, because she felt that she liked me. This was so different from her attitude when she first arrived and I had to push her upstairs, as if she did not want to be here at all. Also at one point I commented on how she had been trapped into kicking, dirtying, and provoking, as she did when she was a baby. Perhaps this happens at home with her mother. Ann said 'Yes, it does happen'. Ann left the session shouting happily to me 'Goodbye' while running downstairs to meet her mother.

This session is centred from the beginning around the complex problems of the early feeding situation which are stirred up by the announcement of the mother's absence. At the beginning Ann seems so invaded and dominated by despair and anger that no communication seems possible. She is provocative and rejects every query and remark I make. But still she is able to show her expectation that I will pick her up (carry her upstairs in my arms) and give her what she needs, food. But she cannot take anything in for two main reasons. The first is the irritation and anger she transfers from her relationship with her mother to me. Only by fighting can she allow herself to have some closeness to me, yet the desire for it is possible to sense.

The other reason for her difficulty in taking anything in from me is based on much more depressive experiences. When she let herself slide down on to the floor after having realized that the balls 'do not bounce' and says in despair, 'they have not given me anything to eat', she seems to express her early experience with her mother's breasts which are not bouncing with milk but are in such a state that they cannot feed her. When I spoke of her early experience, which I linked with her being sent to the nursery, Ann began to have some contact with herself and with me, i.e. she began to differentiate her experiences with me from her early depressive experience with the breast. From the material of other sessions I got a picture of Ann's phantasy that she had done something to mother's breast, damaged it in some way. She felt that the mother could not stand her any more, she was exhausted by her and thus sent her away into the nursery. But this is not clear in this session and I leave it aside. What is more obvious is that when Ann seems to experience the analyst as somebody who is able to stand her irritation, anger and provocation, and can speak of them, and at the same time sees and speaks of her vital demand for food and proximity and of her fear of loss, then she feels contained and understood and her feelings towards me change. She becomes able to speak of her anger and her desires, and to remember her childhood history. She is more able to differentiate me from her early objects and thus can use me as a containing and understanding object. The standing and understanding changed her feelings and transformed me from a menacing object into a lovely peach that she knew that she liked, could name, and could actively ask for.

This move towards the active expression of liking, wanting or even demanding the object is important because Ann frequently shows a tendency to become very passive. This passivity is often related to a hopeless state of mind and sometimes becomes erotized into a kind of pleasure through wallowing in a regressive, despairing mood. She relinquishes her ego and tries to make me act actively instead. This is shown in the session when in despair she hangs on to the pipe, aware that there is danger, but showing that she is not going to do anything about it. If I do not catch her she will let herself fall and either hurt herself or die. In this way she often tries to mobilize me to do things for her that she would be quite able to do herself. My impression is that she uses this a lot with her parents. She has her asthmatic crises, her legs hurt, she is so upset that her mother goes to sleep with her in the same room, and brings everything into the bed for her. She then bosses and enslaves her mother, which makes the relationship with her only worse and her sense of guilt more intense.

Although Ann expressed some of her needs fairly directly in this session, some of them were communicated by what Klein (1952) has described as projective identification. It was important to understand and verbalize this to her. My experience of sensing that something important was happening, and of not being informed of it, probably corresponded to Ann's experience of apprehension, of secrecy about her mother's trip, about which she had been informed only at the last minute. In addition my anxiety concerning the loss of a loved person was stimulated by Ann when she hung on the pipe. The pencil-box was slung at my face as a menacing object, expressing, to my mind, Ann's early experience of a threatening breast nearing her face.

During the session I had been putting into words what I understood of these different communications and this, together with standing her anger, seemed to have given Ann a sense of being contained which then enabled her to speak to me of her different feelings, anger as well as need. She was able to introject at that moment a containing, robust object who could stand and face both need and anger. This not only strengthened her ego, but made communication possible with the external world as well as with her internal world.

Final comments

I have tried to show the nature of some of the processes involved in the weakening and strengthening of the child's ego in relation to its objects, as I have observed it in the analytical relationship. For the ego to become robust and strong, and to ensure the integration of the drives and their psychic representatives, love and hate, the individual has to be able to introject a containing object which becomes the core of his or her own ego. Unless the analyst understands and verbalizes the obstacles which are in the way of this introjection — which in Ann's case were her early menacing and depressive experiences of the non-containing object — the child has difficulty with this introjection and consequently has difficulties in developing his own, independent ego with which he can begin to deal with life and its adversities. Yet, independent and strong ego functioning is our main criterion when we think of the terminability of an analysis.

To end with, I shall consider a few points that are relevant to our discussion about containing, communication and terminability, as I have observed and described in these few sessions with Ann.

1. The splitting processes we observe in the first series of sessions is not just a 'falling apart'. Ann actively cuts off and fragments her mental functions and feelings and those of her object. This is fuelled by the death drive and might become a serious obstacle to the ego's development.

2. When Ann cuts off and freezes her feelings towards me, she also loses contact with her own internal world. She loses her ability to

215

discriminate, to know what she likes and does not like. Her actions became impulsive and are no longer guided and controlled by those ego trends which are able to know through her own perceptions something of the nature of her internal as well as external objects and her feelings and wishes towards them.

3. Some of Ann's ego functions seem to continue undisturbed and 'order the chaos' through 'intellectual mastery' (Freud 1937, p. 228). Ann was capable of good generalization and logic when she made 'sets'. But this was largely cut off from her feelings and from her object-relatedness.

4. We can also observe a secondary erotization when Ann with a cruel expression destroys the face representing her own mind, or when she cynically repeats the song of joy and sweetness about Christmas at a moment when everything is in pieces. She seems to get caught up into a sado-masochistic excitement which might become self-perpetuating.

5. Only when Ann can experience the analyst as standing and understanding her most intolerable impulses and feelings, as originally experienced in her early object relations, does she become able to introject not only what the analyst is interpreting but the very functions of the analyst: perceiving, standing up against, intuiting, thinking, speaking. This introjection of an object which contains through all these functions then becomes part of her ego.

6. Through this introjection Ann's feelings towards me change. From a menacing object, I change into a liked and desired one. Ann becomes more able to perceive, to feel what she likes and dislikes, loves and hates. She is more able to speak of her childhood history and feelings. One hopes that this introjection will help her to find suitable object relations in future instead of being stuck with those into whom she projects her own unbearable feelings, becoming dependent on, yet alienated from, them.

7. What I am describing is like a cross-section showing the shifts of a relationship in a session and does not imply any permanent modification in Ann's ego structure. This last session is only after one year of analysis! Ann has to be able to test her new object again and again, introject it, destroy it, and mourn it. By the continuous repetition of these processes, Ann gradually acquires trust in her analyst's capacity and desire to hold and contain all her feelings. She can then move towards actively containing and taking responsibility for her own self.

Summary

The author discusses the relation between certain qualities of communication and containment in the analytical relationship and how these can lead to changes in the child patient's ego either in the direction of greater integration or in the direction of increased splitting and regression. These shifts are described through the case material of the analysis of the seven-year-old girl, Ann. When the analyst did not understand Ann's particular anxiety, she cut off her capacity to perceive, feel, and communicate. When, on the contrary, she experienced her analyst as somebody who was able to stand and understand her need and anger and to speak of them to her, this seemed to give her a sense of being contained, and enabled her to introject not only the analyst's interpretations but also her functions of perceiving, intuiting and thinking, that is to say an object who contains through these functions. This object becomes part of the child's own ego through repetitive experience of being contained and understood in all kinds of emotional situations. This in turn broadens the child's capacity to communicate with the external world as well as with her internal world.

References

Bion, W.R. (1962) 'A theory of thinking', *International Journal of Psycho-Analysis*, 43: 306–10; and in *Second Thoughts*, London: Heinemann (1962); also in *Melanie Klein Today: Volume 1*, London: Routledge (1988).

Freud, S. (1937) 'Analysis terminable and interminable', SE 23, 209–53.

Klein, M. (1946) 'Notes on some schizoid mechanisms' in *Developments in Psycho-Analysis*, London: Hogarth Press (1952); also in *The Writings of Melanie Klein*, vol. 3: 1–24, London: Hogarth Press (1975).

——— (1952) 'On identification' in *The Writings of Melanie Klein*, vol. 3, 141–75.

PART FOUR

The application of Kleinian ideas in other fields of work

Introduction

ELIZABETH BOTT SPILLIUS

Using the ideas of psychoanalysis to illuminate aspects of other fields of work, especially literature and the study of society, has a venerable tradition started of course by Freud. Klein herself and Joan Riviere extended this work, especially in the field of literature. Klein's later colleagues have continued to make contributions in this area, though the volume of such work is decreasing. This is balanced, however, by gradually increasing interest in Kleinian ideas in the fields of literary and art criticism, philosophy, among certain social scientists, and in the fields of psychiatry, group relations, and the helping professions.

In the field of literature Hanna Segal is the main Kleinian contributor. Her early paper 'A psycho-analytical approach to aesthetics' (1952) is a notable exploration of artistic creativity in relation to the depressive position, a theme which she continued to explore in 'Delusion and artistic creativity' (1974, reprinted here), in 'Psychoanalysis and freedom of thought' (1977b), and in 'Joseph Conrad and the mid-life crisis' (1984). Indeed, interest in the relation between the depressive position and creativity informs much of her work, especially that on symbolism. (See especially 'Notes on symbol formation', 1957, reprinted in Volume 1.) Elliott Jaques' paper 'Death and the mid-life crisis' (1965, reprinted here) is also focused on the depressive position, especially on the reworking of it in the middle phase of life and the role of this reworking in creativity. Apart from Segal and Jaques, however, the post-Klein generation has been much less active in applying the ideas of Kleinian analysis to literature and creativity. There are two recent exceptions: Arthur Hyatt Williams (1986) has examined Coleridge's *The Ancient Mariner* in the light of Klein's views on the paranoid-schizoid and depressive positions and John Steiner (1985) discusses Sophocles' drama *Oedipus Rex* psychoanalytically, not so much, however, to show the relevance of Kleinian theory to Sophocles' work of art but more to show the relevance of the work of art to psychoanalysis.

Much work has been done by Kleinian analysts in the field of the study of society: by Money-Kyrle in psychoanalytic commentaries on ethics and politics (1951, 1961, 1978) and more recently by Segal (1987) in a Kleinian commentary on nuclear war; by Bion in his work on groups (1961) which has had a profound influence on group therapy and group relations training (Rice 1965, Pines 1985); Kleinian ideas have been used at the Tavistock Institute of Human Relations by Jaques, Menzies Lyth and others in the empirical study of institutions and planned institutional change; several Kleinian analysts have worked at the Tavistock Clinic in the field of developing new methods of treatment appropriate to the needs of the National Health Service. Very little of the work in this last field has been systematically published, but it takes two characteristic forms: the development of a consultative relationship between a Kleinian analyst and a person or group working in another helping profession, and the development, often disapproved of by 'purer' colleagues, of psychotherapy training schemes instead of psychoanalysis to meet the demands imposed by the Health Service.

Certain trends of change are apparent in Kleinian applied psychoanalysis both in the field of literature and in social science. In the field of literature the most obvious change is how few Kleinian analysts now write about it themselves. Segal is the exception; literature and psychoanalysis have always been her twin preoccupations. In the social field there has been virtually a disappearance, again with the exception of Segal's nuclear war paper, of commentaries on society, politics, and ethics by Kleinian analysts who are not simultaneously specialists in the fields concerned. Increasingly one finds that if sociological studies and commentaries are made by Kleinian analysts, these analysts have also been trained in the disciplines that they are writing about. This is true, for example, of Elliott Jaques (1948, 1951, 1955, 1956), Isabel Menzies Lyth (1960, 1965, 1969, 1970, 1982, 1985, and in press), Riccardo Steiner (1985), John Hill (Hill and Trist 1955), Turquet (1975), and myself (1968, 1976).

A second major trend is that the use of Kleinian ideas by workers in other fields is now being carried out mainly by specialists in the field concerned who have been analysed and/or have a special interest in Kleinian psychoanalysis. This is the case in the fields of philosophy (Wollheim 1969, 1974, 1980, 1984), art criticism (Stokes 1978), literary criticism (Harris Williams 1987, Waddell 1986), film criticism (Gabbard and Gabbard 1987), feminism (Sayers 1987), politics (Frosh 1987, Rustin

1982, Rustin and Rustin 1984, and to some extent Lasch 1981), anthropology (Cantlie 1968, 1985), adult psychotherapy (Wittenberg 1970, Herman 1987), child psychotherapy (The *Journal of Child Psychotherapy* and studies of specific pathologies, e.g. Frances Tustin on autism 1972, 1981, 1986), and, finally, the study of institutions. The study of institutions, especially at the Tavistock Institute of Human Relations, includes a vast number of studies most of which use Klein's ideas at least to some extent. Most of these studies were inspired, directly or indirectly, by Eric Trist who is at present preparing a comprehensive history of the work (Trist, in press).

In brief, work in other fields that uses Kleinian ideas is now increasingly being done by the disciplines concerned, not by a Kleinian analyst from the perspective of his or her consulting room. There are good reasons for this trend. Conviction about analytic ideas comes from the empirical situation in which the ideas are grounded, that is, from the consulting room. These ideas so enrich the imagination that they may give the unwary analyst an intense sense of the truth not only of his analytic method of investigation but also of the relevance of its findings to other fields. But each of these other fields has its own empirical situation which needs study in its own right. A group or institution, for example, does not function in exactly the same way as an individual or a dyad; the truths that apply to the individual or dyad may be limiting factors for the group but are not determining. Generalizations about group, institution, and culture are on another level which the psychoanalyst cannot study in the consulting room. Even Freud's forays into other fields in *Leonardo* (1910), *Totem and Taboo* (1911), and *Group Psychology and the Analysis of the Ego* (1921) added comparatively little to art criticism, anthropology, and sociology but enormously enriched psychoanalysis. Similarly, even Segal's paper on aesthetics (1952), which has probably had more influence on other fields than any other Kleinian paper, is even more important to psychoanalysis than to the other fields, for it is a cornerstone in Kleinian thinking about creativity, symbolism, and the depressive position.

I do not mean to assert that psychoanalysis has had no effect on other disciplines or on Western culture generally. It is obvious that no writer, artist, or social scientist can work today without having been influenced by Freud's ideas, but the ideas have spread, I believe, not because of his specific works in the applied field but because of his great seminal ideas about the mind and the human condition. Klein's ideas are coming to be known outside the narrow circle of psychoanalysis in the same way.

It is hardly surprising that other disciplines react badly to those psychoanalysts, Kleinian and others, who invade their territory without having learned about the field from the discipline's own point of view and with what is often seen as a reductive approach (Jordan 1986, Harris Williams 1986). The usual reaction of other disciplines to psychoanalytic commentaries is silently to ignore them. But this is more than compensated for by the developing tendency for members of other disciplines to use ideas from psychoanalysis in their own way, and increasingly to use Kleinian ideas.

For the Kleinian analyst who is interested in fields other than psychoanalysis there is thus a conflict which each analyst solves in his or her own way. Perhaps the most usual solution is for the analyst to stay in his or her consulting room, developing ideas about theory and technique through clinical work without, in his or her capacity as analyst, expressing interest in other fields; if such interest is expressed, it comes from the analyst as person rather than as analyst. A few analysts, like Segal, continue to make analytic ventures in other fields. Some, like Isabel Menzies Lyth, myself, and a number of analysts who are also psychiatrists continue to work in the other fields and to use analytic ideas when appropriate. But whatever the solution, the conflict is present for all.

Four papers illustrate different types of application of psychoanalytic ideas in other fields by Kleinian analysts. The first two can be described as psychoanalytic commentaries on other fields, though commentaries that I think are both of interest to the other fields and of importance to Kleinian theory.

Elliott Jaques' 'Death and the mid-life crisis' (1965) extends Segal's ideas of the intrinsic connection between creativity and the depressive position in describing the life crisis that typically occurs in the life of the creative artist as he or she faces emotionally the reality of eventual death and declining powers, which involves a reworking of the depressive position.

Segal's paper 'Delusion and artistic creativity' (1974) extends and develops the ideas she put forward in 'A psycho-analytic approach to aesthetics' (1952), this time in a psychoanalytic view of Golding's *The Spire* which discusses the fine line that distinguishes the reparation of artistic creativity which is based on psychic and external reality and the manic reparation of delusion based on omnipotence and self-interest. Like Freud's psychoanalytic commentaries on literature, this paper is rich in insights for psychoanalysis, insight especially into the psychic bases of omnipotence.

The next two papers illustrate the work of Kleinian analysts who are also trained in other disciplines.

In 'Psycho-analysis and ceremony' (Spillius, but under the name of Bott, 1968) I use psychoanalytic ideas to add another dimension of understanding to an anthropological analysis of ceremony in a small-scale society, stressing particularly the role of the ceremony and its accompanying myths in expressing but also containing anxiety and several types of contradictory social principle. As a dream is to the individual, so a ceremony can be to a social group: a symbolic means of stating and partly resolving contradictions and conflicts.

Isabel Menzies Lyth's paper 'A psycho-analytic perspective on social institutions' is here published for the first time. It is a concise statement of her method of consultancy to institutions, a method based on years of work with many different sorts of organization. Her earliest published work in this field (1960) is a classic study of nurses' anxieties and defences in a teaching hospital, a study which gives vivid empirical illustrations of Jaques' 1955 paper 'Social systems as a defence against persecutory and depressive anxiety' in which he applies Klein's concepts of the paranoid-schizoid and depressive positions and their defences to a discussion of institutions. Menzies Lyth has used this basic orientation in her many subsequent studies (Menzies Lyth, in press), each time using whatever psychoanalytic ideas were relevant to the specific empirical problem presented by the institution in its setting.

Death and the mid-life crisis

ELLIOTT JAQUES

This paper was originally published in the *International Journal of Psycho-Analysis*, 46: 502–14.

In the course of the development of the individual there are critical phases which have the character of change points, or periods of rapid transition. Less familiar perhaps, though nonetheless real, are the crises which occur around the age of 35 — which I shall term the mid-life crisis — and at full maturity around the age of 65. It is the mid-life crisis with which I shall deal in this paper.

When I say that the mid-life crisis occurs around the age of 35, I mean that it takes place in the middle thirties, that the process of transition runs on for some years, and that the exact period will vary among individuals. The transition is often obscured in women by the proximity of the onset of changes connected with the menopause. In the case of men, the change has from time to time been referred to as the male climacteric, because of the reduction in the intensity of sexual behaviour which often occurs at that time.

Crisis in genius

I first became aware of this period as a critical stage in development when I noticed a marked tendency towards crisis in the creative work of great men in their middle and late thirties. It is clearly expressed by Richard Church in his autobiography *The Voyage Home*:

> There seems to be a biological reason for men and women, when they reach the middle thirties, finding themselves beset with misgivings, agonizing inquiries, and a loss of zest. Is it that state which the

226

medieval schoolmen called *accidie*, the cardinal sin of spiritual sloth? I believe it is.

This crisis may express itself in three different ways: the creative career may simply come to an end, either in a drying-up of creative work, or in actual death; the creative capacity may begin to show and express itself for the first time; or a decisive change in the quality and content of creativeness may take place.

Perhaps the most striking phenomenon is what happens to the death rate among creative artists. I had got the impression that the age of 37 seemed to figure pretty prominently in the death of individuals of this category. This impression was upheld by taking a random sample of some 310 painters, composers, poets, writers, and sculptors, of undoubted greatness or of genius. The death rate shows a sudden jump between 35 and 39, at which period it is much above the normal death rate. The group includes Mozart, Raphael, Chopin, Rimbaud, Purcell, Baudelaire, Watteau ... There is then a big drop below the normal death rate between the ages of 40 and 44, followed by a return to the normal death rate pattern in the late forties. The closer one keeps to genius in the sample, the more striking and clearcut is this spiking of the death rate in mid-life.

The change in creativity which occurs during this period can be seen in the lives of countless artists. Bach, for example, was mainly an organist until his cantorship at Leipzig at 38, at which time he began his colossal achievements as a composer. Rossini's life is described in the following terms:

His comparative silence during the period 1832—1868 (i.e. from 40 to his death at 74) makes his biography like the narrative of two lives — swift triumph, and a long life of seclusion.

Racine had thirteen years of continuous success culminating in *Phèdre* at the age of 38; he then produced nothing for some twelve years. The characteristic work of Goldsmith, Constable, and Goya emerged between the ages of 35 and 38. By the age of 43 Ben Jonson had produced all the plays worthy of his genius, although he lived to be 64. At 33 Gauguin gave up his job in a bank, and by 39 had established himself in his creative career as a painter. Donatello's work after 39 is described by a critic as showing a marked change in style, in which he departed from the statuesque balance of his earlier work and turned to the creation of an almost instantaneous expression of life.

Goethe, between the ages of 37 and 39, underwent a profound change in outlook, associated with his trip to Italy. As many of his biographers have pointed out, the importance of this journey and this period in his life cannot be exaggerated. He himself regarded it as the climax to his life. Never before had he gained such complete understanding of his genius and mission as a poet. His work then began to reflect the classical spirit of Greek tragedy and the Renaissance.

Michelangelo carried out a series of masterpieces until he was 40: his 'David' was finished at 29, the decoration of the roof of the Sistine Chapel at 37, and his 'Moses' between 37 and 40. During the next fifteen years little is known of any artistic work. There was a creative lull until, at 55, he began to work on the great Medici monument and then later on 'The Last Judgement' and frescoes in the Pauline Chapel.

Let me make it clear that I am not suggesting that the careers of most creative persons either begin or end during the mid-life crisis. There are few creative geniuses who live and work into maturity, in whom the quality of greatness cannot be discerned in early adulthood in the form either of created works or of the potential for creating them: Beethoven, Shakespeare, Goethe, Couperin, Ibsen, Balzac, Voltaire, Verdi, Handel, Goya, Dürer, to name but a very few at random. But there are equally few in whom a decisive change cannot be seen in the quality of their work — in whose work the effects of their having gone through a mid-life crisis cannot be discerned. The reactions range all the way from severe and dramatic crisis, to a smoother and less troubled transition — just as reactions to the phase of adolescent crisis may range from severe disturbance and breakdown to relatively ordered readjustment to mental and sexual adulthood — but the effects of the change are there to be discerned. What then are the main features of this change?

There are two features which seem to me of outstanding importance. One of these has to do with the mode of work; the second has to do with the content of the work. Let me consider each of these in turn. I shall use the phrase 'early adulthood' for the pre-mid-life phase, and 'mature adulthood' for the post-mid-life phase.

Change in mode of work

I can best describe the change in mode of work which I have in mind by describing the extreme of its manifestation. The creativity of the twenties and the early thirties tends to be a hot-from-the-fire creativity. It is intense and spontaneous, and comes out ready-made. The spontaneous effusions of Mozart, Keats, Shelley, Rimbaud, are the prototype. Most of the work seems to go on unconsciously. The conscious production is rapid, the pace of creation often being dictated by the limits of the artist's capacity physically to record the words or music he is expressing.

A vivid description of early adult type of work is given in Gittings' biography of Keats:

Keats all this year had been living on spiritual capital. He had used and spent every experience almost as soon as it had come into his possession, every sight, person, book, emotion or thought had been converted spontaneously into poetry. Could he or any other poet have lasted at such a rate? . . . He could write no more by these methods. He realized this himself when he wished to compose as he said 'without fever'. He could not keep this high pulse beating and endure.

By contrast, the creativity of the late thirties and after is a sculpted creativity. The inspiration may be hot and intense. The unconscious work is no less than before. But there is a big step between the first effusion of inspiration and the finished created product. The inspiration itself may come more slowly. Even if there are sudden bursts of inspiration, they are only the beginning of the work process. The initial inspiration must first be externalized in its elemental state. Then begins the process of forming and fashioning the external product, by means of working and reworking the externalized material. I use the term sculpting because the nature of the sculptor's material – it is the sculptor working in stone of whom I am thinking – forces him into this kind of relationship with the product of his creative imagination. There occurs a process of interplay between unconscious intuitive work and inspiration, and the considered perception of the externally emergent creation and the reaction to it.

In her note 'A character trait of Freud's', Riviere (1958) describes Freud's exhorting her in connection with some psychoanalytic idea which had occurred to her:

Write it, write it, put it down in black and white . . . get it out, produce it, make something of it – *outside you*, that is; give it an existence independently of you.

This externalizing process is part of the essence of work in mature adulthood, when, as in the case of Freud, the initially externalized material is not itself the end product, or nearly the end product, but is rather the starting point, the object of further working over, modification, elaboration, sometimes for periods of years.

In distinguishing between the precipitate creativity of early adulthood and the sculpted creativity of mature adulthood, I do not want to give the impression of drawing a hard and fast line between the two phases. There are of course times when a creative person in mature adulthood will be subject to bursts of inspiration and rapid-fire creative production.

Equally there will be found instances of mature and sculpted creative work done in early adulthood. The 'David' of Michelangelo is, I think, the supreme example of the latter.

But the instances where work in early adulthood has the sculpted and worked-over quality are rare. Sometimes, as in scientific work, there may be the appearance of sculpted work. Young physicists in their twenties, for example, may produce startling discoveries, which are the result of continuous hard work and experimentation. But these discoveries result from the application of modern theories about the structure of matter — theories which themselves have been the product of the sculpted work of mature adulthood of such geniuses as Thomson and Einstein.

Equally, genuinely creative work in mature adulthood may sometimes not appear to be externally worked over and sculpted, and yet actually be so. What seems to be rapid and unworked-over creation is commonly the reworking of themes which have been worked upon before, or which may have been slowly emerging over the years in previous works. We need look no farther than the work of Freud for a prime example of this process of books written rapidly, which are nevertheless the coming to fruition of ideas which have been worked upon, fashioned, reformulated, left incomplete and full of loose ends, and then reformulated once again in a surging forward through the emergence of new ideas for overcoming previous difficulties.

The reality of the distinction comes out in the fact that certain materials are more readily applicable to the precipitate creativity of early adulthood than are others. Thus, for example, musical composition, lyrical poetry, are much more amenable to rapid creative production than are sculpting in stone or painting in oils. It is noteworthy, therefore, that whereas there are very many poets and composers who achieve greatness in early adulthood — indeed in their early twenties or their late teens — there are very few sculptors or painters in oils who do so. With oil paint and stone, the working relationship to the materials themselves is of importance, and demands that the creative process should go through the stage of initial externalization and working-over of the externalized product. The written word and musical notation do not of necessity have this same plastic external objective quality. They can be sculpted and worked over, but they can also readily be treated merely as a vehicle for the immediate recording of unconsciously articulated products which are brought forward whole and complete — or nearly so.

Quality and content of creativity

The change in mode of work, then, between early and mature adulthood, is a change from precipitate to sculpted creativity. Let me now consider for a moment the change in the quality and content of the creativity. The change I have in mind is the emergence of a tragic and philosophical content which then moves on to serenity in the creativity of mature adulthood, in contrast to a more characteristically lyrical and descriptive content to the work of early adulthood. This distinction is a commonly held one, and may perhaps be considered sufficiently self-evident to require little explication or argument. It is implied, of course, in my choice of the adjectives 'early' and 'mature' to qualify the two phases of adulthood which I am discussing.

The change may be seen in the more human, tragic and less fictitious and stage quality of Dickens's writing from *David Copperfield* (which he wrote at 37) onwards. It may be seen also in the transition in Shakespeare from the historical plays and comedies to the tragedies. When he was about 31, in the midst of writing his lyrical comedies, he produced *Romeo and Juliet*. The great series of tragedies and Roman plays, however, began to appear a few years later; *Julius Caesar, Hamlet, Othello, King Lear,* and *Macbeth* are believed to have been written most probably between the ages of 35 and 40.

There are many familiar features of the change in question. Late adolescent and early adult idealism and optimism accompanied by split-off and projected hate, are given up and supplanted by a more contemplative pessimism. There is a shift from radical desire and impatience to a more reflective and tolerant conservatism. Beliefs in the inherent goodness of man are replaced by a recognition and acceptance of the fact that inherent goodness is accompanied by hate and destructive forces within, which contribute to man's own misery and tragedy. To the extent that hate, destruction, and death are found explicitly in early adult creativeness, they enter in the form of the satanic or the macabre, as in Poe and in Baudelaire, and not as worked-through and resolved anxieties.

The spirit of early adult creativeness is summed up in Shelley's *Prometheus Unbound*. In her notes on this work, Shelley's wife has written:

> The prominent feature of Shelley's theory of the destiny of the human species is that evil is not inherent in the system of the Creation, but an accident that might be expelled . . . God made Earth and Man perfect, till he by his fall 'brought death into the world, and all our woe'. Shelley believed that mankind had only to will that there should be no evil in the world and there would be none. . . . He was attached to this idea with fervent enthusiasm.

This early adult idealism is built upon the use of unconscious denial and manic defences as normal processes of defence against two fundamental

231

features of human life — the inevitableness of eventual death, and the existence of hate and destructive impulses inside each person. I shall try to show that the explicit recognition of these two features, and the bringing of them into focus, is the quintessence of successful weathering of the mid-life crisis and the achievement of mature adulthood.

It is when death and human destructiveness — that is to say, both death and the death instinct — are taken into account, that the quality and content of creativity change to the tragic, reflective, and philosophical. The depressive position must be worked through once again, at a qualitatively different level. The misery and despair of suffering and chaos unconsciously brought about by oneself are encountered and must be surmounted for life to be endured and for creativity to continue. Nemesis is the key, and tragedy the theme, of its recognition.

The successful outcome of mature creative work lies thus in constructive resignation both to the imperfections of men and to shortcomings in one's own work. It is this constructive resignation that then imparts serenity to life and work.

The Divine Comedy

I have taken these examples from creative genius because I believe the essence of the mid-life crisis is revealed in its most full and rounded form in the lives of the great. It will have become manifest that the crisis is a depressive crisis, in contrast to the adolescent crisis, which tends to be a paranoid-schizoid one. In adolescence, the predominant outcome of serious breakdown is schizophrenic illness; in mid-life the predominant outcome is depression, or the consequences of defence against depressive anxiety as reflected in manic defences, hypochondriasis, obsessional mechanisms, or superficiality and character deterioration. Working through the mid-life crisis calls for a reworking through of the infantile depression, but with mature insight into death and destructive impulses to be taken into account.

This theme of working through depression is magnificently expressed in *The Divine Comedy*. This masterpiece of all time was begun by Dante following his banishment from Florence at the age of 37. In the opening stanzas he creates his setting in words of great power and tremendous psychological depth. He begins:

In the middle of the journey of our life, I came to myself within a dark wood where the straight way was lost. Ah, how hard it is to tell of that wood, savage and harsh and dense, the thought of which renews my fear. So bitter is it that death is hardly more.

These words have been variously interpreted; for example, as an allegorical reference to the entrance to Hell, or as a reflection of the poet's state of mind on being forced into exile, homeless and hungry for justice. They may, however, be interpreted at a deeper level as the opening scene of a vivid and perfect description of the emotional crisis of the mid-life phase, a crisis which would have gripped the mind and soul of the poet whatever his religious outlook, or however settled or unsettled his external affairs. The evidence for this conclusion exists in the fact that during the years of his early thirties which preceded his exile, he had already begun his transformation from the idyllic outlook of the *Vita Nuova* (age 27—29) through a conversion to 'philosophy' which he allegorized in the *Convivio* written when he was between 36 and 38 years of age.

Even taken quite literally, *The Divine Comedy* is a description of the poet's first full and worked-through conscious encounter with death. He is led through hell and purgatory by his master Virgil, eventually to find his own way, guided by his beloved Beatrice, into paradise. His final rapturous and mystical encounter with the being of God, represented to him in strange and abstract terms, was not mere rapture, not simply a being overwhelmed by a mystical oceanic feeling. It was a much more highly organized experience. It was expressly a vision of supreme love and knowledge, with control of impulse and of will, which promulgates the mature life of greater ease and contemplation which follows upon the working-through of primitive anxiety and guilt, and the return to the primal good object.

Dante explicitly connects his experience of greater mental integration, and the overcoming of confusion, with the early infantile relation to the primal good object. As he nears the end of the 33rd Canto of 'Paradiso', the climax of his whole grand scheme, he explains:

> Now my speech will come more short even of what I remember than an infant's who yet bathes his tongue at the breast.

But the relationship with the primal good object is one in which reparation has been made, Purgatorio has been traversed, loving impulses have come into the ascendant, and the cruelty and harshness of the superego expressed in the inferno have been relieved. Bitterness has given way to composure.

In Dante, the result of this deep resolution is not the reinforcing of manic defence and denial which characterizes mystical experience fused with magic omnipotence; but rather the giving up of manic defence, and consequent strengthening of character and resolve, under the dominion of love. As Croce has observed:

What is not found in the 'Paradiso', for it is foreign to the spirit of Dante, is flight from the world, absolute refuge in God, asceticism. He does not seek to fly from the world, but to instruct it, correct it, and reform it ... he knew the world and its doings and passions.

Awareness of personal death

Although I have thus far taken my examples from the extremes of genius, my main theme is that the mid-life crisis is a reaction which not only occurs in creative genius, but manifests itself in some form in everyone. What then is the psychological nature of this reaction to the mid-life situation, and how is it to be explained?

The simple fact of the situation is the arrival at the mid-point of life. What is simple from the point of view of chronology, however, is not simple psychologically. The individual has stopped growing up, and has begun to grow old. A new set of external circumstances has to be met. The first phase of adult life has been lived. Family and occupation have become established (or ought to have become established unless the individual's adjustment has gone seriously awry); parents have grown old, and children are at the threshold of adulthood. Youth and childhood are past and gone, and demand to be mourned. The achievement of mature and independent adulthood presents itself as the main psychological task. The paradox is that of entering the prime of life, the stage of fulfilment, but at the same time the prime and fulfilment are dated. Death lies beyond.

I believe, and shall try to demonstrate, that it is this fact of the entry upon the psychological scene of the reality and inevitability of one's own eventual personal death, that is the central and crucial feature of the mid-life phase — the feature which precipitates the critical nature of the period. Death — at the conscious level — instead of being a general conception, or an event experienced in terms of the loss of someone else, becomes a personal matter, one's own death, one's own real and actual mortality. As Freud (1915) has so accurately described the matter:

> We were prepared to maintain that death was the necessary outcome of life. ... In reality, however, we were accustomed to behave as if it were otherwise. We displayed an unmistakable tendency to 'shelve' death, to eliminate it from life. We tried to hush it up. ... That is our own death, of course. ... In the unconscious everyone is convinced of his own immortality.

This attitude towards life and death, written by Freud in another context, aptly expresses the situation which we all encounter in mid-life. The reality of one's own personal death forces itself upon our attention and can no longer so readily be shelved. A 36-year-old patient, who had been in analysis for seven years, and was in the course of working through a deep depressive reaction which heralded the final phase of his analysis some eighteen months later, expressed the matter with great clarity. 'Up till now', he said, 'life has seemed an endless upward slope, with nothing but the distant horizon in view. Now suddenly I seem to have reached the crest of the hill, and there stretching ahead is the downward slope with the end of the road in sight — far enough away it's true — but there is death observably present at the end'.

From that point on this patient's plans and ambitions took on a different hue. For the first time in his life he saw his future as circumscribed. He began his adjustment to the fact that he would not be able to accomplish in the span of a single lifetime everything he had desired to do. He could achieve only a finite amount. Much would have to remain unfinished and unrealized.

This perspective on the finitude of life was accompanied by a greater solidity and robustness in his outlook, and introduced a new quality of earthly resignation. It reflected a diminishing of his unconscious wish for immortality. Such ideas are commonly lived out in terms of denial of mourning and death, or in terms of ideas of immortality, from notions of reincarnation and life after death, to notions of longevity like those expressed by the successful 28-year-old novelist who writes in his diary, 'I shall be the most serious of men, and I shall live longer than any man'.

Unconscious meaning of death

How each one reacts to the mid-life encounter with the reality of his own eventual death — whether he can face this reality, or whether he denies it — will be markedly influenced by his infantile unconscious relation to death — a relationship which depends upon the stage and nature of the working through of the infantile depressive position, as Melanie Klein discovered and vividly described (1940, 1955). Let me paraphrase her conclusions.

The infant's relation with life and death occurs in the setting of his survival being dependent on his external objects, and on the balance of power of the life and death instincts which qualify his perception of those objects and his capacity to depend upon them and use them. In the depressive position in infancy, under conditions of prevailing love, the good and bad objects can in some measure be synthesized, the ego becomes more integrated, and hope for the re-establishment of the good object is experienced; the accompanying overcoming of grief and regaining of security is the infantile equivalent of the notion of life.

Under conditions of prevailing persecution, however, the working through of the depressive position will be to a greater or lesser extent inhibited; reparation and synthesis fail; and the inner world is unconsciously felt to contain the persecuting and annihilating devoured and destroyed bad breast, the ego itself feeling in bits. The chaotic internal situation thus experienced is the infantile equivalent of the notion of death.

Ideas of immortality arise as a response to these anxieties, and as a defence against them. Unconscious phantasies of immortality are the counterpart of the infantile phantasies of the indestructible and hence immortal aspect of the idealized and bountiful primal object. These phantasies are equally as persecuting as the chaotic internal situation they are calculated to mitigate. They contain omnipotent sadistic triumph, and increase guilt and persecution as a result. And they lead to feelings of intolerable helplessness through dependence upon the perfect object which becomes demanding of an equal perfection in behaviour.

Does the unconscious, then, have a conception of death? The views of Melanie Klein and those of Freud may seem not to correspond. Klein assumes an unconscious awareness of death. Freud assumes that the unconscious rejects all such awareness. Neither of these views, taken at face value, is likely to prove correct. Nor would I expect that either of their authors would hold to a literal interpretation of their views. The unconscious is not aware of death *per se*. But there are unconscious experiences akin to those which later appear in consciousness as notions of death. Let me illustrate such experiences.

A 47-year-old woman patient, suffering from claustrophobia and a variety of severe psychosomatic illnesses, recounted a dream in which she was lying in a coffin. She had been sliced into small chunks, and was dead. But there was a spider's-web-thin thread of nerve running through every chunk and connected to her brain. As a result she could experience everything. She knew she was dead. She could not move or make any sound. She could only lie in the claustrophobic dark and silence of the coffin.

I have selected this particular dream because I think it typifies the unconscious fear and experience of death. It is not in fact death in the sense in which consciously we think about it, but an unconscious phantasy of immobilization and helplessness, in which the self is subject to violent fragmentation, while yet retaining the capacity to experience the persecution and torment to which it is being subjected. When these phantasies of suspended persecution and torture are of pathological intensity, they are characteristic of many mental conditions: catatonic states, stupors, phobias, obsessions, frozen anxiety, simple depression.

A case of denial of death

In the early adult phase, before the mid-life encounter with death, the full-scale reworking-through of the depressive position does not as yet necessarily arise as a part of normal development. It can be postponed. It is not a pressing issue. It can be put to one side, until circumstances demand more forcibly that it be faced.

In the ordinary course of events, life is full and active. Physiologically, full potency has been reached, and activity — social, physical, economic, sexual — is to the fore. It is a time for doing, and the doing is flavoured and supported to a greater or lesser degree — depending on the emotional adjustment of the individual — by the activity and denial as part of the manic defence.

The early adult phase is one, therefore, in which successful activity can in fact obscure or conceal the operation of strong manic defences. But the depressive anxiety that is thus warded off will be encountered in due course. The mid-life crisis thrusts it forward with great intensity, and it can no longer be pushed aside if life is not to be impoverished.

This relationship between adjustment based upon activity in the early adult phase, and its failure in mid-life if the infantile depressive position is not unconsciously (or consciously, in analysis) worked through again, may be illustrated in the case of a patient, Mr N, who had led a successful life by everyday standards up to the time he came into analysis. He was an active man, a 'doer'. He had been successful in his career through intelligent application and hard work, was married with three children, had many good friends, and all seemed to be going very well.

The idealized content of this picture had been maintained by an active carrying on of life, without allowing time for reflection. His view was that he had not come to analysis for himself, but rather for a kind of tutorial purpose — he would bring his case history to me and we would have a clinical seminar in which we would conduct a psychoanalytic evaluation of the case material he had presented.

As might be expected, Mr N had great difficulty in coping with ambivalence. He was unconsciously frightened of any resentment, envy, jealousy, or other hostile feelings towards me, maintaining an attitude of idealized love for me and tolerant good nature towards every attempt on my part to analyse the impulses of destructiveness, and the feelings of persecution which he was counteracting by this idealization.

When we finally did break through this inability to cope with ambivalence — indeed a pretty complete unfamiliarity with the experience — it emerged that, in all his relationships, his idealization was inevitably followed by disappointment — a disappointment arising out of failure to

237

get the quality of love he was greedily expecting in return, and nursed by the envy of those whom he idealized.

It was out of the analysis of material of this kind that we were able to get at the reflection in the analysis of his early adult mode of adjustment. He admitted that he was ill, and that unconscious awareness of his illness undoubtedly was the main reason for his seeking analysis. Being active, and overconcerned for others, were soporifics, to which he had become addicted. Indeed, he confessed, he had resented my analysis taking this defensive addiction away from him. He had secretly entertained ideas of stopping his analysis 'because all this thinking about myself, instead of doing things, is no good. Now I realize that I have been piling up my rage against you inside myself, like I've done with everyone else'.

Thus it was that during the first year of his analysis, the patient lived out many of the techniques which had characterized his early adult adjustment. It was with the onset of the Christmas holiday that the unconscious depressive anxiety, which was the main cause of his disturbance in mid-life, came out in full force. It is this material that illustrates the importance of the depressive position and unconscious feelings about death in relation to the mid-life crisis.

He had shown definite signs before the holiday of feelings of being abandoned, saying that not only would he not see me, but his friends were to be away as well. Three days before the end of the holiday, he telephoned me and, in a depressed and tearful voice, asked if he could come to see me. I arranged a session that same evening.

When he came to see me, he was at first afraid to lie on the couch. He said that he wanted just to talk to me, to be comforted and reassured. He then proceeded to tell me how, from the beginning of the holiday, a black gloom had settled upon him. He yearned for his mother to be alive, so that he could be with her and be held and loved by her. 'I just felt completely deserted and lost', he said. 'I sat for hour after hour, unable to move or to do any work. I wanted to die. My thoughts were filled with suicide. Then I became terrified of my state of mind. That's why I 'phoned you. I just had never conceived it as even remotely possible that I could lose my self-control like this.' Things were made absolutely unbearable, he then explained, when one of his children had become nearly murderously aggressive towards his wife a few days before. His world seemed to have gone to pieces.

This material, and other associations, suggested that his wife stood for the bad aspect of his mother, and his son for the sadistic murderous part of himself. In his fear of dying, he was re-experiencing his own unconscious phantasies of tearing his mother to pieces, and he then felt abandoned and lost. As I interpreted on these lines, he interjected that the worst thing was the feeling of having gone to pieces himself. 'I can't stand it', he said, 'I feel as though I'm going to die'.

I then recalled to him a dream he had had just before the holiday, which we had not had time to analyse, and which contained material of importance in the understanding of his infantile perception of being dead. In this dream he was a small boy sitting crying on the kerb in his home town. He had dropped a bottle of milk. It lay in jagged shattered bits in the gutter. The fresh good milk ran away, dirtied by contact with the muck in the gutter. One of his associations to the dream was that he had broken the bottle by his own ineptness. It was no use moaning and crying over the spilt milk, since it was himself, after all, who had caused the damage.

I related his dream to his feeling of being abandoned by me. I was the bottle of milk — containing good milk — which he destroyed in his murderous rage because I abandoned him and went dry. He unconsciously felt the Christmas holiday as losing me, as he felt he had lost his mother and the good breast, because of his ineptness — his violence and lack of control — and his spoiling me internally with his anal muck. He then felt internally persecuted and torn to pieces by the jagged bits of the bottle, representing the breast, myself, and the analysis; as Klein (1955, p. 313) has expressed it, 'the breast taken in with hatred becomes the representative of the death instinct within'.

I would conclude that he had unconsciously attempted to avoid depression by paranoid-schizoid techniques of splitting and deflecting his murderous impulses away from me, through his son against his wife. These techniques had now begun to fail, however, because of previous analytical work with respect to his splitting and denial. Whereas he had been able to deny what in fact turned out to be a pretty bad situation in his home, by perceiving it merely as the product of his own projections, he now became filled with guilt, anxiety, and despair, as he began to appreciate more that in reality the relationships at home were genuinely intolerable and dangerous, and were not just a projection of his own internal chaos and confusion.

During the succeeding months, we were able to elaborate more fully his attitude towards death as an experience of going to pieces.

A connection between his phobic attitude to death and his escape into activity was manifested, for instance, in his recalling one day a slogan that had always meant so much to him — 'Do or die'. But now it came to him that he had always used his own personal abbreviation of the slogan — simply 'Do'. The possibility of dying just did not consciously exist for him.

On one occasion he demonstrated at first hand how his fear of death had caused him always to retreat from mourning. A friend of his died. The patient was the strong and efficient one, who made all the necessary arrangements, while friends and family stood about helplessly, bathed in tears and paralysed with sorrow. He experienced no feeling — just clear-headedness and a sense of action for the arrangements which had to be made. He had always been the same, had done the same when his father and his mother had died. More than that, however, when I interpreted his warding-off of depression by means of denial of feeling and refuge in action, he recalled an event which revealed the unconscious chaos and confusion stirred within him by death. He remembered how, when a cousin of his had suddenly collapsed and died a few years before, he had run back and forth from the body to the telephone to call for a doctor, oblivious of the fact that a small group of people had gathered about the body, and not realizing that everyone but himself was perfectly aware that his cousin was quite dead, and had been for some time before he arrived upon the scene.

The chaos and confusion in the patient in connection with death, I would ascribe to his unconscious infantile phantasies equivalent to death — the phantasies of the destroyed and persecuting breast, and of his ego being cut to pieces.

Mainly, I think, because of the love he got from his father, probably reinforcing his own innate good impulses and what he has had described to him as good breast-feeding in the first five weeks with his mother, he had been able to achieve a partial working through of the infantile depressive position, and to develop his good intellectual capacities. The partial character of his working through was shown in the extent of his manic denial and activity, and his excessive use of splitting, introjection and projection, and projective and introjective identification.

During the period of early adulthood — the twenties and early thirties — the paranoid-schizoid and manic defence techniques were sufficiently effective. By means of his apparent general success and obsessional generosity, he was able to live out the role of the good mother established within, to nurture the good part of himself projected into others, to deny the real situation of envy and greed and destructiveness expressed by him as his noxiousness, and to deny the real impoverishment of his emotional life, and lack of genuine love and affection in his behaviour as both husband and father.

With the onset of mature adulthood in his mid-thirties, his defensive techniques began to lose their potency. He had lost his youth, and the prospect of middle age and of eventual death stimulated a repetition and a reworking-through of the infantile depressive position. The unconscious feelings of persecution and annihilation which death represented to him were re-awakened.

He had lost his youth. And with both his parents dead, nobody now stood between himself and the grave. On the contrary, he had become the barrier between his children and their perception of death. Acceptance of these facts required constructive resignation and detachment. Unconsciously such an outlook requires the capacity to maintain the internal good object, and to achieve a resigned attitude to shortcomings and destructive impulses in oneself, and imperfections in the internal good object. My patient's unconscious phantasies of intolerable noxiousness, his anxieties of having polluted and destroyed his good primal object so that he was lost and abandoned and belonged nowhere, and his unconscious phantasies of the badness of his internalized mother as well as his father, precluded such detachment and resignation. The psychological defences which had supported his adjustment in early adult life — an adjustment of a limited kind, of course, with a great core of emotional impoverishment — failed him at the mid-life period when, to the persecutory world in which he unconsciously lived, were added his anxieties about impending middle and old age, and death. If he had had a less well established good internal object, and had been innately less constructive and loving, he might have continued his mature adult life along lines similar to his early adult type of adjustment; but if he had, I think his mid-life crisis would have been the beginning of a deterioration in his character, and bouts of depression and psychosomatic illness, due to the depth and chronicity of his denial and self-deception, and his distorted view of external reality.

As it has worked out, however, the positive factors in his personality make-up enabled him to utilize his analysis, for which he developed a deep sense of value and appreciation. The overcoming of splitting and fragmentation first began to show in a session in which, as out of nowhere, he saw two jagged edged right-angled triangles. They moved together, and joined to make a perfect square. I recalled the dream with the broken bits of bottle to him. He replied, 'It's odd you should mention that; I was just thinking of it. It feels like the bits of glass are coming together'.

Evasion of awareness of death

One case history does not of course prove a general thesis. It can only illustrate a theme, and the theme in this instance is the notion that the circumstances met by this patient at the mid-life phase are representative of a general pattern of psychological change at this stage of life. The extent to which these changes are tied up with physiological changes is a question I am not able to tackle. One can readily conjecture, however, that the connection must be an important one — libido, the life-creating impulse, represented in sexual drive, is diminishing, and the death instinct is coming relatively more into the ascendant.

The sense of the agedness of parents, coupled with the maturing of children into adults, contributes strongly to the sense of ageing — the sense that it is one's own turn next to grow old and die. This feeling about the age of parents is very strong — even in patients whose parents died years before there is the awareness at the mid-life period that their parents would then have been reaching old age.

In the early adult phase of life, contemplativeness, detachment, and resignation are not essential components of pleasure, enjoyment and success. Manically determined activity and warding off of depression may therefore — as in the case of Mr N — lead to a limited success and pleasure. Splitting and projection techniques can find expression in what are regarded as perfectly normal patterns of passionate support for idealized causes, and equally passionate opposition to whatever may be felt as bad or reactionary.

With the awareness of the onset of the last half of life, unconscious depressive anxieties are aroused, and the repetition and continuation of the working through of the infantile depressive position are required. Just as in infancy — to quote Klein again (1940) — 'satisfactory relations to people depend upon the infant's having succeeded against the chaos inside him (the depressive position) and having securely established his "good" internal objects', so in mid-life the establishment of a satisfactory adjustment to the conscious contemplation of one's own death depends upon the same process, for otherwise death itself is equated with the depressive chaos, confusion, and persecution, as it was in infancy.

When the prevailing balance between love and hate tends more towards the side of hate, when there is instinctual defusion, there is an overspill of destructiveness in any or all of its various forms — self-destruction, envy, grandiose omnipotence, cruelty, narcissism, greed — and the world is seen as having these persecuting qualities as well. Love and hate are split apart; destruction is no longer mitigated by tenderness. There is little or no protection from catastrophic unconscious phantasies of annihilating one's good objects. Reparation and sublimation, the processes which underlie creativeness, are inhibited and fail. And in the deep unconscious world there is a gruesome sense of invasion and habitation by the psychic objects which have been annihilated.

In primitive terms, the process of sculpting is experienced partly as a projective identification, in which the fear of dying is split off and projected into the created object (representing the creative breast). Under the dominance of destructiveness the created object, like the breast, is felt to

remove the good or valuable element in the fear of dying, and to force the worthless residue back into the infant. The infant who started with a fear that he was dying ends up by containing a nameless dread (Bion 1962).

The conception of death is denuded of its meaning, and the process of sculpted creativity is stopped. It is the experience of a patient who, having created a work of art by spontaneous effusion, found that 'it goes dead on me; I don't want to have anything more to do with it; I can never work on it further once it is outside, so I can never refine it; it completely loses its meaning for me — it's like a strange and foreign thing that has nothing to do with me'.

The ensuing inner chaos and despair is unconsciously phantasied in terms akin to an inferno: '*I came to myself within a dark wood . . . savage and harsh and dense.*' If this state of mind is not surmounted, hate and death must be denied, pushed aside, warded off, rejected. They are replaced by unconscious phantasies of omnipotence, magic immortality, religious mysticism, the counterpart of infant phantasies of being indestructible and under the protective care of some idealized and bountiful figure.

A person who reaches mid-life, either without having successfully established himself in marital and occupational life, or having established himself by means of manic activity and denial with consequent emotional impoverishment, is badly prepared for meeting the demands of middle age, and getting enjoyment out of his maturity. In such cases, the mid-life crisis, and the adult encounter with the conception of life to be lived in the setting of an approaching personal death, will likely be experienced as a period of psychological disturbance and depressive breakdown. Or breakdown may be avoided by means of a strengthening of manic defences, with a warding off of depression and persecution about ageing and death, but with an accumulation of persecutory anxiety to be faced when the inevitability of ageing and death eventually demands recognition.

The compulsive attempts, in many men and women reaching middle age, to remain young, the hypochondriacal concern over health and appearance, the emergence of sexual promiscuity in order to prove youth and potency, the hollowness and lack of genuine enjoyment of life, and the frequency of religious concern, are familiar patterns. They are attempts at a race against time. And in addition to the impoverishment of emotional life contained in the foregoing activities, real character deterioration is always possible. Retreat from psychic reality encourages intellectual dishonesty, and a weakening of moral fibre and of courage. Increase in arrogance, and ruthlessness concealing pangs of envy — or self-effacing humbleness and weakness concealing phantasies of omni-potence — are symptomatic of such change.

These defensive phantasies are equally as persecuting, however, as the chaotic and hopeless internal situation they are meant to mitigate. They lead to attempts at easy success, at a continuation on a false note of the early adult lyricism and precipitate creation — that is, creation which, by avoiding contemplation, now seeks not to express but to avoid contact with the infantile experience of hate and of death. Instead of creative enhancement by the introduction of the genuinely tragic, there is emotional impoverishment — a recoil away from creative development. As Freud incisively remarked: 'Life loses in interest, when the highest stake in the game, life itself, may not be risked.' Here is the Achilles heel of much young genius.

Working through the depressive position

When, by contrast, the prevailing balance between love and hate is on the side of love, there is instinctual fusion, in which hate can be mitigated by love, and the mid-life encounter with death and hate takes on a different hue. Revived are the deep unconscious memories of hate, not denied but mitigated by love; of death and destruction mitigated by reparation and the will to live; of good things injured and damaged by hate, revived again and healed by loving grief; of spoiling envy mitigated by admiration and by gratitude; of confidence and hope, not through denial, but through the deep inner sense that the torment of grief and loss, of guilt and persecution, can be endured and overcome if faced by loving reparation.

Under constructive circumstances, the created object in mid-life is experienced unconsciously in terms of the good breast which would in Bion's (1962) terms

> moderate the fear component in the fear of dying that had been projected into it and the infant in due course would re-introject a now tolerable and consequently growth stimulating part of its personality.

In the sculpting mode of work the externally created object, instead of being experienced as having impoverished the personality, is uncon-sciously re-introjected, and stimulates further unconscious creativeness. The created object is experienced as life-giving. The transformation of the fear component in the fear of dying into a constructive experience is forwarded. The thought of death can be carried in thinking, and not predominantly in projective identification, so that the conception of death can begin to find its conscious realization. The reality-testing of death can be carried out in thinking, separated partly from the process of creating an external object. At the same time the continuing partial identification of the creative sculpting with the projection and re-introjection of the fear of dying gives a stimulus to the sculpting process because of its success in forwarding the working through of the infantile projective identification with a good breast.

Thus in mid-life we are able to encounter the onset of the tragedy of personal death with the sense of grief appropriate to it. We can live with it, without an overwhelming sense of persecution. The infantile depressive position can be further worked through unconsciously, supported by the greater strength of reality-testing available to the nearly mature individual. In so reworking-through the depressive position, we unconsciously regain the primitive sense of wholeness — of the goodness of ourselves and of our objects — a goodness which is sufficient but not idealized, not subject to hollow perfection. The consequent feeling of limited but reliable security is the equivalent of the infantile notion of life.

These more balanced conditions do not, however, presuppose an easy passage through the mid-life crisis. It is essentially a period of purgatory — of anguish and depression. So speaks Virgil:

Down to Avernus the descent is light. But thence thy journey to retrace, there lies the labour, there the mighty toil by few achieved.

Working through again the infantile experience of loss and of grief gives an increase in confidence in one's capacity to love and mourn what has been lost and what is past, rather than to hate and feel persecuted by it. We can begin to mourn our own eventual death. Creativeness takes on new depths and shades of feeling. There is the possibility, however, of furthering the resolution of the depressive position at a much deeper level. Such a working through is possible if the primal object is sufficiently well established in its own right and neither excessively idealized nor devalued. Under such circumstances there is a minimum of infantile dependence upon the good object, and a detachment which allows confidence and hope to be established, security in the preservation and development of the ego, a capacity to tolerate one's shortcomings and destructiveness, and withal, the possibility of enjoyment of mature adult life and old age.

Given such an internal situation, the last half of life can be lived with conscious knowledge of eventual death, and acceptance of this knowledge, as an integral part of living. Mourning for the dead self can begin, alongside the mourning and re-establishment of the lost objects and the lost childhood and youth. The sense of life's continuity may be strengthened. The gain is in the deepening of awareness, understanding and self-realization. Genuine values can be cultivated — of wisdom, fortitude and courage, deeper capacity for love and affection and human insight, and hopefulness and enjoyment — qualities whose genuineness stems from integration based upon the more immediate and self-conscious awareness and acceptance not only of one's own shortcomings but of one's destructive impulses, and from the greater capacity for sublimation which accompanies true resignation and detachment.

Sculpted creativity

Out of the working through of the depressive position, there is further strengthening of the capacity to accept and tolerate conflict and ambivalence. One's work need no longer be experienced as perfect. It can be worked and reworked, but it will be accepted as having shortcomings. The sculpting process can be carried on far enough so that the work is good enough. There is no need for obsessional attempts at perfection, because inevitable imperfection is no longer felt as bitter persecuting failure. Out of this mature resignation comes the serenity in the work of genius, true serenity, serenity which transcends imperfection by accepting it.

Because of the greater integration within the internal world, and a deepening of the sense of reality, a freer interaction can occur between the internal and the external worlds. Sculpted creativity expresses this freedom with its flow of inspiration from inside to outside and back, constantly repeated, again, and yet again. There is a quality of depth in mature creativity which stems from constructive resignation and detachment. Death is not infantile persecution and chaos. Life and the world go on, and we can live on in our children, our loved objects, our works, if not in immortality.

The sculpting process in creativity is facilitated because the preparation for the final phase in reality-testing has begun — the reality-testing of the end of life. For everyone, the on-coming years of the forties are the years when new starts are coming to an end. This feeling can be observed to arise in a particularly poignant way by the mid-forties. This sense of there being no more changing is anticipated in the mid-life crisis. What is begun has to be finished. Important things that the individual would have liked to achieve, would have desired to become, would have longed to have, will not be realized. The awareness of on-coming frustration is especially intense. That is why, for example, the issue of resignation is of such importance. It is resignation in the sense of conscious and unconscious acceptance of inevitable frustration on the grand scale of life as a whole.

This reality-testing is the more severe the greater is the creative ability of the individual, for the time scale of creative work increases dramatically with ability. Thus the experience is particularly painful in genius, capable of achieving vastly more than it is possible to achieve in the remaining years, and therefore frustrated by the immense vision of things to be done which will not be done. And because the route forward has become a cul-de-sac, attention begins its Proustian process of turning to the past, working it over consciously in the present, and weaving it into the concretely limited future. This consonance of past and present is a feature of much mature adult sculpting work.

The positive creativeness, and the tone of serenity which accompany the successful endurance of this frustration, are characteristic of the mature production of Beethoven, Goethe, Virgil, Dante, and other giants. It is the spirit of the 'Paradiso', which ends in words of strong and quiet confidence:

But now my desire and will, like a wheel that spins with even motion, were revolved by the Love that moves the sun and other stars.

It is this spirit, on a smaller scale, which overcomes the crisis of middle life, and lives through to the enjoyment of mature creativeness and work in full awareness of death which lies beyond — resigned but not defeated. It is a spirit that is one criterion of the successful working through of the depressive position in psychoanalysis.

References

Bion, W.R. (1962) *Learning from Experience*, London: Heinemann; reprinted in paperback, Maresfield Reprints, London: H. Karnac Books (1984).

Freud, S. (1915) 'Thoughts for the times on war and death', SE 14.

Klein, M. (1935) 'A contribution to the psychogenesis of manic depressive states' in *The Writings of Melanie Klein*, vol. 1, London: Hogarth Press (1975) 262—89.

——— (1940) 'Mourning and its relation to manic depressive states' in *The Writings of Melanie Klein*, vol. 1, 344—69.

——— (1955) 'On identification', in *The Writings of Melanie Klein*, vol. 3, London: Hogarth Press (1975), 141—75.

Riviere, J. (1958) 'A character trait of Freud's' in J.D. Sutherland (ed.), *Psycho-Analysis and Contemporary Thought*, London: Hogarth Press.

2

Delusion and artistic creativity: some reflections on reading *The Spire* by William Golding

HANNA SEGAL

This paper was first published in 1974 in the *International Review of Psycho-Analysis*, 1: 135—41.

This essay has no pretensions to literary criticism, nor is it an attempt to 'psychoanalyse' a book, or, through the book, its author. It is an attempt to use the material of a novel to further a psychoanalytic investigation into the origin and the nature of artistic endeavour. It is a continuation of a trend of thought I started in my paper 'A psycho-analytical approach to aesthetics' (Segal 1952). In particular, it is concerned with the shadowy area in which originate both the psychotic delusion and the artistic creation.

The Spire, a novel by William Golding (1964), is a story set in the Middle Ages, of the endeavours of Jocelin, Dean of the Cathedral, to build a 400—foot spire, as he has heard that this has been done in France. Despite the opposition of his chapter, and advice that such a spire cannot be built because the church has no foundations and the structure no strength, he is certain that he can translate his vision into reality. He has been vouchsafed a vision which convinces him that he has been chosen by God for this task. His conviction that he has been so chosen is also nourished by the fact that his promotion to his present position has been miraculously fast. He is supported by an angel, who 'warms his back'. Roger Mason is the only man capable of building such a spire, but he is, to begin with, doubtful, and later is completely opposed to the plan. Jocelin must compel him to do the building.

Apart from Jocelin, there are four main protagonists: Roger Mason and his wife Rachel, Pangall, an old servant of the cathedral, and his beautiful young wife, Goody. Jocelin compares them to the four pillars of the cathedral: 'My spire will stand on them as on the four pillars.' Pangall is old and crippled, Goody young and beautiful and Jocelin's favourite —

his 'golden child'. He had arranged her marriage to Pangall, but the marriage is sterile because, as becomes clear later, of Pangall's impotence. Roger Mason is the powerful builder, Rachel his earthy counterpart; but that marriage too is sterile, as Rachel later confesses to Jocelin, because 'she always laughs at the crucial moment'.

When the novel starts, we are carried by Jocelin's exultation: he is full of power and conviction about his mission; he radiates a god-like patronizing love, which includes his enemies as well as his friends. But right from the start one can feel the underlying anxiety and tension, and his mood very quickly becomes irritable as his plans are opposed or his authority seems flouted.

He exults in his imagination of his cathedral. He contemplates the model:

> The model was like a man lying on his back. The nave was his legs placed together, the transepts on either side were his arms outspread. The choir was his body; and the Lady Chapel, where now the services would be held, was his head. And now also, springing, projecting, bursting, erupting from the heart of the building, there was its crown and majesty, the new spire. They don't know, he thought, they can't know until I tell them of my vision!

Four portraits of Jocelin are to adorn the four faces of the spire.

From the beginning of the book, he meets with opposition from his chapter, from Pangall and from Roger Mason. Pangall accuses him of ruining and defiling the cathedral, built by Pangall's fathers and forefathers, and he complains of the workmen's desecration of the cathedral and mockery of himself. Mason opposes the building of such a tall tower because, according to him, the structure of the cathedral has no strength to support it. But Jocelin ignores the chapter's and Pangall's complaints, as well as Mason's realistic warnings. He has noticed Mason's interest in Goody and realizes that this gives him power to hold the man. Guiltily but exultantly, he thinks, 'I've got him in a net'.

The story of the building and possible final collapse of the spire is marked by several climaxes which make the underlying symbolism of the story clearer: the first climax comes when Roger Mason, having decided to dig to the foundation of the cathedral to gauge its strength, opens up a pit and slowly the cathedral starts filling with the stench of the dead. There is no foundation, and when the floors are removed, the subterranean waters start moving. And the earth creeps. There is a dramatic moment when the foundations begin to collapse. Pangall complains to Jocelin that he is the butt of the workmen's mockery. Just before the waters start moving, Jocelin gets a glimpse of the workmen chasing

Pangall, one of them holding the model of the cathedral between his legs, with the spire 'sticking out obscenely'. He half sees Pangall pushed about and later disappearing into the pit. He also has a glimpse of Goody, part naked, covered by her flaming-red hair. But he immediately represses the sight, is unclear about what he has seen, and becomes confused. After the opening of the pit, Pangall disappears and Roger again begs to be let go. But Jocelin is more convinced than ever of his mission: if the cathedral has no foundations it is but further confirmation that it is miraculous. He also realizes that with Pangall's disappearance Roger is finally caught in the net. He sees Roger and Goody 'as in a tent'.

From the moment of the opening of the pit, Jocelin's folly becomes more apparent. His confusion increases. He spends more and more time up on the building's tower, watching the building of the spire. Somewhere on the tower Roger has his 'swallow's nest', in which Goody visits him. Another climactic moment occurs when Jocelin overhears their intercourse and becomes acutely aware of his jealousy and his guilt.

Parallel to his angel, Jocelin has also his devil, and the devil which torments him with sexual feelings attains more power. He has a masturbatory phantasy in a state of semi-sleep, waking up from which he realizes with horror his sexual feelings towards Goody as well as his homosexual feelings towards the young sculptor who is engaged on his portrait. He feels his angel begins to exhaust him by recurring and increasing hotness in his back, and at times the angel becomes indistinguishable from the devil. He is occasionally threatened by the emergence of the memory of what he saw at the pit, but inevitably represses it again and becomes more confused. The structure of the spire begins to collapse, and another climax is reached, when Jocelin finds Goody in the throes of childbirth — red hair and red blood fusing in his mind — a dramatic childbirth which leads to the death of Goody and the child. His guilt at what he has done to Goody and Roger begins to break through, but more than ever it is important to finish the spire, to justify such sacrifice: 'This I have done for Him through love.' Roger works gloomily now on the spire, having nowhere else to go, but things progressively deteriorate: the cathedral is deserted, the workmen take part in devil-worship, the countryside is desolate, and the pillars of the cathedral begin to sing. Jocelin pins his hopes on the Nail from the Cross that was promised to him by the bishop; but when the bishop comes and offers him the Nail, his main business is a court of inquiry into Jocelin's fitness to continue as Dean.

Simultaneously he receives a visit from his aunt. The aunt has been the king's mistress, and it was largely her money that provided for the building of the spire. In exchange, she wanted to be buried in the cathedral; Jocelin manipulates for the money but refuses her request, as to him it would be defiling the cathedral. Now, however, she comes

251

alarmed by reports about his health. The crucial moment in their conversation comes when he says, 'After I was chosen by God ...' And she laughs, saying, 'Who chose you — God? *I* chose you', and describes how after a particularly happy love-making, because they were happy and wanted to spread their happiness, she and the king decided to elevate him to his post. At that moment the basis of Jocelin's conviction is shaken: he has not been chosen by God but by this sinful, despised couple. From that moment a complete collapse sets in: his doubts and guilt break through and illness 'breaks his spine'; crippled by illness he crawls on all fours to Roger Mason to beg his forgiveness, but Roger, lying drunk and despairing in his digs, only curses him. In a semi-confused state, but with an awful clarity, he confesses that the pit, 'the cellarage knew it all'; it knew that he had made Goody marry Pangall because he knew of the man's impotence. He also knew that Pangall was murdered at the pit.

He is brought home and nursed physically and mentally by Father Adam, whom he always called Father Anonymous because of his humility. And it is only then that he describes the details of his vision, in which the spire represented his prayer reaching Heaven, to which Father Anonymous replies sadly, horrified, 'They never taught you to pray'.

A synopsis is always very unsatisfactory. For those who know the book it must seem a very thin account of the real thing. To those who have not read it, it does hardly convey the richness and complexity of the themes.

I have chosen only such elements of the narrative that will illustrate my own view of it. The cathedral obviously represents Jocelin himself. This is clear from his first seeing the model of the cathedral as a human body; and it is his own face that will adorn the spire. That the erect spire represents the penis and potency becomes even clearer when the workman pursuing Pangall sticks the spire 'obscenely between his legs'. The sexual phantasies involved in the building of the spire are both clear and complex. Heterosexually the spire-penis is meant to reach Heaven-mother (after Goody's death Jocelin has a phantasy of the spire reaching Goody in heaven and she is confused in his mind with the Virgin Mary). Seen homosexually, the spire is an offering to God the Father. His relationship with God is felt in quite physical terms. The angel that warms his back, and becomes later indistinguishable from the devil, is felt as a sexual penetration by God. Towards the end, when the angel and devil fuse, he feels that the angel 'kicks him in the arse'. There is also a homosexual relationship in which he does not submit to God or the angel, but *is* God to another man. The sculptor who sculpts his face and follows him round is a dumb young man with a permanently open and humming mouth, and it is his face and mouth that get confused with

Goody's genital in Jocelin's masturbation phantasy. The spire, however, represents not only his potency but also his omnipotence. He represents it to himself as an offering to God, but it is clear throughout that it is his own penis-spire that is to dominate the landscape, to reach heaven and to stand for ever as an object of universal admiration.

This building, of his own self and his own omnipotent potency, is done on the basis of the total destruction of his parents. He says himself, with anguish, 'How many people at that moment are built into this cathedral!' His parents are represented by the two sterile couples, Pangall and Goody, Roger and Rachel: in one couple the man is impotent; in the other, the woman. As his plan develops, he further destroys these couples, allowing for the murder of Pangall and the unfaithfulness of Roger. As Roger tells him, the four pillars are hollow: they cannot support his spire. The hollow pillars are the hollow, sterile marriages, representing what he has made in his phantasy of his parents' sexuality. But to build this spire he needs Roger's strength: to build his own potency he must reconstruct in his internal world a potent father and marriage; he brings Roger and Goody together to form a couple. This bringing of the sexual parents together is done, however, entirely under his control. They are in his 'tent'. He overcomes his extreme jealousy by acquiring control over their sexuality and gratifying his own desires by projective identification. He puts his heterosexual feelings into Roger and uses him to possess Goody, and his feminine feelings into Goody, through whom he imprisons and entraps Roger. He gets his own sexual satisfaction, like a voyeur, through watching them, controlling them, and identifying with them. Their union results in a baby, but this is not allowed: the baby dies and kills Goody in the process, and Jocelin thinks that it is his sudden appearance in Goody's room which brought about that death. The sexual parents, manipulated by Jocelin, are not allowed to build a baby: they are only allowed to build Jocelin's spire.

Jocelin's building of the spire is the building of a delusion — the delusion that the parents never had potency or creativity. (The 'cellarage', as he calls it, of the cathedral contains nothing but dead bodies.) If the cathedral is Jocelin, the cellarage is his unconscious, containing nothing but a phantasy of dead bodies ('the cellarage knew').

Wherever the signs of sexual potency are found they are destroyed anew, like Roger's and Goody's baby. Jocelin's aim is to be the only and wholly controlling partner of both father and mother, and only his spire is allowed intercourse with either. It pretends to be an offering to God, but it is only an offering to his own power. I said that the cathedral represented Jocelin himself, but this is only partly true. In fact the cathedral was there before him, as Pangall bitterly reminds him: it represents also the body of his mother and the potency of his father, which he ruthlessly destroys to create his own spire. The spire is supposed to be a completion of the cathedral, but in fact the cathedral is sacrificed to it. It represents a phantasy of taking over his mother's body and the sexual powers of his father to use them for his own needs, as he uses Roger and Goody.

This structure cannot be maintained for reasons of guilt and reasons of psychic and external reality. The basis of his structure is that there was no sex between the parents. When his aunt tells him how she and the king had chosen him, it represents to him the statement that he was not chosen by God but was born out of ordinary happy love-making between the sexual parents, as represented by the king and the aunt whom he condemns and despises. Confronted with this knowledge, he realizes that the whole foundation of his inner world, represented by the cathedral, was false. He has to admit that the sexual parents existed and that it is he in his own mind who has murdered them. The spire sways and threatens to collapse. Despair sets in, and the collapse of his omnipotent phantasy becomes the collapse of himself, as he had developed no other relation to his internal parents that he could turn to: 'they never taught him to pray.'

Described in that way, one could see the book as a case history of a manic delusion and its collapse. But of course a good novel is never just that. It describes universal problems that can be seen from many angles. I think that in the author's mind the book was to illustrate problems of true and false faith, as exemplified by Jocelin and Father Anonymous. But, as in every work of art, the novel contains also the story of its own creation and it expresses the problems, conflicts and doubts about the author's own creativity. The agonizing question that the artist poses himself is: 'Is my work a creation or a delusion?' The story of Jocelin can be seen as exposing the common roots of delusion and artistic creativity and the differences between them. Why was Jocelin's spire a delusion and not a great artistic creation? Is it accidental that it is going to collapse? What did Jocelin have in common with the artist? And in what way did he differ? Jocelin exclaims at one point, 'There is no innocent work'. Is the artist's work different from Jocelin's? I agree with him that there is no innocent work, and the artist's work, in particular, has one of its roots in destructiveness.

Adrian Stokes, in his book *The Invitation in Art* (1965), emphasizes that at the beginning of every artistic creation is an act of aggression: the sculptor has to break and chip the stone, the painter and the writer feel that they defile the white canvas or paper with the first stroke of the brush or pen; and from that moment they feel committed to the restoration represented by completing the work of art. In 1952, in 'A psychoanalytical approach to aesthetics', I put forward the theory that the artist's work is a way of working through the depressive position — that stage of development when the infant begins to relate to his mother and soon to other people in his environment as to whole and separate persons, in contrast with an earlier stage, where no such clear perception exists. Confronted with the wholeness and separateness of the parents, the infant, and later the child, experiences the impact of his own ambivalence towards them. In that he experiences separation, jealousy and envy, he hates them and in his mind attacks them. As at that early stage of development the infant feels his wishes and phantasies to be omnipotent, he feels that the parents thus attacked become fragmented and destroyed, and he introjects them as such into his internal world. This is one aspect of the infant's 'cellarage'. But in that he also loves his parents and needs them, this destruction brings about feelings of mourning, loss, guilt, and a longing to undo the damage done and to restore in his mind the parents to their original state, reparative impulses come into play. When the child becomes aware of the parental intercourse and fertility, the reparation involves restoring to them in his mind their full sexual potency and fertility. It is in this situation, in the 'cellarage', that are rooted the creative urges. The artist in particular is concerned with the task of creating a whole new world as a means of symbolic restoration of his internal world and his internal family. It is clear that the artist and the creator of the delusion are close to one another in the vividness of their feeling of the destruction of their whole inner world and their need to create a complete world anew. The artist's compulsion to create may at times be as overriding and ruthless as Jocelin's. There is a beautiful description of this aspect of creativity in Patrick White's *The Vivisector* (1970). His mother says of the young painter, 'You were born with a knife in your hand, or rather in your eyes'.

The artist, whatever his medium may be, creates an illusion, but at times it comes close to a delusion; his created world becomes to him so real, as in the famous story about Dumas, who rushed out of a room sobbing, 'I have killed my Porthos', when he was describing the death of his hero. So both the artist and the person suffering from a delusion start with a common cellarage: the destruction of the parental couple in their phantasy and their internal world; and both have the overriding need to recreate a destroyed and lost structure.

Here, however, the similarity ends and the differences begin. Jocelin does not aim, in his creation, at restoring any objects: what he is creating is an ideal picture of himself, including an omnipotent potency, at the expense of the parental figures. He seems to be serving God, but it is his spire, standing for a part of his own body, which is to reach heaven omnipotently. He bears an extraordinary resemblance to a patient I have in analysis who has a mono-delusion and has created in his mind an extraordinarily complex delusional system centring on his supposed 'mission', but who in real life has achieved nothing (Segal 1972). The artist, on the other hand, is concerned primarily with the restoration of his objects. Proust, for instance, says that a book, like a memory, is 'a vast graveyard where on most of the tombstones one can read no more the faded names'. To him, writing a book is bringing this lost world of loved objects back to life: 'I had to recapture from the shade that which I had felt, to re-convert it into its psychic equivalent, but the way to do it, the only one I could see, what was it but to create a work of art.' Jocelin has some awareness of where he went wrong in his creation, when, towards the end of the book, he says, 'But what is heaven if I can't reach it, holding them each by the hand?' He refers to Roger and Goody, destroyed by him and standing for his sexual parents, whom he never restored in his internal reality. From this difference, restoring the object rather than the self, follow the crucial differences between the artist's and the psychotic's relation to his creation and the means which he employs. To begin with, the creative artistic process lessens the guilt of the original destructiveness by real creation. When the artist in Patrick White's book is asked why he painted a cruel portrait of his crippled sister, he answers, 'I had my painterly reasons: these come first, of course. Then I think I wanted to make amends — in the only way I ever knew — for some of my enormities'. This answer expresses both the original attack and the amends, as does the picture itself in its cruelty and its beauty. This aspect of attack and amends recurs constantly in *The Vivisector*. For instance, the painter's mistress dies in an accident, probably due to his cruelty, and for years after her features reappear in various forms in his work.

The delusion-formation, on the other hand, perpetuates the guilt by repeating the crime, as in Jocelin's case his repetitive destruction of the parental sexual couple and their child.

Also, in that the work of art primarily represents the object and not the self, the artist can visualize a separation between himself and the completed work. He can finish it and move on to the next one. It is an important part of overcoming the depressive anxieties and completing the reparation, to allow the object to be separate once again. This enables the artist to have a certain objective detachment from his work and a critical attitude to it. He is never completely identified with it. Very important consequences follow from this: unlike Jocelin, he does not become confused: in allowing the object to become separate he allows differentiation between his internal world and the external world, and is therefore aware of what is phantasy and what is reality. In that way his work is not only not confused with him, it is also not completely identified and not confused with his phantasy objects. He can see it as a symbol, and as a symbol it can be used for communication (Segal 1957).

To Jocelin the cathedral and the spire are him. The artist is aware that his creations symbolize aspects of his internal world: they are neither him nor entirely his internal objects. This enables the artist to have a reality-sense. If the artist succeeds and Jocelin fails, it is because the artist, as we know, is a supreme artisan: he does not confuse his wishes and his phantasies with realities: he has a reality-appreciation of his material, which Jocelin completely lacks. Where Jocelin relies on infantile omnipotence and magic, the holy Nail from the Cross, the artist relies on his reality-sense, and by reality-sense I mean reality-sense in relation naturally to the external world, but also and primarily in relation to his own psychic world. Where Jocelin aims at maintaining an unconscious delusion that he is the source of omnipotence, the artist seeks to restore an internal truth. Jocelin, in his view of himself as chosen by God, is as blind to his own nature and his inner realities as he is to the material realities of the cathedral. When he feels threatened by the emergence from repression of the memory of what happened at the pit, the murder of Pangall, he flees up the tower, where he recovers peace. His creation is an escape from realities, external and internal. The artist, on the other hand, is always in search of the psychic truth: he explores the world externally, and even more internally, searches for the understanding of the cellarage, as Golding is doing in his book.

What is the difference between Jocelin, and William Golding who wrote the book? Jocelin must represent something of the author, in the sense in which Flaubert said, 'Madame Bovary, c'est moi'. The cellarage which represents Jocelin's unconscious must be well known to the author, who can describe it with such feeling and depth. Yet Jocelin is clearly not all that there is to his author: the author must have fully encompassed and overcome that part of himself represented by Jocelin and seen it fully related to all his objects, past and present. Jocelin is but one part of Golding — it is the cathedral as a whole, and the novel as a whole, which represents the author's internal world and its conflicts; Mason, the artisan and potent man in particular, represents both a potent internal father and the potent part of the artist in the artisan. Father Anonymous represents the humility with which the artist views himself in relation to his task. Jocelin is wholly narcissistic; his creator is obviously aware of the reality of human relationships and capable of reintegrating what has been split and destroyed in the act of writing his book.

Where Jocelin's spire will soon collapse, William Golding's cathedral and spire stand complete, containing and bringing to life a whole new world in which we can become engrossed. But the theme itself which William Golding chose is significant: the collapse of his work is always a threat of which the artist is aware. And here Golding describes a particular threat which must be experienced by every artist. Artists are often accused of being narcissistic, which is a great misconception, but the particular kind of omnipotent narcissism represented by Jocelin must be a temptation that they probably have always to struggle with and to overcome.

References

Golding, W. (1964) *The Spire*, London: Faber & Faber.

Segal, H. (1952) 'A psycho-analytical approach to aesthetics', *International Journal of Psycho-Analysis*, 33: 196–207; also in *The Work of Hanna Segal*, New York: Jason Aronson, 185–206; reprinted in paperback, London: Free Association Books (1986).

—— (1957) 'Notes on symbol formation', *International Journal of Psycho-Analysis*, 38: 391–7; also in *The Work of Hanna Segal*, 49–65 and *Melanie Klein Today:* volume 1, London: Routledge (1988).

—— (1972) 'A delusional system as defence against the re-emergence of a catastrophic situation', *International Journal of Psycho-Analysis*, 53: 393–401.

Stokes, A. (1965) *The Invitation in Art*, London: Tavistock Publications.

White, P. (1970) *The Vivisector*, London: Cape.

3

Psychoanalysis and ceremony[1]

ELIZABETH BOTT SPILLIUS

This paper, in a shortened form, was first given in 1967 as one of the
Winter Lectures on Psycho-Analysis to members of the general public. It
was first published in the present form in 1968 in *The Psychoanalytic
Approach*, ed. J.D. Sutherland, London: Baillière, Tindall & Cassell and
was reprinted in 1972 in *The Interpretation of Ritual: Essays in Honour of
A.I. Richards*, ed. J.S. La Fontaine, London: Tavistock Publications.

I am convinced that a knowledge of unconscious mental processes gained
from the practice of psychoanalysis can deepen and enrich understanding
of social behaviour. But I have not written this paper to prove or even
to illustrate this conviction. I have written it in an attempt to understand
a particular event, the kava ceremony of the Kingdom of Tonga in the
South Pacific. This ceremony is a social event and as such involves
groups, roles, and social differentiation as well as conscious and
unconscious feelings. In order to understand it to my satisfaction I found
I had to use ideas derived both from social anthropology and from
psychoanalysis.

What I am saying, in effect, is that the problem in question should take
priority over one's loyalty to a particular profession or professions,
whether that problem is concerned with the understanding of a patient,
of a ceremony, of social stratification, of political behaviour, or whatever
it may be. Of course professional training shapes one's interests and
limits one's selection of topics for study. In view of my double training
as an anthropologist and a psychoanalyst it is not surprising that I have
selected a problem that concerns both professions. The analysis of
ceremonies falls within the traditional domain of anthropology, but it has
also stirred many psychoanalysts to speculative efforts in applied
psychoanalysis.[2]

In the course of trying to understand and interpret the kava ceremony
it has repeatedly occurred to me that a ceremony has much in common

with a dream. A dream is a condensed and disguised representation of unconscious thoughts and wishes. A ceremony is a condensed and partially disguised representation of certain aspects of social life. A dream and a ceremony both serve a double and contradictory function: they release and communicate dangerous thoughts and emotions; but at the same time they disguise and transform them so that the element of danger is contained and to some extent dealt with. An effective ceremony protects society from destructive forms of conflict; an effective dream protects the sleeper from anxiety.

Of course there are important differences between a dream and a ceremony. A dream is the product of an individual; a ceremony is the product of a group. Dreams reflect unconscious thoughts. Some of the ideas and emotions expressed in ceremonies are unconscious, but many others are not so much unconscious as unformulated. Just as one can speak a language correctly without being able to formulate its grammatical rules, so one can play one's part in social life and in a ceremony without understanding how all the parts and principles fit together. Further, many of the symbolic statements made in a ceremony concern social norms and values of which the participants are consciously aware.

The basic events of the kava ceremony are very simple. A group of people pound up the root of a kava plant, mix it with water, and drink it. But all this is done according to a fixed ceremonial procedure that has hardly varied for at least 160 years. We have a good description of the ceremony dating from 1806 (Mariner 1818, vol. 2, pp. 172–96) and the verbal orders and the actions performed have hardly changed at all, with one important exception. The kava root used to be chewed and then mixed with water, whereas nowadays it is pounded with stones.

The botanical name of the kava plant is *Piper methysticum*. It contains several chemical constituents and there is considerable controversy about their physiological effects. The general conclusions are that it has a slight tranquillizing and anaesthetic action, though the effects are very mild. Tongans, however, treat kava as if it were strong stuff. And so it is, but the strength comes from society, not from the vegetable kingdom.[3]

Before I describe the ceremony, here are a few background facts about the Kingdom. Tonga is a Polynesian society consisting of about 150 small islands with a population of about 70,000 people in 1960. It has a Treaty of Friendship with Great Britain, but has always been independent, never a colony, a fact of which Tongans are very proud. The people have been Christian for 130 years and virtually everyone can read and write. Tongans practise subsistence farming on smallholdings, with coconuts and bananas as the main cash crops. There are no extremes of wealth or poverty. For the past 100 years government has assumed the form of a constitutional monarchy. Anyone who saw Queen Sālote of

Tonga at the coronation of Queen Elizabeth in 1953 will not be likely to forget her. She is as memorable in Tonga as she is in Britain. She died in December 1965 and was succeeded by her eldest son, the present King Tāufa'āhau Tupou IV.

Description of the ceremony

The basic form of the kava ceremony is always the same, though it may vary from a small informal gathering of four or five people to a huge assemblage of several hundred people. It can be dressed up or down as the occasion requires. It takes place on many different sorts of occasion: when men visit each other just to talk; when welcoming home relatives who have been away; in courtship; at weddings; at certain points in a funeral; at the appointment of a king and later on at his coronation; and similarly at the appointment of a chief and on the occasion when he first presents himself and his villagers to his king.

Figures 1 and 2 show the seating at an informal and at a formal ceremony. The participants sit cross-legged, with the chief whose title is genealogically the most senior at the head of the circle. He has an official called a matāpule on either side of him. These matāpule are the hereditary ceremonial attendants of chiefs, their duties being to conduct their chief's kava ceremony and to give and receive gifts on his behalf. The matāpule have never held political authority. The chiefly title holders, on the other hand, used to have political authority, though nowadays much of it has been transferred to the central government.

The rest of the main circle (*'alofi*) is composed of other chiefs and matāpule sitting alternately. There are always more matāpule than chiefs, however, so that after the first few places matāpule sit next to one another. In the part of the main circle nearest the bowl (*fasi tapu* and *fasi tou'a*) some chiefs and matāpule sit in pairs, and some minor chiefs sit on their own.

In theory the seating of the various chiefs in the main circle demonstrates the genealogical position of their titles relative to that of the presiding chief. The title of the presiding chief is supposed to be genealogically senior, and the other chiefly titles in the main circle are supposed to have been derived from his line at later points in time. Although each chiefly titleholder sits as an individual, he also represents the village over which he has titular authority. In Tongan idiom he is more than a representative; the title is the embodiment of the village and its history.

In a large formal ceremony all the people in the main circle have to have been formally appointed to chiefly or matāpule titles. Women, who

Figure 1 Schematic diagram of seating at small informal kava ceremony

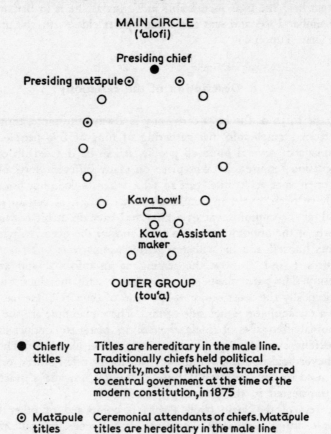

MAIN CIRCLE
('alofi)

Presiding chief

Presiding matāpule ⊙

Kava bowl

Kava   Assistant
maker

OUTER GROUP
(tou'a)

● Chiefly   Titles are hereditary in the male line.
   titles   Traditionally chiefs held political
          authority, most of which was transferred
          to central government at the time of the
          modern constitution, in 1875

⊙ Matāpule   Ceremonial attendants of chiefs. Matāpule
   titles   titles are hereditary in the male line

○ Non-titleholders

do not normally hold titles or wield political authority, thus do not sit in the main circle. (The Queen, who held the ruling title, Tu'i Kanokupolu, was of course an exception to this general rule. In the traditional system kings and chiefs were almost invariably men, but British rules of succession to the kingship were adopted in 1875.) In a small informal ceremony the people in the main circle do not have to have been formally appointed to titles; they can use the name of a matāpule title they are descended from, or, failing that, they can use their personal names. Women can therefore sit in the main circle on such informal occasions if they want to.

The kava bowl is opposite the presiding chief. The bowl is three or

Figure 2 Schematic diagram of seating at formal royal kava ceremony

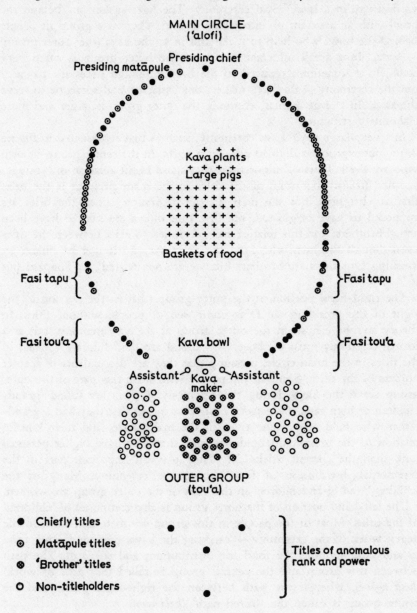

MAIN CIRCLE
('alofi)

Presiding chief

Presiding matāpule

Kava plants
Large pigs

Baskets of food

Fasi tapu

Fasi tapu

Fasi tou'a

Kava bowl

Fasi tou'a

Assistant

Kava maker

Assistant

OUTER GROUP
(tou'a)

● Chiefly titles

◎ Matāpule titles

⊗ 'Brother' titles

○ Non-titleholders

} Titles of anomalous rank and power

four yards away from the chief in a small ceremony, some two hundred yards away in a large royal ceremony. The kava maker sits behind the bowl with an assistant on either side of him. There is a group of people behind the bowl who help to make and serve the kava (the 'outer group' — *tou'a*). In a small informal ceremony the outer group is often very small. It is sometimes reduced to the bare minimum necessary to carry out the ceremony — the kava maker, one assistant, and someone to serve the kava. In a large formal ceremony the outer group is larger and more elaborately structured.

In a very large royal kava ceremony, such as that represented in Figure 2, the outer group is divided into three parts. In the centre group sit men who are the holders of minor titles that stand in the relation of 'younger brother' (*tehina*) to certain of the titles in the main circle. It is the titles that are brothers, not the men. In the beginning, when the titles are supposed to have originated, the first titleholders are said to have been actual brothers, and this relation has continued to exist between the titles even though the men who hold the titles may no longer be linked by kinship. 'Our titles are brothers but we are not related', as Tongans put it.[4]

The right-hand portion of the outer group (that is, the portion to the right of the presiding chief) is composed of people without titles. In theory anyone can sit in the outer group at a kava ceremony, but at a formal ceremony most of those who attend are the 'children' (*fānau*) of the titles in the main circle, meaning that they are descendants of former holders of the titles. Some of the people who sit in this part of the outer group serve the kava during the ceremony. Others are called 'grandchildren of high rank' (*makapuna 'eiki*). This means that they had a grandfather who held one of the titles in the main circle, and their kinship relation to the present titleholder is such that they have higher personal rank than the current titleholder. They play an important part in the ceremonial distribution of food during the ceremony. Many of the 'children' and 'grandchildren' in this part of the outer group are women.

The left-hand portion of the outer group is also composed of 'children' of the titles. Most of the people in this group are men, and they do the heavy work of the ceremony — carrying the kava, pigs, and other food in and out, dividing the food for distribution, and so forth. The path between this group and the central group is called the 'path of work' (*hala ngāue*), whereas the path between the right-hand group and the centre group is called the 'sacred path' (*hala tapu*).

Finally, at a formal royal ceremony, there are certain very important chiefly titles that are seated right at the back, behind the outer group (see Figure 2).

To summarize the salient facts about the seating: the chief whose title is genealogically senior sits at the head of the main circle; the rest of the main circle is made up of formally appointed titleholders, chiefs and matāpule, sitting alternately. The titles of the chiefs in the main circle are supposed to be genealogically junior to the title of the presiding chief. The outer group is composed, first, of men who hold minor chiefly titles that stand in the relation of 'younger brother' to the titles in the main circle and, second, of men and women without titles who are the 'children' and in a few cases also the 'grandchildren' of the titles in the main circle.

The first thing that happens in the ceremony is that people come in and seat themselves. Kava plants and sometimes food are presented to the presiding chief and placed in the centre of the circle (see Figure 2). The traditional food to go with the kava is sugar cane, but vast quantities of pigs and other cooked food are presented along with it. Nowadays the sugar cane is often omitted. In a formal ceremony the food is meticulously counted and thanks for it are chanted by the matāpule. Then the presiding matāpule tells someone in the outer group to take a kava plant from in front of the presiding chief down to the bowl end, where it is split up, cleaned, and then pounded by the kava maker. (Traditionally small bits of the kava root were handed to people in the outer group who chewed it, spat it out neatly on to a leaf, and then handed it back to the kava maker who put it in the bowl.) The kava maker puts the pounded kava root in the bowl and begins to knead it with his hands, and water is poured in by the kava maker's assistants — all of these actions being carried out according to fixed ceremonial orders chanted by the presiding matāpule. The pouring in of the water is one of the most sacred moments of the ceremony and all conversation stops. Then the matāpule calls out to mix the kava and to strain it. While the kava maker is straining the kava conversation is resumed, speeches may be made, and if there is food some of it is ceremonially divided and distributed to each titleholder in the main circle. The titleholders do not eat their food, however. They call for their respective 'grandchildren of high rank' to come from the outer group and take the portions of food away. Then all the remaining food is ceremonially given to the matāpule on the left of the presiding chief, who orders men from the outer group to take it away. After the ceremony is over this food is divided among the participants.

Eventually, after the flurry of activity in distributing and removing the food, the kava maker's assistant calls out that the kava is clear and the matāpule gives the order for servers to come from the outer group with cups. A cup of kava is taken to each person in the main circle and to several in the outer group. Generally when the serving is completed the ceremony is ended. It may be continued, but in this case the second serving is directed by the matāpule on the chief's left. An informal kava ceremony may go on all night, alternating from right to left.

To recapitulate the sequence of ceremonial operations: the participants seat themselves; kava and food are presented and counted; a kava root is pounded and placed in the bowl; the kava is kneaded and water is poured in; the kava is strained, to the accompaniment of conversation or speeches and the distribution and clearing away of food; finally, cups of kava are served.

The first kava ceremony I saw was a small informal one, so informal that I did not realize it was a ceremony. I noticed an old man mumbling away from time to time — in fact he was giving ceremonial orders — and I saw that there were occasional lulls in the conversation, but I thought they were natural pauses not especially sacred moments in a ceremony. The first royal ceremony I saw was an entirely different affair. From the first moment when the food and kava were brought in with cries of 'Tue, tue, tue tue, tue — e — e', and the matāpule chanted their thanks, the atmosphere was electric — charged with an intense feeling of being together in a group. The kava, the ceremony, and the group were sacred — *tapu*. I have never felt anything like it in our own society except at the coronation of Queen Elizabeth, where it seemed to me that our mutual indifference to anything outside our own little circle was lost for a moment in a common feeling of being one nation.

How does one set about understanding such a ceremony? It is not much use asking people point-blank what it means any more than it would be useful to ask an individual what his dream means. To such questions Tongans reply politely, 'It is our custom', and that is the end of the matter. What one should not do, either with a dream or a ceremony, is plunge headlong into arbitrary interpretations of symbolism. While this may be a useful intellectual exercise for the anthropologist or the psychoanalyst, it does not bring him much closer to the new and unique bit of reality he is trying to understand. It would be like trying to interpret a dream without knowing anything about the dreamer — no associations, no transference, no background knowledge of the dreamer's current life and childhood.

To understand a ceremony one needs to know something about the social context. One can also learn a lot by listening to what people say spontaneously and following up their leads. One can ask certain direct questions, such as why people sit where they sit, why the kava is used instead of another plant, or what the properties of kava are, without running into the blank wall of 'It is our custom'. One can ask people to explain the differences between one type of kava ceremony and another. I think this process of exploration is analogous to the use of patients' associations to dreams.

In the course of talking around the ceremony several informants told me the myth of the origin of kava, which proved to be a useful lead. I recorded two versions of the myth and there are others in the literature (Gifford 1924, pp. 71–5). Their points of similarity and difference helped to clarify the central theme of the myth but I only have time for one version, which is the one recorded by the late Queen Sālote.

The myth of the origin of kava

One day the King of Tonga went fishing with a friend. They did not catch anything, and as they were tired and hungry they called in at the little island of 'Eueiki to get something to eat. At that time there was only one couple living on the island and they had one child, a daughter, whose name was Kava'onau. (In some versions the name is abbreviated to 'Kava'.) She had leprosy. It was a time of famine and the only food the couple had left was a large kape plant (*Alocasia macrorrhiza*) which stood near the beach. When the King landed he sat down to rest against this plant. When the couple realized who their guest was they set about making an earth oven, but when they came to get their sole remaining food plant they could not use it because the King was leaning on it. The King's friend saw the couple hit something in their house and bring it out to be baked in the earth oven. He saw that they had killed their daughter because they had nothing else to give their King. The King's friend told the King what the couple had done. The King was deeply moved by their sacrifice. He rose up immediately and returned to the main island, telling the couple to bury their child properly.

Two plants grew from the grave, one from the head and one from the foot. One day the couple saw a mouse bite the first plant, stagger a bit, and then bite the second plant, after which he recovered his balance.

One day Lo'au came to the island and the couple told him all that had happened. (Lo'au is a figure who turns up in Tongan legend and mythology at times when social institutions are being established or changed. He tells the people how to organize their social life and then fades from view. He is thought of as human, not a god, and he is called the 'carpenter of the land', which, freely translated, means the establisher of social customs.)

When Lo'au heard the couple's story he sat in silence for a time, deeply moved, and then he spoke in poetry telling them what they should do. They must take the two plants to the King and give him Lo'au's instructions about how the plants should be used. The one from the head was to be used to make a drink, and that was the kava, and the other was to be eaten with the drink, and that was the sugar cane. The couple did as Loʻau had told them. At first the King thought their plant might be poisonous. He had one of his matāpule taste it first. But on finding it was all right he directed the people to carry out Loʻau's instructions.

And so kava was made for the first time and the rules and procedures for making it were established.

Tongans say that the origin of the kava from the leprous girl explains some of its properties. The shoots of the kava plant grow, split, and become limey and grey like the skin of a leper, and the skin of those who drink too much kava becomes grey and scaly like the skin of a leper. There are other linguistic links with the idea of kava as a poison. *Kavafisi* and *kavahaha* are creepers used as fish poisons. The word 'kavahia' means to be nauseated. Some informants told me that they felt nauseated when they drank strong green kava, and nausea is said to have been the Tongan reaction to attempts to copy the Fijian custom of *actually* eating human flesh.[5] At the same time, in other contexts Tongans said that kava loosened the tongue and made one feel pleasantly relaxed. Thus there is a series of associations between kava, tranquillity, leprosy, poison, nausea, and cannibalism. It may seem odd that tranquillity should appear alongside ideas of poison, nausea, and cannibalism, but I hope the reasons for this strange juxtaposition will become clearer as the exposition proceeds.

Interpretation

The first point is that *the kava ceremony is one of a series of ceremonies that clarify social principles and social roles*. In the kava ceremony the principle of stratification by titles is marked off as clearly as possible from all other forms of social differentiation. This aspect of the ceremony is conscious and explicit. Many Tongans told me, 'Everything in the kava ceremony goes by titles'.

In the traditional political system, chiefly titles carried formal political authority. A chiefly titleholder had the right and obligation to rule and to represent all the inhabitants of a given territory. The kava ceremony displayed the political relationships of titles to one another.

This emphasis on titles only makes sense when one knows that in the traditional system, and to a considerable extent today as well, there were two other systems of social differentiation that were very important in everyday life though they played a very minor role in the kava ceremony; these two other systems of social differentiation were political power and personal rank.[6]

Any man who could gather about him a large and industrious group of relatives and friends could become a political leader in the traditional system. This dimension of political power cut across the system of titles. Some powerful leaders did not hold titles. Some chiefly titleholders were strong leaders of large and powerful local groups; others were politically unimportant.

The third system, that of personal rank, is the same today as it was in the traditional system. The rewards of high rank are gifts of food and elaborate gestures of deference from people of lower rank. By and large, high rank is more highly esteemed than political power or political authority. Power and authority mean work and responsibility; high rank means pure privilege.

Personal rank depends not on whether one holds a title, but on sex, seniority, and descent. Sisters have higher rank than their brothers; elder siblings have higher rank than younger siblings; and the descendants of sisters have higher rank than the descendants of their brothers. Unlike a system of social class such as we are familiar with in our society, the Tongan system of rank is such that no two individuals can have the same rank. The society is not divided into ranked groups or categories; rather the conception is one of a line from the person of highest rank at the top to the person of lowest rank at the bottom. Moreover, a personal rank is relative to the relationships involved. A man may be an 'aristocrat' ('eiki) at one funeral and a lowly kitchen worker at another, depending on how he is related to the deceased.,

Unlike titles, which are normally inherited in the male line, personal rank is inherited from both parents. To be a great aristocrat means that one is descended, preferably through a line of eldest sisters, from the eldest sister of the former sacred King, the Tu'i Tonga, a title that is now defunct. Even the principles of rank in themselves may sometimes conflict. If a man marries a woman who is a great aristocrat and his sister marries a lowly commoner, the children of the respective marriages will be in a contradictory situation. According to one principle the children of the sister will have higher rank than the children of her brother, but according to the other principle (that descent from Tu'i Tonga's sister confers high rank) the children of the brother will have higher rank. The resolution of such contradictions depends on the situation and the people involved, and gives rise to much gossip, ill-feeling, and amusement.

Like the dimension of political power, personal rank cuts across the other dimensions of stratification. The tendency was very marked in the traditional system. Many men of high rank did not hold titles or political power. Some titleholders were of high rank, some of low rank. Some powerful leaders were of high rank, others of low rank.

The discrepancy between rank and political power was incorporated into the traditional political hierarchy. The sacred King, the Tu'i Tonga, held the most senior title and was of very high personal rank; only his sisters and their children were of higher personal rank. But his political power was very limited. Secular authority was wielded by a second king, the Tu'i Kanokupolu, which is the title of the present ruling line. The Tu'i Kanokupolu title was genealogically junior to that of the Tu'i Tonga, and the individual incumbents of the Tu'i Kanokupolu title were of much lower personal rank than the sacred king, but their political power was much greater. They were supposed to rule the kingdom on behalf of the Tu'i Tonga. The recurrent practice of a particular type of marriage between the two royal houses ensured that the sacred king continued to be of higher personal rank than the secular king; personal kinship ties thus reinforced the relationship between the titles.

In the traditional system the object of the social and political game was to use one's standing in one system to increase one's standing in the others, marriage being one of the main devices for doing so. The process took several generations. Increasing the rank of one's descendants was the ultimate goal, but it was unwise in the long run to concentrate on rank alone. The disappearance of the former sacred kingship is a case in point. The kava ceremony provided a snapshot of the process; it showed where the manoeuvring for position had got to at any particular moment, at least as far as the system of formal titles was concerned.

In the modern social and political system the principle of independent but overlapping dimensions of stratification has been retained, though the content has changed. The system of personal rank continues unaltered. Education, however, has supplanted the old system of power and unofficial political leadership. Education is the new pathway to political authority and to higher rank for one's descendants.

The system of chiefly titles and political authority has also changed. In 1875 at the time of the Constitution most of the authority of the chiefly titleholders was transferred to the central government. In compensation for their loss, about forty of the more important and powerful chiefs were given the new European title of 'noble' (*nopele* in Tongan) and were given a special position in the central government. They could elect seven of their peers to the legislative assembly. At the present time being a noble gives one a considerable initial advantage in acquiring political authority, though one must also be educated.

The system of noble titles thus provides a link between the old and the new systems of formal government. The kava ceremony has changed accordingly. It used to be a ceremonial statement of political authority; now it is a statement of continuity between the new political system and the old. As before, principles of personal rank and political power are almost entirely excluded from the ceremony. People are seated and served according to their titles, not according to their personal rank, education, or position in government.

In the beginning I found the constant contradictions of rank, titles, and government authority difficult to grasp. Tongans assured me it was perfectly simple if one had grown up with it. But one thing that helps to keep it simple is ceremonies. Ceremonies mark off one social principle from the others and keep each principle clear in everyone's mind. At government feasts people are seated primarily according to their position in government; a commoner of low rank who is a Cabinet minister will be seated at the Queen's table. At funerals, duties depend mainly on the principles of kinship and personal rank. In the kava ceremony titles are what matter, and power and personal rank play a very minor role. Thus, if the same set of people were involved in the three types of ceremony, they would assume different positions and would have very different relationships with one another in each ceremony. Hence the kava ceremony cannot be understood on its own; it is part of a complex of ceremonies.[7]

I have repeatedly said that power and personal rank are 'virtually' excluded from the kava ceremony. The qualifying objective needs explanation. Although titles are dominant in the ceremony and are supposed to be seated and served according to their genealogical seniority, there are certain features of the seating and the ceremonial procedure that link the system of titles to the principles of political power and personal rank.

Certain important titles are in an anomalous relation to the present kingship. Two of these titles were originally senior to the title of the present king. A third title had a good claim to the throne at one period. A fourth title, although always junior to the present ruling line, had a remarkably able and ambitious series of incumbents in the eighteenth and early nineteenth centuries. One of them broke away from the secular king (the Tu'i Kanokupolu) and became a virtually independent ruler of the northern islands. The power of this particular titleholder, in other words, far outstripped the official political authority of his title. By a series of marriages to aristocratic women, the line increased the personal rank of its incumbents until, in the late nineteenth century, the personal rank of the current incumbent was considerably higher than that of the King himself. In the royal ceremony at the present time, all four of these titles are seated far away at the back, twenty yards or so behind the outer group (see Figure 2). Both their distinctiveness and their anomalous position are thus emphasized. They do not fit in.

There is one event in the ceremonial procedure itself that draws attention to the principle of personal rank. This is the moment when the 'grandchildren of high rank' are called from the outer group to collect the portions of food allocated to the titleholders in the main circle. It is a reminder to all concerned that although the chiefs and nobles hold the titles, they have relatives who are of higher personal rank.

The kava ceremony thus displays the system of titles, with passing references to the two other principles of social differentiation, personal rank and political power. It demonstrates the separateness of the three principles and at the same time shows how they coexist.

We have no historical information on how this particular form of differentiated social principles developed. It was in full flower at the time of Captain Cook's visits. He confessed himself bewildered by the system, though he gives a clear description of behaviour from which the operation of the three principles of authority, power, and rank can be inferred.

Although the historical development of the system remains obscure, some of its effects can be observed in operation. It preserves social continuity while at the same time providing opportunities for flexibility and individual initiative. For individuals it provides a ready-made defence and a mode of adaptation to a general problem that Freud outlined long ago in *Totem and Taboo* (1913): how are subordinates to reconcile themselves to the fact that they hate and envy the authority ('father') whom they also need and love. In the Tongan system 'authority' is split up and dispersed so that no one, not even the King, can be on top all the time. However great a man may be in one dimension, someone else will be greater in some other dimension or some other context. What you lose on the swings you gain on the roundabouts. Further, the system is such that it is difficult, even today, to mobilize consistently opposed groups of 'haves' and 'have-nots'. But it would be a mistake to regard the splitting of authority, rank, and power as a 'solution' to the problem of ambivalent feelings towards authority, for it seems very likely that each of the three systems generates its own complex of envy and rivalry. The system may generate more hatred than it disperses.

There are many indications in everyday life that Tongans are very sensitive about problems of authority and conflict. People avoid open expression of disagreement, while at the same time seeing to it that the authorities concerned find out indirectly about the issues involved. For example, people will agree to fulfil what they consider to be unreasonable demands by a person in authority or a person of high rank, but they will then fail to carry out the desired activity. If confronted by their lack of conformity, they disappear, or find a reasonable excuse or say they did not understand what was required of them. 'They have been leading us around for generations', as one eminent noble put it.

Possibly one factor in this general sensitivity to conflict and avoidance of open expression of it is that Tonga is an island, or rather a group of islands in close communication with one another. In a comparatively isolated group of islands more of an effort has to be made to contain and resolve internal conflicts than on a large land mass where dissidents and persecuted groups can move away without actually leaving the society. And if the controls break down and violence actually breaks out on an island, as it did in Tonga in the early nineteenth century, the island is in for a blood bath that few can escape.

The second major point about the kava ceremony is that *it is a conserving and conservative institution*. This aspect of the ceremony is less explicit than the emphasis on titles. It is unformulated though certainly not unconscious.

The seating and serving order of the kava ceremony are a partial substitute for a written history, for the seating of each title, especially in the royal kava ceremony, is supposed to be explainable in terms of actual historical events. I was so intrigued by this aspect of the ceremony that I spent many months asking titleholders why they sat where they did in the royal kava ceremony. I was frustrated and puzzled to find that many titleholders did not know why they sat where they did. Eventually it dawned on me that this in itself was the significant point. Forgetting is selective. The seating of titles that are still politically important is known and understood. The reasons for the seating are forgotten if the titles are politically unimportant today.

Personal rank and political power can change very quickly in Tonga; it takes a long time for the titles and the kava ceremony to catch up. Two or three generations of 'bad' marriages can drastically reduce the personal rank of the man who holds a title, but the title itself and its position in the kava ceremony are hardly affected. Once a drop in personal rank is combined with a drop in the political power and influence of the titleholder, however, the rank of the title and its position in the kava ceremony gradually begin to decline as well. People start to forget the reasons for the seating of the title. Its position in the circle may be changed to accommodate a more important title. Eventually unimportant titles cease to be appointed and even their ceremonial place is forgotten.

Occasionally there is a massive reshuffle of seating arrangements to take account of changes in political power. This happened after the death of the last sacred king in 1865. While the sacred kingship was still in existence, the kava circle of the secular king, the Tu'i Kanokupolu, included only those titles that were derived from the Tu'i Kanokupolu line and were genealogically junior to the Tu'i Kanokupolu title. But when the sacred kingship lapsed in 1865 and the Tu'i Kanokupolu became the sole king, the titles derived from the Tu'i Tonga line had to be fitted into the Tu'i Kanokupolu's kava circle, even though many of these titles were genealogically senior to the title of the Tu'i Kanokupolu. This conflict between actual political power and the genealogical seniority of titles was surmounted by a sort of legal fiction. Before he died the last Tuʻi Tonga transferred his sacred prerogatives to the Tuʻi Kanokupolu. There is some doubt, however, about how he disposed of his kava prerogatives. Some say that he handed these over to the 'King of the Second House', a very ancient title that stands in the relation of 'brother' to the Tuʻi Tonga title. The difficulty was solved by a marriage between the Tuʻi Kanokupolu line and the 'King of the Second House' line, the end result being that the 'King of the Second House' title is now held by the Royal Family, and the present incumbent is the King's younger brother.

Thus the kava ceremony changes to take account of changes in the power of titles, but it changes more slowly than the rank and power of individuals, and the changes are phrased as much as possible in the idiom of titles and their genealogical seniority.

The third major point about the ceremony is that *it expresses a fundamental contradiction*. We were first alerted to this aspect of the ceremony by comparing the many different social contexts in which it takes place. One thing all these social situations have in common is a confrontation of people of different status. In everyday life these people can be expected to harbour feelings of jealousy and resentment about their differential privileges. At the same time, in spite of the antagonisms, during the ceremony there is a strong feeling of being at harmony together in a group. As Tongans put it, 'You do not drink kava with an enemy'.

In brief, the ceremony says, 'We are all united', but it also says, 'We are all different'. And the element of difference contains another contradiction, for it makes two contrary communications. It says, 'We are differentiated and interdependent', but it also says, 'We are unequal. Our titles differ in seniority. And some of us do not have titles at all'. In other words the kava ceremony expresses ambivalence — the simultaneous presence of contradictory feelings. I do not mean that each participant in the ceremony becomes consciously aware of the sort of emotional ambivalence that I have described. Most people seemed to be more aware of feelings of unity and harmony than of feelings of antagonism and rivalry — or at any rate more willing to talk about feelings of unity and harmony. The feelings of antagonism showed themselves more in what people did than in what they said. At formal ceremonies we observed many minor breaches of *tapu*. One's hands should be clasped in one's lap throughout the ceremony, for example, but our photographs show that people often moved their hands about. Similarly people are not supposed to talk in a very formal ceremony, but people were whispering away almost all the time — usually uncomplimentary remarks about the way the ceremony was being conducted.

Within the prescribed events of the ceremony there is only a little scope for the formal expression of conflict, envy, and jealousy. For example, there is one titleholder whose duty it is to see that the kava is well prepared and that everyone behaves properly. In 1959 the incumbent of this title was a man of comparatively low personal rank; he aimed his sharpest reprimands at two titleholders of very high personal rank, men whom he would never have dared to challenge in any other social context. But he was not alone; all the men of low rank relished his performance. Even in this case, the titleholder concerned was not ceremonially obliged to abuse the men of high rank. What he did was left to his own initiative.

In other words, the formal, prescribed events of the ceremony emphasize unity and harmony. Rivalry, jealousy, and envy are widely and consciously felt, to varying degrees, but their expression is either unofficial or is left to individual initiative.[8]

The myth of the origin of the kava helps to elucidate the contradictory attitudes implied in the ceremony. When the late Queen was reflecting on this myth she said it expressed the mutual sacrifice and understanding between ruler and subjects that was essential to keep Tonga united and strong. It was this mutual sacrifice and understanding the kava ceremony was commemorating. I agreed with this interpretation, but said I thought the myth also expressed suspiciousness and hostility between ruler and subjects. The couple sacrificed their most precious possession, their daughter, but she did have leprosy; eating her might have harmed the King. The King's refusal to eat her was partly an act of generosity, but he was also protecting himself. And when the couple brought in the plant, he thought at first that it might be poisonous. If I had thought of it at the time, I might have added that the couple's sacrifice was an insult to the King, for to call someone a 'man eater' is a common insult in Tonga. And, in addition to everything else, spitefulness is implied in the couple's heroic act. It is as if they were saying to their King, 'Look at the dreadful thing you have made us do'.

After some discussion the Queen said that such suspiciousness between ruler and subjects was probably inevitable and natural. Perhaps what the myth and the ceremony meant was that mutual understanding and sacrifice were possible in spite of doubt and suspicion.

This was as far as I got with the myth while we were still in Tonga. After we left I wished I had asked many other questions about it, for it now seems to me that there are many other levels of meaning and feeling in it. If I were doing the study again I would ask why the little island of 'Eueiki? Why the famine, the cannibalism, and, above all, the leprosy, all of which are known in Tonga but have always been rare. Why the particular food plant, the kape, and what of the many different triangular situations mentioned in the various versions of the myth? There is one issue that I think worth including even though I did not explore it fully at the time. The myth seems to deal with the progression of psychic experience from a very primitive level in which good and bad are confused and contaminated to one in which good and bad are better differentiated, so that it becomes possible to distinguish the symbol from the object. The burial, in other words, transforms the contaminated, sacrificed girl into the two plants, the kava, which is still potentially poisonous, and its antidote, the sugar cane.[9]

The kava myth helps us to understand what the plant symbolizes and why Tongans regard it as strong stuff, but it does not throw much light on the actual events of the ceremony — the pounding, pouring in of water, serving, etc. For this we must turn, very briefly, to another myth that almost paraphrases some of the events of the kava ceremony. The explicit claim of this myth to relevance in connection with the kava ceremony is that it is concerned with the origin of the system of titles that the kava ceremony ceremonially displays. None of my informants pointed out the close parallel between the events of the kava ceremony and the events of the myth, though I was told the myth in the context of discussing the ceremony so that there was obviously an associative link. I myself was only half aware of the connections between the myth and the ceremony while I was still in Tonga, I think this half-awareness is similar to Tongans' feeling about the myth. A connection is dimly felt without being explicitly thought out.

The story of the myth is simple and melodramatic. A god from the sky has intercourse with a woman of the earth and a son is born, called 'Aho'eitu. When he grows up he wants to see his father and, following instructions from his mother, he climbs up to the sky by a giant iron-wood tree. 'Aho'eitu is enthusiastically welcomed by his father, who thinks at first that 'Aho'eitu is a god of even higher rank than himself. The father then sends his new-found son, without introduction, to see his other sons in the sky, presumably the sons of sky mothers. When 'Aho'eitu's half-brothers see everyone admiring 'Aho'eitu because of his beauty, and when they hear rumours that he is their father's son, they tear 'Aho'eitu to pieces and eat him up. The father suspects what they have done. He calls for a wooden bowl and makes his sons vomit into it. This is very reminiscent of the former custom of chewing the kava, of the statements that kava sometimes makes people feel like vomiting, and of the linguistic association with nausea. The sons vomit up 'Aho'eitu's flesh and blood, they confess, and the father sends people to collect the bones and the head, which are also put in the bowl. Water is poured into the bowl, as in the kava ceremony. The pouring in of the water, as I have noted above, is one of the most sacred moments of the ceremony. After some time 'Aho'eitu begins to take shape and finally sits up in the bowl. Then the father calls all his sons together and tells them that 'Aho'eitu will go back to the earth to become the first king of Tonga, the first Tu'i Tonga. At this point, the myth says, affection awakens in the hearts of the brothers, and they plead with their father to be allowed to go with 'Aho'eitu. The father agrees. Four of the brothers go down to earth to serve 'Aho'eitu as his matāpule. The fifth and eldest brother cannot be king, the father says, because he is guilty of murder, but he will be the King of the Second House (Tu'i Fale Ua). If 'Aho'eitu's line should die out then the King of the Second House will become King. (This is the rationale for the belief, mentioned above, that the last Tu'i Tonga bequeathed his kava prerogatives to the King of the Second House.) There are several other myths and legends that purport to show that all through Tongan history the descendants of the King of the Second House tried to murder 'Aho'eitu's descendants in order to wipe out his line.

Using the leads provided by this myth, I think that the chewing or, nowadays, the pounding of the kava is a symbolic repetition of psychic cannibalism, representing a desire both to get possession of the qualities of the beautiful envied brother and son and to destroy him. This mixture of admiration, greed, and destructive envy is a familiar theme from the analysis of the cannibalistic phantasies of patients. But of course in the ceremony it is kava that is pounded or chewed, not a person; this symbolic transformation is taken up in the kava myth.

The idea that the pounding of the kava may represent cannibalistic destruction of an envied object, a brother or son, is consistent with the fact that the people in the outer group, who used to chew and now help to pound the kava, stand in the relation of 'child' or 'younger brother' to the titleholders of the main circle.[10] In other words, the kava plant is presented to the presiding chief as 'Aho'eitu was presented to his father. The father then sends the kava/son to be destroyed. The destruction is carried out by 'children', though perhaps also by 'younger brothers' (of the 'father') — an indication that people in the 'father' category are involved in the destruction. The father's envy and destructiveness are hinted at in the myth, for the father at first thinks his son is of higher rank, and then sends him to his other sons without introduction. He immediately suspects his other sons of murder and cannibalism, as if the thought were not far from his own mind. So far as I could discover none of this is conscious. That is, participants in the ceremony are aware to some extent of their envy and jealousy of one another, and most of them know the two myths, but they do not consciously link the two sets of knowledge.

In the 'Aho'eitu myth incorporation and destruction are followed by healing water and the awakening of good feeling. Once this has taken place the kava is served, that is, the experience can be reincorporated in a form that is soothing and tranquillizing. But the transformation is not always successful, for strong green kava sometimes makes people want to vomit. In other words, the method of preparing the kava can be seen as an effort to convert envy and jealousy into remorse and affection, to change poisonous feelings into feelings of tranquillity and harmony. But other myths and legends make it clear that envy and jealousy can never be overcome entirely and permanently, just as they can never be eradicated from everyday life. The feelings appropriate to cannibalism are here to stay. Envy, greed, and jealousy are always with us, but so are admiration and remorse. Conflict is inevitable. The kava ceremony states the particular Tongan variant of this general human dilemma and tries to communicate the idea that the forces of love can be made stronger than the forces of hate, at least temporarily. Once again, people do not think all this out consciously. They feel there is something good about the ceremony, something healing, but no one phrases it in terms of reparation to a damaged object and the reincorporation of the whole experience.

As with the kava myth, there are many other possible interpretations of the 'Aho'eitu myth. One version of the myth, for example, goes into considerable detail about the way the brothers threw 'Aho'eitu's head into a bush, which caused the bush to become poisonous. Perhaps this is a way of talking about castration, with the customary theme of power residing in the cut-off head/phallus. There is a great deal of ambiguity in the myth about who is killing whom. Obviously the half-brothers kill 'Aho'eitu, but he is the father's favourite so they are attacking the father as well. The father himself sends 'Aho'eitu to his death, as I have indicated above. And what of the mother far away in Tonga? 'Aho'eitu is her only son, so she is being attacked and perhaps destroyed. But it is she who tells 'Aho'eitu how to get to heaven in the first place. And what of the link with the kava myth itself in which a daughter is destroyed? Is it a daughter only or also a mother in disguise?

I do not think one can select any particular interpretation as the 'right' one. None of them can be 'proved' or 'disproved', at least not by the methods appropriate to the consulting room, nor by any other method that I could think of at the time. In the consulting room, where the two partners to the relationship are supposed to be discovering psychic truth, however painful and improbable, one can make interpretations about unconscious cannibalism or unconscious desires to castrate a brother, and judge from the patient's reactions whether the interpretations are close to home or wide of the mark. One always has the transference situation, of which one has direct experience, as a yardstick against which the manifest content of the patient's material can be compared. In Tonga I was often aware of transference, especially of the more obvious aspects of it: the attitude that I was a foreigner with whom a cultural 'front' had to be kept up; attempts to 'use' me in one way or another to gain some social end; the feeling that I was a sympathetic outsider with whom emotional burdens could be shared. But I never felt it appropriate to interpret the transference. I was prepared to raise such issues as the likelihood of hostility between ruler and subjects, particularly with a very secure and much-loved monarch, but I was not prepared to try out interpretations of cannibalism or castration with anyone, so unprepared, in fact, that I could hardly think of such interpretations intellectually until I had left the field. The social situation I was in did not sanction such endeavours.

From among the many possible interpretations, I have emphasized the theme of cannibalism and reparation, of the destruction and restoration of a brother/son, because it seemed to me the most obvious, the most consistent with the events and the status differentials of the ceremony, and the most in accord with constellations of envy and rivalry in other aspects of Tongan social life. It helped to order the facts in a new and comparatively simple pattern that I had not seen before. But it seems very likely that at various times and to various Tongans any or all of the variants described above might be unconsciously meaningful. The ambiguity of myths and ceremonies is part of their point. It gives individuals some leeway to play with experience, to make culture their own possession.

The particular beauty of the kava ceremony, at least for me, is that it deals with problems on so many different levels at the same time. It clarifies social principles and roles. It puts a temporary brake on certain types of rapid change. It states and partly resolves problems of dependence and envy, and of interdependence and rivalry, some aspects of which are generated by the peculiarly Tongan system of social stratification, and some by the universal human attributes of having a capacity for thinking and feeling and being brought up in a society.

Small-scale societies tend to have multidimensional ceremonies of this type more frequently than we do. This suggests that time and continuity of shared experience are needed to build a ceremony that can transmit messages on many different levels at the same time. A long history of interpersonal contact and conflict makes possible the development of a symbolic statement in which universal human experiences are meaningfully linked with unique social circumstances.

In conclusion, I hope that I may have been able to interest you in taking a fresh look at ceremonies in our own society — at the coronation, for example, or at the elaborate ceremonial installation of the Lord Mayor of London as compared to the absence of ceremony in the installation of the head of the Greater London Council, at the Communion

Service, at weddings, funerals, New Year's Eve parties, and so forth. Are roles dramatized and clarified? Is there a sense of continuity with the past? Is a symbolic form of expression provided for unspoken, or unformulated, or unconscious thoughts? Does the ceremony show other aspects that the kava ceremony does not display?

Even in the lecture situation in which we find ourselves, it seems to me there is a ceremonial component. There is some dramatization of roles, though it is not nearly so complex as in the kava ceremony. There is not much sense of continuity with the unique past history of British society, but there *does* seem to be symbolic expression of unspoken thoughts. I would gather from your presence and your attentiveness that you are here because of sympathetic interest in the subject, but it would be surprising if interest and curiosity were not accompanied by criticism, doubt, and at least some measure of hostility both towards the subject and towards the speakers. Similarly, the speakers experience a complex mixture of feelings. The conventional arrangements of lectures like these — the raised platform, the physical distance between speaker and audience, the loudspeakers, the chairman, the introductions, the applause, the questions — are partly necessary for purely practical reasons, but they also provide a setting that both expresses contradictory feelings and keeps them under control.

Notes

1   The Foundations Fund for Research in Psychiatry generously provided me with a fellowship to analyse and write up the material of this paper. I am deeply indebted to the many Tongans who helped me to record and understand the ceremony and to the several colleagues with whom I have discussed the interpretations of it, especially Miss Pearl King, Miss Isabel Menzies Lyth, Ms Audrey Cantlie, and my ex-husband, James Spillius.

2   Many anthropologists, especially in Britain, do not share my view that understanding of unconscious mental processes is relevant to the analysis of social events. They are particularly apprehensive that psychoanalysts will attempt to explain social events in terms of individual needs. Their attitude is paralleled by the psychoanalyst's conviction that the complex events of the consulting room cannot be reduced to the level of neuro-anatomy. See especially Leach (1958); Lévi-Strauss (1964), especially Chapter 3; Gluckman (1964); Turner (1964); and Fox (1967).

3   For discussion of the chemical constituents and physiological action of kava see especially Keller and Klohs, 1963. Dr C.R.B. Joyce,

Reader in Psycho-Pharmacology at the University of London has very kindly reviewed the literature for me and reports the following conclusions: 'All in all, my impression remains firm that this substance is not remarkable for its pharmacological activity; that such active properties as it contains have not been isolated so far (there is more activity on animals in the watery or chloroform extract, for example, than in any so far identified substance); and that the whole situation is a remarkable example of the placebo phenomenon in a wide and important social setting.' Personal communication, May 1967.

4 A similar institution is found among certain Bantu tribes. A.I. Richards (1950) calls it 'positional succession'; I. Cunnison (1956) calls it 'perpetual kinship'.

5 Tongans say that cannibalism was not indigenous to Tonga, but that early in the nineteenth century groups of young Tongan warriors visited Fiji, adopted the practice of eating slain enemies, and continued to practise this custom when they returned home to Tonga. The new custom was not adopted with enthusiasm and was soon abandoned.

6 The analysis of these three principles of social differentiation, political authority (titles), political power, and personal rank was first worked out by my ex-husband, James Spillius, and was presented to the Tenth Pacific Science Congress at Honolulu in 1961 in a paper entitled 'Rank and political structure in Tonga'.

7 This complex of ceremonies is a striking example of what Max Gluckman has called the 'ritualization' of social relations in small-scale ('tribal') societies. He attributes this 'ritualization' [to] ... the fact that each social relation in a subsistence economy tends to serve manifold purposes ... it is from this situation that I see emerging the relatively great development of special customs and stylised etiquette to mark the different roles that a man or woman is playing at any one moment' (Gluckman 1962, 26–7).

8 In recent years anthropologists have devoted much attention to conflict and ambivalence and their expression in religion and ritual as well as in everyday affairs. See especially Fortes (1959); Gluckman (1955, 1963 (especially the Introduction and Chapter 3 entitled 'Rituals of rebellion in South-East Africa') and 1965, (especially Chapter 6 entitled 'Mystical disturbance and ritual adjustment')); Leach (1965); Turner (1957 and 1964).

One problem of particular relevance is that some rituals incorporate conflict directly into the prescribed events of the ritual whereas others, like the kava ceremony, imply conflict but do not prescribe its enactment. But a comparative discussion of this topic would lead me too far from the immediate problem of the kava ceremony.

9 On the differentiation of 'good' and 'bad' as part of normal psychic development, see especially Bion (1957, 1958 and 1962). See also Hanna Segal (1964). On the differentiation of symbol from object see Hanna Segal (1957).

10 The early accounts of kava ceremonies in which the kava was chewed instead of pounded do not specify whether the chewing was done only by the 'children' in the outer group or also by the 'younger brothers'. All we know is that the people who did the chewing were in the outer group and that a considerable number of them took part in the chewing. Nowadays only the kava maker does the actual pounding.

References

Bion, W.R. (1957) 'Differentiation of the psychotic from the non-psychotic personalities', *International Journal of Psycho-Analysis*, 38: 266–75; and also in *Second Thoughts*, London: Heinemann (1967) 86–92; reprinted in paperback, Maresfield Reprints, London: H. Karnac Books (1984); and in *Melanie Klein Today* volume 1, London: Routledge (1988).

—— (1958) 'On hallucination', *International Journal of Psycho-Analysis*, 39: 341–9; also in *Second Thoughts*, 65–85.

—— (1962) 'A theory of thinking', *International Journal of Psycho-Analysis*, 43: 306–10; also in *Second Thoughts*, 110–19; and in *Melanie Klein Today* volume 1, London: Routledge (1988).

Cunnison, I. (1956) 'Perpetual kinship: a political institution of the Luapulu peoples', *Rhodes-Livingstone Journal*, 20.

Fortes, M. (1959) *Oedipus and Job in West African Religion*, Cambridge: Cambridge University Press.

Fox, R. (1967) '*Totem and Taboo* reconsidered', in E.R. Leach (ed.) *The Structural Study of Myth and Totemism*, ASA Monograph 5, London: Tavistock Publications.

Freud, S. (1913) *Totem and Taboo*, SE 13, London: Hogarth Press.

Gifford, E.W. (1924) *Tongan Myths and Tales* in Bernice P. Bishop Museum Bulletin 8, Oxford: Blackwell.

Gluckman, M. (1955) *Custom and Conflict in Africa*, Oxford: Blackwell.

—— (1962) 'Les rites de passage' in M. Gluckman (ed.) *Essays on the Ritual of Social Relations*, Manchester: Manchester University Press.

—— (1963) *Order and Rebellion in Tribal Africa*, London: Cohen & West.

—— (ed.)(1964) *Closed Systems and Open Minds*, London and Edinburgh:

Oliver & Boyd.

——— (1965) *Politics, Law and Ritual in Tribal Society*, Oxford: Blackwell.

Keller, F. and Klohs, M.W. (1963) 'A review of the chemistry and pharmacology of the constituents of *Piper methysticum*', *Lloydia*, 26 (1).

Leach, E.R. (1958) 'Magical hair', *Journal of the Royal Anthropological Institute*, 88: part 2.

——— (1965) 'The nature of war', *Disarmament and Arms Control*, 3 (2).

Lévi-Strauss, C. (1964) *Totemism* (trans. R. Needham), London: Merlin Press.

Mariner, W. (1818) *An Account of the Natives of the Tonga Islands*, (2nd edn), 2 vols (ed. John Martin), London: John Murray.

Richards, A.I. (1950) 'Some types of family structure amongst the Central Bantu', in A.R. Radcliffe-Brown and D. Forde (eds), *African Systems of Kinship and Marriage*, London: Oxford University Press.

——— (1956) *Chisungu: A girl's initiation ceremony among the Bemba of Northern Rhodesia*, London: Faber & Faber.

Segal, H. (1957) 'Notes on symbol formation', *International Journal of Psycho-Analysis*, 38: 391–7; also in *The Work of Hanna Segal*, New York: Jason Aronson (1981), 60–5; reprinted in paperback, London: Free Association Books (1986); and in *Melanie Klein Today* volume 1, London: Routledge (1988).

——— (1964) *Introduction to the Work of Melanie Klein*, London: Heinemann.

Spillius, J. (1961) Unpublished paper, 'Rank and political structure in Tonga' presented to the Tenth Pacific Science Congress, Honolulu.

Sutherland, J.D. (ed.) (1968) *The Psychoanalytic Approach*, London: Baillière, Tindall & Cassell.

Turner, V.W. (1957) *Schism and Continuity in an African Society*, Manchester: Manchester University Press.

——— (1964) 'Symbols in Ndembu ritual' in M. Gluckman (ed.), *Closed Systems and Open Minds*, London and Edinburgh: Oliver & Boyd.

4

A psychoanalytic perspective on social institutions

ISABEL MENZIES LYTH

This paper was first given as one of a series of Freud Memorial Lectures at University College, London on 20 October 1986. It is here published for the first time, and will also be published in *The Dynamics of the Social: Selected Papers of Isabel Menzies Lyth*, in 2 vols, London: Free Association Books.

Psychoanalysts have been interested in society and its institutions since ever there were psychoanalysts. Freud himself set the pattern as appears in a number of papers, notably 'Totem and taboo' (1913). However, these early contributions were mainly by armchair scientists and not yet by practitioners. Fenichel wrote that social institutions arise through the efforts of human beings to satisfy their needs, but social institutions then become external realities, comparatively independent of individuals, that affect the structure of the individual (Fenichel 1946). This is a profound remark and stresses two elements that have been amply demonstrated in institutional practice. Institutions once established may be extremely difficult to change in their essentials and they do actually modify the personality structure of their members temporarily or permanently. Indeed, to change the members one may first need to change the institution.

Later the situation changed, much stimulated by the Second World War when new institutions were needed to support the war effort. Significant developments came from two converging directions, from psychoanalysts and psychiatrists of a similar dynamic orientation who ventured into the field of institution building and extended their skills, and from social scientists who became increasingly aware of the value of psychoanalytic insights in their work. This was a powerful partnership. It has continued, involving in particular psychoanalysts with a social science background and social scientists who have added a psychoanalytic element to their practice by long personal analysis and extensive study. So the psychoanalytic perspective implies psychoanalysis per se and not only psychoanalysts.

The psychoanalytic view of groups and institutions owes much to early pioneers in group work like Bion and Foulkes (Bion 1961; Foulkes 1948). They began the important task of bridge building between psychoanalysis and groups and institutions. Other notable contributors are psychoanalysts like Elliott Jaques and social scientists like E.L. Trist, A.K. Rice, E.J. Miller and A. Bain. It is invidious to mention names but these people have most influenced my own theory and practice.

Bion emphasizes how difficult it is for human beings to relate to each other in a realistic way in a joint task (1961). He describes the human being as a group animal: as such he cannot get on *without* other human beings. Unfortunately, he cannot get on very well *with* them either. Yet he must establish effective co-operation in life's tasks. This is his dilemma. Understanding his attempts at solving this dilemma, at evading it or defending himself against the anxieties it arouses are central to the understanding of groups and institutions since these become permanent features of institutions. Such understanding is central also to practice oriented to helping institutions and their members to solve the dilemma more effectively and function better.

My title covers a vast topic. I have decided, therefore, to limit myself mainly to the contribution of psychoanalysis to institutional practice, usually called consultancy, to practice, as in psychoanalytic practice, oriented to facilitating change for the benefit, hopefully, of the client. I will now try to set out the main ways in which derivatives from or parallels to psychoanalytic practice appear in psychoanalytically oriented institutional consultancy.

Most important is a deep conviction about the existence of the unconscious such as most easily comes through having an analysis oneself. This was how it came to Freud as he pursued the difficult course of his self-analysis. A useful alternative experience is an intensive and lengthy membership of a group where the work is based on psychoanalytic principles as applied to group phenomena and directed towards increasing insight into group process. There is no harm in having both. They are different and complementary, the latter leading more directly into work with institutions.

Such experience develops the capacity to recognize and understand the manifestations of the unconscious mind, both content and dynamics, in the conscious thoughts, feelings, speech and behaviour of the people one is working with — and in ourselves. One also learns to recognize its presence in the institution itself. In institutions, significant elements of both content and dynamics are likely to be held in common by members, derived from a shared external situation and possibly common internal situations, through conscious and unconscious collusive interaction between them. I have described elsewhere how the external realities of nursing stimulate powerful anxieties in all nurses to do with unconscious phantasies of ill, injured, dying and dead people (Menzies 1970). In institutional practice such understanding is extremely useful in orienting oneself to the nature of the situation. It is fairly unlikely, however, that one would interpret it directly to the client, as a psychoanalyst might to a patient. I cannot imagine that Trist and Bamforth took up with the coal-miners they worked with some of the cruder interpretations one hears about what the miners are doing, such as tearing out the contents of their mothers' insides (Trist and Bamforth 1951). True or not, such interpretations are irrelevant or even an insult. Perhaps more important than content in any case are the dynamic processes that go on in institutions at both conscious and unconscious levels. Of particular significance are the defences developed to deal with anxiety-provoking content and the difficulties in collaborating to accomplish the common task. These defences appear in the structure of the institution itself and permeate its whole way of functioning.

It is obvious that people do not say what they really mean even when they honestly and sincerely say what they consciously think, let alone when they do not. Neither patients nor clients are likely to be absolutely sincere and honest, although they become increasingly so if work is going well and trust in the analyst or consultant is growing. In the institutional setting it is not always unconscious thought and feelings one needs to understand, but also the implicit; what is not being said. Thoughts conscious in some people, or even shared in twos and threes, are not openly shared with everyone in a work situation where they could be realistically and constructively used. A manager said of a meeting with others at the same level that they had been able to say things to each other that previously they had only been able to say to friends in private. He commented on how valuable that had been.

Bain gives a good example of this kind of thing (1982). In the initial stages of his work in Baric, a computer processing company, he heard a great deal about what operators felt was wrong with their life at work and the action necessary to put it right; for example, more flexible hours, being allowed to chat as they might in an office job, free tea and coffee, and so on. Little was said at first about experiences in the job itself. Bain was not convinced that these complaints were really the substance of the matter. He felt there must be something more basic and significant concerning the job and job-centred experiences. It seemed this had somehow got out of focus so that while the workers felt intuitively that there was something wrong with the job they could not at first formulate it. With Bain's help they became increasingly able to focus on the job itself and their experience of it. A rather terrible picture emerged: loss of the sense of self or fears of this, loss of awareness of what was going on although they continued to function, feeling like an automaton or like the machine they worked on, irritation, boredom, alienation, depersonalization. This was more convincing and suggested that action to ameliorate matters needed to be directed at the work situation itself and not, or not only, at the fringe benefits. It is, unfortunately, only too common for situations of the kind Bain describes to develop in institutions, large and small, with a failure to diagnose the real nature of the problem. Remedies of the kind at first requested by the Baric operators are then instituted. Their beneficial effect is quite likely to be slight and disappointment considerable. Sadly, this process may be repetitive. The ineffectual remedies may be tried time and again with only minor modifications, leaving the core problem virtually untouched.

I think what may be happening is something like this. There is within the job situation a focus of deep anxiety and distress. Associated with this there is despair about being able to improve matters. The defensive system collusively set up against these feelings consists, first, in fragmentation of the core problem so that it no longer exists in an integrated and recognizable form consciously and openly among those concerned. Secondly, the fragments are projected on to bits of the ambience of the job situation which are then consciously and honestly, but mistakenly, experienced as the problem about which something needs to be done, usually by someone else. Responsibility has also been fragmented and projected often into unknown others, 'Them', the authorities. One meets this same process frequently in psychoanalysis when a patient feels himself to be up against an intractable problem and believes he cannot manage the feelings associated with it. Such defensive reactions to institutional problems often mean the institution cannot really learn. The solutions tried before had failed, but they will work this time — as though there is a kind of magic about them. Effective resolution can only come when the institution, with or without the help of a consultant, can address itself to the heart of the matter and not only to its ambience and introduce relevant changes there.

The relation of the consultant to the client institution that facilitates the elucidation of such situations strikingly resembles Freud's recommendations about the way the psychoanalyst may best gain access to his patient's mind (Freud 1911—15). I recently found the following statement which puts forward a view very close to my own. It is from a review by Almansi of a book by Wallace, *Freud and Anthropology* (Almansi 1986) and it says, 'All in all, Wallace believes that Freud's most valuable gift to anthropology was the clinical method of psychoanalysis itself and the unequalled insights it provides'. Freud recommends 'evenly suspended attention', not directing one's attention to anything in particular, not making a premature selection or prejudgement about what is significant, which might distract one's attention from whatever *might turn out to be* the most significant feature. If one can hold to this attitude something will — hopefully — evolve that begins to clarify the meaning of what the patient is showing the analyst. Bion takes Freud's advice seriously and has developed the point further (1970). He recommends eschewing memory and desire, not consciously summoning up memories about the patient or what has previously happened: or previous understanding about the patient, desires for him or for the progress of the analysis, or for that matter for oneself. These would also interfere with the evenly suspended attention needed to be in touch with the patient and the evolution of meaning.

Bain also stresses the value of ignorance and adds that, even if one is not ignorant, a 'cultivated ignorance' is essential to the role of the social consultant (1982). In my paper on work done in the Royal National Orthopaedic Hospital (RNOH), I talk of the need to take a fresh look at the situation, to set aside habitual ways of looking at things, to blind oneself to the obvious, to think again (Menzies Lyth 1982). This state-ment suggests that it is beneficial if the client too can foster these attitudes so that consultant and client together can work towards the emergence of new meanings and appropriate action. In other words, the consultant may, indeed should, encourage the members of his client institution to speak as freely and widely as they can about their work situation, relationships and experiences, something akin to psychoanalytic free association. In the initial exploratory survey of the nursing situation we invited nurses to talk about the presenting problem — difficulties in the deployment of student nurses in practical training — but invited them also to talk about anything at all that seemed to them significant in their experience of nursing (Menzies 1970). It was this invitation that evoked much of the material that led to our deeper understanding of the work and training situation, particularly the anxiety situations and the socially structured defences developed to cope with them.

The strain of this way of working is considerable for the consultant as it is for the analyst. One does not have many props since one has at least temporarily abandoned such conventionally useful things as memory, consciously set objectives and theory; they are in the background only and not to be used for guidance in the field. One exists most of the time in a state of partially self-imposed ignorance which may feel profound, frightening and painful. One needs faith that there is light at the end of the tunnel even when one does not have much hope. Bion writes mov-ingly of this experience elaborating on a quotation from Keats describing 'negative capability', that is 'when a man is capable of being in uncertain-ties, mysteries and doubts, without any irritable reaching after fact and reason' (Bion 1970).

What compounds this experience is its repetitiveness. If we can hold on to our ignorance with evenly suspended attention, meaning will probably emerge and we will experience the reward of at least one mystery or part of a mystery solved, uncertainty and doubt dispersed. But it will not last, especially if one communicates one's understanding to the client who accepts one's interpretation and is prepared and able to proceed again into the unknown. One is thrown back again on ignorance, uncertainty and doubt and must experience the process all over again. One may need to give a good deal of support to the client to go along with the process, especially a client who is accustomed to using the 'expert' and expects him to produce a definitive answer quickly. If one resists this pressure, one may be bitterly attacked as though one is delinquently withholding goodies to which the client is entitled. Or failing that, the client clutches at straws and magical unrealistic answers. I have often had the experience while consulting to a group that I was the only person in the room who did not know what was going on. The group members 'knew' i.e. had abandoned ignorance. Fortunately, people can identify with the model presented by the consultant and learn to work this way so that collaboration in the process becomes progressively easier and more rewarding to both parties. Patients are similar. A new patient may ask an analyst to tell him what to do about a problem or how to use an interpretation, an experienced patient knows, even if he may not like it, that he has to take responsibility and work out what to do for himself.

This brings me to another way that psychoanalytically orientated consultancy runs in parallel with psychoanalysis, the initiative for taking appropriate action as insights and meaning evolve lies with the client. Just as the patient makes his own life decisions without advice or suggestion, the client makes his own decisions about change and is responsible for implementing them. Ultimately he has to take the consequences. Not that it always feels like that especially if the action is unwelcome to some people. At the Royal National Orthopaedic Hospital the ward sister, caring for the welfare of her child patients and acting properly within her management authority, ruled that no hospital staff from outside the ward should visit the children in the Cot Unit unless they had a task to perform for them. The sister and her staff did not think that casual visitors were good for the children. This rule distressed and angered many well-disposed hospital staff who had visited the children to cheer them up and encourage them. The rule was known as the 'Tavistock rule', the anger about it was diverted on to the Tavistock and away from the ward sister who was liked and respected by her colleagues.

The analyst's or consultant's responsibility lies in helping insights to develop, freeing thinking about problems, helping the client to get away from unhelpful methods of thinking and behaving, facilitating the evolution of ideas for change, and helping him to bear the anxiety and uncertainty of the change process. This feature is notable in psycho-analytically orientated consultants and others whose work has been influenced by them. They stay around. Other consultants without that orientation are more likely to do their investigations and send their report to their client — a blueprint of what he should do about his problems. The consultant then leaves his client to do what he can about it on his own. This seems to happen surprisingly often, for example, in the repetitive attempts to reorganize the British health and social services. It is unlikely to work: the client is left on his own with what may well be the most difficult part of the task. It would be unthinkable to give a patient a detailed report on his psychopathology, instruct him as to what he should do about it and send him away to do it.

I find it as unthinkable to leave a client institution in a similar situation. Serious change in a social institution inevitably involves restructuring the social defence system and, as Jaques has described, this implies freeing underlying anxieties until new defences, or, better, adaptations and sublimations are developed (Jaques 1955). There is a sense in which all change is felt as catastrophic even when it is rationally recognized as for the better, since it threatens the established and familiar order and requires new attitudes and behaviour, changes in relationships, a move into a comparatively unknown future (Bion 1970). At this point, the problem of containment seems central: the presence of someone who can give strength and support, continue the process of developing insight and help define the exact nature of desirable changes.

Some of the changes that institutions make actually bring their members into more direct and overt contact with difficult tasks and stressful situations than before. I am postulating that this is a good thing, not a bad thing, since it allows workers to deploy their capacities more fully. This happened in the RNOH when the Cot Unit changed from multiple indiscriminate caretaking (a care-system in which all the nurses care 'indiscriminately' for all the patients in a ward) to case-assignment. This removed a traditional defence against anxiety. Nursery nurses were more intimately and intensely in contact with patients and families. This in fact strengthened them and fostered maturation. But, while the change was going on, they needed help, support and training to develop and sustain new ways of coping with stress in themselves as well as patients and families, e.g. by confrontation and working through its meaning.

I am indebted to Bain for helping me formulate my ideas on the func-tion of the consultant who follows a dynamic approach to institutional practice (Bain 1982). He states that the institutional consultant must concern himself with three kinds of analysis, role analysis, structure analysis, and work culture analysis. Of these, work culture analysis appears the most closely related to psychoanalysis. It considers such things as attitudes and beliefs, patterns of relationships, traditions, the psychosocial context in which work is done and how people collaborate in doing it. However, a second look may show that both roles and structure are infiltrated and partially determined by dynamics familiar to psychoanalysis. For example, the content of roles is partially determined by projection systems which contribute to the view taken by themselves and others of the incumbents of the different roles and of the roles themselves. Anxieties about one's capacity to do one's job are projected downwards into subordinates and their roles. This is linked with a tendency to filch their capacities so subordinates' capacities are underestimated and their roles diminished. Projection of one's capacities upwards also takes place along with an expectation that one's superiors will take over one's responsibilities as well, so that anxiety about one's capacity to do one's job properly is relieved. Anxieties about whether one's subordinates are capable and trustworthy — partly arising from one's own projections — may lead to unduly narrow and rigid prescription of their roles and to unnecessarily close supervision. This is not a magical process, messages are conveyed through attitudes and action: little interchanges like 'I will do that for you', the tone of voice conveying that 'you' are not really capable of doing it and 'I' am. The effects of such attributions can sometimes be seen in roles at all levels in a structure as was found in the nursing service of the general teaching hospital the author studied (Menzies 1970). But they are probably the most obvious in the lowest rung of the hierarchy where the role content may be well below the capacity of the workers. Bain found this strikingly in Baric as we did among student nurses in the general teaching hospital. Similar factors influence structure: diminution of the content of roles may lead to too many levels in the hierarchy with people doing jobs that people below them could easily do, and to too many supervisors.

This three-pronged analysis may seem very different from what goes on in a psychoanalysis which, as I said above, may appear to be more analogous to work culture analysis. I do not think this is so, however. Psychoanalysis is directly concerned with the patient's internal world as he shows it to the analyst. This internal world consists of images and phantasies, conscious and unconscious, of other people, the self and interpersonal relationships, of roles and role relationships, all of which exist within a structure. It is a social system, an imaginary institution. Psychoanalytic exploration of this internal world changes it, i.e. the patient's personality. The internal changes are reflected in changed relationships with the external world. For example, analysis of internal role systems leads to changes in the roles the patient operates, how he operates them or both. Membership of a psychoanalysis like membership of other social institutions changes the structure of the personality (Fenichel 1946).

One difference between psychoanalytic practice and psychoanalytically orientated consultancy lies in real differences between the two situations. The patient takes action in the external world himself and copes with the way he and the changes in him affect and are affected by real people and situations that facilitate or inhibit his efforts. If and when an institution uses a consultant to facilitate institutional change, individuals or even small groups with whom he is working cannot usually take decisions or initiate action on their own. Other people and groups need to be involved if understanding and insights are to grow and relevant action take place. Role and structure analysis need to be explicit and related to each other and to work culture analysis; they go hand in hand. Further, the work must usually range fairly widely throughout the institution. People who affect and are affected by change need to be overtly involved. The work cannot be too narrowly restricted to the group or unit where the problem is said to exist. Significant changes in the so-called problem area require counterbalancing changes in surrounding areas if they are to be effective and lasting.

Bain found in Baric that the level of the operators' role could only be raised if other roles and the structure were also changed, with less supervision, fewer supervisory roles, and so on. Similarly in the RNOH a significant change in the nursery nurses' role had to be balanced by change in the roles of the staff nurse and ward sister. They delegated more patient and family care to the nursery nurses and themselves became more involved in management, technical nursing, support and training. The nursery nurses also took over certain aspects of the social worker's role in family care while she trained and supported them. Similarly, work was done with other wards and departments both to help develop attitudes consistent with those in the Cot Unit itself and to assist in desirable role and structure modification. The health service being what it is, results were somewhat limited: unnecessary supervisors could not be removed, for example, since the health service decreed they should be there.

Rather frequently in institutional consultancy one or two types of analysis are neglected and the consultant concentrates on the other two or one. Psychoanalytically orientated workers may and often do concentrate exclusively or almost so on some form of work culture analysis orientated to achieving significant attitude change. This can make their work inadequate, useless or even harmful. This happens only too often, for example, in sensitivity or support groups aimed at helping care-takers to be more understanding and sensitive both to themselves and clients. Such attitude change is not hard to achieve: care-takers basically want to be like that. The problem is that the existing roles and structure may make it virtually impossible to deploy their changed attitudes. For years, student nurses have been exhorted to 'nurse the whole patient as a person'. This is usually what the student wants to do. But the role system and the institutional structure in nursing, especially multiple indiscriminate care-taking, too often make it impossible to do this. The danger is that people become disappointed, frustrated and disillusioned. Attitudes change back in defence against these feelings and in line with the demands of the institutional system. Or people cannot tolerate the system and leave. The consultants and what they stand for may be discredited.

The author's job-title and role in two therapeutic communities caring for delinquent and deprived children illustrate the point. I was a management consultant. My task was continuously to explore with the staff the therapeutic impact of the roles and structure in the institution and help modify them so that the institution as a whole became more therapeutic. In other words, therapy was understood by the staff and by me as the impact of the whole institution on the children and not only activities more usually regarded as therapeutic or developmental, such as counselling or education; staff sensitivity was not enough. Work culture analysis was not neglected but was carried out mainly by another consultant (Mrs Barbara Dockar-Drysdale, formerly of the Mulberry Bush School) who particularly handled staff attitudes to children, their own reactions and so on. The division was not rigid and, perhaps strangely, it worked. Too many therapeutic communities appear to lack sufficient awareness of role and structural factors and therefore their therapeutic impact is diminished because these are inadequate (Menzies Lyth 1985).

By contrast, the consultant who lacks a psychoanalytic orientation may well confine himself to role and structure without even having sufficient understanding of the contribution of unconscious content and dynamics to them. He may well suggest changes in role and structure without the backing of the requisite changes in work culture. Indeed attention to work culture might not support his ideas about role and structure. This is likely to prevent anything effective happening. There seems to be a crying need for work culture analysis if real improvement is to be effected in the health and social services.

Psychoanalytic practice and consultancy differ in ways that mean the consultant may not be able to follow Freud's wise precepts fully. The psychoanalyst refrains as far as possible from contact with the patient outside the analysis and with his relatives and friends. He is to be as much as possible a mirror that reflects the patient back to himself and shows nothing about the analyst. This is recommended for the protection of the patient and the analysis, to give freedom for phantasy and to help the patient follow his own direction. Desirable as this is in institutional consultancy, it is possible only to a limited extent. One usually has to function in the client's territory so that one shares activities and places in a perfectly ordinary way — coffees, drinks, meals, canteen, lavatories. It is inevitably more sociable and it may be difficult to fend off ordinary human curiosity about oneself without seeming or even being offensive. One can hardly avoid contact with spouses or relatives especially when staff and families as well as their clients are resident (for example, in hospitals and other residential institutions). A.K. Rice said his clients became his friends — fair comment; but yet, one has to try to keep one's distance, not to get too drawn in, and, of course, not to let one's own or one's clients' social feelings interfere with the work. Holding the balance of one's social and work relationships is often a problem. One may be perceived by some as being too much in the pockets of others. Who does one eat with in the canteen, and why? Does one mix enough socially with the lowest level workers? It is conventional for higher managers to entertain outside consultants — dinner in the matron's flat, not the student nurses' canteen. One has to wend one's way carefully through these intricacies noting that they are likely to have an effect on the transference and counter-transference and on one's own transference to the client. It is important to understand what that effect is.

Transference is still an important concept even if it gets a bit cluttered by the greater real presentation of oneself to one's clients. To further the work, it may be essential to draw such transference phenomena into work culture analysis especially when they lead to suspicion of bias. This will not necessarily be easy or welcome. Careful attention to the counter-transference is also necessary; one's own bias may make careful observation and deduction more difficult.

Here another difference between psychoanalysis and consultancy is helpful. One need not work alone. An institutional consultancy may, in any case, be too big an undertaking for one person. The advantages of having at least one colleague are inestimable. Indeed, it is not really advisable to work alone. It is an old Tavistock Institute principle that it takes a group to study a group: or, at least, a person working alone needs his own consultant 'to come home to'. As regards transference and counter-transference, two people can be very useful in helping each other sort them out, check and recheck them and disentangle each other from relationships that interfere with work or from attitudes inconsistent with consultancy. Several times after I had done a long continuous spell of work in the RNOH I would begin to get too possessive of the children and too identified with the hospital. I would begin to talk about 'our children'. My colleague, Tim Dartington, would say, 'They are not our children, you know'. That was all that was needed to remind me of my place. Two or more people give added richness to interpretation of the data. Their perspectives are different, their field experiences are different since they do not always work alongside each other. Their relationships with different members of the client institution are different. Two people are much more than twice one in my experience. I have done a great deal of useful work in cars, buses and trains going to and from the field with colleagues, and am grateful to these colleagues for the insights they have helped me develop.

Note-taking and keeping of records are another example of differences. Freud discouraged the analyst from making notes during sessions since it would involve selection of data and would interfere with evenly suspended attention. Having a colleague in the field allows other possibilities. One can split the roles, one person conducts the discussion with evenly suspended attention while the other takes notes, inevitably selectively. But his selective notes may be useful afterwards in conjunction with memory from evenly suspended attention in recording significant aspects of what went on and keeping track of the vast amount of data one collects in the field.

And, lastly, the question of reports. As remarked earlier, one does not give written reports to patients. I have also criticized the practice of sending the blueprint type of report to clients. However, reports do have their usefulness in certain forms and in certain settings. A written report may be a useful mnemonic. It would never, however, be my first report. First, its contents would have been reported verbally in a face-to-face situation where one can work with their effect on the client, tackle resistance to their acceptance as a means to further understanding, stand corrected and amend conclusions if one is wrong, and so on. The final document is likely to be a distillation of joint work between the client and oneself. This was what I did regularly in one of the children's communities (The Cotswold Community: Principal, Richard Balbernie). I worked there two consecutive days a month, sent a 'field-note' outlining where I thought we had got to and giving them something to work on by themselves until my next visit. I had sufficient trust and respect for that particular client to feel this was a safe and helpful way of working.

A complication is that one may be obliged to write reports, for example, if one is being financed by a research grant. In the RNOH we had to submit annual and final reports to the Department of Health and Social Security who financed the work. The same principle applied. The reports crystallized discussions with the Project Steering Committee and other people in the hospital and were approved by them before being sent. The question of confidentiality is implicit in this and affects wider publication. One cannot disguise an institution effectively as a rule. One's clients are literate and interested in themselves and entitled to be told where the work will be published. This means that results can only be professionally and ethically published when contents have been agreed and consent given for publication. Sometimes one cannot publish.

The end of a consultancy is rather like the end of an analysis. One needs to work through termination to ensure that the patient or client will be able to carry on by himself. This means more than simply sustaining the gains that have been made or that the person has solved the problem he originally brought. It means that the patient or client can continue to make progress on his own through having 'learned' a method of tackling problems which will survive the departure of the analyst or consultant and facilitate creative developments in the future. Bain was rewarded by a follow-up study in Baric which showed that the method of tackling problems had been sustained and creative solutions to other problems were found. Similarly, in the RNOH. After we left, Mavis Young Remmen, the ward sister, and her staff reorganized the care of latency children in a unit separate from the Cot Unit where we had worked together. The exciting thing was that this was not a slavish copy of the model we had developed together but a different model realistic-ally related to the needs of latency children and taking into account the differences in resources, notably that all Cot Unit staff were permanent whereas the latency unit was mainly staffed by transitory student nurses.

Conclusion

I want to return briefly to Fenichel's view that the membership of an institution affects the personality structure of its members. They introject and identify with the institution, the more so the more malleable the members. This is why the design of children's institutions is so important (Menzies Lyth 1985). Members become like the institution in significant ways — by introjecting and operating its characteristic defence mechanisms, sharing common attitudes, carrying on traditional types of relationships. If an individual cannot achieve this identification he is unlikely to remain a member. If he remains too different then he is likely to be rejected by the institution because he does not 'fit'. If he tries to conform to something which is too foreign to him, he may find it too stressful and leave. Over 30% of student nurses give up training mostly of their own volition, because they cannot follow the institutional model which is regressive. Labour turnover was over 400% per annum in the day nursery where Bain and Barnett worked (1986). Note the plight of children who usually cannot opt to leave if they are placed in an institu-tion which is a bad model.

Unfortunately, I have come to a depressing conclusion, that institutions have a natural tendency to become bad models for identification and the bigger the institution the more likely this is. I have already suggested reasons why this should be so, the basic difficulties human beings have in co-operating effectively together, the anxieties these arouse and the defences against the anxieties. The defences are only too likely to be powerful and primitive and to provide bad models for identification. As psychoanalysts we know that a person's mental health is intimately linked with the conscious and unconscious anxieties he experiences and the methods he uses to deal with them. Illness is linked with excessive use of defences, usually primitive, as against other methods like sublimation, development of skills and engagement in constructive anxiety-related activities. Excessive use of regressed defences is the model many institutions offer. The risk tends to be greater where situations of real danger occur such as in coal-mining or where there is shared impact of great human suffering as in the humane institutions.

However, all is not lost. Some institutions manage quite well in spite of everything and establish healthy functioning by their own efforts. Trist's and Bamforth's work in coal-mining demonstrates this, a natural experiment. Two neighbouring coal mines had the same kind of coal seams and used the same technology. By chance they had developed very different social systems. There were dramatic differences in the human experiences in the two systems, for example, in labour turnover, absenteeism and sickness rates as well as in more subtle social indicators. There was also a dramatic difference in coal production, one mine producing nearly twice as much coal per man-shift as the other.

Work in consultancy has shown that other institutions can be helped to change so that they become better places to be in and better models which help their members to become more mature people, more able to act effectively and constructively and reap the rewards of that, and to have a richer experience of life in general. People of all ages have developed and expanded their horizons: work in children's institutions aimed at providing better developmental situations for the children had a considerable spin-off in the development and maturation of the adults who cared for them. Another by-product is that the institution itself becomes more effective — productivity increases if it is that kind of institution — as in the coal mine. It is as though the institution's 'ego' strengthens as defences are modified and it copes more effectively with its real-life tasks.

One can also begin to establish principles — or theories — about what is a healthy institution: principles, not blueprints; just as one has theories about what constitutes a healthy personality: the avoidance of overuse of regressed defences, more adaptation and sublimation, the ability to confront and work through problems, opportunities for people to deploy their full capacities, neither more nor less than they can manage, opportunity to have realistic control over their own life in the institution although taking the needs of others duly into account, independence without undue supervision, visible relation between work and rewards. The principles are not so new — it is implementing them that is the problem.

Which brings me to a last point — the psychoanalytically-orientated or 'clinical' way of working pays a large bonus in research results. It was from clinical practice that Freud's theories developed. Similarly, from institutional clinical practice a great deal of important institutional theory has developed. Working 'clinically' often gives access to data that may be denied to the 'pure' research worker studying the institution for his own purposes or withheld because in the narrower research context it is not seen to be relevant.

References

Almansi, R.J. (1986) 'Review of *Freud and Anthropology*, Psychological Issues Monograph 55 by Edwin R. Wallace', *Journal of the American Psychoanalytical Association*, 34, no. 3.

Bain, A. (1982) *The Baric Experiment*, Occasional Paper No. 4, London: Tavistock Institute of Human Relations.

—— and Barnett, L. (1986) *The Design of a Day Care System in a Nursery Setting for Children under Five*, Occasional Paper No. 8, London: Tavistock Institute of Human Relations.

Bion, W.R. (1961) *Experience in Groups*, London: Tavistock Publications, and New York: Basic Books.

—— (1970) *Attention and Interpretation*, London: Tavistock Publications; reprinted in paperback, Maresfield Reprints, London: H. Karnac Books (1984).

Fenichel, O. (1946) *The Psychoanalytic Theory of Neuroses*, London: Routledge & Kegan Paul.

Foulkes, S.H. (1948) *Introduction to Group-Analytic Psychotherapy*, London: Heinemann.

Freud, S. (1911—15) 'Papers on technique', SE 12, London: Hogarth Press.

—— (1913) *Totem and Taboo*, SE 13, London: Hogarth Press.

Jaques, E. (1955) 'Social systems as a defence against persecutory and depressive anxiety', in M. Klein, P. Heimann, and R. Money-Kyrle, (eds) *New Directions in Psycho-Analysis*, London: Tavistock Publications; paperback, Tavistock Publications (1971); also reprinted by Maresfield

Reprints, London: H. Karnac Books (1985).

Menzies, I.E.P. (1970) *The Functioning of Social Systems as a Defence against Anxiety*, Tavistock Pamphlet No. 3, London: Tavistock Institute of Human Relations.

Menzies Lyth, I. (1982) *The Psychological Welfare of Children making Long Stays in Hospital*, Occasional Paper No. 3, London: Tavistock Institute of Human Relations.

—— (1985) 'The development of the self in children in institutions', *Journal of Child Psychotherapy*, vol. 11, no. 2.

Trist, E.L. and Bamforth, K.W. (1951) 'Some social and psychological consequences of the Longwell method of coal-getting, *Human Relations*, 4.

References to general introduction and other introductory material

Bick, E. (1962) 'Child analysis today', *International Journal of Psycho-Analysis*, 43: 328—32; also 168—76 of this volume.
—— (1964) 'Notes on infant observation in psychoanalytic training', *International Journal of Psycho-Analysis*, 45: 558—66.
—— (1968) 'The experience of the skin in early object relations', *International Journal of Psycho-Analysis*, 49: 484—6; also in *Melanie Klein Today: Volume 1*, London: Routledge (1988).
Bion, W.R. (1955) 'Language and the schizophrenic', in M. Klein, P. Heimann and R. Money-Kyrle (eds), *New Directions in Psycho-Analysis*, London: Tavistock Publications, 220—39; paperback, Tavistock Publications (1971); also reprinted by Maresfield Reprints, London: H. Karnac Books (1985).
—— (1957) 'Differentiation of the psychotic from the non-psychotic personalities', *International Journal of Psycho-Analysis*, 38: 266—75; also in *Second Thoughts*, London: Heinemann (1967), 43—64; reprinted in paperback, Maresfield Reprints, London: H. Karnac Books (1984) and in *Melanie Klein Today: Volume 1*, London: Routledge (1988).
—— (1961) *Experiences in Groups*, London: Tavistock Publications, and New York: Basic Books.
—— (1962) *Learning from Experience*, London: Heinemann; reprinted in paperback, Maresfield Reprints, London: H. Karnac Books (1984).
—— (1967) 'Notes on memory and desire', *The Psychoanalytic Forum*, 2: 272—3 and 279—80; also 17—21 of this volume.
Bott, E. See Spillius.
Brenman, E. (1980) 'The value of reconstruction in adult psychoanalysis', *International Journal of Psycho-Analysis*, 61: 53—60.

Brenman Pick, I. See Pick.

Cantlie (Hayley), A. (1968) 'The ox and the cucumber', *Man*, 3: 262—71.

—— (1985) 'Encounter with Kali', unpublished paper.

Daniel, P. (1984) 'The miscarriage of masculinity as seen in the analysis of a 4 year old boy', unpublished paper given to the Weekend Conference of English—Speaking Members of European Psycho-Analytic Societies, 14 October.

—— (1985) 'An infant observed becomes a child in analysis', unpublished paper given to the British Psycho-Analytical Society, December.

Folch, T. Eskalinen de (1983) 'We — versus I and you', *International Journal of Psycho-Analysis*, 64: 309—20.

—— (1988a) 'Communication and containing in child analysis: towards terminability', *International Journal of Psycho-Analysis*, 69: 105-12; also 206—17 of this volume.

—— (1988b) 'Guilt bearable or unbearable: a problem for the child in analysis', *International Review of Psycho-Analysis*, 15: 13—24.

Freud, S. (1910) *Leonardo da Vinci and a Memory of his Childhood*, SE 11: 59—137. (*Standard Edition of the Complete Psychological works of Sigmund Freud*, London: Hogarth Press (1950—1974).)

—— (1911) *Totem and Taboo* SE 13: 1—161.

—— (1912) 'Recommendations to physicians practising psychoanalysis', SE 12: 111—20.

—— (1921) *Group Psychology and the Analysis of the Ego*, SE 18: 67—143.

Frosh, S. (1987) *The Politics of Psychoanalysis*, London: Macmillan.

Gabbard, K. and Gabbard, G.O. (1987) 'The science fiction film and psychoanalysis: *Alien* and Melanie Klein's night music', in M. Charney and J. Reppen (eds), *Psychoanalytic Approaches to Literature and Film*, Cranbury, NJ: Associated University Presses, 171—9.

Grinberg, L. (1962) 'On a specific aspect of counter-transference due to the patient's projective identification', *International Journal of Psycho-Analysis*, 43: 436—40.

Harris, M. (1965) 'Depression and the depressive position in an adolescent boy', *Journal of Child Psychotherapy*, 1, 3: 33—40; also 158—67 of this volume.

Harris Williams, M. See Williams.

Hayley, A. See Cantlie.

Heimann, P. (1950) 'On countertransference', *International Journal of Psycho-Analysis*, 31: 81—4.

Herman, N. (1987) *Why Psychotherapy?* London: Free Association Books.

Hill, J.M.M. and Trist, E.L. (1955) 'Changes in accidents and other absences with length of service', *Human Relations*, 8: 121—52.

Hughes, A. (1988) 'The use of manic defence in the psycho-analysis of

a ten-year-old girl', *International Review of Psycho-Analysis*, 15: 157—64.
Jaques, E. (1948) 'Interpretive group discussion as a method of facilitating social change', *Human Relations*, 1: 533—49.
—— (1951) *The Changing Culture of a Factory*, London: Tavistock Publications.
—— (1955) 'Social systems as a defence against persecutory and depressive anxiety', in M. Klein, P. Heimann, and R.E. Money-Kyrle (eds), *New Directions in Psycho-Analysis*, London: Tavistock Publications, 478—98; paperback, Tavistock Publications (1971); also reprinted by Maresfield Reprints, London: H. Karnac Books (1985).
—— (1956) *The Measurement of Responsibility*, London: Tavistock Publications.
—— (1965) 'Death and the mid-life crisis', *International Journal of Psycho-Analysis*, 46: 502—14; also 226 of this volume.
Jordan, E. (1986) 'The poem as patient', *Free Associations*, 7: 111—17.
Joseph, B. (1975) 'The patient who is difficult to reach', in P.L. Giovacchini (ed.), *Tactics and Techniques in Psychoanalytic Therapy*, vol. 2: *Countertransference*, New York: Jason Aronson, 205—16; also 48—60 of this volume.
—— (1978) 'Different types of anxiety and their handling in the analytic situation', *International Journal of Psycho-Analysis*, 59: 223—8.
—— (1983) 'On understanding and not understanding: some technical issues', *International Journal of Psycho-Analysis*, 64: 291—8.
—— (1985) 'Transference: the total situation', *International Journal of Psycho-Analysis*, 66: 447—54; also 61—72 of this volume.
Klein, M. (1957) *Envy and Gratitude*, in *The Writings of Melanie Klein*, vol. 3: *Envy and Gratitude and Other Works*, London: Tavistock; and reprinted by London: Hogarth Press (1975), 176—235; in paperback, New York: Dell Publishing Co. (1977).
—— (1961) *Narrative of a Child Analysis*, in *The Writings of Melanie Klein*, vol. 4, London: Hogarth Press.
Lasch, C. (1981) 'The Freudian Left and cultural revolution', *New Left Review*, 129: 23—34.
Malcolm, R. See Riesenberg Malcolm.
Meltzer, D. (1967) *The Psychoanalytical Process*, London: Heinemann.
—— (1973) *Sexual States of Mind*, Strathtay, Perthshire: Clunie Press.
Meltzer, D., Bremner, J. Hoxter, S., Weddell, D. and Wittenberg, I. (1975) *Explorations in Autism*, Strathtay, Perthshire: Clunie Press.
Menzies Lyth (Menzies) I.E.P. (1960) 'A case-study in the functioning of social systems as a defence against anxiety. A report on the nursing service of a general hospital', *Human Relations*, 13: 95—121; reprinted as *The Functioning of Social Systems as a Defence against Anxiety*, Tavistock Pamphlet No. 3, London: Tavistock Institute of Human Relations (1970).

—— (1965) 'Some mutual interactions between organizations and their members', *Psychotherapy and Psychosomatics*, 13: 194—200.

—— (1969) 'The motor cycle: growing up on two wheels', in H.S. Klein (ed.), *Sexuality and Aggression in Maturation*, London: Baillière, Tindall & Cassell, 37—49.

—— (1970) 'Psychosocial aspects of eating', *Journal of Psychosomatic Research*, 14: 223—7.

—— (1982) *The psychological welfare of children making long stays in hospital: an experience in the art of the possible*, Occasional Paper No. 3, London: Tavistock Institute of Human Relations.

—— (1985) 'The development of the self in children in institutions', *Journal of Child Psychotherapy*, 11, 2: 49—64.

—— (In press) *The Dynamics of the Social: Selected Papers of Isabel Menzies Lyth*, in 2 vols, London: Free Association Books.

Money-Kyrle, R.E. (1951) *Psychoanalysis and Politics*, London: Duckworth Press.

—— (1956) 'Normal counter-transference and some of its deviations', *International Journal of Psycho-Analysis*, 37: 360—6; and in *The Collected Papers of Roger Money-Kyrle*, 330—42; also 22—33 of this volume.

—— (1961) *Man's Picture of his World*, London: Duckworth.

—— (1968) 'Cognitive development', *International Journal of Psycho-Analysis*, 49: 691—8; also in *The Collected Papers of Roger Money-Kyrle*, 416—33.

—— (1978) *The Collected Papers of Roger Money-Kyrle*, ed. D. Meltzer with the assistance of E. O'Shaughnessy, Strathtay, Perthshire: Clunie Press.

O'Shaughnessy, E. (1981) 'A commemorative essay on W.R. Bion's theory of thinking', *Journal of Child Psychotherapy*, 7, 2: 181—92; also 177—90 of this volume.

—— (1983) 'Words and working through', *International Journal of Psycho-Analysis*, 64: 281—9; also 138—51 of this volume.

—— (1986) 'A three-and-a-half year old boy's melancholic identification with an original object', *International Journal of Psycho-Analysis*, 67: 173—9.

—— (1988) 'The invisible Oedipus complex'. This paper was first given in September 1987 at a Kleinian conference on the Oedipus complex organized by Professor J. Sandler at the Psychoanalysis Unit of University College, London. It is being simultaneously published in R. Britton, M. Feldman, and E. O'Shaughnessy, *The Oedipus Complex Today: Clinical Implications*, London: H. Karnac Books; also 191—205 of this volume.

Pick, I. Brenman (1985) 'Working through in the counter-transference', *International Journal of Psycho-Analysis*, 66: 157—66; also 34—47 of this volume.

Pick, I. Brenman and Segal, H. (1978) 'Melanie Klein's contribution to child analysis: theory and technique', in J. Glenn (ed.), *Child Analysis and Therapy*, New York: Jason Aronson, 427—49.

Pines, M. (ed.) (1985) *Bion and Group Psychotherapy*, London: Routledge & Kegan Paul.

Piontelli, S. (1986a) *Backwards in Time*, Strathtay, Perthshire: Clunie Press.

———— (1986b) 'Pre-natal life and birth as reflected in the analysis of a two year old psychotic girl'; unpublished paper read to the British Psycho-Analytical Society, May.

———— (1987) 'Infant observation from before birth', *International Journal of Psycho-Analysis*, 68: 453—63.

Racker, H. (1968) *Transference and Countertransference*, London: Hogarth Press; in paperback, Maresfield Reprints, London: H. Karnac Books (1982).

Rice, A.K. (1965) *Learning for Leadership*, London: Tavistock Publications.

Riesenberg Malcolm, R. (1970) 'The mirror: a perverse sexual phantasy in a woman seen as a defence against a psychotic breakdown', published in Spanish as 'El espejo: una fantasia sexual perversa en una mujer, vista como defensa contra un derrumbe psicotico', *Revista Psicoanalisis*, 27: 793—826; also (in English) 115—37 of this volume.

———— (1981) 'Melanie Klein: achievements and problems. (Reflections on Klein's conception of object relationship.)' Published in Spanish as 'Melanie Klein: logros y problemos', *Revista Chilena de Psicoanalisis* 3: 52—63. Also published in English in R. Langs (ed.), *The Yearbook of Psychoanalysis and Psychotherapy*, vol. 2, 306—21, New York: Gardner Press (1986).

———— (1986) 'Interpretation: the past in the present', *International Review of Psycho-Analysis*, 13: 433—43; also 73—89 of this volume.

Rosenfeld, H. (1986) 'Transference-countertransference distortions and other problems in the analysis of traumatized patients'; unpublished talk given to the Kleinian analysts of the British Psycho-Analytical Society, 30 April.

———— (1987) *Impasse and Interpretation*, London: Tavistock Publications.

Rustin, M. (1982) 'A socialist consideration of Kleinian psychoanalysis', *New Left Review*, 131: 71—96.

Rustin, M. and Rustin, M. (1984) 'Relational preconditions of socialism', in Richards, B. (ed.), *Capitalism and Infancy*, London: Free Association Books, 207—25.

Sayers, J. (1987) 'Melanie Klein, psychoanalysis, and feminism', *Feminist Review*, 25: 23-37.

Segal, H. (1950) 'Some aspects of the analysis of a schizophrenic', *International Journal of Psycho-Analysis*, 31: 268—78; also in *The Work of*

Hanna Segal (including a postscript, 1980), New York: Jason Aronson (1981), 101–20; reprinted in paperback, London: Free Association Books (1986). Also 96–114 of this volume.

—— (1952) 'A psycho-analytical approach to aesthetics', *International Journal of Psycho-Analysis*, 33: 196–207; also in *The Work of Hanna Segal*, 185–206.

—— (1957) 'Notes on symbol formation', *International Journal of Psycho-Analysis*, 38: 391–7; also in *The Work of Hanna Segal*, 49–65 and in *Melanie Klein Today: Volume 1,* London: Routledge (1988).

—— (1967) 'Melanie Klein's technique', in B.B. Wolman (ed.), *Psychoanalytic Techniques*, New York: Basic Books; also in *The Work of Hanna Segal*, 3–24.

—— (1974) 'Delusion and artistic creativity', *International Review of Psycho-Analysis*, 1: 135–41; reprinted in *The Work of Hanna Segal*, 207–16; also 249–58 of this volume.

—— (1977a) 'Countertransference', *International Journal of Psychoanalytic Psychotherapy*, 6: 31–7; also in *The Work of Hanna Segal*, 81–7.

—— (1977b) 'Psychoanalysis and freedom of thought', inaugural lecture, Freud Memorial Visiting Professor of Psychoanalysis, University College, London, 1977–8, published by H.K. Lewis, London; also in *The Work of Hanna Segal*, 217–27.

—— (1980) 'Postscript to "Some aspects of the analysis of a schizophrenic"', in *The Work of Hanna Segal*, 119–20.

—— (1982) 'Mrs Klein as I knew her', unpublished paper read to the Tavistock Clinic meeting to celebrate the centenary of the birth of Melanie Klein, July.

—— (1984) 'Joseph Conrad and the mid-life crisis', *International Review of Psycho-Analysis*, 11: 3–9.

—— (1987) 'Silence is the real crime', *International Review of Psycho-Analysis*, 14: 3–12.

Spillius (Bott) E. (1968) 'Psychoanalysis and ceremony', in J.D. Sutherland (ed.), *The Psychoanalytic Approach*, London: Baillière, Tindall & Cassell, 52–77; reprinted in J.S. La Fontaine (ed.), *The Interpretation of Ritual Essays in Honour of A.I. Richards*, London: Tavistock Publications, 205–37 and 277–84; also 259–83 of this volume.

—— (1976) 'Hospital and society', *British Journal of Medical Psychology*, 49: 97–140.

Steiner, J. (1985) 'Turning a blind eye: The cover-up for Oedipus', *International Review of Psycho-Analysis*, 12: 161–72.

Steiner, R. (1985) 'Some thoughts about tradition and change arising from an examination of the British Psycho-Analytical Society's controversial discussions', *International Review of Psycho-Analysis*, 12: 27–71.

Stokes, A. (1978) *The Critical Writings of Adrian Stokes*, 3 vols, London: Thames & Hudson.

Trist, E. (In press) *The Social Engagement of Social Science*, Philadelphia: The University of Pennsylvania Press.

Turquet, P.M. (1975) 'Threats to identity in the large group', in L. Kreeger (ed.), *The Large Group: Therapy and Dynamics*, London: Constable, 87—144.

Tustin, F. (1972) *Autism and Childhood Psychosis*, London: Hogarth Press.

—— (1981) *Autistic States in Children*, London: Routledge & Kegan Paul.

—— (1986) *Autistic Barriers in Neurotic Patients*, London: H. Karnac Books.

Waddell, M. (1986) 'Concepts of the inner world in George Eliot's work', *Journal of Child Psychotherapy*, 12, 2: 109—24.

Williams, A.H. (1986) '*The Ancient Mariner*: opium, the saboteur of self-therapy', *Free Associations*, 6: 123—44.

Williams, M. Harris (1986) '"Knowing" the mystery: against reductionism', *Encounter*, June, 48—53.

—— (1987) *A Strange Way of Killing: The Poetic Structure of Wuthering Heights*, Strathtay, Perthshire: Clunie Press.

Wittenberg, I. (1970) *Psychoanalytic Insight and Relationships: A Kleinian Approach*, London: Routledge & Kegan Paul.

Wollheim, R. (1969) 'The mind and the mind's image of itself', *International Journal of Psycho-Analysis*, 50: 209—20.

—— (1974) 'Identification and imagination', in R. Wollheim (ed.), *A Collection of Critical Essays*, New York: Anchor Books, 172—95.

—— (1980) 'The good and the bad self: the moral psychology of British idealism and the English school of psychoanalysis', in Freny Mehta (ed.), *The Scientific Consensus and Recent British Philosophy*, Bombay: Bombay Popular Prakashan, 3—34.

—— (1984) *The Thread of Life*, London: Cambridge University Press.

Name Index

Abraham, K. 166
Almansi, R.J. 287
Anderson, R. 156
Andreas-Salomé, L. 20

Bach, J.S. 227
Bain, A. 285, 286; on institutional
  consultancy 290–2, 296
Balzac, H. de 228
Bamforth, K.W. 286, 297
Barnett, L. 296
Baudelaire, C. 227, 231
Beethoven, L. van 228, 247
Bick, E. 155, 156, 168–7
Bion, W.R. 28, 32 n.2, 243–4, 282
  n.9; and containment 11–13, 75,
  134; on counter-transference 11, 28;
  and groups 222, 285; on memory
  and desire 7, 9, 17–21, 288; on
  patient-analyst interaction 59, 139,
  178, 186, 206: on projective
  identification 59, 139, 178, 186,
  206–7; and psychosis 34, 94, 115,
  178–80, 183–4; and reverie 75,
  179, 186, 187; on thinking 7,
  177–89
Blum, H. 88 n.3
Bott, E., see Spillius, E. Bott
Bremner, J. 155
Brenman, E. 15–16, 88 n.3
Brenman, I., see Pick, I. Brenman
Brierley, M. 20–1
British Psycho-Analytical Society 2,
  31 n.2, 156, 168–9

Cantlie, A. 223, 280 n.1
Chopin, F. 227
Church, R. 226
Coleridge, S.T. 221
Conrad, J. 221
Constable, J. 227
Couperin, F. 228
Croce, B. 233

Daniel, P. 157
Dante Alighieri 231–4, 247
Dartington, T. 294
Darwin, C. 21
Deutsch, H. 49
Dickens, C. 231
Donatello 227
Dürer, A. 228

Einstein, A. 230

Federn, P. 112, 113
Fenichel, O. 284, 292, 296
Flaubert, G. 257
Folch, T. Eskelinen de 157, 206–17
Fortes, M. 281 n.8
Foulkes, S.H. 285
Fox, R. 280 n.2
French, T.M. 20
Freud, A. 168
Freud, S. 42, 88, 221, 229–30, 298;
  on analytic process 15, 61, 109, 189,
  206; and anthropology 223, 272,
  284, 287; on counter-transference
  170; on death 234, 236, 244; on ego

Subject Index

acting-in 7, 15, 95, 144, 203
acting-out 36, 45, 94, 102, 118, 144
  by analyst 8, 38, 53, 55; in
  transference 50–1, 53, 59–60, 71,
  121–3
adhesive identification 156
adolescence 199, 232
  depression in 156, 158–66
aesthetics 221, 223–4, 249, 254
affect 32 n.8, 198, 200
  flatness of 159, 166; split-off 36,
  174, 197, 208
aggression, aggressiveness 8, 23, 254
alpha function 39
ambivalence 166, 237, 246, 255
  and guilt 29, 158; towards authority
  272
analyst 32 n.6, 32 n.8, 199–200
  anxiety in 18, 41, 52–3, 171, 215;
  collusion by 50, 94, 144, 193;
  feelings of 9–12, 25, 31, 37, 45–6,
  175; idealization of 16, 32 n.6, 161,
  201, 237; identification of, with
  patient 12, 23, 27, 30, 170–1;
  manipulation of 51, 59; neutrality of
  23, 41, 43, 46; parental role of
  23–4, 29–30, 38, 41, 196–7, 200;
  reparative drive in 11, 23–4, 28,
  30–1, 41
analytic relationship 7, 24, 78, 111,
  148, 159
  and communication 13–14, 54,

74–5, 178; interpretation and
  15–16, 75, 78, 85–6, 104, 139,
  184; and projective identification 35,
  61, 139; and transference 5, 73, 201;
  and unconscious phantasy 12, 13,
  30, 78, 86
analytic situation 6, 13, 14–15,
  103–4
anthropology 223, 224–5, 287; *see also*
  ceremony
anxiety 14, 20, 56, 118, 201, 225
  in analyst 18, 41, 52–3, 171, 215;
  about death 127; and defence 71, 78,
  79, 149, 232, 286, 297; depressive
  158, 165, 225, 232, 238, 256; and
  disintegration/fragmentation 53, 115,
  125; persecutory 41, 166, 170, 225,
  243; projection of 43, 53, 68, 174,
  291; sexual 44; split-off 193;
  unconscious 24, 50, 61, 171, 297
asthma 207, 214
attention, evenly suspended 287–8,
  289, 295

bed-wetting 172, 173
borderline disorder 8, 45
breast 180–1, 236
  as container 134, 135, 162; early
  experience of 136, 214, 215, 239,
  240, 245
cannibalism 268, 277–8, 281 n.5
case histories, *see* clinical material